The Ralph Nader Congress Project is the most ambitious Nader undertaking to date, and the most comprehensive survey of the national legislature in our time. Begun in 1972, it took shape from interviews with the members of the 92nd and 93rd Congresses, with hundreds of congressional staff members, with lobbyists and federal officials. The result is a provocative and timely analysis of congressional committees directly and crucially involved in domestic legislation. Earlier works of the Congress Project include the set of profiles of individual members published in 1972 and updated in 1974, which were called "perceptive observations of the inner workings of Congress" by *The New York Times*, and the best-selling paperback, *Who Runs Congress?*, published in 1972 and updated in 1975.

THE MONEY COMMITTEES

This book is printed on 100 percent recycled paper

The Ralph Nader Congress Project

The Judiciary Committees: A Study of the House and Senate Judiciary Committees

The Commerce Committees: A Study of the House and Senate Commerce Committees

The Environment Committees: A Study of the House and Senate Interior, Agriculture, and Science Committees

The Money Committees: A Study of the House Banking and Currency Committee and the Senate Banking, Housing, and Urban Affairs Committee

The Revenue Committees: A Study of the House Ways and Means and Senate Finance Committees and the House and Senate Appropriations Committees

Ruling Congress: A Study of How the House and Senate Rules Govern the Legislative Process

A Study of the House Banking and Currency Committee and the Senate Banking, Housing, and Urban Affairs Committee

Lester M. Salamon, DIRECTOR

The Ralph Nader Congress Project

Grossman Publishers

A DIVISION OF THE VIKING PRESS
NEW YORK   1975

THE
MONEY
COMMITTEES

Copyright © 1975 by Ralph Nader

First published in 1975 by Grossman Publishers
625 Madison Avenue, New York, N.Y. 10022

Published simultaneously in Canada by
The Macmillan Company of Canada Limited

Printed in U.S.A.

Library of Congress Cataloging in Publication Data

Ralph Nader Congress Project.
    The money committees;

    Includes bibliographical references and index.
    1. United States. Congress. House. Committee on
Banking and Currency. 2. United States. Congress.
Senate. Committee on Banking, Housing, and Urban Affairs.
3. Monetary policy—United States. I. Title.
JK1430.B32R34   1975   328.73'07'65   75-14416
ISBN 0-670-48526-8

To the memory of my father,
VICTOR WILLIAM SALAMON,
who taught me about the world of finance
the hard way

Contributors

Lester M. Salamon, Project Director
Robert Fusfeld
Michael Massey
Nancy Masuelli
Kerry Vandell

Contents

FOREWORD BY LESTER M. SALAMON   xv

INTRODUCTION BY RALPH NADER   xxi

MEMBERS OF THE BANKING
COMMITTEES   xxvii

1 Why the Banking Business Is Everyone's Business   1

2 The Arena: The Banking Committees and Their
Legislative Context   26

3 Banking on Congress: The Bank Holding
Company Act of 1970   84

4 Brick by Brick: Housing and Urban Policy   146

5 Cowboys Who Lasso Themselves: The
Battle Against Inflation   311

6 The Banking Committees and the Future:
Conclusions and Recommendations   340

xi

TABLES

1 Types and Numbers of Commercial Banks,
December 31, 1972   6

2 Total Number and Assets of U.S. Financial Intermediaries,
December 31, 1972   8

3 Comparison of Assets of Big Three Auto Manufacturers and
the Three Largest Commercial Banks, 1972   10

4 U.S. Companies in Which a New York Commercial Bank Is the
Largest Stockholder, 1972   13

5 Ownership of Stock in Major U.S. Corporations by New York
Banks, 1972 (Partial List)   14

6 Research Reports Issued by the House Banking and Currency
Committee, 1963–72 (Partial List)   34

7 Constituencies of House Banking Committee Members,
92nd Congress   47

8 House Banking Committee Ideology as Reflected in
Floor-Vote Ratings, 1971   48

9 House Banking Committee Voting Blocs on Social-Welfare
Issues, 92nd Congress   50

10 Proportion of House Banking Committee Membership,
U.S. Metropolitan Population, and Commercial Bank Assets
Accounted for by Six States, 92nd Congress   51

11 Comparison of House and Senate Banking Committee
Budgets, 89th-92nd Congresses   61

12 Mandated Agency Reports Issued by the Senate Banking
Committee, 1965–72   64

13 Senate Banking Committee Ideology as Reflected in
Floor-Vote Ratings, 1971   72

14 Senate Banking Committee Voting Blocs,
92nd Congress   74

15 The Growth of Commercial Bank Branching,
1900–1966   93

16 Merger Approval under the Bank Merger Act, 1960–63   98

17 Santa Maria Del Mar, Biloxi, Miss., FHA
Project 065-44803   171

18 Ideology and Constituency Base of Senate Housing
Subcommittee Membership, 92nd Congress   179

19 Ideology and Constituency Base of Senate Housing
Subcommittee Membership, 93rd Congress   180

20 Ideology and Constituency Base of House Housing
Subcommittee Membership, 93rd Congress   182

21 *Ideology and Constituency Base of House and Senate HUD–*
Space Science–Veterans Appropriations Subcommittees
Membership, 92nd and 93rd Congresses 184

NOTES 367

INDEX 391

is a situation ripe for special interest or executive dominance, and for the compromising of broad public interests.

The purpose of this book is to explore how the Banking committees have coped with this situation, and what the consequences have been for the shape of public policy in the areas under their jurisdiction; in other words, to show how the structure of legislative decision-making as well as the political dynamics of the legislative process, which have been amply scrutinized in the recent scholarly literature on the Congress, actually affect the content of policy. Given this focus, it is natural that the congressional committee should be our unit of analysis, since it is at the committee level that most policy decisions are made in Congress.

Chapter 1 sets the stage for this analysis by examining some of the key policy issues within the Banking committees' bailiwick in an effort to show how Banking committee decisions affect our daily lives. Chapter 2 then provides an overview of the committees themselves, focusing especially on their leadership patterns, member backgrounds and orientations, decision-making norms and procedures, styles of staff usage, relations with outside people and groups, and other factors that define the internal dynamics of these decision-making arenas. In Chapters 3–5 we turn to the substance of committee decision-making, with detailed case studies of committee action in the fields of bank regulation (Chapter 3), housing and urban development policy (Chapter 4), and economic stabilization and price control policy (Chapter 5). Unlike traditional case studies, however, we have endeavored to go beyond the recitation of individual legislative histories to examine the overall thrust of policy in each area as it has evolved historically, and to analyze the structure of the "policy subsystem"—the set of executive agencies, interest groups, and related political forces—that importantly constrain policy choices. In this way, we have sought to overcome some of the shortcomings of the case study approach by emphasizing the ongoing character of policy disputes, the underlying constellations of political forces at work in each arena, and the broader dynamics of committee decision-making behavior. In Chapter 6, finally, we draw some conclusions about the performance of the Banking committees, and suggest a program of change that we believe could importantly improve committee output.

Although we have sought to be comprehensive in our treatment of these committees, considerations of space and time inevitably imposed limitations of which readers should be aware. In the first place, the comprehensive approach we adopted in the substantive policy chapters necessarily limited the number of decisions and policy areas we could scrutinize within the confines of a single book. We attempted to choose the policy areas that are most important, both in terms of impact on the public welfare and in terms of the time the committees devoted to them. Within each policy area, moreover, we typically examine more than one piece of legislation. Even so, several important areas of committee decision-making could not be treated at length here, including consumer credit policy, mass transit, small business assistance programs, loan guarantees to major corporations like Lockheed, and the regulation of the securities industry (which is a Banking Committee responsibility in the Senate, but not in the House). Material was gathered on most of these areas in the course of our research, however, and finds reflection throughout the text, especially in Chapters 1, 2, and 6. In the case of three of these subjects—consumer credit, mass transit, and small business—detailed case studies were prepared. Although these chapters had to be deleted for reasons of space, their contents inform the analysis throughout.

A second limitation arises from the time span covered here. Most of the primary research that forms the basis of this book took place in 1972, during the second session of the Ninety-second Congress. During this period interviews were conducted with almost the entire staffs and most of the members of both the House and the Senate Banking committees as well as with representatives of the key interest groups and executive agencies with which these committees regularly interact. While the Ninety-second Congress consequently provides the primary focus of the analysis, however, many of the interviews and most of the discus-

sion have been updated at least through the Ninety-third Congress
(1973–74).

Since 1974, however, some significant changes have taken place
in the Banking committees. Most important, at the start of the
Ninety-fourth Congress, in 1975, the chairmanship of both committees suddenly changed hands, as Henry Reuss (D., Wis.)
unseated Wright Patman (D., Tex.) as chairman in the House,
and William Proxmire (D., Wis.) replaced John Sparkman
(D., Ala.) in the Senate when the latter chose to assume the post
of Foreign Relations Committee chairman instead. In addition,
William Widnall (R., N.J.), ranking minority member of the
House Banking Committee, was not reelected in 1974, which
produced a leadership turnover in that committee on the minority
side as well. These leadership turnovers, coupled with the more
general alteration in the congressional balance of power produced
by the first post-Watergate congressional elections in 1974, can be
expected to lead to some changes in Banking committee behavior,
changes that will not be reflected in this book. At the same time,
however, one of the central themes that has emerged from our
work is that Banking committee behavior is significantly constrained by certain structural characteristics of Congress and by the
broader political context within which these committees operate.
Under such circumstances, the alterations in committee behavior
and committee output that will ultimately be produced by this
change of leadership may be far less extensive than we might be
tempted to believe. While it is still too early to determine whether
this is true, the analysis presented here should provide the base
line against which such a judgment can be made.

In an important sense, this book represents a group effort.
During the summer of 1972, four young researchers recruited
through the Nader Congress Project—Robert Fusfeld, Michael
Massey, Nancy Masuelli, and Kerry Vandell—provided invaluable
assistance, poring over committee hearing records, interviewing
staff and committee members, and preparing draft memoranda on
various aspects of committee operation. Although this final product

is the work of a single pen and reflects about fourteen months of work beyond the initial summer, I want to acknowledge the invaluable contributions made by these four able researchers, especially in the preparation of Chapters 3 and 5. Also important was the contribution of editor Carol Wieland, whose careful reading of the text added much to both substance and style. In addition, I want to express my gratitude to the members and staffs of the House and Senate Banking Committees, who, almost without exception, gave generously of their time, despite busy schedules, to respond to our questions and provide us with needed materials on committee activities. Finally, special thanks are due my wife, Lynda, not only for all those things for which authors are always indebted to their spouses—for putting up with weird writing schedules, overbearing deadlines, and distracted stares—but for some extra things as well. In certain respects, the burdens she bore in connection with this project were more onerous than those on me, and I will always be grateful for the strength with which she shouldered them.

The nineteenth century, it is said, was the age of the legislature, but the twentieth century is the age of the executive. Yet no one can study the United States Congress at close range without coming away with at least grudging respect for this institution and those who serve in it for their success in maintaining a degree of viability that far exceeds that of most other legislative bodies in the world. For all its faults, and they are many, the Congress is a human institution, with vast idiosyncracies and innumerable special arrangements that allow the institution to make headway despite serious problems and that make it necessary to subject every generalization to qualification. Although we have tended to stress the weaknesses of Congress in this account, we have also appreciated the important sources of strength in the institution and the particular circumstances that sometimes underlie the actions which elicit our critical observations. It is precisely because we believe that Congress has immense reservoirs of strength and

Introduction

There is a saying around Capitol Hill that "the banks never lose." This study of the House and Senate Banking Committees draws a dynamic picture of how the people almost always lose. It is a story of how the power of the banking and housing industries works in intricate but purposive ways to promote and sustain a multibillion-dollar subsidy state, insulated from both taxpayer and consumer accountability and from a good deal of market competition. The cash registers for this subsidy state and the friends of these lords of banking are the little-surveyed Senate Banking, Housing and Urban Affairs Committee and the House Banking and Currency Committee.

In recent years, one of these committees has become less pliable, largely due to the ascension of Representative Wright Patman to the chairmanship of the House committee in 1963. It took populist Patman several years to produce studies of bank power and build an island of defense and reform within the often hostile environment of his own committee majority. By the late sixties he launched some basic challenges to the commercial banking industry which brought forth a broad spectrum of lobbying efforts, especially from the large New York banks and their trade association. For once in their long history of securing rubber-stamping servants in the Congress, the large banks had to use their influence more overtly and more urgently. Campaign contributions were rewards for "good behavior" in Congress. Information about gifts, liquor, women, free flights to tropical resorts, tickets to sports events, and many other "freebies" supplied to many committee staffs in Congress, including past banking committee staffs, has only recently been disclosed. Alliances with bank regulatory agencies, the retention of former committee staff as lobbyists, and offers of stock, directorships, or easy loans to members of Congress, are some of the techniques used to preserve or expand banking power. And a great deal of power it is, far more than the public realizes.

As Professor Lester Salamon, the director of this study, emphasizes: "[T]hrough trust-fund investments, stock ownership, and interlocking directorships, a relatively small number of commercial banks exercise vast influence over the underlying corporate structure of the American economy, both within the banking industry and outside." About fifty commercial banks have more assets than those held by the remaining 14,000 commercial banks in the country. The fifty include First National City Bank, Chase Manhattan Bank, Bank of America, Morgan Guaranty Trust Company, Chemical Bank, and Bankers Trust Company. The growth of their assets in the past five years has been phenomenal; so have their international operations and the range of their holding company structures. If the large utilities and the oil, chemical, auto, airline, railroad and armaments companies bow to anyone, they bow to the giant money centers in New York, which are among their major shareholders and creditors as well as being timely boosters for them in Washington.

The Congress must not only deal with the direct claims made upon it by the banks. The legislature also has to exercise its authority toward the very close relationships and influence which the banks have with the Federal Reserve, the Comptroller of the Currency, and other bank or bank-related agencies. If there were antitrust laws prohibiting the merger of government and business, the first enforcement effort would be toward the complex web of interests and personnel exchanges of the banks and the Federal Reserve system. Here is where major decisions affecting the supply and distribution of credit and capital are made in Olympian aloofness, where inflation is heightened or cooled, where millions of families and individuals are told what interest rates they have to pay. As the following pages describe, the commercial banks have more influence in fact over the Federal Reserve and its monetary policy—with its impact on housing, urban development, and credit distribution—than the president and the Congress. For the bankers are the daily constituency that shapes the Federal Reserve through formal committees, private advocacy, and what sociologists call "peer group bonding," with their colleagues shuttling into and out of the Federal Reserve system. This identity of interests is shielded from outside penetration by the "independent" status of the Federal Reserve within the federal government—its self-funding appropriations process separate from the Congress, its exclusion from audit by the General Accounting Office, the permissive climate of secrecy that Washington has always accorded matters relating to money and banking, and the unparalleled length—fourteen years— of the term of office for the presidentially appointed members of the Board of Governors.

Where financial institutions are found, the housing industry is not far away. This affinity explains why the Banking committees have jurisdiction over public housing, urban renewal, housing loan guarantees, water and sewer grants, housing subsidies, the Model Cities program, urban mass transit, and many other federal urban programs. Also tied in with jurisdiction over financial institutions by the committees is the ever widening field of consumer credit with its issues of disclosure, privacy, fraud, and, with electronic techniques, the growing separation of consumers from direct expenditures of their monies.

As more large banks created their own corporate parent—the bank holding company—over the past fifteen years, their acquisitions of nonbank-related businesses have provoked opposition from such interests as insurance, leasing, and travel. In particular, insurance agents fear being squeezed out by the bank holding company sprawl. As a result, before and after the epic struggle, described in this volume, over bank holding company legislation in the late sixties, segments of the insurance industry have become steady opponents of bank moves into their areas of business. They now concentrate their opposition on what they consider very permissive pro-banking regulation by the Federal Reserve under the 1970 Bank Holding Company Act, which delimits the businesses banks can acquire or develop. But as the traditional territorial and line-of-business restrictions on commercial banks are repealed, it is likely that countervailing forces within the small banking community and outside the banking industry will become more active. The Banking committees now witness a more diverse array of lobbying forces than was previously the case when bankers stuck more to their last. Such interindustry conflict, however, rarely redounds to the advancement of consumer interests, though it may restrain further concentration of banking power that would reduce the consumers' rights to competition, efficiency, and equity in the merchandising of money. But such conflict does not serve to expose or lead to the prosecution of the business crimes that epidemically rage through the housing subsidy programs and other financial institutions that are finally receiving some media attention.

Although the details about consumer victimization are coming out more and more in hearings and reports completed by the various banking subcommittees, the results of these hearings produce either no legislation or weak laws that are even more weakly enforced. The mystique of banks and matters financial has been a persistent camouflage against public understanding of the role of these institutions in shaping the economy of workers and consumers. The educational system and daily experience revolve around money and training or effort to acquire it; yet millions of people do not understand how financial corporations make, handle, and transfer money. It is to Wright Patman's credit that he understood this vacuum in public understanding. One of his first acts as House Banking Committee chairman was to issue a "Primer on Money" pamphlet that was distributed in large numbers to schools, teachers, students, and other citizens requesting copies. He has fought tirelessly against the congressional abdication of responsibility to the executive branch of government, especially against the Federal Reserve's "independence" from accountability. The mystique of money and banking again. The members of Congress are considered, Patman said, "competent enough to pass on the use of nuclear missiles, the appropriations and expenditures of government, the drafting of young men into the services and into war, but not to pass on monetary matters."

During the twelve years of his chairmanship Patman was stymied in no small way by the strong industry control of the counterpart Senate Banking Committee. With the switch of Senator John Sparkman from the head of the Senate unit to the Foreign Relations Committee in January 1975, the leadership of the Senate committee was assumed by Senator William Proxmire, but Patman was ousted by the House revolt of that same month: he and two other chairmen were voted out of their posts by the House Democratic Caucus. It was ironic that the revolt against seniority included Patman, a wry, active octogenarian and dean of the House of Representatives whose populism and drive to probe and legislate had not dimmed. The man who started the demise of Wilbur Mills by challenging him on the house floor and blocking the "Christmas tree" tax package in 1972, who first obtained the facts about the collapse of the Penn Central, who led the Congress in the Watergate investigation right after the notorious break-in until blocked by his own committee majority, was not deemed dynamic and effective enough by the new members of the House, and these freshmen threw their considerable numerical weight behind Henry Reuss for chairman. Reuss has been a frequent supporter of Patman, but, unlike Patman, he is considered more of a compromiser and less critical of banking concentration and the Federal Reserve.

On the Senate side, the new chairman finds himself constrained by the Sparkman legacy of small staff and budget. Under Sparkman, much staff work was accomplished by the American Bankers Association (which takes up an entire column of telephone listings in the Washington telephone book) and other trade association employees. With the infusion of consumer-sensitive replacements under the direction of staff chief Kenneth McLean, some long overdue reform proposals are likely to be reported out by the committee to the Senate floor, but the staff budget, by virtue of the necessary work load and by comparison with other Senate committees, is held at low levels by pro-banking senators. Proxmire is determined to conduct more thorough oversight of the banking and housing agencies. Although the committee grudgingly approved a new oversight subcommittee, it refused Proxmire's request for an adequate staff. When one hurdle is overcome, the always lurking bank lobby manages to install another one.

It should not be surprising that in a society which presumes to call itself democratic, the ultimate appeal must be to an active public. It does not have to be a very large public, as population numbers go, but there should be a representative and informed and persistent quality associated with its growth. It could start with students intent on reforming the management of big and little money—other people's money, as Brandeis called it—in the economy. It could start with labor unions whose pension funds are controlled by large bank managers. It could start with consumer groups around the country. It could start with proposals to create new and different financial institutions controlled in fact by the depositors. But start it must if money—the taproot of power —is to cease being paid or deposited by people in ways that work against their own interests.

Ralph Nader

Members of the Banking Committees

xxvii

Majority:	*Minority:*
Williams	Brooke
McIntyre	Packwood
Mondale	Brock
Cranston	

Subcommittee on Housing and Urban Affairs

Majority:	*Minority:*
Sparkman, Chm.	Tower
Proxmire	Bennett
Williams	Brooke
McIntyre	Packwood
Mondale	Roth
Cranston	Brock
Stevenson	Taft
Gambrell	

Subcommittee on International Finance

Majority:	*Minority:*
Mondale, Chm.	Packwood
Sparkman	Bennett
Williams	Brooke
Cranston	Roth
Stevenson	Taft
Gambrell	

Subcommittee on Production and Stabilization

Majority:	*Minority:*
Cranston, Chm.	Brock
Sparkman	Tower

Majority:	*Minority:*
Proxmire	Bennett
McIntyre	Packwood
Stevenson	Taft
Gambrell	

Subcommittee on Securities

Majority:	*Minority:*
Williams, Chm.	Brooke
Proxmire	Tower
Mondale	Bennett
McIntyre	Packwood
Stevenson	Roth
Gambrell	

Subcommittee on Small Business

Majority:	*Minority:*
McIntyre, Chm.	Roth
Sparkman	Tower
Proxmire	Brooke
Williams	Brock
Mondale	Taft
Cranston	

SENATE COMMITTEE ON BANKING, HOUSING, AND URBAN AFFAIRS, NINETY-THIRD CONGRESS

Majority:	*Minority:*
John Sparkman, Chm. (Ala.)	John Tower (Tex.)
William Proxmire (Wis.)	Wallace F. Bennett (Utah)

Majority:	*Minority:*
Harrison A. Williams, Jr. (N.J.)	Edward F. Brooke (Mass.)
Thomas J. McIntyre (N.H.)	Bob Packwood (Oreg.)
Alan Cranston (Calif.)	Bill Brock (Tenn.)
Adlai E. Stevenson III (Ill.)	Robert Taft, Jr. (Ohio)
J. Bennett Johnston, Jr. (La.)	Lowell P. Weicker, Jr. (Conn.)
William D. Hathaway (Maine)	
Joseph R. Biden, Jr. (Del.)	

Subcommittee on Consumer Credit

Majority:	*Minority:*
Proxmire, Chm.	Brock
Sparkman	Bennett
Johnston	Brooke
Hathaway	

Subcommittee on Financial Institutions

Majority:	*Minority:*
McIntyre, Chm.	Bennett
Sparkman	Tower
Proxmire	Brock
Williams	

Subcommittee on Housing and Urban Affairs

Majority:	*Minority:*
Sparkman, Chm.	Tower
Proxmire	Brooke
Williams	Packwood
Cranston	Taft
Stevenson	

Subcommittee on International Finance

Majority:	*Minority:*
Stevenson, Chm.	Packwood
Cranston	Brock
Hathaway	Taft
Biden	

Subcommittee on Production and Stabilization

Majority:	*Minority:*
Johnston (Chm.)	Taft
Stevenson	Tower
Hathaway	Weicker
Biden	

Subcommittee on Securities

Majority:	*Minority:*
Williams, Chm.	Brooke
Proxmire	Bennett
McIntyre	Weicker
Biden	

Subcommittee on Small Business

Majority:	*Minority:*
Cranston, Chm.	Weicker
Sparkman	Tower
McIntyre	Packwood
Johnston	

HOUSE COMMITTEE ON BANKING AND CURRENCY, NINETY-SECOND CONGRESS

Majority:

Wright Patman, Chm. (Tex.)
William A. Barrett (Pa.)
Leonor K. Sullivan (Mo.)
Henry S. Reuss (Wis.)
Thomas L. Ashley (Ohio)
William S. Moorhead (Pa.)
Robert G. Stephens, Jr. (Ga.)
Fernand J. St. Germain (R.I.)
Henry B. Gonzalez (Tex.)
Joseph G. Minish (N.J.)
Richard T. Hanna (Calif.)
Tom S. Gettys (S.C.)
Frank Annunzio (Ill.)
Thomas M. Rees (Calif.)
Tom Bevill (Ala.)
Charles H. Griffin (Miss.)
James M. Hanley (N.Y.)
Frank J. Brasco (N.Y.)
Bill Chappell, Jr. (Fla.)
Edward I. Koch (N. Y.)
William R. Cotter (Conn.)
Parren J. Mitchell (Md.)
William P. Curlin (Ky.)

Minority:

William B. Widnall (N.J.)
Florence P. Dwyer (N.J.)
Albert W. Johnson (Pa.)
J. William Stanton (Ohio)
Ben B. Blackburn (Ga.)
Garry E. Brown (Mich.)
Lawrence G. Williams (Pa.)
Chalmers P. Wylie (Ohio)
Margaret M. Heckler (Mass.)
Philip M. Crane (Ill.)
John H. Rousselot (Calif.)
Stewart B. McKinney (Conn.)
Norman F. Lent (N.Y.)
Bill Archer (Tex.)
Bill Frenzel (Minn.)

Subcommittee on Bank Supervision and Insurance

Majority:

St. Germain, Chm.
Moorhead

Minority:

Johnson
Wylie

Majority:	Minority:
Annunzio	Crane
Griffin	Rousselot
Brasco	Archer
Chappell	Lent
Koch	
Cotter	
Curlin	

Subcommittee on Consumer Affairs

Majority:	Minority:
Sullivan, Chm.	Dwyer
Stephens	Wylie
Gonzalez	Williams
Minish	Heckler
Hanna	Archer
Annunzio	McKinney
Hanley	
Chappell	
Koch	

Subcommittee on Domestic Finance

Majority:	Minority:
Patman, Chm.	Widnall
Minish	Blackburn
Hanna	Crane
Gettys	Brown
Annunzio	Williams
Rees	Frenzel
Henley	
Brasco	
Mitchell	

Subcommittee on Housing

Majority: | *Minority:*

Majority:
Barrett, Chm.
Sullivan
Ashley
Moorhead
Stephens
St. Germain
Gonzalez
Reuss
Minish

Minority:
Widnall
Dwyer
Brown
Stanton
Blackburn
Heckler

Subcommittee on International Finance

Majority:
Gonzalez, Chm.
Reuss
Ashley
Moorhead
Hanna
Rees
Hanley
Brasco
Cotter

Minority:
Johnson
Stanton
Crane
Frenzel
Lent
Archer

Subcommittee on International Trade

Majority:
Ashley, Chm.
St. Germain
Gettys

Minority:
Blackburn
Brown
Johnson

Majority:	*Minority:*
Rees	Rousselot
Griffin	McKinney
Hanna	Lent
Koch	
Mitchell	
Curlin	

Subcommittee on Small Business

Majority:	*Minority:*
Stephens, Chm.	Stanton
Barrett	Williams
Sullivan	Wylie
Gettys	Heckler
Griffin	Rousselot
Chappell	McKinney
Cotter	
Mitchell	
Curlin	

HOUSE COMMITTEE ON BANKING AND CURRENCY, NINETY-THIRD CONGRESS

Majority:	*Minority:*
Wright Patman, Chm. (Tex.)	William B. Widnall (N.J.)
William A. Barrett (Pa.)	Albert W. Johnson (Pa.)
Leonor K. Sullivan (Mo.)	J. William Stanton (Ohio)
Henry S. Reuss (Wis.)	Ben Blackburn (Ga.)
Thomas L. Ashley (Ohio)	Garry Brown (Mich.)
William S. Moorhead (Pa.)	Lawrence G. Williams (Pa.)

Majority:

Robert G. Stephens, Jr. (Ga.)
Fernand J. St. Germain (R.I.)
Henry B. Gonzalez (Tex.)
Joseph G. Minish (N.J.)
Richard T. Hanna (Calif.)
Tom S. Gettys (S.C.)
Frank Annunzio (Ill.)
Thomas M. Rees (Calif.)
James M. Hanley (N.Y.)
Frank J. Brasco (N.Y.)
Edward I. Koch (N.Y.)
William R. Cotter (Conn.)
Parren J. Mitchell (Md.)
Walter E. Fauntroy (D.C.)
Andrew Young (Ga.)
John Joseph Moakley (Mass.)
Fortney H. Stark (Calif.)
Lindy Boggs (La.)

Minority:

Chalmers P. Wylie (Ohio)
Margaret M. Heckler (Mass.)
Philip M. Crane (Ill.)
John H. Rousselot (Calif.)
Stewart B. McKinney (Conn.)
Bill Frenzel (Minn.)
Angelo D. Roncallo (N.Y.)
John B. Conlan (Ariz.)
Clair W. Burgener (Calif.)
Matthew J. Rinaldo (N.J.)

Subcommittee on Bank Supervision and Insurance

Majority:

St. Germain, Chm.
Annunzio
Barrett
Hanley
Brasco
Cotter
Moakley
Ashley
Moorhead

Minority:

Rousselot
Johnson
Wylie
Williams
Roncallo
Rinaldo

Subcommittee on Consumer Affairs

Majority:	*Minority:*
Sullivan, Chm.	Wylie
Fauntroy	Heckler
Mitchell	McKinney
Barrett	Rinaldo
Gonzalez	Roncallo
Young	Burgener
Stark	
Moakley	
Koch	

Subcommittee on Domestic Finance

Majority:	*Minority:*
Patman, Chm.	Crane
Annunzio	Widnall
Minish	Blackburn
Gettys	Frenzel
Rees	Conlan
Fauntroy	Rinaldo
Stark	
Ashley	
Stephens	

Subcommittee on Housing

Majority:	*Minority:*
Barrett, Chm.	Widnall
Sullivan	Brown
Ashley	Stanton

Majority:	*Minority:*
Moorhead	Blackburn
Stephens	Heckler
St. Germain	Rousselot
Gonzalez	
Reuss	
Hanna	

Subcommittee on International Finance

Majority:	*Minority:*
Gonzalez, Chm.	Johnson
Reuss	Stanton
Moorhead	Crane
Rees	Frenzel
Hanna	Conlan
Fauntroy	Burgener
Young	
Stark	
Stephens	

Subcommittee on International Trade

Majority:	*Minority:*
Ashley, Chm.	Blackburn
Rees	Brown
Mitchell	Johnson
St. Germain	McKinney
Hanna	Frenzel
Koch	Conlan
Young	
Moakley	
Sullivan	

Subcommittee on Small Business

Majority:	*Minority:*
Stephens, Chm.	Stanton
Mitchell	Williams
Koch	Heckler
Gonzalez	Rousselot
Gettys	Burgener
Annunzio	Roncallo
Hanley	
Brasco	
Cotter	

Subcommittee on Urban Mass Transportation

Majority:	*Minority:*
Minish, Chm.	Brown
Gettys	Widnall
Hanley	Williams
Brasco	Wylie
Koch	Crane
Cotter	McKinney
Young	
Moakley	
Stark	

THE MONEY COMMITTEES

1

Why the Banking Business Is Everyone's Business

For most Americans, the world of banking is a land apart, only barely comprehensible to the layman's mind and of signal irrelevance to his daily concerns. In fact, however, the world of banking is at the center of American economic life, affecting every citizen every day in a host of direct and indirect ways. The availability of housing, the growth or stagnation of whole geographic regions, the viability of small businesses, the pace of corporate take-overs, the ability of local governments to build schools and parks—all these and more are substantially affected by the decisions of the men who run the nation's banks. This is so because in a capitalist economy like that in the United States, capital—or credit—is the key to all economic activity; it is the commodity necessary for all

1

economic transactions. As the major suppliers of credit and the chief controllers of the flow of capital, the banks and other "financial intermediaries" are consequently the linchpin of the whole American economic system. By 1974, these institutions controlled an immense $1.9832 trillion worth of assets—more than one and a half times as much as is produced by all corporations, businesses, and other enterprises in the United States together each year.[1] As a result of this pivotal function and these immense resources, financial institutions have more influence over the stability, growth, and shape of the national economic order than any other single type of private institution in the country.

Because of the crucial economic function that they perform, banks have been singularly successful in wrapping themselves in the warm embrace of public protection. Each wave of economic distress with which the economic history of this nation is studded has left behind a new tier of legal provisions aimed at strengthening the banking system and insulating it from the harsh realities of economic misfortune. What has come down to us today, consequently, is a private industry supported by an immense, intricate web of governmental protections and regulations at both state and national levels, a "dual banking system" in which banks can choose which set of authorities—state or national—to obey.

The profound economic importance of the banking industry combined with this intimate involvement of the government in its operations has inevitably placed ominous responsibilities upon Congress. And within Congress, these responsibilities fall squarely on two committees: the Banking and Currency Committee in the House and the corresponding Banking, Housing and Urban Affairs Committee in the Senate. Though operating in relative obscurity because of the complexity of their subject matter, these committees decide some of the most fundamental issues confronting Congress and the nation. A brief look at just four of the issues under the jurisdiction of these committees—economic concentration, inflation, housing and urban development, and consumer finance—should demonstrate this point beyond question.

THE PUBLIC STAKE IN BANKING COMMITTEE DECISIONS

Economic Concentration and Competition

Perhaps the most fundamental issue confronting the Banking committees arises from the impact that financial institutions have on the basic structure of the American economy. Because of their immense assets and their resulting control over the flow of credit to government, business, and consumers, financial institutions exercise vast influence over the degree of monopoly or competition throughout the American economy.

Some of this influence is limited by the existence of competition among financial institutions themselves. Instead of a single, monolithic body, the American financial industry consists of a collection of different institutional types: commercial banks, savings and loan associations, mutual savings banks, credit unions, pension funds, finance companies, and insurance companies. Each of these institutions emerged in response to a felt need at a particular time, so that the financial structure that has come down to us today is less the product of any grand design than of a succession of ad hoc adjustments. As Treasury Secretary William E. Simon recently noted, "We have a banking structure which has been largely constructed by historical accident and one which has been reworked and patched up typically only in times of financial crisis."[2]

Probably the oldest and most important of these institutions are the commercial banks, which were chartered by states early in the nation's history to provide a basic currency of exchange in the form of bank notes and thus finance the nation's economic activity. Although the commercial banking system has changed dramatically since those early days, the basic, unique function of commercial banks remains the same: providing most of the stuff we use as money. This now takes the form of demand deposits (checking accounts) instead of "bank notes." Indeed, within limits set by governmental authorities, commercial banks actually "create" money, by accepting deposits from individuals or businesses and loaning out all but a fraction (the "reserves") to borrowers, creating new balances in the checking accounts of the borrowers in the process.*[3] Ninety percent of the money supply in use today has been created in this way, making the commercial banks the pivotal actors in determining both the size of the money supply and its distribution among competing potential uses. As one basic textbook explains:

> By making loans and investments [commercial banks] add to the supply of funds in the credit market, and by reducing their loans and investments they reduce the supply of funds. By their lending and investing activities commercial banks

* For those unfamiliar with how a fractional reserve system allows banks to *create* money, the following example should help. Assume that all banks keep 15 percent of all deposits as reserves against withdrawals and loan out the remaining 85 percent. Now, if Citizen A deposits $1000 in Bank 1, which holds $150 in reserve and loans out the remaining $850 to Citizen B, who deposits it in Bank 2, which in turn holds 15 percent ($127.50) and loans out the remaining $722.50 to Citizen C, who deposits it in Bank 3, and so on, the result will be that the commercial banking system as a whole will have generated $6,666.67 in capital out of the original $1,000 deposit. The table below illustrates this:

	Amount deposited in checking account	Amount loaned	Reserve
Bank 1	$1,000.00	$ 850.00	$ 150.00
Bank 2	850.00	722.50	127.50
Bank 3	722.50	614.12	108.38
Bank 4	614.12	522.00	92.12
Bank 5	522.00	443.70	78.30
Bank 6	443.70	377.14	66.56
Bank 7	377.14	320.57	56.67
Bank 8	320.57	272.48	48.09
Bank 9	272.48	231.60	40.88
Bank 10	231.60	196.86	34.74
Total for 10 banks	$5,354.11	$4,550.97	$ 803.14
Total for all other banks (for banks 11-end)	$1,312.56	$1,116.70	$ 196.86
Total for Banking System	$6,666.67	$5,666.67	$1,000.00

affect the volume of funds available for lending, the level of interest rates, and the volume of aggregate spending for both consumption and investment.[4]

Although all of the 13,928 commercial banks in existence as of December 31, 1972, perform this same basic role, there are some important differences among them reflecting the diversity of the bank regulatory structure. Unlike all other corporations, which operate exclusively under state charters, banks since 1863 have had the option of securing federal charters administered by the comptroller of the currency instead. Although Congress clearly intended to eliminate state banks entirely, and enacted a severe tax on state bank notes in 1865 to achieve this end, the shift from bank notes to demand deposits as the basic form of currency in the latter nineteenth century frustrated this goal. As a result, only 4,613 commercial banks operate under national charters, while 9,315 are state banks operating under the varied regulations of the different states. But the 4,613 national banks account for close to 60 percent of all commercial bank assets. In addition, 1,092 of the state banks voluntarily belong to the Federal Reserve System, the central banking apparatus Congress created in 1913 to stabilize the commercial banking system. These state member banks also participate in federal deposit insurance and thus fall under the jurisdiction of the Federal Deposit Insurance Corporation (FDIC), as do an additional 8,017 state nonmember banks (banks not part of the Federal Reserve System) which have voluntarily joined the FDIC network.[5] In terms of legal status and regulatory structure, therefore, there are really four different classes of commercial banks, as depicted in Table 1, below. Nevertheless, as Table 1 shows, 98.5 percent of all banks, controlling 99.1 percent of all commercial bank assets, fall under some form of federal regulation and hence are subject to Banking Committee jurisdiction.

The other types of financial institutions are more specialized than the commercial banks. Indeed, for the most part they took

TABLE 1.

Types and Numbers of Commercial Banks,
December 31, 1972

Type of bank	Regulatory bodies bank is subject to*	Number of banks	Percent of all commercial bank assets controlled
National banks	b, c, d	4,613	58.1
State member banks	a, c, d	1,092	19.9
State insured banks	a, d	8,017	21.1
State noninsured banks	a	206	0.9
Total		13,928	100.0

* a = State banking authority
 b = Comptroller of the Currency (Federal)
 c = Federal Reserve Board
 d = Federal Deposit Insurance Corporation
SOURCE: Board of Governors of the Federal Reserve System, *Annual Report,
1973*, p. 298.

root in the financial nooks and crannies that the commercial banks ignored. For example, the traditional preference of the commercial banks for demand deposits—on which no interest is paid—and for short-term loans—which do not tie up capital for long—opened the way in the late nineteenth century for the emergence of specialized "savings intermediaries" (mutual savings banks, savings and loan associations, etc.) which sought to attract the savings of individuals and small businesses by paying interest to depositors and putting the money to productive use, mostly in the home mortgage market.[6] The personal savings account thus came into vogue, giving birth to a whole new branch of the financial industry. And as personal incomes have risen, particularly since World War II, so have the fortunes of the savings intermediaries. The assets of the savings and loan industry skyrocketed from $8.7 billion in 1945 to $243.6 billion in 1972, so that a set of institutions that controlled only 3 percent of all financial institution assets in 1945 controlled close to 15 percent twenty-seven years later.[7] The traditional lack of interest of commercial banks in consumer finance also opened the way for the growth of credit unions, finance companies, and the like.

Pension funds and insurance companies are somewhat different types of institutions. They receive their funds from premiums or automatic payroll deductions and are thus not in competition for deposits with commercial banks and savings banks. They typically invest most of their funds in common stock, which banks are forbidden to do. Yet these institutions control sizable blocks of capital and have increasingly turned to direct lending to corporate clients, much like commercial banks.[8] Moreover, they are in at least indirect competition with banks, since many people see insurance policies and savings accounts as alternative forms of savings.

Although this pluralistic character of the financial industry guarantees a degree of competition, it does so only partially, for behind the façade of pluralism lie some ominous aggregations of economic power. In the first place, although the $1.9832 trillion of financial-institution assets are spread among a variety of types of institutions, one type clearly dominates the field: the commercial banks. As Table 2 indicates, commercial banks alone control close to half of all assets in financial institutions (particularly if we include finance companies, which get most of their capital from commercial banks). If we deduct pension funds and insurance companies, and consider only "depository institutions," moreover, commercial bank dominance is even greater—accounting for over two-thirds of all depository-institution assets.

Not only are financial-institution assets generally concentrated in the hands of commercial banks, but commercial bank assets are themselves concentrated in the hands of a fairly small number of banking titans. Of the almost 14,000 commercial banks in existence as of 1972, for example, 50—less than one-half of one percent—controlled 50 percent of all commercial-bank assets.[9] Even this understates the degree of concentration, for the large banks have devised a host of ways to extend their influence over

TABLE 2.

Total Number and Assets of U.S. Financial Intermediaries,
December 31, 1972

| | | Assets | |
Institution	Number	Amount (billions)	Percent of total
Commercial Banks	13,928	$ 716.9	43.3
Savings and Loan Associations	5,448	243.6	14.7
Life Insurance Companies	1,805	239.4	14.5
Mutual Savings Banks	486	100.6	6.1
Finance Companies	(n.a.)*	73.7	4.5
Investment Companies	(n.a.)*	59.8	3.6
Credit Unions	23,134	24.8	1.5
Private Pension Funds	(n.a.)*	123.7	7.5
State and Local Government Pension Funds	(n.a.)*	72.2	4.4
Totals		$1,654.7	100.0

* (n.a.) = not available.

SOURCES: U.S. Bureau of the Census, *Statistical Abstract of the U.S.* (1973), pp. 447–451; U.S. Savings and Loan League, *1973 Savings and Loan Fact Book*, p. 53.

other banks while still preserving the outward signs of competition. A 1967 study of the ownership of 48 commercial banks in 10 large metropolitan areas showed, for example, that more than 10 percent of the stock of 30 of these banks was actually owned by supposedly competing banks. The largest bank in Cleveland, for instance, not only controlled one-third of all bank deposits in the city but also owned major blocks of stock in its three competitors, and had interlocking directorates as well with no fewer than seven large insurance companies.[10] A report of the Senate Committee on Government Operations issued in December 1973 illustrates the extent of this concentration vividly. On the basis of responses to a letter from Senator Lee Metcalf (D., Mont.) requesting information on the 30 largest stockholders of the nation's largest banks, the committee report notes that

bank nominees* dominate the holdings of the 30 top security holders in banks. More than one-fourth of the stock in
Wells Fargo was reported held by 21 unidentified bank nominees. The top 30 security holders in J. P. Morgan, holding
more than one-fourth of the stock in that bank, included 22
unidentified bank nominees. Fifteen percent of the stock in
Chase Manhattan was reported held by 22 unidentified bank
nominees. *The reported bank holdings, in most instances,
were several times greater* than the combined holdings of
other institutional and individual investors among the top
security holders.[11]

It is true that concentration—defined as the percent of the
market dominated by a single firm or by the top three firms—is
not as great in the commercial banking industry as it is in some
others, like automobiles. But the sheer size of the individual firms
in the banking field constitutes an enormous concentration of
power. For example, General Motors, the largest industrial corporation in the United States, with assets of more than $18 bil-
lion, resembles a scrawny adolescent compared to the largest
commercial bank, Bank of America, which has assets of $34
billion.[12] In fact, GM, Ford, and Chrysler—the Big Three automobile manufacturers and three of the largest firms in the nation
—have just barely more assets *together* than the largest commercial bank *by itself*; and the top three commercial banks outdis-
tance the Big Three auto firms in terms of assets by two and a
half to one (see Table 3).

These massive aggregations of economic power inevitably give
the barons of commercial banking substantial influence over the
structure of the corporate economy. For the most part, this influence is indirect: it operates through traditional bank loan activity
and is a function of bank decisions to extend or withhold loan
money to particular corporate clients and for particular purposes.

---

* Bank nominees, as noted below, are "street names" or aliases used by
commercial bank trust departments in recording their stock ownership.

TABLE 3.

Comparison of Assets of Big Three Auto Manufacturers and
the Three Largest Commercial Banks, 1974

Top Three Auto Manufacturers		Top Three Commercial Banks	
Name	Assets (billions)	Name	Assets (billions)
General Motors	$20.5	Bank of America	$51.2
Ford	14.2	First National City Bank	44.9
Chrysler	6.7	Chase Manhattan Bank	34.5
Total	$41.4	Total	$130.6

SOURCE: *Fortune*, May 1975, p. 10.
Moody's Bank and Finance Manual, 1975, p. a 52.

The massive wave of conglomerate formations that swept the
American economy in the 1960s, for example, was largely financed by commercial-bank assets. But banks influence the corporate structure more directly as well, despite the fact that they
are formally forbidden to acquire stock in nonbanking businesses.
Trust-department investments, interlocking directorates, and
bank holding companies are three of the mechanisms through
which this influence operates. In 1970 more than 3,400 banks
had trust departments, that is, departments that administer es-
tates, pension funds, or other similar funds deposited with the
bank for safekeeping and professional management. These departments controlled assets worth an astounding $288 billion as
of 1970, most of it in common stock of major corporations. And
of these 3,400 bank trust departments, 52 controlled 68 *percent*
of all bank trust assets.[13] As a recent *Yale Law Journal* article
notes, this massive concentration of resources places these giant
trust departments "among the most powerful (and most anony-
mous) of our nation's financial institutions. . . . They manage
assets substantially exceeding the assets of the largest one hundred corporations in the United States. In fact, bank trust departments have larger securities portfolios than all other institutional
investors combined. As a result, certain commercial banks have
the power to control major corporations."[14]

This extensive bank influence is systematically concealed from view, however, by a bizarre system of "street names" that the banks use to record their stock ownership. In its report to the Federal Power Commission (FPC) in 1972, for example, the Long Island Lighting Company (LILCO) listed Kane & Co., Cudd & Co., Carson & Co., Reing & Co., and Genoy & Co. as among its top ten stockholders. All five of these curious-sounding companies showed the same Church Street Post Office station in New York as their address. When a *Newsday* reporter investigated the matter, he discovered that the first two—located at P.O. Box 1508—were really "street names" for the Chase Manhattan Bank, while the latter three—located at P.O. Box 491 at the same post office station—were really "street names" for Morgan Guaranty Trust Company. Thus five of the top ten stockholders recorded by this large utility company turned out in reality to be two giant New York banks.[15]

In an effort to unravel this corporate charade, the Senate Committee on Government Operations staff in 1973 analyzed the ownership reports submitted by various industries to their respective federal regulatory authorities, as well as responses to a corporate ownership inquiry sent to 324 major U.S. corporations by Senator Lee Metcalf. Once the various "street names" reported on these forms were translated into actual owners, a startling picture emerged of extensive concentration of ownership of U.S. corporations by a relative handful of mammoth commercial banks. Of the thirty largest stockholders recorded by the Burlington Northern Railroad in its 1972 report to the Interstate Commerce Commission (ICC), for example, eleven turned out to be "fronts" for four large banks—Bankers Trust (New York), Chase Manhattan (New York), the Bank of New York, and State Street Bank (Boston). Together, these four banks controlled 25 percent of Burlington's voting stock, enough to ensure them control of the company. This same pattern was evident across the board—in broadcasting, in airlines, in electric utilities, in retailing companies, in industrials. The hand of the bankers was everywhere, most frequently in a controlling role. Thus, of 132 companies that indicated their largest stockholder in response to Senator Metcalf's inquiry, 58 recorded a name that turned out to be a commercial bank, and in 40 of these cases, the largest stockholder turned out to be one of four giant New York banks (see Table 4).

Since ownership of 5 percent of the stock of a widely held company of the sort recorded here is typically taken as sufficient to exercise control, the data reported in Table 4 represent an amazing picture of corporate control on the part of the New York banking community. In fact, of eighty-nine major companies that reported their thirty largest stockholders in response to Senator Metcalf's letter, sixty-five reported New York banks in control of at least 5 percent of their stock. And in forty-eight of these cases, or well over half, the New York banks controlled over 10 percent of the stock. In short, as noted in Table 5, some of the largest corporations in the American economy are really the possessions of a relatively small group of powerful commercial banks.

Although banks claim that they do not exercise any control as a consequence of this massive ownership of corporate enterprise, this conclusion is hard to sustain. Indeed, even the Commission on Financial Structure and Regulation appointed by President Nixon in 1970 conceded in its recent report that, "When a bank holds a sizable amount of a corporation's equity securities, it could have a significant influence on the management of that enterprise."[16] Leaving nothing to chance, the bankers frequently institutionalize this management influence by serving on the boards of the corporations in which their trust departments own sizable chunks of stock. Thus, four of the board members of the Long Island Lighting Company were also directors of banks that owned large blocks of LILCO stock. On an even larger scale, sixteen of the twenty-three directors of the ill-fated Penn Central Railroad, the nation's largest transportation company, were also directors of commercial banks that owned Penn Central stock and had loaned money to Penn Central.[17] In short, through trust-

TABLE 4.

U.S. Companies in Which a New York Commercial Bank Is the Largest Stockholder, 1972
(Partial List)

Largest stockholder and company	*Percent of company's voting stock held by largest stockholder*
Chase Manhattan Bank:	
Atlantic Richfield	4.5
General Electric	3.6
RCA	4.2
Union Carbide	5.2
Litton Industries	9.0
Monsanto	7.4
United Airlines	8.3
American Airlines	9.0
Northwest Airlines	6.9
National Airlines	8.4
Burlington and Northern	6.7
Southern Railway	8.3
Long Island Lighting	5.1
Florida Power and Light	3.6
Safeway Stores	10.5
First National City Bank:	
Xerox	6.1
Bendix	10.9
Virginia Electric & Power	5.6
Pennzoil United	7.5
Carolina Power & Light	7.0
First National Bank of Dallas	10.2
Morgan Guaranty Trust Company:	
United Aircraft	7.0
R.H. Macy	6.2
Travelers Insurance	6.0
Bankers Trust Company:	
Mobil Oil	6.1
Continental Oil	5.8

SOURCE: Senate Government Operations Committee, *Disclosure of Corporate Ownership* (1973), p. 25.

TABLE 5.
Ownership of Stock in Major U.S. Corporations by New York Banks,
1972 (Partial List)

Companies	Percent of stock held by New York banks within the 30 largest stockholders	Percent of stock held by 30 largest stockholders
Oil Companies:		
Mobil Oil	17.4	29.0
Atlantic Richfield	11.7	26.3
Continental Oil	13.3	30.8
Industrials:		
Ford Motor	11.2	35.7
General Electric	14.0	21.1
Westinghouse	11.7	23.1
Union Carbide	12.9	26.7
Litton Industries	11.9	45.5
Caterpillar Tractor	13.2	30.0
Monsanto	12.4	31.9
United Aircraft	20.6	44.7
Xerox	19.8	31.9
Warner-Lambert	14.3	28.3
Airlines:		
United Airlines	21.9	47.1
American Airlines	30.8	44.6
Pan American	13.6	49.2
Northwest Airlines	22.5	53.0
Braniff Airlines	17.1	56.1
Railroads:		
Burlington & Northern	30.0	36.0
Southern	18.5	40.2
Chicago-Rock Island & Pacific	78.1	92.0
St. Louis-San Francisco	19.8	48.2
Rio Grande Industries	19.2	54.2
Seaboard Coast Line	15.8	40.1
Utilities:		
American Electric Power	13.3	25.5
Virginia Electric Power	16.1	29.9
Pennzoil United	18.6	40.9
Texas Utilities	11.0	25.8
Continental Telephone	15.2	29.4
Western Union	17.8	43.0
Retailing Companies:		
Safeway Stores	18.4	33.5
Grand Union	12.6	45.2
R.H. Macy	15.5	44.5

SOURCE: Senate Government Operations Committee, *Disclosure of Corporate Ownership* (1973), pp. 26–27.

fund investments, stock ownership, and interlocking directorships, a relatively small number of commercial banks exercise vast influence over the underlying corporate structure of the American economy, both within the banking industry and outside.

The formation of bank holding companies provides yet another, and even more direct, way for banks to extend their economic control. By setting up a holding company, which is a separate corporate entity with the power to acquire other businesses,* a bank can effectively escape the legal prohibitions against bank acquisition of nonbanking activities through the simple expedient of having the parent holding company do the acquiring for it. During the 1960s in particular, expansion-minded banks moved actively into the holding-company form of operation. By 1969, in fact, 40 percent of all commercial bank deposits in the United States were controlled by such holding companies.[18]

What is the meaning of this concentration of corporate control in the hands of the nation's large commercial banks? To what extent does it represent a harmful aggregation of economic power? What are its implications for the level of competition throughout the economy? To what extent should it be regulated by government? The public stake in the answers to these questions is immense, and it is the Banking committees in Congress that ultimately have the responsibility to respond. Chapter 3 analyzes how they have exercised this responsibility by examining the legislative history of the Bank Holding Company Act of 1970, probably the most significant antitrust legislation in a generation.

Interest Rates, Monetary Policy, and Inflation

The Banking committees, as part of their responsibility over the banking system, also have jurisdiction over monetary policy—the set of policy tools that determine the level of money supply and hence the rate of interest. To say that the committees have *juris-*

---

* A bank holding company is any association, corporation, or trust that holds a controlling interest in one or more banks and therefore controls the policy of the bank or banks.

diction over "monetary policy" is not to say that they *control* this policy, however; for Congress has essentially surrendered this control to the Federal Reserve Board and its affiliated twelve regional Federal Reserve Banks, as well as to commercial banks generally.

The Federal Reserve Board determines the supply of money to be made available for investment and consumption in three basic ways: by selling and purchasing U.S. government obligations; by setting the proportion of total deposits that commercial banks must keep on hand as a reserve against withdrawals (the "reserve requirement"), and by setting the rate at which commercial banks can borrow money from the Federal Reserve (the "discount rate"). All three of these mechanisms set the amount of "reserves" available to commercial banks, and hence the maximum amount of credit in the economy. It is then up to the banks themselves to decide whether to extend loans up to the permissible limit or keep their reserves on deposit in a regional Federal Reserve Bank. Through these mechanisms the "Fed" and the commercial banks determine directly the amount of capital available for investment and the level of interest rates, and indirectly the rate of inflation and the pace of economic growth. As the Federal Reserve Board itself noted in one of its publications, "the Federal Reserve, through its influence on credit and money, affects indirectly every phase of American enterprise and every person in the United States."[19] The public stake in these decisions is thus substantial, especially since it is public authority that gives the whole operation its force and effectiveness.[20]

Nevertheless, the decision-making structure responsible for these decisions is amazingly impervious to systematic public control. The Federal Reserve System is run by a seven-member Board of Governors chosen by the president with the consent of the Senate. However, these governors are appointed for fourteen-year terms each and are thus effectively insulated from detailed public control. The determination of Federal Reserve policy is shared between the Board and the presidents of the twelve regional Federal Reserve Banks, who are in turn selected by the directors of these regional banks, most of them private bankers and large businessmen in their respective regions. Every three weeks, the Fed's Board of Governors meets with the regional bank presidents in what is known as the "Open Market Committee" to decide the basic contours of monetary policy, particularly whether government securities should be purchased or sold. These decisions directly affect the reserves available to the banking system, and hence the amount of money available for investment and the resulting level of interest rates, degree of price stability, and rate of economic growth.

Yet the only thing open about the Open Market Committee is its name. The Board of Governors and the regional Reserve Bank presidents meet in strictly guarded secrecy. No congressman or member of the president's cabinet, no member of the Council of Economic Advisers or the Office of Management and Budget, and no representative of the press is allowed to sit in on these meetings, let alone to participate actively. Nor can influence be exerted through other channels. Even the rudiments of power Congress enjoys over some administrative agencies through its control of budgets is unavailable *vis-á-vis* the Fed, for the Fed supports itself out of the revenue it receives as interest on the U.S. government bonds it holds. As of 1972, for example, the Fed owned $71 billion of U.S. government bonds, from which it received interest payments in excess of $4 billion.[21] It does not need appropriations from Congress.

The rationale advanced for Federal Reserve independence is the need to insulate monetary policy from short-run political pressures.[22] But the result is that one of the two major instruments of national economic management is beyond the control of the elected political leadership. While the president, his economic advisers, and the Congress may be moving in one direction through "fiscal policy"—the control of government spending and debt—the Fed and the commercial banks remain free to cancel out these efforts through a monetary policy that moves in the opposite direction entirely. As one Stanford University economist put it, "It is like having two managers for the same baseball team, each manager independent of the other."[23]

In fact the commercial banks may actually have more influence on the formation of monetary policy than the president and Congress. They dominate the boards of the twelve regional Federal Reserve Banks;[24] their representatives sit in the Open Market Committee; and they select members of an Advisory Council established by law to keep the Fed in touch with the views of bankers. Beyond this, an intricate web of informal relationships ties the Federal Reserve System to the private banking community in ways that influence the Fed's view of the world. As one Fed governor put it:

> I think there are lots of relationships between the Federal Reserve and bankers because they are both in essentially the same business and so they speak a common language in a great many respects, and the Federal Reserve engages in supervisory operations which bring them in close contact with the bankers.[25]

With interest rates rising to unprecedented heights despite the onset of a recession, the wisdom of this pattern of policy-making must come under serious question. And it is the Banking committees that have the responsibility for providing the answers, since it is to them that Congress as a whole has delegated jurisdiction over this critical area. Chapter 5 explores how they have dealt with this responsibility, focusing particularly on their handling of wage-and-price-control legislation in 1970–73.

Housing, Urban Development, and the Distribution of Credit

In the process of influencing the overall *supply* of credit, and hence the interest rate, the Federal Reserve and the commercial banks also influence the *distribution* of capital among different sectors of the economy and different regions of the country. Despite the public role they perform and the public protections they enjoy, bankers insist on the freedom to operate like other businessmen, that is, to seek to sell their product—in this case, money—at the highest possible price. In the process, they can effectively deny some types of borrowers the access to credit that they need for economic sustenance.

If allocating credit on the basis of profit were the same as allocating it on the basis of social need, there would be no problem with this system. But some of the socially most important sectors of the economy are at a competitive disadvantage in bidding for capital. Large corporations, for example, can pass along the costs of higher interest rates to their customers. Small businessmen, local governments, and home buyers—all of them equally in need of capital—cannot. What is more, bankers prefer to deal with the large-scale corporate borrowers, with whom they can establish on-going, large-lot credit activities, than with the administratively more costly and inevitably less permanent small-business and home-mortgage customers. As a consequence, bankers typically give first preference to their large corporate accounts, leaving the small fry to scramble for the rest. As one economist observed about the home mortgage market, "The volume of mortgage credit is a sort of residual, in that home buyers can obtain only that volume of credit which remains after the more volatile and persistent demands of corporations have been satisfied."[26] A similar pattern applies to small businessmen and local governments.

The results of this system of credit distribution are apparent in the erratic shifts in the flow of credit to these socially important but economically disadvantaged sectors. Five times between World War II and 1972, for example, housing starts plummeted as interest rates rose and financial institutions reduced the capital available for mortgage lending. A sixth such cyclical decline seems well under way at this writing. And each of these setbacks has hurt low- and moderate-income housing even more severely than housing in general. In short, the continuing decay of American urban centers and the persistence of widespread housing blight can be attributed in substantial measure to the way financial institutions distribute credit among competing claimants.

In an effort to ease some of the strains caused by this situation, the federal government inaugurated a series of housing and urban development—as well as small-business-assistance—programs during the New Deal and shortly thereafter. Because financial-institution operations were a major cause of the problems these programs were to address, and because the programs relied heavily upon these institutions for solutions, it was only natural that the Banking committees should acquire jurisdiction. In addition to their other responsibilities, therefore, the Banking committees function as the major arenas in Congress for shaping federal policy on the critical issue of the future of the city. Public housing, urban renewal, urban planning assistance, Federal Housing Administration (FHA) loan guarantees, water and sewer grants, housing subsidies, the Model Cities program, urban mass transit, new-town assistance, and a host of other federal urban programs all fall within their realm of responsibility. In fact, with the intensification of the urban crisis in the past decade and a half, the Banking committees have been spending more than half their time each year on housing and urban development matters. In the process, the Housing subcommittees of these two committees have emerged as major actors in their own right. They are the only subcommittees in Congress with jurisdiction over all the programs of a cabinet department—the Department of Housing and Urban Development. So important have these responsibilities become, in fact, that the Senate committee changed its name in 1970 from Banking and Currency to Banking, Housing and Urban Affairs to signify this new role and lay explicit claim to it for the future. In Chapter 4 we will explore how well these committees have carried out these critical urban responsibilities.

Consumer Credit

A fourth area that demonstrates the public stake in Banking committee activity is consumer credit, which has burgeoned in recent years. Between 1947 and 1971, while total debt in the United States grew five times, consumer debt grew eleven times.[27] By the end of 1971, consumer debt stood at $110 billion, making it in dollar terms the largest of all consumer issues. Of this $110 billion, moreover, 86 percent is controlled by financial intermediaries and only 14 percent by retailers themselves.[28]

What this means is that financial institutions are increasingly interposed between the consumer and the seller, raising a host of crucial new issues. One of these issues is the cost of consumer credit. The prevailing rate of 18 percent interest on outstanding balances plus the hidden 3 to 7 percent service charges that financial institutions charge retailers substantially raise the cost of consumer items and divert to financial institutions a larger share of each consumer dollar. Frequently, retail stores, particularly small ones, find themselves squeezed financially as a consequence— unable to compete without allowing credit-card purchases, but faced with difficult cash-flow problems when they do. Until recently, moreover, banks carefully disguised the true cost of consumer credit to card-holders. Even now, cash customers must pay more because of the existence of credit cards, since retailers typically add the bank-service charges to the price of their goods, whether bought on credit or not. In addition, the growth of consumer credit has fostered the expansion of a large consumer investigation industry whose inquisitional methods and accumulated files of personal data raise troubling civil-liberties questions.

Quite clearly, as the United States continues to move toward a "cashless" society, the way consumer credit is handled will become increasingly important, especially so since public comprehension of the intricacies of interest computation is quite limited and the opportunities for fraud correspondingly great. And it is to the Banking committees in Congress that the public must turn for protection.

ORPHAN ANNIE AND HER DADDY WARBUCKS

Despite the profound public stake in Banking committee decisions, these committees operate in virtual obscurity, far from the
purifying glare of public scrutiny. In this they share a fate similar
to that of other congressional committees, but it is a fate they
exhibit to an unusual degree, for the sheer complexity of Banking
committee subject matter makes it especially difficult for these
committees to generate public interest. The media respond accordingly, relegating Banking committee activities to the nether-
worlds of the financial or real estate sections while reserving
front-page coverage for committees with high "sex appeal," like Foreign Relations. "Even housing legislation gets no coverage to
speak of," conceded veteran *New York Times* reporter John Herbers.[29]

Since publicity competes only with money as the lifeblood of
Congress, inattention by public and press in turn breeds inattention, or worse, among committee members themselves. "The
Banking Committee is not a particularly desirable committee,"
one Senate Banking Committee staffer told us, "because you can't
get any headlines." Poor attendance, high member turnover, and
resulting concentration of power—as we will demonstrate below
—are the result. As Senator Joseph Clark (D., Pa.) put it in
1964, the Banking committees are like Orphan Annie, cut off
from those they need the most and hence largely defenseless in a
hostile world.[30]

But the Banking committees need not make their way in the
world completely alone. Like Orphan Annie, they have their own
Daddy Warbucks, all too eager to smother them in his warm
embrace. Banking committee actions intimately affect some of
the most powerful economic interests in the nation, interests that
long ago learned the wisdom of focusing attention on such decision-making outposts as the Banking committees in Congress.
The bankers in particular are in an unusually good position to

exert influence on Congress. As the editor of a symposium on banking in a respected legal journal recently wrote:

> Banking is a pervasive industry, represented in every town throughout the land and possessing in each locality extraordinary political influence by virtue of its strategic link with the entire business community and the typical status of bank managers as community pillars.[31]

To keep this "extraordinary political influence" on target, moreover, the bankers finance one of the smoothest lobbying operations in Washington, the American Bankers Association. The ABA maintains a research staff of several dozen to keep several steps ahead of information-starved congressional committees, a "government liaison" staff to present industry positions to congressmen and keep track of committee activity, and a "contact-banker" system to bring the all-important local pressure to bear when it is needed. The bankers also contribute actively to political campaigns to make sure that those on the receiving end of this treatment are persons sympathetic to industry views. In addition to campaign war chests generated locally, the bankers contribute to a central campaign finance organization called the Banking Profession Political Action Committee (Bank PAC; this group was called the Bankers Political Action Committee before 1970). As the ABA president pointed out on the eve of the 1972 elections, Bank PAC's mission was to channel the contributions of bankers to "those people who understand . . . the role that banking plays in the functioning of our economy and help them continue in office or get them into office." By "people who understand the role that banking plays," of course, Bank PAC meant people who would support industry positions. "Not to have people *favorably inclined* in relation to something over which they have decision-making power," the ABA president noted, "is just stupid."[32] Numerous members of the Banking committees, including the chairman and ranking minority member on the Senate side, apparently met this test, and were suitably rewarded with Bank PAC support.

The commercial bankers are not alone in showering such affection upon the Banking committees. The savings and loan associations and the home builders have similar resources, and identical inclinations. They too are wired in to local structures of power in every congressional district. They too maintain elaborate research and lobbying operations to immerse committee members in industry positions. They too bring local pressure to bear through intricate local contact networks. And they too reach into ample wallets at election time to reward those who have responded appropriately to their pleadings.

The staff director of the Senate Banking Committee may therefore have been speaking the literal truth when he boasted that, "This Committee fortunately deals with some of the best legislative liaison people [i.e. lobbyists] that money can buy."[33] But fortunate for whom? Intense interest-group involvement in a context characterized by public inattention and press neglect places tremendous strains even on those congressmen determined to resist special-interest pleadings. The tendency over time is to convert the policy-making process into a closed guild, an impervious "policy subsystem" linking interest groups, committee members, and administrative agencies together in an unholy alliance fundamentally at odds with the public's interests. According to some observers, this is precisely what has happened to the Banking committees. As John Herbers put it, "They've locked themselves into an insider's game."[34]

How accurate is this description? How have the Banking committees responded to the intense interest-group pressure they are under? What has determined this response? And what have been the consequences for the shape of public policy in the crucial areas under Banking Committee jurisdiction? These are the questions this book seeks to answer. The first step is to examine the committees themselves—their leadership, memberships, staff resources, decision-making patterns and positions in Congress—for these elements define the arena in which the policy battles are fought, and impart advantages to some competitors over others. Subsequent chapters will then explore the various policy battles that take place in this arena, and the consequences they have for us all.

2

The Arena:
The Banking
Committees and Their
Legislative Context*

Rumor has it that a red carpet was chosen for the House Banking Committee's hearing chamber to hide the blood spilled during chairman Wright Patman's frequent jousts with the nation's money lords. If so, then the mellow hues and somber decor of the Senate Banking Committee's chamber seem equally well chosen, symbolically underlining as they do an important contrast between the two committees. In part, this contrast is a product of the im-

* This chapter was completed before the dramatic leadership changes in the 94th Congress that replaced Wright Patman with Henry Reuss as chairman of the House Banking Committee and John Sparkman with William Proxmire as chairman of the Senate Banking Committee. Although we have made some changes to take account of this leadership turnover, we have left

portant structural differences between the House and the Senate. But in even larger part, it is the product of the fundamental difference between the chairmen of these two committees: between House chairman Wright Patman's rustic populism, with its earthy distrust of the financial wizardry of powerful New York bankers, and Senate chairman John Sparkman's sophisticated Old South urbanity, with its touch of humane paternalism, but also its irrepressible faith in the essential goodness of the man of means.

Because of the impressive powers of the chairman in congressional committees, these differences between Patman and Sparkman strongly influence the structure of decision-making, the pattern of staff activity, and ultimately the work produced in each committee. At the same time, their influence is muted by other committee members and by the overall context in which both committees must function. Taken together, these three elements —leadership, membership, and legislative context—shape the arena in which banking, housing and urban development policies are made in Congress. And since the shape of the arena has an important impact on the outcome of the game,[1] the first step toward understanding congressional policy on bank regulation, monetary affairs, housing, and urban development is to examine how these three elements interact in the case of these two committees. Let us look first at the House.

THE INTERNAL POLITICS OF THE HOUSE BANKING COMMITTEE

Leadership: "The Warrior from Patman's Switch"

In the politics of banking and housing, one man commands attention beyond all others: Wright Patman (D., Tex.), the elder

---

most of the chapter unchanged, first, because too little time has elapsed to assess the new chairman; second, because both Patman and Sparkman left imprints on their committees that are certain to persist for some time; third, because there is need for a clear view of the base line against which to statesman of the House and the chairman of the House Banking Committee from 1963 to 1974. Liberals habitually attack the seniority system in Congress on the ground that it systematically delivers decisive power into the hands of hide-bound conservatives responsible only to special-interest pleadings. Wright Patman is the exception that fights the rule. Looking like a wise old owl, with his round wire-rim glasses and penetrating glare, Patman is a champion of turn-of-the-century Populist radicalism who has functioned for almost half a century as the persistent conscience of the nation's money lords, and a nagging conscience at that. Reflecting the Populist-inspired and Depression-fed hostility toward financial institutions that pervaded his East Texas district when he was first elected in 1928, Patman arrived in Congress determined to challenge the giant banks whose monetary policies and lending practices he held largely responsible for the ruin of countless small farmers and businessmen. One of the earliest manifestations of his zeal was the formal bill of impeachment he brought in January 1932 against long-time Secretary of the Treasury and banker Andrew Mellon on grounds of conflict of interest.[2] When Mellon resigned one month later, ostensibly to accept an appointment as ambassador to England (prompting one overseas acquaintance to wire Patman, "Don't send us a rotten Mellon"), Patman's credibility as an effective adversary of the bank barons was firmly established.

Unlike many other one-time Populists, however, Patman's ardor for the cause has not mellowed with time. On the contrary, his feisty suspicion of the men of money remains as intense today as it was when he first arrived in Congress, prompting one wag on the staff of the Senate Banking Committee to conclude that "Patman must have been frightened by a banker while a fetus."[3] During his long tenure (1942–63) as chairman of the House Select Committee to Investigate the Problems of Small Business,

---

measure any change brought about by the new chairman; and fourth, because many of the features of committee operation analyzed here are sufficiently fundamental to be largely unaffected by the change in leadership.

Patman generated a constant stream of inquiries into the concentration of financial power in the hands of commercial banks and private foundations.[4]

No sooner did Patman take over as chairman of the House Banking Committee in 1963 than he launched a blistering public attack on "superconcentration" in the banking industry and on the Federal Reserve Board, which he characterized as "a pliable instrument for a comparatively few mighty bankers."[*5] Since that date, Patman has transformed the House Banking Committee into a watchdog of the banking industry, investigating and publicizing the links between the bankers and the Federal Reserve System,[7] the pattern of mergers and takeovers among banks,[8] the extent of bank expansion into nonbanking activities,[9] and the interlocking directorates among financial institutions.[10] In the Ninety-first and Ninety-second Congresses alone, Patman sponsored legislation to prevent the expansion of bank holding companies into nonbanking activities,[†] outlaw interlocking directorships among financial institutions,[‡] require banks and pension funds to invest a certain portion of their assets in a National Development Bank that would make low-interest loans to home buyers and local governments,[§] and permit the General Accounting Office (GAO) to audit the Federal Reserve Board.[¶] So intense has Patman's fire been, in fact, that he is regularly accused of carrying out a "ven-

---

* This Patman attack was later reprinted and circulated widely as a booklet entitled *The ABC's of Money*. So widespread was its distribution, in fact, that the American Bankers Association felt obliged to develop its own booklet in reply and to send it out to local bankers with instructions to carry its message to "students and teachers" in particular since "a substantial number of students are writing to the [Banking] Committee and to their Congressmen asking for copies of the Patman speech."[6]

† H.R. 6778, 91st Cong. This bill passed in amended form.

‡ H.R. 5700, 92nd Cong. This bill never came to a vote.

§ H.R. 14639, 91st Cong., 2nd sess. (1970). This bill was part of the Emergency Home Finance Act of 1970, but was ultimately dropped.

¶ This proposal was offered as an amendment to the 1972 housing bill, which was ultimately killed in the Rules Committee. It was then introduced in the 93rd Congress (H.R. 10265) and passed the House in May 1974, but was killed in the Senate.

detta" against the bankers with the aim of destroying the commercial banking system, and the Fed as well.*

What really lies behind Patman's attack, however, is a quite straightforward set of beliefs. In Patman's view, the concentration of tremendous financial resources in the hands of the nation's largest commercial banks keeps interest rates artificially high, distorts the flow of credit in the economy in the direction of large corporate borrowers, and undermines competition throughout the economy.[13] Patman is an advocate of "unit banking"—widely dispersed and independently owned commercial banks, which he believes are more responsive to the needs of local small businesses and consumers than the huge banking complexes with numerous "branch offices" that have come into existence under the regulatory scheme devised during the Depression. The mammoth New York banks that dominate American commercial banking are thus naturally a special object of Patman's ire. "We have had more trouble from the few acres of land comprising Wall Street since this Government was established," he noted recently, "than we have had from any similar land area in any part of the world."[14]

Particularly irksome to Patman is the evidence of commercial-bank expansion into nonbanking activities through trust departments, interlocking directorates, and holding companies.[15] Patman is convinced that such expansion undermines competition by leading bankers to refuse loans to enterprises in competition with those whose stock they own or whose board members and officers sit on the bank's board. Patman claims, in fact, that an effort by several of his constituents to organize a steel plant in Texas in the 1930s was almost scuttled because the directors of the New York banks to which the Texans had to go for capital were also on the boards of directors of the large, established steel companies, and

* The "vendetta" charge came up most recently during debate on Patman's bill to allow GAO auditing of the Fed.[11] When Patman introduced his omnibus H.R. 5700, the Banking Reform Act of 1971 designed to outlaw interlocking directorates among banks, committee member Laurence Williams (R., Pa.) dubbed it the "Banking Destruction Act of 1971."[12]

vice versa.[16] When these banking titans began forming holding companies and expanding into nonbanking businesses during the 1960s, therefore, Patman responded with predictable outrage and alarm, and quickly introduced legislation to bring such financial conglomerates under federal regulation. The growth of financial conglomerates, Patman noted at the outset of hearings on this legislation in 1969, constitutes "one of the most important subjects related to banking and the overall economy that this committee has considered in many years," because "this movement could change the entire economic structure of the United States."[17] (In Chapter 3 we examine the fate of this legislation and its relation to the overall pattern of bank regulation in detail.)

Closely related to this distrust of the massive economic power of the large commercial banks is Patman's deep suspicion of banker influence in the setting of governmental economic policy. Patman's was thus one of the few voices raised in opposition to the 1935 Banking Act, which gave private bankers extensive influence over the network of twelve Federal Reserve District Banks and over Fed policy-making generally. "I am in favor of getting the Government out of private business," he pointed out, "but at the same time I am in favor of getting the bankers out of the Government business."[18] Patman contends, with some justification, that the regional bank structure, coupled with the emergence of the Open Market Committee as the basic Fed policy-making unit, weakened public control of the Federal Reserve System and shifted system powers "from the Federal Reserve Board to groups more closely allied with private banking interests."[19] The recent rapid expansion of the money supply, Patman contends, is evidence of this fact, for it reflects the Fed's traditional concern with "smoothing ups and downs in the cost of short-term loans to banks" despite the resulting pressure this puts on prices.*[20] Pat-

* An alternative explanation for this expansion is that the Fed is increasingly losing control of the size of the money supply because many banks are leaving the system to take advantage of more lax state reserve requirements.[21]

man has thus led the opposition in Congress against the doctrine of Fed "independence," the notion that the Fed must be allowed to operate in secret, free of outside political pressures from either Congress or the president. The members of Congress are considered to be "competent enough to pass on the use of nuclear missiles, the atomic bomb, the appropriations and expenditures of government, the drafting of young men into the services and into war," Patman complains, "but not to pass on monetary matters."[22] Patman's introduction of legislation to subject the Federal Reserve Board to audits by the General Accounting Office during the Ninety-second, and later the Ninety-third, Congress reflects this sentiment. "No member can get any information from the Federal Reserve," Patman argued on the floor of the House during debate on this legislation in 1974. "They will tell a member it is a secret. . . . Meaningful GAO audits will end secrecy and unaccountability in Federal Reserve operations."[23]

Given his strong opinions on the subjects before his committee, it is understandable that Patman takes a vigorous view of his powers as chairman. As he sees it, the powers of the chairman are the only weapons he has to combat the vastly superior political clout of his opponents. "The big banks have built-in intimidation," the chairman explained to us. "They don't have to say a word."[24] Accordingly, Patman has been determined to exploit every scrap of influence the committee chairmanship affords him.

This determination was strengthened, moreover, by the peculiar circumstances under which Patman inherited this position. Although he came to Congress in 1929, Patman did not manage to secure a seat on the Banking Committee until 1937, eight years later. He thus lost the opportunity to begin amassing seniority on this committee as early as he might have. Patman charges that the bankers arranged this deliberately.[25] At the very least, it is clear that it was *not* an absence of openings that was responsible for keeping him off the committee for so long. In fact, Brent Spence, the man Patman ultimately succeeded as Banking Committee chairman, entered Congress in 1931, two years *after* Patman began his service. Yet Spence managed to get on the Banking Committee well before Patman. As a consequence, when committee chairman Henry Steagall died in 1943, it was Spence and not Patman who was next in line for the chairmanship. Thus did the bankers escape twenty extra years of hostile fire from a Banking Committee chairman opposed to the big banks. Indeed, as the years passed, many must have come to believe that they would escape entirely the warrior from Patman's Switch, Texas, or at least that he would be too infirm when he took control to do much damage. What has happened instead is that the delay has given Patman a peculiar sense of urgency and drive. As one banking lobbyist moaned, "Patman must have a deal with the devil not to die until he gets the Fed."[26]

Unlike most committee chairmen, who restrict themselves to timid compromiser or stick-in-the-mud conservative roles,[27] Patman is what might be termed an "activist-initiator" chairman, who has endeavored to give substance to the much-doubted view that Congress can be a coequal branch of government. For those eager to halt the surrender of legislative initiative to the executive branch and private lobbies, Patman's mode of committee leadership may consequently provide a useful object lesson. His use of committee staff, subcommittees, and hearings show how this has been attempted.

Committee Staff. The heart of the Patman operation is his use of staff. Even in the 1950s and early 1960s he was using his position as chairman of the House Select Committee to Investigate the Problems of Small Business to begin assembling a small staff of lawyers and economists to conduct inquiries into financial-institution structure and operations, focusing particularly on commercial-bank trust departments. When he took over as chairman of the Banking Committee in 1963, Patman put the same techniques to work there, but on a larger scale. To do so, however, he had to begin almost from scratch, for chairman Brent Spence had subscribed religiously to that false economy in committee financing that has had so much to do with the decline in

TABLE 6.

Research Reports Issued by the House Banking and
Currency Committee, 1963–72 (Partial List)

Title	Congress	Date of issue
An Alternative Approach to the Monetary Mechanism	88th	Aug. 1964
Bank Holding Companies: Scope of Operations and Stock Ownership	88th	May 1963
Banks Holding Treasury Tax and Loan Account Balances as of October 15, 1963	88th	Dec. 1963
Chain Banking: Stockholder and Loan Links of 200 Largest Member Banks	88th	Apr. 1963
Commercial Bank Reporting Practices to Stockholders	88th	Mar. 1964
Comparative Regulations of Financial Institutions	88th	Nov. 1963
Correspondent Relations: A Survey of Banking Opinion	88th	Oct. 1964
Federal Reserve System After 50 Years	88th	Aug. 1964
Federal Reserve's Attachment to the Free Reserve Requirement	88th	May 1964
Impact of Examination Practices Upon Commercial Bank Lending Policies	88th	Apr. 1964
Money Facts	88th	Sept. 1964
Prevalent Monetary Policy and its Consequences	88th	May 1964
Primer on Money	88th	Aug. 1964
Report on the Correspondent Banking System	88th	Dec. 1964
Structure of Ownership of Member Banks and the Pattern of Loans Made on Hypothecated Bank Stock	88th	Oct. 1964
Study of Federal Credit Programs	88th	Feb. 1964
Twenty Largest Stockholders of Record in Member Banks of the Federal Reserve System	88th	Oct. 1964
Audits of Banks by Public Accountants	89th	Mar. 1966
Investigation into Crown Savings Bank Failure	89th	Feb. 1966
Reorganization of Federal Bank Supervision	89th	Apr. 1965
Bank Stock Ownership and Control	90th	Dec. 1966
Framework of Monetary Policy	90th	Jan. 1967
Acquisitions, Changes in Control, and Bank Stock Loans of Insured Banks	90th	1967
Commercial Banks and their Trust Activities: Emerging Influence on the American Economy (2 vols.)	90th	1967

function to shepherding administration or special-interest bills through Congress, and at worst violate the intent of the 1946 Legislative Reorganization Act, which forbade the use of committee staffs for constituent or campaign work, Patman has pursued a quite different course. He has used his staff resources to do basic background research designed to seize the legislative initiative from the bureaucracy and the private interests and return it to Congress. In the ten years after Patman took over as chairman, the Banking Committee staff produced over thirty independent research reports on various aspects of bank structure, Federal Reserve policy, and federal financial policy (see Table 6). These reports, which provide voluminous data unavailable anywhere else, have already become standard reference works for students of American banking. In the process, they have frequently injected wholly new perspectives into the debate on financial policy and significantly altered the entire legislative environment within which banking and monetary policy is formulated. As a consequence, even his foes credit Patman with being a "remarkable teacher."[29] The series of Banking Committee studies and hearings on the Federal Reserve System in 1963 and 1964, for example, constituted the first serious congressional inquiry into Fed structure and operations in two decades, and nearly led to some basic reforms in Fed decision-making. The detailed inquiries into changing commercial-bank structure in the mid-1960s, culminating in an explosive documentation of the alarming growth of one-bank holding companies, prepared the ground for the passage of probably the most important federal antitrust legislation in two decades, the Bank Holding Company Act of 1970 (discussed in Chapter 3). When the Penn Central, the nation's largest transportation company, collapsed in 1970, only Patman of all the committee chairmen in Congress thought to put congressional staff people to work to find out why. They discovered that the Penn Central was really owned by a block of giant commercial banks, whose directors formed a clear majority on the Penn Central board of directors and milked the railroad for all it was worth during its declining years before unloading their stock on an un-suspecting public under somewhat questionable circumstances just before the ultimate collapse.[30] This report formed the back-drop for Patman's introduction of the omnibus Bank Reform Act of 1971, which was designed to outlaw such interlocks. Not until three years later did the Federal Trade Commission get around to reaching much the same conclusions as the Banking Committee report and bringing suit against the Penn Central management.

Patman's staff also came close to breaking the Watergate case open as early as August 1972, well before the Senate Watergate Committee or even the Washington *Post* put it all together. While the Justice Department fumbled around under the weight of the White House–directed coverup pressures, Patman set his staff to work tracing the funds used to pay off the Watergate burglars. By the end of August, they had developed a remarkably clear picture of the intricate laundering operation this cash underwent as it passed illegally from corporate coffers, through the Committee to Re-elect the President, into H. R. Haldeman's safe, and ulti-mately to the Watergate defendants. Had the Banking Committee membership not been subjected to vigorous White House pressure —which the White House transcripts show was orchestrated from John Dean's office and which ultimately induced a majority of the committee to vote against granting the chairman subpoena power to compel White House and CREEP testimony—the whole sordid story might have surfaced a year earlier than it did.

By setting his staff to work preparing independent research reports, Patman thus endeavors to avoid having his committee and Congress swept along by materials developed by the bankers or their friends in the bureaucracy. His committee is one of the few legislative committees in Congress with trained social scien-tists, instead of just lawyers, on its staff. Indeed, the staff director is a former economics professor. But staffers emphasize that the committee staff reports are not academic exercises; each is geared to a clear legislative purpose.[31] A recent report on bank regu-latory structure is a perfect example. In 1970, during congressional consideration of the bank holding company legislation, President Nixon appointed a Commission on Financial Structure and Regulation (the Hunt Commission) to explore the need for basic changes in the regulatory provisions governing American financial structure. The commission was the brainchild of Treasury Under Secretary Charls Walker, the former executive director of the American Bankers Association, who worked closely with it during 1970 and 1971 and then took charge of developing legislative proposals based on the commission's report. To avoid being outmaneuvered by this blue-ribbon assemblage into accepting the Treasury Department's perspective, Patman put his staff to work developing its own report on financial structure and regulation. As a result, by the time the administration introduced its massive, fifty-six-page Financial Institutions Act in October 1973,[32] Congress had available to it a lengthy staff report of the House Banking Committee that provided the groundwork for a set of regulatory reforms much closer to Patman's views than to those of the Treasury and the ABA.[33] Although no action has yet been taken on these proposals, it seems clear that the availability of the Patman committee report will help raise issues that might otherwise have been avoided. Indeed, this has been the overall consequence of the whole series of House Banking Committee reports: while not always successful in converting a majority in the committee or in the Congress to Patman's side (as we will see below), they have nevertheless forced attention to long-neglected issues and provided Congress with more data and more well-developed points of view against which to judge the issues than would otherwise have been the case—or is the case with most other committees.

This use of staff energies has not been without its costs, however. By keeping the staff under his tight personal control, Patman frustrates committee colleagues who need the benefit of staff assistance themselves. Moreover, there is a kind of "cabal" quality to the Patman staff operation, which alienates committee moderates and leads to suspicions about what the staff is doing and how much it can be trusted by members outside the Patman "inner circle." With staff energies absorbed in investigative reports and in the chairman's perennial battles with the bank regulatory authorities, too little time is left for the important task of personally explaining issues to other members and working with them individually or in small groups to perfect language and otherwise participate in the legislative process in ways that formal committee sessions do not allow. As a consequence, Patman sometimes unnecessarily loses support from members who feel they have been transformed into mere spectators, instead of equal partners, in commiteee deliberations.[34]

In only one case has Patman been forced to surrender control over committee staffing. During Brent Spence's tenure as Banking Committee chairman, the committee's important Housing Subcommittee established a tradition of autonomy under subcommittee chairman Albert Rains (D., Ala.). Central to this tradition was a separate subcommittee staff controlled by the subcommittee chairman and not the full-committee chairman. When Rains retired and William Barrett (D., Pa.) assumed command of the Housing Subcommittee in 1966, Patman sought to alter this tradition and bring the Housing Subcommittee staff under his own control—a move that ultimately failed.

But though Patman lost this battle, he may have won the war, for his penchant for background reports to wrest the initiative from lobbyists and the administrative agencies has rubbed off on the Housing Subcommittee staff as well. For a long time, subcommittee members had been disturbed by their inability to develop a comprehensive overview of the operations and effects of the nation's complex housing programs. The regular hearing and legislative process was not sufficient, so subcommittee members split into three study panels in October 1970 and authorized urban experts to present thirty-six research papers to them. Although the panels were not as successful in providing a comprehensive view as hoped, and though Patman criticized them for their lack of clear legislative focus, the exercise constituted a significant first step away from the subcommittee's bondage to the agencies and their industry clients for information on housing policy.[35]

The Subcommittees. Patman's utilization of Banking Committee subcommittees provides additional evidence of the chairman's activist-initiator style. Before Patman became chairman, the House Banking Committee's subcommittees were designated only by number and given no clear jurisdiction. This pattern suited the generally conservative outlook of chairman Spence, who preferred to keep committee members from establishing proprietary rights to any issue for fear that overly activist legislation might result. The one exception Spence permitted was the Housing Subcommittee, which fellow southerner Albert Rains established and dominated.

When Patman became chairman, he formalized the subcommittee structure. Seven subcommittees were organized, and each was assigned a general subject matter specialty: Domestic Finance, Housing, International Finance, Bank Supervision and Insurance, International Trade, Consumer Affairs, and Small Business. Although Patman claimed the Domestic Finance Subcommittee for himself, he distributed the other subcommittee chairmanships among his senior colleagues. The overall result was to democratize committee structure by creating alternative centers of power within the committee.

But this democratization went only so far. Patman retained the power to determine subcommittee membership and to control the flow of legislation through—or around—the subcommittees. And he has used this power extensively to promote his own policy goals. As one committee staffer put it, "The chairman plays the subcommittees pretty close to his chest." Despite the existence of a Bank Supervision Subcommittee, for example, Patman typically steers important bank regulation proposals to his Domestic Finance Subcommittee or sidesteps the subcommittee stage altogether. Thus, Patman's 1971 proposal to radically restrict interlocking directorates and other tie-in arrangements between banks and other corporations (the Bank Reform Act) went directly to the full committee for hearings, bypassing the subcommittee structure entirely. In fact, of the three major pieces of legislation considered by the Banking Committee in the Ninety-second Congress, only one—the housing bill—received subcommittee scrutiny. The other two—the Emergency Loan Guarantee Act, authorizing the government to guarantee a loan to Lockheed Aircraft, and the Economic Stabilization Act, authorizing wage and price controls—went straight to the full committee. As a result, during the first session of the Ninety-second Congress, the Banking Committee's seven subcommittees taken together clocked only twenty-six days of hearings or executive sessions, ten of them by the Housing Subcommittee alone. The full committee registered thirty-nine days of sessions.[36] In this way, Patman limits subcommittee autonomy and maintains better control over the content of legislation.

Only the Housing Subcommittee has managed to minimize this control, but not without a struggle. As we have seen, by the time Patman assumed command of the committee in 1963, the Housing Subcommittee had already established a tradition of autonomy under the effective leadership of Albert Rains. With jurisdiction over the most exciting subject in the Banking Committee's bailiwick, the Housing Subcommittee has attracted all the senior committee members on both Democratic and Republican sides (except Patman), and has grown steadily in size as additional members clamor for a piece of this action. As a result, Housing Subcommittee bills come to the full committee virtually wired for clearance, a situation Patman has found disconcerting, to say the least. The upshot has been a series of moves to clip the subcommittee's wings. At the opening of the Ninety-second Congress, for example, Patman proposed eliminating a separate budget for the Housing Subcommittee and merging it with the full committee budget—a move that would have given him substantially expanded influence over the subcommittee's staff. When this failed, Patman proposed breaking the subcommittee in two by creating a new subcommittee to handle urban mass transit. This proposal failed as well, despite the support of younger members of the committee like New York's Ed Koch and Baltimore's Parren Mitchell, both of whom were too junior to win seats on the coveted Housing Subcommittee but wanted a greater say on urban policies.* Frustrated, Patman took his revenge by subjecting the subcommittee's proposed 250-page 1972 housing bill to a meticulous line-by-line review in full committee. As Patman explained, "Barrett reported that bill to my committee after two years of study and wanted us to report it out immediately. I said, 'Hell, no!' I'm going to find out what's in that bill."[37] In short, Patman watches the subcommittees like a hawk, relying on them to the extent that they promote his policy goals and systematically bypassing them, or redoing their work, when it suits his purposes better.

He takes the same activist approach to conference committees. Appointing conferees to settle differences between House and Senate versions of a bill is a prerogative of the chairman. And, as one Patman aide confided, Patman uses this prerogative energetically as a "key source of power." Fortuitously, the top three Democrats on the committee aside from Patman (William Barrett, Leonor Sullivan of Missouri, and Henry Reuss of Wisconsin) typically support the chairman on bank-regulation issues. By arranging his conference committees so that these four most senior Democrats are in control, Patman can thus somehow win in conference battles he has lost in his committee. When the full Banking Committee refused to report out a consumer-finance regulation bill in 1970, for example, Patman and his colleagues managed to have it added during a conference with the Senate on another bill, so that the Fair Credit Reporting Act of 1970 went to the House floor without ever being reported out by the House

* This idea was adopted at the start of the 93rd Congress. By this time, however, a plan was already circulating in Congress to strip the Banking Committee of jurisdiction over urban mass transit.

Banking Committee. Thus are the chairman's powers used to promote the chairman's programs.

Hearings. This pattern of subcommittee use is in turn related to the way Patman uses the hearing process. As we have seen, the heart of the Patman "activist-initiator" style of committee leadership is an effort to reassert congressional initiative in the formulation of financial policy. But such an effort is inevitably controversial, requiring considerable changing of outlooks and much reeducation. "Wright Patman's great strength," one committee consultant pointed out, "is that he doesn't mind losing." One reason for this, undoubtedly, is that even if defeated, a novel proposal can have a substantial educational impact. And public hearings are one way to maximize that impact.

Patman makes active use of the educational potential of hearings. He coordinates the hearings with the issuance of major staff reports to ensure clear focus. He draws extensively on outside academic experts instead of relying exclusively on the regular stable of interest-group representatives who typically recite well-known organization positions. And he subjects opposition witnesses from industry or the agencies to Star Chamber–like quizzings and extended lectures. For example, during the hearings on the Bank Reform Act of 1971, Patman lectured Federal Reserve Board Chairman Arthur F. Burns for twenty minutes on the Fed's policy of collecting interest on the government bonds it purchases in the course of its Open Market operations instead of simply retiring the bonds and reducing the federal debt.[38] When Chase Manhattan Bank President David Rockefeller testified on this same bill, Patman treated his colleagues to an extended recital of the elaborate interlocks tying Chase Manhattan to supposedly competing financial institutions and ended up with a stinging rebuke to Rockefeller for Chase's legally questionable unloading of almost half a million shares of Penn Central stock on the basis of inside information just before the railroad's collapse.[39] HUD Secretary George W. Romney received much the same treatment when he arrived in June of 1972 to testify on the proposed 1972 housing bill. No sooner had Romney completed his testimony than Patman launched into a solid five minutes of intricate, prepared questions challenging the whole structure of federal housing policy as reflected in the bill. Under the committee's rule limiting each member to five minutes for questioning each witness, Patman barely had time to read his list of questions, let alone allow Romney to respond.[40] In the process, however, he managed to get some basic, underlying issues formally out on the table, and to require administration responses.

The hearing process, in short, is an integral part of the Patman leadership style, and the chairman consequently approaches it with all the cunning zeal of a country lawyer out to show the city slickers they still have a thing or two to learn. In fact, Banking Committee hearings are in many respects like elaborately staged seminars, with Patman in the role of teacher drawing information out of sometimes reluctant witnesses for the edification of committee members. And for those "students" who do not learn their lessons, this teacher can be a stern disciplinarian indeed.*

Patman also uses his control over hearings and over the committee schedule in the more traditional way, to prevent consideration of disagreeable legislation. In Patman's case the disagreeable legislation is not liberal legislation, as is usual with most committee chairmen, but special-interest legislation. The classic example was the Bank Merger Act of 1966, a bill designed to exempt commercial banks from antitrust regulation and thus to reverse a Supreme Court opinion that definitively held them liable to such

---

* For example, when freshman New York Congressman Edward Koch sought Patman's support for a post on the coveted Housing Subcommittee, Patman refused, reminding Koch that he had failed to support the chairman in opposing a proposal to enlarge the size of the Housing Subcommittee at the start of the 92nd Congress. "But I did support your proposal to break the subcommittee in two and create a separate one for mass transit," protested Koch. "Yes, but you must be more constant in your affections," was Patman's reply.

regulation. Following Senate passage of this bill, Patman simply refused to schedule it for consideration on the House side, hoping thereby to scuttle the proposal. Only a full-fledged committee revolt managed to circumvent the chairman. A similar situation arose in 1971, when the Senate passed a bill virtually emasculating the "class-action" provisions of the 1968 truth-in-lending law, provisions that allowed persons aggrieved by fraudulent consumer-credit practices to bring suit on behalf of all persons similarly affected and thus make the suit financially feasible. Rather than risk surrendering these provisions, which were designed to deter consumer-credit fraud, Patman simply pigeonholed the Senate bill and ultimately killed it.

Through his control of committee staff, subcommittees, scheduling, and hearings, Wright Patman has sought to seize the initiative on Congress' behalf in the area of bank regulation and financial policy. His efforts represent, if nothing else, an effective one-man oversight operation that keeps the bank regulatory agencies to which Congress has delegated so much authority on the defensive. Patman's office is a veritable clearinghouse for complaints from those aggrieved by bank regulatory-authority actions, particularly if those actions favor large commercial banks over smaller competitors or over nonbank financial institutions. Patman's files thus overflow with correspondence with the regulators, and his batting average is generally judged to be high.*

In addition, Patman has been successful in pushing legislation to protect nonbank financial institutions from the power of the commercial banks. Credit unions and savings and loan associations have benefited particularly from his support. Patman's efforts in July 1974 to stop the First National City Bank of New

---

* Typical was the correspondence in 1972 with the Federal Reserve Board over two cases of questionable interlocking directorates that seemed to violate the Bank Holding Company legislation. By raising this issue formally with the Fed, Patman and his staff managed not only to have these two cases declared improper but also to get twelve other cases outlawed by the Fed as well.[41]

York from selling $650 million worth of new certificates of deposit aimed at attracting the savings of small investors who would otherwise put their funds in savings and loan associations is just the latest example of his solicitude for these nonbank "savings intermediaries."[42] Patman's effectiveness in these efforts is immeasurably aided by the presence of a strong savings and loan lobby with extensive influence in Congress.

When it comes to the bank-regulation issues he cares most about, however, Patman's effectiveness has been much more limited. It may be true, as one staffer noted, that "There has not been any antitrust legislation out of Congress in the last twenty-two years, except for what has come from Banking and Currency."[43] But the Banking and Currency Committee's output in this field has itself been small, consisting almost exclusively of the one-bank holding company legislation of 1970, which, as we shall see below, emerged from the legislative process a seriously flawed piece of legislation, from Patman's perspective. But Patman's efforts have not yet succeeded in disrupting the power of bank trust departments, in preventing interlocking directorates among banks or between them and other firms, in putting an end to bank ownership of stock in competing banks, in forcing banks and pension funds to invest a larger portion of their assets in housing or a National Development Bank, in bringing the Federal Reserve under greater congressional control, or even in subjecting the Federal Reserve System to a General Accounting Office audit.

Part of the reason for these defeats undoubtedly lies with Patman's stubbornness and bullheadedness, and his tendency to overstate his case. Some critics charge, for example, that Patman lost a golden opportunity to reshape Federal Reserve structure in 1964 by making much more of the Fed's presumed subservience to the bankers than even those professional economists most hostile to the Fed could endorse.[44] At the same time, however, Patman's frustrations are also a product of the composition of Banking Committee membership.

Membership

There were thirty-seven members on the Banking Committee in the Ninety-second Congress—twenty-two Democrats and fifteen Republicans. For most of these, this committee was their second or third choice—well behind Foreign Affairs and Appropriations, and frequently behind Commerce and Public Works as well. This is understandable, given the committee's jurisdiction; for, except for the housing and urban development programs, service on it yields few fruits that can directly help constituents, and thus help members get reelected. As a consequence, to the extent that this committee has any appeal, it appeals mostly to members with urban districts, who, like Democrat William S. Moorhead of Pittsburgh—one of the few committee members interviewed who indicated that the Banking Committee was his first choice—see in this committee a chance to help local constituents with urban-renewal or housing efforts. As Moorhead pointed out, member-ship on Banking and Currency gives you "more clout with HUD."[45]

The committee's composition reflects this fact: only seven (19 percent) of its thirty-seven members in 1972 represented rural districts; the rest came from central-city or suburban districts, the former accounting for 38 percent of the members, the latter for 43 percent (see Table 7). Even among metropolitan regions,

TABLE 7.

Constituencies of House Banking Committee Members, 92nd Congress

	Central city		Suburbs		Rural		Total	
	Number	Per-cent*	Number	Per-cent*	Number	Per-cent*	Number	Per-cent*
Democrats	13	59.1	3	13.6	6	27.3	22	100.0
Republicans	1	6.7	13	86.7	1	6.7	15	100.0
Total	14	37.8	16	43.2	7	18.9	37	100.0

* Read percentages across.

Banking Committee membership is geographically concentrated. New York and Pennsylvania have four members each on the committee, and Ohio, New Jersey, California, and Texas have three each. These six states alone thus account for 54 percent of House Banking Committee members, considerably more than their 39 percent of the *total* U.S. population but accurately reflecting the fact that these states account for 54 percent of the *metropolitan*-area population in the country.

This heavy representation of mostly northern urban areas on the Banking Committee naturally affects the committee's overall ideological coloration. In a word, this committee tends to be more "liberal" than the House as a whole, as shown in Table 8. As a

TABLE 8.
House Banking Committee Ideology
as Reflected in Floor-Vote Ratings,
1971

Rating of:		Median	Mean	Standard deviation	Chairman
Americans for Democratic Action (Liberal)	Committee members	49	46.2	32.1	24
	Entire House	30	39.6	32.2	xxxx
Americans for Constitutional Action (Conservative)	Committee members	48	47	31	48
	Entire House	54	51.0	31.8	xxxx
Committee on Political Education (Labor)	Committee members	66	58.6	29.9	54.5
	Entire House	50	53.2	33.1	xxxx

consequence, it sometimes has difficulties getting broad House support for its measures.

But Banking Committee liberalism is a relative matter, and the liberal edge on the committee is a fairly narrow one. Though the committee is heavily weighted toward metropolitan constituencies, many of these are Republican-leaning suburban districts unsympathetic to the housing and urban development needs of the central-city poor. Indeed, some of these districts are represented by Goldwater conservatives eager to eliminate the government role in housing altogether—for example, Republicans Benjamin B. Blackburn of Atlanta and John H. Rousselot of Los Angeles. The shift of a few key votes can thus eradicate the committee's slight liberal majority on particular issues. This means that a few key "moderates," like Southern Democrat Robert G. Stephens, Jr., of Georgia and Ranking Republican William B. Widnall of New Jersey, hold the key to liberal majorities on urban legislation in the committee (see Table 9).* The price of committee endorsement of liberal programs, therefore, is accommodation of the views of these pivotal moderate-conservatives.

Even this slim liberal majority on social-welfare measures disappears on bank-regulation issues, however. In attracting congressmen from the urban industrial states, after all, the House Banking Committee simultaneously attracts members from the banking capitals of the country. The six states that account for a majority of Banking Committee members account not only for a majority of the nation's metropolitan population, but also close to half of all its commercial-bank assets, as Table 10 below shows.

Given the leadership role bankers typically play in local politics, it is understandable that many members selected from these districts should be favorably disposed to bank interests. In addition, the party caucuses responsible for committee assignments usually steer members with financial experience to the Banking Committee, so that numerous members have personal business interests in banks. For example, Congressman Bill Chappell, Jr. (D., Fla.), a director and stockholder of a Florida bank, requested assignment to the Judiciary Committee, but was assigned to Banking and Currency instead at the prompting of the Florida delegation.[46] Other Banking Committee members who have been or are now officers or stockholders in banks include Leonor Sulli-

---

* Widnall was defeated in a reelection bid in 1974.

TABLE 9.

House Banking Committee Voting Blocs* on Social-Welfare Issues,
92nd Congress

Liberals	Conservatives	Swing Votes
Wright Patman (D., Tex.)	Tom Gettys (D., S.C.)	Robt. G. Stephens (D., Ga.)
William Barrett (D., Pa.)	Tom Bevill (D., Ala.)	William Widnall (R., N.J.)
Leonor Sullivan (D., Mo.)	Charles Griffin (D., Miss.)	Florence Dwyer (R., N.J.)
Henry Reuss (D., Wis.)	Bill Chappell (D., Fla.)	J. William Stanton (R., Ohio)
Thomas L. Ashley (D., Ohio)	Albert Johnson (R., Pa.)	Garry Brown (R., Mich.)
William S. Moorhead (D., Pa.)	Ben Blackburn (R., Ga.)	
Fernand St. Germain (D., R.I.)	Lawrence Williams (R., Pa.)	
Henry B. Gonzalez (D., Tex.)	Chalmers Wylie (R., Ohio)	
Joseph O. Minish (D., N.J.)	Philip Crane (R., Ill.)	
Richard Hanna (D., Cal.)	John Rousselot (R., Cal.)	
Frank Annunzio (D., Ill.)	Stewart McKinney (R., Conn.)	
Thomas Rees (D., Cal.)	Norman Lent (R., (N.Y.)	
James Hanley (D., N.Y.)	William Archer (R., Tex.)	
Frank Brasco (D., N.Y.)		
Edward Koch (D., N.Y.)		
William R. Cotter (D., Conn.)		
Parren Mitchell (D., Md.)		
Margaret Heckler (R., N.J.)		
William Frenzel (R., Minn.)		

* Based on interest-group ratings on floor votes and interviews.

TABLE 10.

Proportion of House Banking Committee Membership,
U.S. Metropolitan Population, and Commercial
Bank Assets Accounted for by Six States, 92nd Congress

	Committee Members		Percent of total U.S. metropolitan population	Percent of total U.S. bank assets, 1969
	Number	Percent of total		
New York	4	10.8	12.1	20.7
Pennsylvania	4	10.8	7.4	6.0
California	3	8.1	18.3	10.2
Texas	3	8.1	5.5	5.3
Ohio	3	8.1	6.2	4.5
New Jersey	3	8.1	4.6	3.0
Total	20	54.0	54.1	49.7

SOURCE: *U.S. Statistical Abstract*, 1970.

van (D., Mo.), Henry Reuss (D., Wis.), William Moorhead
(D., Pa.), Robert Stephens (D., Ga.), Richard Hanna (D., Cal.),
Tom Gettys (D., S.C.), Thomas M. Rees (D., Cal.), William R.
Cotter (D., Conn.), William Stanton (R., Ohio), and W. R.
Archer (R., Tex.). Still other members have business ties to the
banking industry growing out of practice in law firms with bank
clients, a situation chairman Patman considers "the worst evil in
Congress."[47]

The bank lobby groups take an active part in the committee
recruitment and promotion process. The American Bankers Association, for example, instructs its "contact bankers" in each
congressional district to report extensively on the background and
views of newly elected congressmen, and then urges newcomers
with views congenial to the ABA to seek membership on the
Banking Committee.[48] In return, such members can count on
banker support during elections. On the eve of the 1972 elections,
for example, the director of the ABA's campaign finance arm
made it clear that members of the Banking committees in Congress had a first call on the organization's campaign war chest.[49]

For those members supportive of the bankers' positions, the rewards can be substantial. For example, Republican William Stanton of Ohio, the son of a banker, received contributions to his 1970 congressional campaign from six officers of the First National City Bank of New York, the senior vice president of California's mammoth Bank of America, the Bankers Political Action Committee, and the Cleveland Trust Company, among others. Congressman Thomas L. ("Lud") Ashley (D., Ohio) was similarly blessed, receiving substantial help from the ABA's Bankers Political Action Committee, the Ohio Bankers Committee, and several bank officers.[50]

The upshot of these various pressures and relationships is to disrupt liberal-conservative alignments on bank-regulation issues before the committee. As we will see more fully in Chapter 3, Patman can usually count on support from his three most senior Democratic colleagues on the committee: William Barrett, Leonor Sullivan, and Henry Reuss. Barrett, the second-ranking Democrat, is a wily Philadelphia "ward healer" of the old school whose emotional attachment to the underdog and deep sense of party loyalty regularly place him on Patman's side in showdowns with the bank barons. Sullivan, the third-ranking Democrat, has led the battle for consumer-finance regulation on the committee and has joined Patman in his efforts to regulate interlocking directorates and conflicts of interest in the banking business.[51] Henry Reuss, the fourth-ranking Democrat, is one of the few committee members with sufficient expertise in economics to match wits with Patman, and his support for Patman's efforts to keep tabs on the growth of bank economic power, regulate commercial-bank expansion into nonbanking business, and subject the Fed to greater public control has added an important aura of academic respectability to Patman's program.

But Patman frequently encounters key defections farther down the line. Particularly bothersome to the chairman is the loss of a key group of liberal Democrats and moderate Republicans, a group that one committee staffer terms the "Ivy League liberals"

—people like Lud Ashley, William Moorhead, Richard Hanna, and Tom Rees among the Democrats, and William Stanton and Garry Brown (Mich.) among the Republicans. "These guys come to Congress in their thirties as promising $20,000–$25,000-a-year-attorneys and businessmen with high ideals and great enthusiasm," noted one close observer of the committee.

> But after six or seven years they find themselves approaching middle age with decent incomes but no real security, while their former law partners back home are secure and prosperous. They need $50,000–$150,000 to cover campaign costs every two years, just to stay in office. Since bank funds are easy to get, since bank issues are complex and therefore easy to camouflage, and since these members are socially close to the middle-level business-professional leadership of their communities in which local bankers play so crucial a role, support for banker positions on the committee comes to seem entirely natural.[52]

Many of these members have long-standing business or political relationships with the large commercial bankers in their urban districts. They therefore come to Congress with little of that ingrained hostility to prosperous commercial banks that figures so prominently in Patman's political philosophy, and prefer to err in the direction of laxity toward banks rather than toward regulations that might increase bank competition or restrain bank growth.

Typical of this group is fifth-ranking Democrat Lud Ashley of Toledo, a Yale graduate with a 93 percent cumulative rating from the liberal Americans for Democratic Action. Like many other northern, urban liberals, Ashley has built a substantial part of his congressional career on active promotion of local urban-renewal efforts, which has put him in close working contact with local bankers.[53] Out of this contact has emerged a strong commitment on Ashley's part not to oppose the trends toward bank consolidations, bank mergers, and bank expansion into nonbanking fields, and to stand firm on the principle of Federal Reserve independence from the elected political leadership.[54] Along with the traditional conservative elements on the committee, Ashley and other members of the "Ivy League liberal" clique thus constitute an effective counterweight frustrating Patman's goals.

The 1966 Bank Merger Act episode mentioned above provides probably the most dramatic illustration of the power of this curious anti-Patman coalition. This bill, to exempt commercial banks from coverage under the Sherman and Clayton antitrust laws and thus overrule a 1963 Supreme Court decision, had passed the Senate but was held up in the House by Patman's refusal to hold hearings on it. Under pressure from the ABA, the probank forces on the committee, led by "Ivy League liberals" Ashley, Moorhead, and Hanna, secretly convened a rump session of the committee while Patman was away visiting his ailing wife in the hospital. To avoid detection by Patman's staff, in fact, these dissidents sneaked into the committee hearing room through a rear door and then met with the lights off. Naturally, the insurrection infuriated Patman. Feeling on the committee was so bitter that finally Speaker John McCormack had to come in as peacemaker, and a compromise bill was sent to the floor the following year.

At the opening of the Ninetieth Congress in 1967, the dissidents in the battle of the Bank Merger Act sought to push their victory to completion by proposing a new set of committee rules that would permanently clip the chairman's wings. Among other things, the new rules would have restricted the chairman's power to hire and fire staff, appoint subcommittee members, and authorize the research reports that have been so central a part of the Patman legislative strategy. When it came time for the vote on the new rules, however, the dissidents' majority melted away, the victim of defections among several senior members on both sides of the aisle who apparently objected to weakening an office they might some day inherit. Patman consequently escaped from the episode with a set of compromise rules that left his powers as chairman virtually intact, requiring, for example, only prior "notice" instead of prior approval of forthcoming staff reports. Nevertheless, the embers of the battles of '66 and '67 still smolder close to the surface in this committee, kept alive by the frequent blasts of hostile wind from one side or the other.[55] And as we will see more fully below, the battle lines formed neatly again over the Bank Holding Company Act in 1969, although this time Patman successfully prepared a counterattack on the House floor.

Despite the Banking Committee's twenty-two-to-fifteen Democratic majority, and its generally liberal-progressive cast on standard social-welfare and civil-rights issues, therefore, chairman Patman frequently encounters nothing but frustration in his efforts to promote the bank-regulation, consumer-finance, and Fed-limitation measures he cares most about. His response has generally been to bear down ever more forcefully with the powers that are his as chairman. As a result, members complain bitterly of Patman's autocratic style, his penchant for monopolizing staff resources, consuming too much time at hearings, and ignoring members not in his favor. "The octogenarian doesn't know my name and ignores my calumnies with stoic indifference," complained committee newcomer William Frenzel, a liberal Republican from Minnesota.[56] Patman's long interrogations of committee witnesses regularly provoke impatient despair on the part of his younger colleagues who must sit mutely waiting their turn. When, after one recent Patman harangue, committee witness John Lindsay compared New York City to Alice in Wonderland, conservative Republican Ben Blackburn of Georgia interrupted, "Mr. Mayor, if you want to see Alice in Wonderland, I invite you to return to our committee some time."[57]

The Banking Committee, in short, is not one big happy family. On the contrary, it bristles with antagonisms and tensions, which frequently erupt into brawls. Patman regularly accuses his opponents of selling out to the special interests, while they respond with charges that Patman is an elderly tyrant tilting at imaginary windmills. As one staff member conceded, "Things can get pretty brutal on this committee."

While the House Banking Committee is hardly a well-integrated, harmonious team, however, neither is it a complete free-for-all; for the cleavages that divide the members do not all over-lap neatly, as we have already seen. Enemies on one issue are frequently allies on another, so that all feel some constraint about pushing issues to the limit. On issues like distribution of control over committee staff or matters on which the White House has established a clear partisan position, the committee splits along party lines, particularly since Patman tends to be a strongly parti-san chairman. On traditional social-welfare issues like public housing, traditional party lines break and the conservative coali-tion of southern Democrats and small-town Republicans makes its appearance. Even this alignment disintegrates on banking is-sues, as the "Ivy League liberals" defect to the conservative camp. Finally, on matters affecting the powers of the chairman, Patman can usually count on support from some senior Republi-can conservatives, who perhaps wish to keep the chairman's powers intact in the event of a Republican Congress and their assumption of the chairmanship. In fact, William Widnall, the ranking Republican, takes such an accommodating and propri-etary approach to minority staffing that his partisan colleagues complain almost as much about his staff policy as about Pat-man's. The committee's fifteen Republicans have less than a half dozen professional staff slots on the committee, compared to over twenty for the twenty-two Democrats. Significantly, when the Republicans moved to increase their staff at the outset of the Ninety-second Congress, it was sixth-ranking Republican Garry Brown, and not William Widnall, who raised the issue. Nor has Widnall energetically advanced minority staff involvement in committee business. Minority staffers remain in the background of committee activities, rarely taking an active part even in com-mittee markup sessions.

Were it not for this fluidity and shifting alignments, the House Banking Committee might by now have become completely un-workable as a decision-making unit. What exists instead is a kind of persistent cold-war standoff, with enough underlying tension to provoke frequent disputes—to a large degree due to Patman's penchant for forcing issues—but also enough overlapping of alliances and enmities to preserve minimum working relationships. Clearly, for those who enjoy fiercely competitive sport, the Banking Committee under Patman was one of the best games in town.*

THE INTERNAL POLITICS OF
THE SENATE BANKING COMMITTEE

Compared to the House Banking Committee, with its frequently fierce brawling, the Senate Banking Committee seems a much more placid place. This is largely a consequence of the style and philosophy of its chairman, John Sparkman (D., Ala.). But it is also a result of the more substantial edge that banking and housing lobby supporters enjoy on the committee, a situation that keeps committee mavericks like William Proxmire (D., Wis.)—the only Patman ally on the Senate committee—at bay. The Senate committee has thus been a far more congenial place than its House counterpart for the bankers and their allies, as we will see more fully below. With the accession of Proxmire to the chairmanship in the Ninety-fourth Congress as a result of Sparkman's decision to replace retiring J. William Fulbright (D., Ark.) as chairman of the Senate Foreign Relations Committee, the pattern of committee behavior may change. Nevertheless, an analysis of the general dynamics of Senate Banking Committee operations under Sparkman can shed light on the elements with which Proxmire too will have to contend.

Leadership: The Alabama Fence-Sitter

John Sparkman, chairman of the Senate Banking Committee from 1967 to 1974, shares a southern rural background with Wright Pat-

---

* There is considerable evidence that some of the tension within this Committee subsided during the 93rd Congress, thanks in no small measure to the appearance of a new cadre of generally pro-Patman younger members on

man. But there the similarity ends. Where Patman takes Federal
Reserve independence and growing bank concentration as harmful trends to be fought tooth and nail, Sparkman treats them as
inevitable facts of life to be accepted with equanimity. Where
Patman seeks to raise issues and seize the initiative, Sparkman
prefers to moderate issues and look the other way. Far from being
an activist-innovator, Sparkman is the archetypical consensus
chairman. Perfectly content to let others define the problems and
propose solutions, he typically holds himself above the swirl of
controversy until he can safely intervene as the fatherly conciliator,
delicately picking his way among the positions staked out by others.
Flexibility, not leadership, is thus the hallmark of the Sparkman
style, so much so that one opponent, hearing Sparkman boast
during a campaign that he knew what it meant to wear patched
britches, blurted out, "Sparkman, you'll always have to wear
patched britches, because you'll always be a-bustin' your britches
tryin' to straddle every fence you come to."[58]

Hard as it is on the britches, though, fence-straddling can do
wonders for a political career. For example, Sparkman's flexibility
and moderation so distinguished him from the rest of his obdurate
southern colleagues in the Congress that it earned him the vice-
presidential nomination of his party in 1952—and what other
southern senator could have survived a run with arch-liberal
Adlai Stevenson? These same qualities have enabled Sparkman to
develop an amazing reservoir of good will among some of the
most disparate camps in the Congress. It is therefore natural that
Sparkman should have earned his spurs on the massive omnibus
housing bills that have wended their way through the Byzantine
legislative process every two or three years since 1949, for these
bills are a compromiser's dream. They resemble elaborate Christmas trees which must be trimmed with just enough baubles and
bangles to win the necessary interest-group support without bring-

the committee. Committee members have breathed life into the subcommittees and managed to secure enlarged control over staff selection and assignment, all of these formerly points of dissatisfaction.

ing the whole shaky structure crashing down.* And Sparkman, serving since the 1950s as the chairman of the Senate Banking Committee's Housing Subcommittee, along with fellow Alabamian Albert Rains in the House, early distinguished himself as a past master of this intricate balancing act. In this role, Sparkman has functioned as one of the more moderate southern Democrats, throwing his considerable weight generally to the liberal side in support of federal government involvement in housing and urban development. But Sparkman's liberalism on these issues has been rather narrowly defined, corresponding rather closely to the positions of the home builders and savings bankers who have been the major beneficiaries of federal housing policy, and who comprise an influential segment of Sparkman's Alabama constituency thanks to the postwar southern building boom. As one Sparkman aide pointed out, "Sparkman has always been a housing man. He is much less interested in urban development programs and he knows the mayors hardly at all compared to his relationships with the home builders."[59] Thanks to his pivotal role in securing federal assistance for their industries, in fact, Sparkman has emerged as the darling of the "housing lobby," and as a consequence his campaign coffers never hurt for funds.†

When Sparkman became chairman of the full Banking Committee in 1967, he carried with him the same sensitivity to the needs of key business lobbies that has put him in such good stead in the housing field. At the same time, he carried with him the conciliatory, compromising style he had perfected during twenty years of housing battles. Thus, one of Sparkman's first accomplishments as chairman was to break the bitter logjam that had developed on the committee over the proposed truth-in-lending law, a bill designed to provide consumers information about the cost of credit.

* See Chapter 4 for further elaboration of this point.
† The National Association of Home Builders alone, for example, contributed $3,700 to help Sparkman defeat Republican Winston Blount in Sparkman's unusually tough 1972 reelection campaign. Alabama builders contributed even more, according to reports filed with the Secretary of the Senate.[60]

This legislation had been introduced in every Congress from the early 1960s on by Senator Paul Douglas (D., Ill.), but had been tied up by the adamant refusal of committee chairman A. Willis Robertson (D., W.Va.) to consider it in committee, and by the inability of Douglas to muster the votes to force Robertson's hand.[61] When Sparkman assumed the committee chairmanship following the defeat of Robertson in the 1966 elections, he moved to dissipate the rancor produced by this struggle and scheduled the truth-in-lending bill for committee action. Since by this time Paul Douglas had also been defeated in his reelection bid, it fell to William Proxmire to push the bill for him. By transforming the chairmanship from a barrier into a neutral facilitator of the truth-in-lending legislation, Sparkman thus opened the way for Proxmire and his allies to enact Congress' first major piece of consumer-finance legislation.

While opening the committee up in this way, however, Sparkman has generally lined up on most bank-regulation issues with the committee's powerful conservative bloc, headed by Senators Wallace F. Bennett (R., Utah), John G. Tower (R., Tex.), and William E. Brock III (R., Tenn.). Sparkman's aides may argue, as one did, that what the chairman is trying to do is to "walk a fine line between helping the consumer and making sure what the committee does isn't really harmful to the consumer." But, as we will see more fully below, in practice this has amounted to rather consistent opposition to bank regulation and consumer-finance protection. As a consequence, the Senate committee lacks the antibank aggressiveness of its House counterpart, and the bankers have gratefully responded as generously as have the builders in their zeal to keep the Alabama fence-sitter in office.* The "spirit of compromise" is the governing ethic in the Senate Banking Committee, ranking minority member John Tower publicly confirmed recently,[62] and committee staffers readily agree. "Sparkman is the kind of chairman who tries to make the committee

---

* During 1971 alone, for example, various banking organizations paid $9,715 just in "speaking fees" to Sparkman.

work," one Republican staffer told us. "He sees his function to be to work out the final compromise."[63] Sparkman's organization of staff resources, his use of hearings, and his handling of subcommittees demonstrate the consequences this has for committee output.

Committee Staff. Staff operations in the Senate Banking Committee under Sparkman have followed two guiding principles—frugality and decentralization—both of them reflections of Sparkman's style. Unlike Patman, who pushed persistently for staff expansion in the hopes of wresting the legislative initiative from private interests and the executive branch, Sparkman has been content with a much more limited staff role. Thus, while the House Banking Committee budget climbed from $200,000 to $1.7 millon under Patman, the Senate Committee's investigative budget had reached only $907,000 by the Ninety-second Congress, and $230,000 of this sum was earmarked for a special securities industry study and therefore unavailable for general committee activities (see Table 11).

More important, Senate staff resources are used very differently from the way they are used in the House. Where Patman

TABLE 11.
Comparison of House and Senate Banking Committee Budgets, 89th–92nd Congresses

ongress	Total		Full committee		Housing subcommittee		Securities	
	Senate	House	Senate	House	Senate	House	Senate	House
9th	$395,700	$812,000	$174,700	$435,000	$271,000	$377,000	——	——
0th	530,000	925,000	230,000	550,000	300,000	375,000	——	——
2nd	907,000	1,659,800	332,000	942,500	345,000	717,300	$230,000	——

ɔURCES: House—*Congressional Record*, Mar. 1, 1972, p. H1621.
Senate—*Study of Federal Housing Programs*, Senate Report No. 15, 89th Cong., 1st sess. (1965); *Study of Housing and Urban Affairs*, Senate Report No. 91-46, 91st Cong., 1st sess. (1969); *Authorizing Additional Expenditures by the Committee on Banking, Housing and Urban Affairs for Inquiries and Investigations*, Senate Report No. 92-650, 92nd Cong., 2nd sess. (1972); and committee files.

carefully husbands staff resources for centrally directed inquiries, Sparkman delegates most staff slots to his committee colleagues. Of the twenty-one professional staffers on the Senate Banking Committee, only seven are primarily responsible to Sparkman, three of them working exclusively on the Housing Subcommittee and one serving in a semiadministrative capacity as staff director. The remaining two-thirds of the committee staff slots are dispersed among the more senior members of the committee, seven to Democrats and seven to Republicans. Third-ranking Democrat Harrison J. Williams (N.J.) had three, ranking Republican Tower had two, and other members had one each.

This delegation of staff-selection power naturally serves an integrative function for the committee, shielding Sparkman from the charges of dictatorship that constantly swirl around Patman. In particular, as one Republican staffer put it, "it makes the minority role greater." It also serves an educational function, enabling the senators to keep on top of committee business. As such, it is a symptom of an important disease afflicting this committee: lack of interest and distraction. "Getting a quorum for executive sessions in this committee is like counting baby chicks," staff director Dudley O'Neal reports. "You no sooner get your hands on one of them than another scurries away."[64] Distributing staff slots among the members is a way to cope with this problem by giving members a way to participate in committee deliberations by remote control.

Despite its advantages, this pattern of staff use virtually locks the committee into a passive role as a processor of information provided by others. The staff members have their hands full just keeping their respective members up to date and processing the day-to-day legislative load. This leaves little time at all for the kind of independent inquiries that are the hallmark of the Patman staff operation. Worse still, substantial staff energies on the Senate side are channeled into what is euphemistically termed "case work," the handling of constituent problems with various federal agencies. Under congressional rules, "case work" is supposed to be handled exclusively by the "office staffs" of the members, not by the committee staffs. But neither chairman Sparkman nor ranking Republican Tower adheres to this rule. Senator Sparkman's office staff even has a formal procedure for routing all constituent inquiries about housing and urban programs to Carl A. S. Coan, Sr., staff director of the Banking Committee's Housing Subcommittee, which Sparkman chairs.[65] "We hear a lot from Carl about Alabama, and we naturally try to do everything we can for him," the congressional relations director of HUD told us. "Frankly, I don't understand how he has much time left for anything else."[66] Senator Tower's staff assistant on the Housing Subcommittee estimated that he devotes 30 to 35 percent of his time to "case work." While constituents in Alabama and Texas undoubtedly benefit from this personal attention by high-level professionals, congressional attention to the formulation of national housing and urban development programs suffers. And perhaps more seriously, the practice can create a subtle incentive for staff members to avoid policy proposals that might anger the executive bureaucracy out of fear that such proposals might disrupt the cordial relations necessary for effective case work.

With staff resources limited, spread out, and diverted into constituency work, the Senate committee is significantly weakened before the onslaught of special-interest pleaders. Even scouting operations are difficult to mount, let alone serious independent attacks. The result of this weakness, coupled with Sparkman's conciliatory style and his reluctance to raise embarrassing questions about his committee's clients, is to limit the committee in developing independent sources of information and seizing the legislative initiative. Compared to the more than thirty investigative reports and staff studies issued by the House Banking Committee between 1963 and 1972, the Senate Banking Committee has produced only four, just one of which—a securities industry study issued in February 1972—is of the same genre as the Patman committee's reports. The Senate committee restricts its own investigative impulses to requesting reports from the agencies,

which are then reprinted over the committee's name—a procedure that draws new information into the legislative process at
congressional instigation, but still leaves most of the control in
agency hands. At least nine such reports have been issued as
committee prints since 1965 (see Table 12).

TABLE 12.

Mandated Agency Reports Issued by the Senate
Banking Committee, 1965–72

Title	Congress	Date of issue
A Survey on the Use of Administrative Disbarments of Contractors (prepared by the Attorney General)	89th	Nov. 1965
Government Activities Affecting Small Business: Problems of Small Business Displacement Under Programs of Public Improvement (prepared by the Attorney General)	89th	Dec. 1966
Federal Credit Programs (prepared by the Treasury Department)	90th	Jan. 1967
Mortgage Discounts (prepared by HUD)	90th	Feb. 1967
Study of Mortgage Credit (prepared by various agencies and private individuals)	90th	May 1967
Rehabilitation Programs (prepared by HUD)	90th	Aug. 1967
Housing Partnership (First Annual Report of the National Corporation for Housing Partnerships)	91st	Aug. 1970
Study of International Housing (compilation of reports of several agencies)	92nd	June 1971
State and Local Taxation of Banks (prepared by the Board of Governors of the Federal Reserve System)	92nd	June 1972

Typical was the 1972 report the committee asked the Federal
Reserve Board to prepare on the subject of whether states should
be permitted to tax national banks on the value of their intangible
property (the financial assets that comprise most bank property),
in view of the fact that states *can* tax *state* banks' intangible property. The resulting 691-page report provided an excellent smoke-
screen for the Fed's ultimate recommendation that *all* banks, both
national and state, be exempted from property taxation on in-

tangible property on the ground that banks cannot cheat local assessors as easily as can other businesses and are therefore at an unfair disadvantage.*

That Senate Banking staffers have generated few independent inquiries charting new ground for legislation is not to say that they lack competence. On the contrary, the Senate committee is staffed with some very able individuals, like Carl Coan, staff director of the Housing Subcommittee, and Proxmire assistant Ken McLean. But the pattern of staff activities, reflecting the style of the chairman and the needs of the members, leaves the committee heavily reliant on outsiders for information and initiative.

What is potentially more disturbing, moreover, is that this habit of reliance carries over into staff recruitment and promotion as well. Far more than the House committee, the Senate Banking Committee draws heavily on the lobby groups and executive agencies for its staff, thus blurring the distinctions between legislative and executive branches and between public and private purposes. For example, both Carl Coan, staff director of the Housing Subcommittee, and Dudley O'Neal, staff director of the full committee, are former Federal Housing Administration employees, with close ties to the HUD bureaucracy. Coan's son, in turn, served during the latter 1960s as a high official in HUD responsible for legislative relations, and now works as vice president for congressional relations with the most important lobby group his father's subcommittee must deal with, the National Association of Home Builders. The committee's minority counsel during the Ninety-third Congress, chosen by Senator Tower, is a former Treasury Department official who worked as a staff assistant to Treasury Under-Secretary Charls Walker, a past president of the American Bankers Association and the major advocate of a broad set of bank regulation reforms recommended to the committee in the Treasury Department's proposed Financial

* The report naturally puts this point more genteely: "Tax assessors cannot readily undervalue fixed claims, such as bank assets, to the degree that they can and generally do undervalue other types of assets."[67]

Institutions Act of 1973. Senator Bennett's current staff man on the committee is a former American Bankers Association lobbyist.

Nor is this a one-way street, for committee staffers, having developed contacts with the legislators, frequently end up as paid lobbyists for the interests. Indeed, it seems at times as if the Senate Banking Committee has been a training school for bank lobbyists. When the committee held hearings in 1969 on the one-bank holding company legislation, in fact, the proceedings had all the trappings of a college reunion. No fewer than three former committee staff directors appeared at the hearings in their new roles as industry lobbyists, one for the First National City Bank of New York and the Association of Registered Bank Holding Companies, another for the American Bankers Association, and a third for CIT Financial Corporation. So powerful was this display of career potential, apparently, that Hugh Smith, the primary staffer handling the holding company legislation for Sparkman, quit the committee right after the bill cleared (in watered-down form) to claim his fortune as a bank lobbyist, too. Whether this career pattern influences the behavior of staffers while they are on the committee payroll is difficult to determine definitively. But it hardly creates a strong incentive for staff members to rock the boat or challenge private-interest views, and it provides the interest groups unusual access to internal committee decision-making.

The handling of the Fair Credit Billing Act (S.652) in 1972 provides an excellent example of the advantages such access can provide. S.652, originally proposed by Senator Proxmire to close some loopholes left by the Truth-in-Lending Act of 1968, was quickly seized upon by the bank lobby groups as a vehicle for *limiting* earlier consumer-finance protections, particularly the class-action provisions of truth-in-lending. When Proxmire staffer Ken McLean did not prepare a detailed "agenda" laying out the differences between the Proxmire bill and the bankers' bill, from which members could work in the markup session—on the ground that the bankers' bill so changed the substance that it really constituted a wholly different piece of legislation—former committee staffer Jim Cash, now a lobbyist for the American Bankers Association, came to the rescue with an agenda of his own. Although staff director Dudley O'Neal, an "old friend" of Cash's,[68] considered the ABA agenda to be fair, others complained bitterly that it treated the ABA version as the basic working bill and biased the debate in its favor. And, as it turned out, the bankers' version passed, and Proxmire ended up opposing the bill he originally introduced when it reached the floor for a vote.

Hearings. Although Sparkman has not used the Senate Banking Committee staff to generate new information and take the legislative initiative as Patman has done in the House, he has partially compensated for this by permitting numerous special investigative hearings. Between 1965 and 1972, at least twenty-four such hearings have been conducted, ranging in length from a one-day hearing on the "State of the National Economy" in 1971 to thirteen days of hearings on the "Balance of Payments Problem" conducted intermittently between March and August of 1965. These hearings allow members to raise questions and assemble useful information that the staff lacks the time to assemble for them. In the process, they give the legislators a platform from which to put the heat on reluctant administrators and, much more seldom, private decision-makers.

As devices for generating insight and information, however, hearings are notoriously unsatisfactory. "Hearings are generally boring and not very productive," Senate Banking Committee staff director Dudley O'Neal volunteered,[69] and this is true of special investigative hearings as well as regular hearings on legislation. Witness lists are virtually foreordained because of the obligation to "touch base" with the known organized interests in the field. Moreover, witnesses almost invariably recite well-known organizational positions in their testimony. As one lobbyist explained to us, "There is no incentive for candor in congressional hearings. Everyone else is tooting his organization's horn, so I must, too."[70] As a result, member participation is limited. For example, Senator Harrison Williams was able to attract only two of his ten Subcommittee on Securities colleagues to the first hearings in a special subcommittee study of the securities industry in September 1971. Senator Thomas J. McIntyre (D., N.H.), chairman of the Subcommittee on Small Business, was even less successful, and had to face the representatives of the fuel-oil industry alone during a special hearing on the "Cost and Adequacy of Fuel Oil" the same month.

Far from being a reflection of a spirited investigative instinct, in fact, the Senate committee's special hearings are more a reflection of chairman Sparkman's consensus style. The aim is to give various members a stake in committee operations by making the committee available to their own personal goals and ambitions. If Harrison Williams wants to demonstrate to his constituents a concern for rail mass transit, Sparkman is willing to accommodate by turning the Subcommittee on Housing over to him for three days of exploratory hearings on "The Effect of Railroad Mergers on Commuter Transportation." If Senator McIntyre wants to win plaudits from his Yankee constituents for his concern about their peculiar economic problems, the same avenue is available—and the Senate finds itself treated to hearings on "The Problems of Small Domestic Shoe Manufacturers" (1969), "Foreign Trade Zone Application of the State of Maine" (1968), "The High Cost of No. 2 Heating Oil" (1970), and other equally esoteric topics.

Although these hearings might help build political careers, they are not very useful in developing new insights or giving the committee the legislative initiative. The hearings tend to be flabby and diffuse, sidestepping issues as often as confronting them. In the absence of previous independent, investigative research, they leave the committee the captive of information generated by organizations with an ax to grind.

Subcommittees. Sparkman's "consensus" style is reflected in the Senate Banking Committee's subcommittee operations as well.

Under Sparkman's predecessor, conservative A. Willis Robertson, subcommittees were eliminated when liberals Joseph Clark and William Proxmire came up for subcommittee chairmanships in 1961.[71] Sparkman reversed this decision when he took over in 1967, creating six subcommittees, each chaired by a senior Democrat on the committee (see pages xxvii-xxix). Unlike Patman, however, Sparkman has given the subcommittees relatively free rein, and has allowed his colleagues to use their subcommittees to build their own subject-area reputations. Virtually all of the special inquiries cited earlier, for example, were subcommittee operations. Committee innovators like William Proxmire and Harrison Williams have consequently been able to exploit the subcommittee structure to bring new issues before the committee— Proxmire in the areas of bank regulation and consumer finance and Williams in the field of securities regulation. Committee approval of a $230,000, two-year securities industry study under Williams' direction exemplifies Sparkman's accommodating style. So does the fact that Sparkman enlarged the Housing Subcommittee to include every member of the full committee.

While subcommittees are available to boost reputations and publicize new issues, however, they are rarely arenas of decisive action. Senators have little time to devote to the committee as it is, as one committee staffer noted. Any serious issues that arise during subcommittee consideration, are therefore "bumped to the full committee, where they will have to be reviewed anyway." Like Patman, moreover, Sparkman frequently skips the subcommittee stage altogether. Thus, neither the Economic Stabilization Act of 1971 (wage and price controls) nor the emergency loan guarantee legislation (the Lockheed loan) received subcommittee scrutiny. Indeed, of the 141 bills, resolutions, and joint resolutions referred to the Senate Banking Committee in 1971, only 70 were referred to subcommittees—and 52 of these 70 were referred to the Housing and Urban Affairs Subcommittee, which Sparkman chairs and which is really not a subcommittee at all since it includes all committee members.[72]

Though far more accommodating than his House counterpart, Sparkman is not above using his control over committee scheduling to promote his policy goals or weaken the position of committee colleagues with opposing views. For example, in 1969 he delayed hearings on the Bank Holding Company Act in an effort to scuttle the House-passed bill, and then bypassed subcommittee consideration, at least partly because Financial Institutions Subcommittee chairman William Proxmire had views on this legislation far closer to Wright Patman's than Sparkman's. Other Proxmire proposals have encountered rough sailing just getting on the committee agenda. For example, a controversial proposal to reduce closing costs and title-insurance charges in connection with real estate sales seemed doomed to be pigeonholed throughout much of 1972 until an Evans and Novak article shook it loose.[73] According to one committee staffer, "Sparkman runs the committee through the agenda power."

There is even some speculation that Sparkman's decision to reorganize the committee's subcommittee structure at the outset of the Ninety-third Congress was motivated in part by a desire to limit the influence of potential opponents, particularly William Proxmire. Under this reorganization, two extra subcommittees were added, one on Consumer Credit and one on Minting and Mining. In addition, the size of subcommittees was reduced and the practice of allowing each committee member to serve on five of the six subcommittees discontinued. Finally, subcommittees were authorized to meet concurrently, and committee staffers were assigned to particular subcommittees, instead of serving as general "legislative assistants" for particular members on the full range of committee business. According to the chairman, the purpose of this reorganization was to enhance the role of subcommittees by making them more efficient and thus increase member interest in committee business.[74] The main loser in this reorganization appeared to be second-ranking William Proxmire, the major advocate of bank regulation and consumer-finance protections on the committee. It was Proxmire's Financial Institutions

Subcommittee that was split in two to create the new Subcommittee on Consumer Credit. As one staffer put it, "Sparkman thought Proxmire had too much power." Given the choice of which of the two resulting subcommittees to chair, Proxmire chose Consumer Credit. As a result, by the time the administration's Omnibus Financial Institutions Act reached Congress in October 1973, Proxmire, the committee's chief critic of the banks, was no longer in charge of the subcommittee to which the proposal was assigned. But Proxmire doubts his position was weakened very much by this reorganization. "Sparkman rarely used the Financial Institutions Subcommittee anyway," Proxmire staff assistant McLean noted, "so we didn't really lose very much."[75] In fact, under the new arrangement, Proxmire was able to organize four sets of subcommittee hearings in the first session of the Ninety-third Congress alone, and thus raise a host of consumer-finance issues that might have been blocked earlier.* As chairman of the full committee beginning in the Ninety-fourth Congress, Proxmire should be able to reestablish his authority in the banking area as well.

*Membership: Genteel Maneuverings
and Muted Tensions*

Although Chairman Sparkman's fence-straddling style robs the Senate Banking Committee of clear direction and policy focus, it is well-suited to the ominous problem the chairman faces in holding this committee together enough to have its decisions accepted on the Senate floor. The problem arises from the sharp ideological cleavages that divide the members of this committee. There is, in the first place, a solid bloc of ideological liberals on the committee. Former Illinois Senator Paul Douglas may have been exag-

---

* Hearings were held before Proxmire's subcommittee on the following subjects during the first session of the 93rd Congress: the report of the National Commission on Consumer Finance (two days); inaccurate and unfair credit billing practices (four days); Federal Trade Commission jurisdiction over financial institutions in consumer credit transactions (two days); and credit reporting procedures (five days).[76]

gerating a bit when he wrote that the Senate Banking Committee was one of only two committees "on which the southern over-lords permitted the Northerners to sit."*[77] But the list of liberal mavericks barred from more powerful committees and assigned to Banking and Currency over the past decade and a half is striking, including Paul Douglas himself, Joseph Clark, Jacob Javits (R., N.Y.), Charles Goodell (R., N.Y.), Walter Mondale (D., Minn.), William Proxmire, and Edward Brooke (R., Mass.). As a consequence, the committee has maintained a rather consistent liberal image. Between the Eightieth and Ninetieth Congresses, in fact, only four Senate committees had lower "conservative scores" than Banking and Currency, based on the floor votes of members.† Table 13 below demonstrates that this pattern persisted in

TABLE 13.

Senate Banking Committee Ideology as Reflected in
Floor-Vote Ratings, 1971

Rating of:		Median	Mean	Standard deviation	Chairman
Americans for Democratic Action	Committee Members	30.0	50.0	38.5	19.0
	Entire Senate	41.0	46.6	33.3	xxxx
Americans for Constitutional Action	Committee Members	37.0	41.6	29.4	37.0
	Entire Senate	39.0	43.8	30.2	xxxx
Committee on Political Education	Committee Members	73.0	55.2	30.7	81.9
	Entire Senate	56.0	53.1	27.7	xxxx

the Ninety-second Congress as well. On both the Americans for Democratic Action (liberal) and Committee for Political Education (labor) ratings of member floor votes, the average score of

* The other committee was Labor and Public Welfare.
† "Conservative scores" were computed by taking the average proportion of floor votes of committee members between 1947 and 1968 cast on the conservative side. Only two minor committees (Post Office and District of Columbia) plus Foreign Affairs and Labor and Public Welfare scored lower conservative scores than Banking and Currency.[78]

Banking Committee members was higher than that for members of the Senate as a whole; the reverse was true with regard to the Americans for Conservative Action rating.

But this evidence of committee liberalism is highly deceptive; for the actual liberal majority on the committee is a slim one. In addition to an unusual number of liberal mavericks, the Banking Committee also contains more than its share of outspoken ideological conservatives, like John Tower, Bill Brock, and Wallace Bennett, who is a former president of the National Association of Manufacturers. The six committee members with ADA rankings above 70 percent are thus all but counterbalanced by five members with ADA ratings below 20 percent.* Table 14 depicts the typical "support blocs" that result, and suggests how dependent committee liberals are on a few swing votes, notably Sparkman's.† Given the Sparkman proclivities outlined above, it is understandable that the committee usually ends up endorsing producer-oriented housing programs and giving consumer-finance and bank-regulation issues rough treatment, as we shall see below.

Sparkman's eagerness to achieve a broad consensus within the committee before taking measures to the floor in practice means catering to the views of the committee's most senior Republicans, John Tower and Wallace Bennett, both of them ideological conservatives. Tower typically takes the lead in the housing area. Like Sparkman, he sticks fairly close to the positions advanced by the home builders, a group that not incidentally has great strength in Texas and the rest of the growing South. Since the Republican presidential victory of 1968, moreover, Tower has served as what

---

* This fact is reflected statistically in Table 13, which shows that the standard deviations of member scores on both labor and liberal ratings are larger for the Senate Banking Committee than for the Senate as a whole, suggesting that the ideological gulf in this committee is wider than that in the Senate generally.

† Since few formal committee votes are ever taken in this committee, it is impossible to speak definitively about "voting blocs." Table 14 was therefore constructed on the basis of interviews and floor voting records.

TABLE 14.
Senate Banking Committee Voting Blocs, 92nd Congress

Liberals	Conservatives	Swing Votes
Proxmire (D., Wis.)	Gambrell (D., Ga.)	Sparkman (D., Ala.)
Williams (D., N.J.)	Tower (R., Tex.)	Packwood (R., Ore.)
Mondale (D., Minn.)	Bennett (R., Utah)	
Cranston (D., Cal.)	Roth (R., Del.)	
Stevenson (D., Ill.)	Brock (R., Tenn.)	
Brooke (R., Mass.)	Taft (R., Ohio)	
McIntyre (D., N.H.)		

one staffer termed "the mouthpiece of HUD" on the committee, a position that has been quite compatible with his support for the home builders, who have considerable influence in HUD.* Bennett's forte is banking and finance policy, where he takes a strict free-enterprise position. As one committee staffer put it, "Bennett carries the banner for the bankers in the committee." But Brock and Tower help him hold it aloft.

Liberal dependence on Sparkman, and Sparkman's eagerness to achieve consensus on the committee, thus persistently threaten the slim liberal majority on the committee and frequently overwhelm it. But the liberal edge is disrupted as well by defections within the liberal ranks. In this respect, the Senate Banking Committee is very much like its House counterpart. On consumer-finance and bank-regulation issues in particular, several otherwise liberal votes tend to swing to the conservative side. This is the case, for example, with California's Alan Cranston and New Jersey's Harrison Williams, both liberal Democrats from states with strong commercial-bank influence, and both recipients of substantial bank campaign contributions. As a consequence, Senator William Proxmire, who normally takes the lead on such measures within

---

* The HUD assistant secretary for mortgage credit and housing production beginning in 1969 was the former president of the National Association of Home Builders. For additional information on HUD–home builder links, see Chapter 4.

the committee, frequently finds his liberal colleagues deserting him.

Even on housing and urban issues, however, the liberal camp is not monolithic. Despite the heavy urban responsibilities of the Banking Committee, only eight of the committee's fifteen members in the Ninety-second Congress hailed from states that had larger than average metropolitan population proportions. And three of these members were ideological conservatives philosophically opposed to extensive government involvement in this area (Tower of Texas, Bennett of Utah, and Roth of Delaware, with Taft of Ohio a possible fourth). This situation is no doubt partly a consequence of the tendency of activist, urban liberals to seek posts on more prestigious and publicity-generating committees, a point we will touch on again. What this means, however, is that the fate of the urban poor and of central cities is largely left in this committee to the mercies of liberals from states with less than average metropolitan and central-city populations. Thanks to pressures operating through Democratic Party channels, support can usually be mustered for programs with strong interest-group support. But central-city-oriented programs of the sort advanced in recent years by Senators Brooke and Mondale have encountered much more difficulty. This is particularly true of public housing, as well as of efforts to protect the central-city poor displaced by urban renewal.

Finally, a further problem for the liberal camp on the Banking Committee arises from the relatively low level of member interest in committee work. All Senate committees suffer to some extent from this problem because of the multiple committee assignments of senators, but the Banking Committee suffers disproportionately. One reflection of this is the pattern of member recruitment and departure. Between 1947 and 1965, for example, the Senate Banking Committee gained members from only three Senate committees, all of them minor (District of Columbia, Post Office, and Rules and Administration), but it lost members to six other committees. This suggests that the Banking Committee serves as a kind of temporary way-station for upwardly mobile senators on their way to more prestigious committees.[79] Northern liberals, moreover, seem particularly prone to leave, as evidenced by the hasty departures of such stalwart liberals as Harold E. Hughes (D., Ia.), Edmund S. Muskie (D, Me.), Jacob Javits, and Charles H. Percy (R., Ill.) over the past decade. This pattern continued into the Ninety-second Congress as well, with the loss of five of the committee's fifteen members, four of them to other committees.*

What makes this member turnover so important is the complexity of the issues the Banking Committee considers, and the need this creates for the development of member experience and expertise if the private lobbies are not to dominate the process completely. Yet, as one Republican staffer conceded, on banking issues, among the liberals, "only Proxmire has any real competence," though Senator Adlai E. Stevenson III (D., Ill.) is not far behind. In the housing sphere, Mondale and Brooke are the only liberals deeply involved. On both issues, the rest, lacking deep interest or experience, tend to play it safe by supporting the moderate position, usually represented by Sparkman. Thus is a liberal majority transformed into a moderate, and even conservative, one.

In short, although the tensions on the Senate Banking Committee are potentially as strident as those on the House Committee, they are muted by the slimness of the liberal edge, the importance of the moderate swing vote, the chairman's passion for consensus, the fissures within the liberal ranks, and the relative inexperience and disinterest of many liberal members. Combined with Sparkman's compromise style of leadership as reflected in the organization of staff work, the handling of hearings, and the use of subcommittees, this standoff within the committee is a perfect prescription for inaction, or worse.

* In addition, Mondale departed at the beginning of the 93rd Congress.

THE LEGISLATIVE CONTEXT

What transpires in the Banking committees is not simply a function of the styles of the chairmen and the ideologies and attachments of the members, however. It is also a function of the broader legislative context, the two houses of Congress. A number of characteristics of this congressional environment vitally affect the Banking committees' operations.

Fragmented Committee Jurisdictions

The pattern of committee jurisdiction is one of the most important of these influences. Congressional policy-making is rigidly compartmentalized according to elaborate, painstakingly negotiated rules that set the boundaries of committee jurisdiction. But the divisions of responsibilities among committees frequently bear no relationship to the way the problems appear in the real world. The result is that different committees may develop competing partial solutions to the same complex problem and end up canceling each other out.

The Banking committees suffer seriously from this endemic congressional malady. For example, though generally responsible for federal housing policy, they have no control over the most massive federal housing program of all: the $5.5 billion worth of benefits provided to homeowners through the income-tax deductions for mortgage interest and property taxation.[80] While the Banking committees are eagerly passing legislation to expand American exports, other committees are hard at work devising duties and quotas that ultimately have the opposite effect. The Banking committees can formulate mass-transit-assistance programs to keep cars off congested city streets, but their work comes to nought thanks to the Public Works committees' promotion of highway programs that bring more cars back on the roads.

Committee jurisdictions are more a product of historical accident and personal idiosyncrasy than of rational design. For example, when William Fulbright was chairman of the Senate Banking Committee in the 1950s, he made foreign economic policy a major focus of committee work. But when Fulbright left to assume the chairmanship of the Foreign Relations Committee, he took a substantial share of this responsibility with him, creating a perennial jurisdictional dispute. By the same token, mass transit became a Banking Committee responsibility largely because Senator Harrison Williams, who took the initiative on this issue in the early 1960s, was on the Senate Banking Committee and managed to upstage the Commerce and Public Works committees, neither of which had shown any interest in what was then a small field. In the interim, the field has blossomed into a multibillion-dollar vineyard for the Banking committees to tend.*

Rational or not, jurisdictional lines, once set, are difficult to change. Every scrap of new jurisdiction is a new source of power for a committee and its chairman, and is defended with fervor. Most importantly, programs come to be devised with jurisdictional issues very much in mind. Should federal housing policies be redesigned to provide direct housing allowances instead of cumbersome production subsidies and loan guarantees? Perhaps so, but then the Banking committees would be in danger of losing jurisdiction over their most important programs to the Labor and Public Welfare committees, which oversee all welfare programs. Should the highway trust fund be tapped to support urban mass transit? Yes, on principle; but no if it means surrendering jurisdiction over mass-transit programs to the Public Works committees, which have legislative responsibility for this fund. Should the Federal Trade Commission or the Federal Reserve Board admin-

* In the 93rd Congress, the House Banking Committee created a special subcommittee on mass transit to accommodate the request of younger committee members for an opportunity to participate more fully in some aspects of the committee's urban policy responsibilities. However, this subcommittee was short-lived, for one of the few proposals that survived the largely abortive committee reform effort sponsored by Representative Richard Bolling (D., Mo.) in the 93rd Congress was one shifting urban mass transit from the Banking Committee to a new House Committee on Public Works and Transportation. Mass transit remains a Banking Committee responsibility in the Senate.

ister the truth-in-lending law? It depends on which league you prefer to play in, for FTC is in the Commerce Committee's bailiwick, not the Banking Committee's. In short, every program is screened not only for its substantive content, but also for its jurisdictional implications, sometimes with harmful results. But there is even more; for the Congressional committees that develop legislation do not control the legislation's funding. "Authorization committees," like the Banking committees, only establish programs and set maximum spending limits; they cannot actually appropriate the money needed to put the programs in operation. Whether the programs are funded, and, if so, at what level, are decisions made by the Appropriations committees, and really by the semiautonomous subcommittees into which they are split. No fewer than five different Appropriations Committee subcommittees have jurisdiction over programs authorized by the Banking committees. Their actions can easily undo what the Banking committees have laboriously worked out, thereby frustrating integrated policy design and program implementation. In fact, Banking committee housing programs have almost always been severely underfunded by the Appropriations committees, particularly in the House, so that committee members come to feel like Sisyphus, laboriously pushing their legislative rocks to the top of the hill, only to see them pushed over the side again.

Going Along to Get Along

In addition to the jurisdictional tangle, the Banking committees must take account of the requirements for floor approval of committee proposals. We have already suggested what this implies for housing and urban development policy-making: since both of the Banking committees are more liberal on the whole than their respective parent bodies, special efforts have to be made to shape committee proposals in a way that will win solid moderate and conservative support. The name of the game, therefore, is appeasement of key committee conservatives—men like Robert Stephens and William Widnall in the House, and John Sparkman and John Tower in the Senate. The all-too-frequent result, however, is to suffuse liberal-sounding programs with deeply conservative content, as we will see in detail below. What is more, because congressmen are elected by separate local constituents, the incentives are great to disperse potential program benefits instead of concentrating them for maximum impact, and to allow substantial leeway for local implementation and control.* In the process, broad national purposes bow to narrow, parochial ones, and efforts to promote national objectives encounter overwhelming obstacles.

In the consumer-finance and bank-regulation area, the dynamics at work are somewhat different. Thanks to the rise of the consumer movement, advocates of regulatory measures stand a worse chance in committee than on the floor of the two houses, where they can generate press attention and throw the spotlight on recalcitrant members. The bank lobby, as a consequence, focuses its fire at the committee stage, where it can frequently torpedo proposals before they ever reach the floor or make them so complicated that they cannot be comprehended. The task for proponents of such measures, like Patman and Proxmire, is therefore to get them out of committee in the first place, and then to build sufficient publicity to secure passage on the floor. Even with the powers of the chairman at his command, Patman has had difficulty doing this. For more than a decade, for example, Patman has been trying to pass legislation authorizing the General Accounting Office to audit the Federal Reserve System, a proposal sternly opposed by the Fed and the commercial banks. In desperation, Patman managed to tack the proposal on to the 1972 housing bill during the committee markup session one day prior to the 1972 Republican National Convention, when several key Republican opponents were absent. When the housing bill died in

---

* As political scientist Morton Grodzins has written, "Now, as in the first days of the republic, the local as opposed to the national orientation of most members of the national Congress leads to legislation that gives important responsibilities to states and localities."[81]

the Rules Committee, however, Patman was back to square one. Finally, in the first session of the Ninety-third Congress, he narrowly managed to secure a committee majority to report out his pet proposal, but then was treated to another lengthy delay at the hands of the Rules Committee, which waited nine months before reporting the bill to the floor. In fact, the Rules Committee only moved when it did because the Senate Banking Committee had just vetoed a companion bill on the same subject the week before, thus making it clear Patman's measure would go nowhere even if it cleared the House, as it finally did on May 30, 1974.

Rules

A third set of extracommittee influences that affect Banking Committee action are the formal rules that guide legislative procedure. Theoretically, rules are neutral and passive in their impact, but in practice they have important substantive consequences, usually delivering advantages to those opposed to congressional action.* For example, when House rules were changed in 1970 to forbid attaching bills not yet passed by the House to conference committee reports, advocates of consumer-finance legislation in the House suffered a major defeat. Under the previous rules, consumer-finance legislation blocked in the House Banking Committee could still be brought to the House floor for a vote by tacking it on to other legislation under consideration in House-Senate conferences. The Fair Credit Reporting Bill of 1970, which regulated credit-reporting firms and set limits on access to credit reports, would probably not have passed had it not been for this provision in the rules, since opponents had the measure firmly bottled up in the House Banking Committee. Now that the provision has been eliminated, getting consumer-finance protections to the House floor is more difficult.

* As one textbook on Congress notes, "[Congressional rules] need to be understood in their *political* context, as instruments in the exercise of political power. . . . Never wholly neutral, rules benefit some groups and disadvantage others. They are, commonly, one of the many faces of minority power."[82]

Workload

Banking Committee performance is also influenced by the tremendous crush of work and the broad array of responsibilities piled on these committees. In addition to their responsibilities in the areas of housing, urban development, urban planning, mass transit, bank regulation, consumer credit, and monetary policy, the Banking committees are in charge of small-business-assistance programs, disaster-relief loans, all federal government loan programs to international agencies like the International Bank for Reconstruction and Development (the World Bank), wage and price controls, and defense-production activities. Altogether, eleven separate government agencies fall wholly, or partly, under the jurisdiction of these two committees—including *all* of the Department of Housing and Urban Development, the Federal Reserve System, the Federal Deposit Insurance Corporation, the Federal Home Loan Bank Board, the Office of Emergency Preparedness, and the Small Business Administration, as well as sizable portions of the Departments of Treasury and Commerce. Although members of both committees have sought to cope with this broad array of responsibilities through specialization—that is, by following the lead of one or two key members who take responsibility for a particular subject matter—the sheer bulk of the workload, given the available staff, makes it difficult to exercise meaningful policy guidance and oversight over more than a few subjects. And some subjects simply get lost between the slats. As one House staff member put it, "Frankly, we can't keep up with things. The Export-Import bill comes up every year and we don't have a chance to look at it thoroughly ever. Hell, it's a joke."[83] As a result, the committees of necessity must look to others for help, particularly the bureaucracy and the lobby groups.

This, then, is the arena within which banking and urban policy is made in Congress—two committees with quite different personalities and internal dynamics operating within a common legislative context characterized by confusing jurisdictions, a premium on accommodation, rules that facilitate obstruction, and a crushing workload that discourages systematic policy evaluation and congressional initiative. Not surprisingly, the shape of federal banking and urban policy significantly reflects these features of the arena in which they have been fought out. Chapters 3, 4, and 5 should demonstrate how.

3

Banking on Congress:
The Bank
Holding Company Act
of 1970

In mid-1968 the American financial community was rocked by the news that the First National City Bank of New York, at that time the nation's third largest commercial bank and now its second largest, was totally reorganizing its corporate structure and reconstituting itself as part of a bank holding company—a corporate entity with the power to acquire other businesses in addition to the bank, just like the giant conglomerates that were taking over large segments of the rest of the U.S. economy in the 1960s. No sooner

NOTE: This chapter benefited greatly from the assistance of Robert Fusfeld, who conducted many of the interviews and prepared a preliminary draft of the latter portion.

84

had the First National City Bank news been digested than similar announcements began to issue from the board rooms of the nation's other banking titans, signaling the most rapid, fundamental alteration of American banking structure in history. Within six months, in fact, 34 of the 100 largest banks in the nation announced their reorganization as holding companies, so that by early 1969, over 40 percent of all U.S. commercial bank deposits were controlled by holding companies, compared to only 13 percent at the beginning of 1968.[1] In some states, the resulting holding-company predominance was even more striking: 62 percent control of all bank deposits in New York, the nation's financial capital; 65 percent in California; 60 percent in Rhode Island; 55 percent in North Carolina.[2] According to a House Banking Committee report issued early in 1969, a total of 684 one-bank holding companies (holding companies owning only one bank) were in existence or planned as of September 1, 1968. Of these, 578 also owned one or another of about 20 different kinds of financial nonbanking businesses like insurance companies; and 397 were engaged in 99 different nonfinancial activities, ranging from agriculture to manufacturing.[3] A basic transformation of American commercial banking was clearly under way, with implications that are still not fully understood.

So dramatic were these developments, in fact, that they touched off one of the most extensive and significant legislative battles over bank-regulation policy in more than a decade, and led ultimately to the enactment of the Bank Holding Company Act Amendments of 1970. At issue in this battle was nothing less than the question of what constitutes the business of banking; whether, given the governmental assistance they receive and the legally protected public role they are supposed to perform, commercial banks should be allowed to acquire and operate data-processing and equipment-leasing firms, set up insurance and travel agencies, establish retail-clothing chains, move into the steel-fabrication business, buy agribusiness complexes, and generally participate directly in the conglomerate craze sweeping the corporate landscape. Also at issue, indirectly, was the question whether, in order to preserve competition in the banking industry, limits should be placed on the forty-year trend toward concentration of control within the banking industry itself.

Advocates on one side of these issues argued that the bank-holding-company movement was a welcome sign of renewed vigor on the part of the commercial-banking industry. They held that it represented an adaptation to unnecessarily rigid restrictions, which artificially prevented banks from profiting from the competitive advantages they enjoyed as "financial shopping centers"; that it permitted banks to pay better salaries and thus attract better talent; and that it provided an outlet for the capital banks were accumulating in the 1960s.[4] Those on the other side of these issues argued that most of the competitive advantages banks enjoyed were really bestowed by public authority; that bank takeovers of nonbanking businesses threatened the stability and viability of the banking system itself and had been outlawed for precisely this reason following the debacle produced by heavy bank investments in the stock market in the 1920s; that competitors of bank-acquired firms would be at a severe disadvantage since the parent banks could extend cheap credit to their subsidiaries while denying it to the competitors of these subsidiaries, and make loans to other borrowers contingent on having these borrowers do business with the banks' various subsidiaries; and that this bank "imperialism" therefore threatened to undermine competition throughout the economy.[5]

With the issues thus posed, the stage was set for one of the most fascinating legislative battles over bank-regulation policy in more than a decade, a battle that offers some of the most revealing insights available into the operations of the Banking committees in Congress and into the politics of national banking policy generally. The purpose of this chapter is to explore these insights in detail. To do so, it is necessary to put the story of the Bank Holding Company Act Amendments of 1970 in context, by examining briefly the historic relationship between government and banking that gave rise to the holding-company phenomenon, by exploring the history of bank holding companies and the governmental response to them prior to 1969, and by analyzing the reasons for the surge in bank-holding-company formations in the late 1960s.

UNCLE SAM AND THE BANK BARONS: REGULATION FOR WHOM?

Given the crucial role that banks play in American economic life, there has never been much question about the need for some governmental supervision to protect the public's stake in these institutions. From the very earliest times, therefore, bankers were required to secure government charters testifying to their competence, verifying the adequacy of their capital stock, and specifying the permissible range of activities for which they could use depositors' money. As the country's financial structure has grown more complex with the emergence of new types of financial institutions, so has the network of legal provisions governing bank operations. In broad terms these provisions have done two things: first, they have created "protected markets" for each of the various types of financial institutions; and second, they have defined the conditions that these institutions must meet to enjoy the benefits afforded by these "protected markets." The holding-company device, as we will see more fully below, emerged as a way for commercial bankers to evade some of these conditions without surrendering the "protected-market" benefits they enjoyed as commercial banks. In this sense, bank holding companies are a product of the overall regulatory framework governing bank activities. Four features of this regulatory framework in particular are important to an understanding of the one-bank holding company battle of 1970: (1) the "protected-market" feature itself; (2) the premium that existing regulations place on stability over competition within each protected market; (3) the "divide and rule" potentials built into the administrative structure; and (4) the wall that has traditionally been maintained between banking and other types of business.

Financial Feudalism: The Protected Markets of Banking

The American banking system, as Chapter 1 suggested, is less a coherent and integrated entity than a welter of hybrid institutional types, each with its own organizational peculiarities and roles. Historical accident, not planning, gave birth to this complexity, as new institutions evolved to perform roles created by new situations. Government, for its part, has rigidified this complexity. As each new institutional type made its appearance, it clamored for protection against potential competitors who might usurp its newfound role. Commercial banks feared "factoring" houses, savings banks feared commercial banks, credit unions feared both savings banks and commercial banks. Since all of these institutions performed public roles, public authority felt obliged to respond, at least to the point of certifying the capability and solvency of the institution. But the resulting government charters, while imposing regulations, were really grants of limited monopoly power, empowering the chartered institution to engage in activities prohibited to others. The overall result has been to create a financial structure resembling the feudal contours of the medieval guild system, with specialized institutions operating in sheltered markets behind protective barriers erected by government.

The commercial banks were naturally the first to partake of this arrangement, and managed to carry off the biggest prize: a monopoly on demand deposits (checking accounts), which constitute most of what we use as money. Given the trend toward a check-oriented society, this monopoly gives commercial banks a virtually certain hold on at least part of the business of every enterprise and household in the nation. More than that, thanks to the Banking Acts of 1933 and 1935, which prohibited all federally affiliated banks (i.e., national banks, state member banks, and state insured banks) from paying interest on demand deposits, this monopoly gives commercial banks a free source of funds.⁶ Not only are commercial banks insulated from competition from other types of financial institutions, which are not allowed to offer checking-account services, therefore, but they are also prevented from competing among themselves for demand deposits on a price basis.⁷ Because the price they pay for their money is lower, they are in a position to charge lower interest rates on loans than are other financial institutions and also to pay higher interest rates to attract savings deposits.

Savings bankers have also had impressive success in securing protective shelters for their business. The savings banks, as we have noted, emerged to tap the small pools of household savings not being actively sought by commercial banks and to put these savings to work in the home-mortgage market. To aid in this endeavor, they secured government sanctions to corner the residential-mortgage market and exemptions from income taxes so long as they keep most of their assets in residential mortgages. More important, to counter the competitive advantage of commercial banks in bidding for savings dollars, the savings banks managed to have limits imposed on the interest rates *commercial banks* could pay on savings deposits, and to have these limits set at a percentage point below what the savings banks were paying. They thus insulated themselves from competition from their fiercest competitors, a move that was justified on the ground that since commercial banks make relatively few mortgage loans, the promotion of the socially desirable goal of improved housing required governmental assistance in channeling savings into the savings banks.* In return, the savings banks surrendered the right to make short-term commercial loans.

These and other guild-like restrictions on which financial insti-

---

* That this shelter has worked is apparent in the fact that as savings and loan assets have skyrocketed—from 3.6 percent of all financial institution assets in 1945 to 15.6 percent in 1972—so too has the amount of residential mortgage credit outstanding—from 9.5 percent of all credit outstanding in 1947 to 23.7 percent in 1972. As of 1972, savings and loan associations accounted for 44.3 percent of all residential mortgage loans outstanding, compared to 14.6 percent for commercial banks.⁸

tutions can do what, and when, have transformed the financial marketplace into a series of sheltered provinces with little competition among them. As a recent staff report of the House Banking Committee notes:

> The availability of vital financial services and credit at all times is needlessly restricted and its cost is often inflated because financial institutions are forced to occupy restricted areas in the credit markets rather than being encouraged and allowed to compete on the broadest possible basis. Indeed, the effect of restrictions on the structure of financial institutions is so pronounced that the financial industry as a whole is comprised of types of institutions which have either been given initial monopoly control over vital credit and financial service areas or are needlessly restricted from providing a fuller range of important services.[9]

Stability Before Competition

So long as there is active competition, easy entry, and no collusion within each of these "protected markets," the potentially harmful effects of this arrangement can be partially offset. However, the overall thrust of American bank regulation, at least since the 1930s, has been in the opposite direction.

During the nineteenth century, as efforts were made to make banking services available across a growing nation, public authority was generally employed to promote bank expansion. "Free banking laws," which opened the bank-chartering process to all who could meet certain basic requirements, and an active "chartering competition" between state and federal authorities, were the order of the day. As a consequence, the number of banks expanded rapidly, reaching thirty thousand by 1920.[10]

Since that date, however, things have changed quite substantially. The financial depression of the late 1920s and early 1930s, which obliterated fifteen thousand banks, gave rise to a profound conviction that the nation was "over-banked," a conviction that quickly became enshrined in a wholly new regulatory climate aimed, as one writer has put it, at "preserving banks, not banking competition."[11] Federal policy on chartering, "branching," and bank mergers illustrates this post-Depression, anticompetitive regulatory stance quite clearly.

Chartering. Under the "free banking laws" in force until the fourth decade of the twentieth century, bank regulators had little discretion in granting bank charters. So long as applicants had the requisite capital and could provide evidence of their trustworthiness, the granting of a charter from state or federal officials was fairly automatic. The passage of the 1935 Banking Act changed this practice fundamentally by formally incorporating into the chartering process the so-called "convenience and needs test."[12] Henceforth, the comptroller of the currency was obliged to determine the community's "need" for a bank by assessing the impact of a potential new bank on the business of existing banks in an area, and to reject a charter application whenever an existing bank was doing a decent job and would stand to lose business if a new bank were chartered. Not only did this standard apply to federal charters; it also extended to state banks through a provision of the law that prohibited the Federal Reserve Board from accepting new state banks into the Federal Reserve System, or the Federal Deposit Insurance Corporation from extending deposit insurance to nonmember state banks, unless the "convenience and needs" test was met.

As interpreted by the banking authorities, this new standard spelled the end of free banking in the United States by erecting an immense barrier to entry into the banking business and thus protecting existing banks from competition. The prevailing philosophy was succinctly summarized by an Oregon bank supervisor who told a Joint Economic Committee hearing in 1952, "I do not believe that . . . I should approve a second bank . . . where it seems evident that the existing bank would be weakened by the loss of a portion of the existing business."[13] As a consequence, the rate of new bank charters declined substantially during the post-1935 period. Indeed, in twenty-five of the thirty-one years from 1936 through 1966, the number of new banks created by state and federal officials combined was less than the number that went out of business through mergers, absorptions, or suspensions; thus the net number of banks in the country declined absolutely during each of these years.[14] Instead of the 30,000 banks in existence in the late 1920s, there were only 14,172 by the end of 1973.[15] Even within their sheltered market, in other words, commercial bankers were further sheltered against the competition of potential newcomers.

Branching. While tightening the provisions on new charters, the New Deal bank legislation loosened the provisions on "branching," the setting up of numerous "branch offices" by parent banks. Prior to 1933, with but a few exceptions, all national banks, and most state banks, were required to be "unit banks"—separate corporate entities operating out of a single full-service office. The unit-banking requirement, by restricting the geographic reach of individual banks, helped promote competition and sustain smaller banks. The theory was that local banks were more responsive to local business needs and more knowledgeable about loan applicants, and that giant banks with numerous branches spread across a state, or even many states, would severely undermine bank competition and lead to inflated prices for bank services.

However, unit banking ran afoul of the pro-protection spirit of the New Deal bank legislation, which was more concerned about the instability that might arise from numerous moderate or small unit banks than it was about the anticompetitive effects of transforming these banks into branches of large banking complexes. Accordingly, over the objections of the smaller banks, the 1933 Banking Act authorized national banks to establish branches wherever state law allowed state banks to do so. Though not eliminating branching restrictions completely, this provision has led to their significant liberalization, as bankers in one state secure more liberal restrictions, which lead in turn to demands from bankers in other states for equal treatment. By 1967, as a result, only ten

states held to the traditional "unit-banking" principle that was almost universally practiced before 1930. In the process, as the number of separate banks has declined and the number of branches has
expanded, American banking structure has been transformed from
a primarily unit-banking system to a primarily branch-banking system. While branch banks accounted for less than 6 percent of all
bank offices in 1920, they accounted for about 66 percent in 1966
(see Table 15). By 1966, in fact, 66 percent of all bank offices were
controlled by only 25 percent of all banks.

TABLE 15.
The Growth of Commercial Bank Branching, 1900–1966

Year	Unit banks	Branch banks	Branches	Total number of bank offices	Branch offices as percent of total
1900	12,340	87	119	12,546	1.6
1920	29,761	530	1,281	31,572	5.7
1940	13,575	959	3,531	18,065	24.9
1960	11,143	2,329	10,216	23,688	53.0
1966	10,457	3,313	16,648	30,418	65.6

SOURCE: Gerald C. Fischer, *American Banking Structure* (New York: Columbia University Press), p. 31.

Scholars dispute whether branching has enhanced or retarded
bank competition, but the fact that the "convenience and needs"
test applies to branches as well as to new banks suggests that the
primary motivation for branching has not been to extend competition, for new branches are disallowed where they might compete
seriously with existing banks.

Despite the vast liberalization on branching, however, expan-
sionist bankers still remain dissatisfied. Only nineteen of the fifty
states allow statewide branching and only a handful allow branching across state lines.[16] As we will see, the holding-company
device has served as a way to circumvent these remaining branching barriers.

Merger Policy and the Emasculation of Anti-Trust Protections.

As if the barriers to entry and the permission to expand the banking system through branching instead of through the formation of new banks were not sufficient, the regulatory effort to guarantee bank stability finds expression as well in the generally permissive treatment of mergers, acquisitions, and other techniques for industry concentration. During the past forty years, as we have seen, the American commercial banking system underwent a fundamental structural transformation from a highly competitive unit-banking system to a more concentrated branch-banking system. While charter restrictions and liberalized branching laws contributed to this transformation, a mammoth and continuing merger trend among banks provided the basic thrust. Between 1920 and 1941, for example, almost half of the 16,000 banks that ceased operations were absorbed by their former competitors.[17] An additional 2,150 mergers took place between 1954 and 1966, a rate of about 165 mergers per year.[18] This trend shows no sign of abating: in 1970, for example, 165 banks ceased operations, 155 of them due to "absorptions, consolidations and mergers."[19] As a consequence, of the 14,000 commercial banks in the nation in 1969, the largest 100 controlled close to half of all deposits,[20] and the largest 50 controlled half of all assets.[21] In numerous local areas, moreover, the degree of concentration is even greater than these national figures suggest, since the local markets are frequently dominated by one or two banking giants.

But mergers, absorptions, and resulting concentration of asset control represent only the tip of the iceberg of anticompetitive behavior on the part of banks. In addition to these more visible forms of concentration, banks have traditionally engaged extensively in such practices as collusive price-fixing through so-called clearinghouse agreements. Other extensive ties bind smaller banks to their larger competitors even in the absence of formal mergers or price-fixing. Through the "correspondent system," for example, smaller banks maintain interest-free "bankers' balances" in the larger banks, and receive in return check clearance, loan participation, and other benefits. In the process, they develop a mutuality of interest that blunts their competitive drive. What may appear to the outsider to be a competitive local banking market consisting of numerous separate banks may therefore really be a tightly knit network consisting of a single dominant institution and its affiliated "correspondent banks." Add to this the extensive pattern of interlocking directorates among banks, and the widespread practice of bank ownership of the stock of "competing" banks noted in Chapter 1, and the true measure of the success of the Depression-born effort to avoid excessive bank competition becomes clear.[22]

How have these arrangements continued in the face of explicit language in the Clayton Antitrust Act that prohibits price-fixing (Section 2), acquisition of competing companies if the result is to reduce competition significantly (Section 7), and interlocking directorates (Section 8); and that explicitly gives the Federal Reserve Board concurrent authority with the Department of Justice to enforce these prohibitions so far as banks are concerned? The answer is that the courts and the Congress have taken pains to exempt banks from antitrust coverage, and the bank regulatory authorities have been all too willing to look the other way. Despite the massive merger trend and the resulting fundamental transformation of banking structure over the past forty years, for example, not until 1948 did the Board of Governors of the Federal Reserve Board initiate its first (and, to date, its only) proceeding under Section 7 of the Clayton Act. It took the Justice Department another eleven years to bring *its* first case against a bank merger. The reason for this somnolent attitude was not any lack of evidence of anticompetitive mergers in potential violation of the Clayton Act. Rather, the major reason was the Supreme Court's earlier acceptance of two curious arguments advanced by the bankers: first, that while banking supplied an "instrument of commerce," it was not itself commerce and hence was not subject to antitrust legislation enacted pursuant to Congress' power to regulate commerce (a distinction without a difference if there ever was one); and second, that because Congress had enacted specific statutes to cover banks, it did not intend for banks to be covered by the general language of the Clayton Act.[23] A third barrier to the use of antitrust provisions against banks arose from the language of the Clayton Act itself, which mentioned only those mergers effected by the acquisition of "stock or share capital," and thus seemed to exempt most bank mergers, which are typically accomplished without stock acquisition.[24] These court precedents and legislative language discouraged the Justice Department from actively pursuing litigation against bank mergers under the antitrust legislation. But since none of the banking legislation on the books addressed itself to the competition issue, the result was to leave banks effectively unfettered in their merger activities, regardless of the effects on competition.

When the Supreme Court reversed itself on the first of these issues in 1944 (the *Southeastern Underwriters* case) and on the second in 1953 (*U.S.* v. *Morgan* and the *Transamerica* case), it opened the flood gates for a barrage of Justice Department suits raising antitrust objections to pending bank mergers. In desperation, the bankers turned to Congress for relief. At the same time, *opponents* of bank mergers were also turning to Congress to try to close the loophole in the Clayton Act concerning stock acquisition. In the Celler-Kefauver Act of 1950, Congress closed this loophole in part by extending coverage to anticompetitive mergers accomplished through *asset acquisition* instead of *stock acquisition*—a slim technical distinction. But the 1950 act closed this loophole only for corporations under the jurisdiction of the Federal Trade Commission, which did not seem to include banks.[25] As bank-merger activity increased in the 1950s, therefore, pressure mounted to clarify the law again.

As it turned out, pro-merger, anticompetition forces won. With the Senate Banking Committee in the lead, Congress passed the 1960 Bank Merger Act, which ostensibly brought bank mergers under federal control, but which really aimed to continue bank exemption from antitrust coverage despite the new turn in Supreme Court decisions. The act pursued this objective in two ways: (1) by vesting responsibility over bank mergers in the three bank regulatory agencies (the Comptroller, the Fed, and the FDIC) rather than in the Justice Department, where the desirability of competition was taken far more seriously; and (2) by establishing a mammoth loophole in the form of a directive to weigh the anticompetitive aspects of a potential merger against a set of so-called "banking factors" (including the ubiquitous "convenience and needs" test), which were designed to protect bank stability and profitability.[26]

In their administration of this act, the regulatory agencies have made active use of this loophole by refusing to reject merger proposals on the ground of their effect on competition. In fact, between 1960 and 1966, the "regulators" approved 1,001 out of 1,035 merger requests and rejected only 34. And this was true despite the fact that, according to one study, the Justice Department found antitrust problems in 52 percent of the mergers approved by the Comptroller of the Currency, in 41 percent of those approved by the FDIC, and in 38 percent of those approved by the Federal Reserve Board during the period 1960–1963.[*][27] Table 16 summarizes this early experience under the Bank Merger Act.

Distressed by this pattern of regulatory laxness, the Justice Department initiated ten separate antitrust actions against bank mergers between February 1961 and February 1966 in an effort to test the bankers' legal argument that the Bank Merger Act superseded the Clayton Act so far as banks were concerned. In the landmark *Philadelphia Bank* case decided in 1963, the Supreme Court supported the Justice Department's view. In a strongly worded opinion, Associate Justice William J. Brennan,

---

* The Comptroller has responsibility for mergers involving national banks. The Federal Reserve Board has responsibility for mergers involving state banks that belong to the Federal Reserve System, i.e., "state member banks." And the FDIC has responsibility for mergers involving state nonmember banks that are covered by federal deposit insurance.

TABLE 16.

Merger Approval under the Bank Merger Act, 1960–63

Agency	Applications approved	Applications denied	Rate of approval	Proportion of approvals disputed by Justice Department
Comptroller	240	9	96.1%	52%
FDIC	96	0	100.0%	41%
Federal Reserve	86	12	87.7%	38%
Totals	422	20	95.5%	46%

SOURCE: George R. Hall and Charles F. Phillips, Jr., *Bank Mergers and Regulatory Agencies: Application of the Bank Merger Act of 1960* (Washington: Federal Reserve Board, 1964), pp. 31–60.

Jr., turned on its head the bankers' argument that their coverage by substantial government regulation exempted them from antitrust coverage. "The fact that banking is a highly regulated industry critical to the nation's welfare makes the play of competition not less important but more so," wrote Brennan for the Court:

> If the businessman is denied credit because his banking alternatives have been eliminated by mergers, the whole edifice of an entrepreneurial system is threatened; if the costs of banking services and credit are allowed to become excessive by the absence of competitive pressures, virtually all costs, in our credit economy, will be affected; and unless competition is allowed to fulfill its role as an economic regulator in the banking industry, the result may well be even more governmental regulation.[28]

Once again, however, the bankers successfully turned to Congress for protection. The Senate Banking Committee in particular was sympathetic, but the bankers also managed to generate sufficient support in the House Banking Committee to overwhelm the opposition of chairman Wright Patman in the celebrated Bank Merger Act battle mentioned in Chapter 2. The resulting Bank

Merger Act Amendments of 1966 effectively countermanded the Supreme Court's *Philadelphia Bank* case decision by writing into the law two key provisions: the first authorized the bank regulatory agencies to approve anticompetitive mergers so long as "the anti-competitive effects . . . are clearly outweighed in the public interest by the probable effect of the transaction in meeting the convenience and needs of the community to be served"; and the second explicitly required *the courts*, and not just the banking agencies, to apply this same standard—and not the standards of the antitrust laws—to future cases involving bank mergers.[29]

In short, preoccupied with the protection of bank stability, the federal government has functioned over the past forty years as a protector of banks against the rigors of competition. Through limitations on bank charters, liberalization of branching restrictions, and the emasculation of antitrust protections as they apply to banks, the federal government has actively promoted the long-term trend toward greater concentration of control within the commercial-banking system. As we will see, moreover, the bank holding company falls squarely within this same tradition, for it was designed to allow banks to evade even the restrictions that remain on branching and mergers.

The Dual Banking System and the Three Musketeers of Regulation

That bank-regulation policy has operated in this way is in substantial measure a consequence of the complex institutional structure created to administer it. As we have already noted, the earliest banks in the United States were state banks operating under state charters and subject to state regulations. With the passage of the Banking Act of 1863 establishing a system of national charters, and the failure of state-chartered banks to succumb from a federal tax on state bank notes in 1865, a "dual banking system" came into existence. Under this peculiar manifestation of American federalism, bankers can choose whether to organize their enterprises under state or federal charters, and thus whether to subject themselves to state or federal controls. What is more, they can change their minds as often as they wish, switching from state to federal to state status, or vice versa, whenever this seems propitious. Instead of a single set of bank regulations in the United States, therefore, there are fifty-one separate ones—one for each state plus the federal set.[30]

Even at the federal level, moreover, the regulatory apparatus is splintered. As the federal government assumed new roles in the field of banking, it created new institutions to perform these roles: the Office of the Comptroller of the Currency in 1863 to issue national bank charters and oversee the solvency of national banks; the Federal Reserve Board and Federal Reserve System in 1913 to regulate the supply of money in the economy and oversee the fractional reserve system; and the Federal Deposit Insurance Corporation in 1935 to provide insurance to bank depositors. While all federally chartered banks must belong to the Federal Reserve System and the FDIC, state banks can also join the Federal Reserve System, or join the FDIC without belonging to the Federal Reserve System. Since only about two hundred small state banks do not participate in federal deposit insurance, virtually all banks are today under some sort or federal jurisdiction, producing a complex and overlapping pattern of controls.

One might expect that the bankers would object to this overlapping of regulatory jurisdictions. But nothing could be further from the truth; for the bankers have learned the lesson of Caesar in Gaul: divide and conquer. The checks and balances built into the system of bank regulation provide infinite opportunities for bankers to play one set of regulators off against the other, producing what one writer has termed a "competition in laxity."[31] The classic pattern is for state-chartered banks to seek liberalizations of the bank regulations in their state, which leads federally chartered banks in the same state to seek parity from federal banking authorities, which leads in turn to demands from federally chartered banks in other states for similar treatment, and ultimately to changes in state regulations in these other states as well. The system of regulation is thus no stronger than its weakest link.* No wonder the dual banking system has become a cherished icon for the money lords. "The checks and balances which are inherent in the dual banking system," a resolution at the 1962 American Bankers Association convention thus asserted, "have served as a deterrent to inappropriate or unduly burdensome actions on either the State or National level."[33]

This same divide-and-conquer strategy works among the three musketeers of bank regulation at the federal level as well. At least one of these agencies, the comptroller of the currency, has traditionally served as a kind of in-house spokesman for nationally chartered commercial banks, fighting off the encroachments of state banks and endeavoring to improve the competitive position of national banks. Indeed, it has seemed at times as if the comptroller's office is an arm of the powerful American Bankers Association, and comptrollers who have failed to play the role have not lasted long in office.† The Federal Reserve Board has been somewhat less accommodating, but the whiplash created by the comptroller's liberality is hard to resist. As we will see below, one of the central issues in the bank holding company battle in 1970 concerned the question of whether administrative jurisdiction

* A typical example of this dynamic is being played out at this writing. Under both state and federal law, banks must maintain reserves against deposits in order to avoid "runs" on the bank. However, national banks, as well as state member banks, are required by the Federal Reserve to hold these reserves in "sterile" or nonearning balances on deposit at the Fed. In contrast, numerous states allow their nonmember banks to count earning assets (like U.S. government bonds) as reserves. Since the yield on Treasury bonds has risen to more than 7 percent, the advantages accruing to state nonmember banks has become quite substantial. As a result, numerous banks have opted out of the Federal Reserve System—104 banks in 1973 alone. In response, pressures are now building among member banks to have the Fed pay member banks interest on deposits held by the Fed.[32]
† The fate of Comptroller John Skelton Williams, who served from 1914 to 1921, demonstrates how the bankers guarantee "moderate, cooperative attitudes" in the Comptroller's office. When Williams began to "crack down" on the bankers, they appealed to friendly congressmen and the very existence of the bureau itself was put in jeopardy until Williams resigned.[34] The case of James Saxon in the early 1960s is similar.

should be centralized in the Federal Reserve Board or splintered among the three federal regulatory agencies, as it is with other aspects of bank regulation. The bankers preferred the latter course.

The Wall Between Banking and Commerce

The one substantial price bankers have had to pay for their sheltered existence has been a set of regulations on how they conduct their business. These include specifications on appropriate accounting procedures, directives on the proportion of deposits that must be held as reserves against withdrawals, and restrictions on the relative shares of different types of assets (government bonds, commercial loans, real estate loans, etc.) banks can hold in their portfolios.

Perhaps the most important of these restrictions, however, is the one that establishes a rather rigid line between banking and nonbanking businesses and forbids banks to cross this line. Growing out of the Depression-born concern about banks that speculated heavily in the stock market and suffered accordingly, and out of a fear that bank expansion into nonbanking businesses could disrupt competition throughout the economy, this wall between banking and commerce was explicitly written into the Glass-Steagall Act of 1933.[35] Under this act, commercial banks are forbidden from investing in equity-type securities (common stock), and from operating nonbanking businesses. In addition, severe limits were placed on commercial-bank involvement in traditionally risky types of investment, such as real-estate speculation, and on bank purchases of certain corporate bonds. Bankers were also subjected to limits on the proportion of their total assets they could loan to a single borrower.[36] The aim throughout was to limit the risk to which bank depositors were exposed by bank investment practices, and to avoid bank interference with competition outside the sphere of banking proper. As one high Justice Department official put it in testimony before the Senate Banking Committee during consideration of the Bank Holding Company Act in 1970:

We have in this country a traditional policy of separating commercial banking from other areas of economic activity. This policy rests on a number of considerations: First, the desire to ensure the solvency of banks. Second, a fear that affiliations between banking and nonbank institutions would impair competition by creating unjustified competitive advantages. Third, a general concern about overall economic concentration. We believe that this traditional policy is sound.[37]

Is Bigger Better?

The overall thrust of bank-regulation policy for more than a generation has been to prevent "excessive" competition among financial institutions by limiting the entry of new firms, encouraging the replacement of small unit banks by larger firms operating numerous branches, and creating sheltered markets within which the various types of financial institutions can operate free from outside competition even from other types of financial intermediaries. The basic transformation of American banking structure facilitated by this pattern of regulation has been defended on grounds that it allows greater economies of scale and that larger banking institutions actually provide better customer service and compete more effectively than the small unit banks of old. In point of fact, however, the evidence is extremely skimpy and frustratingly inconclusive.* One set of researchers argues that price performance is similar in branch and unit banks; that branch banks produce a higher volume of loan activity per dollar of assets and extend banking services over a larger area; and that branch banks as a whole have certain economies of scale.[39] Another set argues that the quality of customer service tends to

---

* According to one student of bank structure, Gerald Fischer, "At present the bank supervisor must make decisions regarding banking competition knowing surprisingly little about how, with whom, or where banks compete. The legislator must write laws and the courts must interpret these statutes with the public interest in mind, and yet the available information concerning so fundamental a question as the performance by different forms of bank organization and by size of bank is extremely limited."[38]

decline significantly when banks expand or undergo mergers and that the presumed economies of scale do not exist.[40]

Arguing the merits of these changes on efficiency grounds alone, however, may be misleading, for even those who find economic advantages in bank concentration acknowledge the dangers these advantages bring with them. "The price society must pay for the various efficiencies and other advantages of branch banking is an unavoidable concentration of financial power," one noted authority on the subject has written. "Whether society wishes to pay this price cannot be determined by economic considerations alone."[41]

The battle over the Bank Holding Company Act of 1970 represented a classic confrontation over precisely this point. The emergence of the bank holding company represents just the latest manifestation of the overall trend toward concentration in banking touched off by the Depression. In addition, the holding-company phenomenon, particularly in the 1960s, constituted a massive challenge to one of the few remaining prohibitions on commercial-bank expansionism: the prohibition against bank involvement in nonbanking business. Against this background on the framework of bank regulation generally, therefore, it is time to look in detail at the bank holding company phenomenon itself and at the efforts to regulate this phenomenon prior to 1970.

"WHATEVER YOU WANT
FROM THE YEARS AHEAD"

Group Banking

Although group banking—the central ownership and operation of a string of banks—made its appearance as early as the late nineteenth century in the United States, it was not until the late 1920s that this phenomenon became a significant feature of American banking. The chief motivation for forming such entities was the desire to evade state and federal prohibitions on branch banking.

Until the passage of the 1933 Banking Act, as we have seen, nationally chartered banks were forbidden to operate full-service branches, and most states put severe limits on branching as well. Even after the passage of the 1933 law, which represented a compromise between advocates of wide-open branching and supporters of the pure unit-banking system, most states continued to outlaw branching across state lines, and national banks operating in these states were held to a similar limitation.

The holding company, a form of group banking, offered a way around these restrictions. By setting up a separate corporate entity not governed by these regulations on state or nationally chartered banks, and having this new entity acquire the banks, bankers or any other enterprise could secure ownership of a host of banks anywhere in the country. By 1929, 28 such banking groups were known to exist, with control of 511 banks. These 511 banks, constituting only 2 percent of all commercial banks in existence at the time, controlled 10 percent of the nation's bank deposits.[42]

Originating as they did in an effort to evade federal and state law in a way that raised the specter of massive monopolization of credit facilities, bank holding companies operated from the start under a cloud of suspicion. However, when the collapse of the banking system during the Great Depression turned governmental attention to the problem of promoting bank stability instead of promoting bank competition, the bank holding company question receded into the background. The 1933 Banking Act consequently treated the holding company form of organization quite mildly, despite the spectacular collapse of a number of these group-banking syndicates during the Depression.* Under this act,

---

* The story of one of these collapses is recounted in the House report on the 1956 Bank Holding Company Act in dramatic fashion: "In 1930 the head of the Guardian National Bank of Commerce of Detroit appeared before your committee and boastfully told of the new era that had been brought to the Detroit area through acquisitions by holding companies of carefully selected, well-managed and strong banks; how, through the supermanagerial ability of the men who dominated the holding company stronger institutions, better-managed institutions, more profitable institutions, render-

bank holding companies were required to register with the Federal Reserve Board and secure the Fed's permission to vote the bank stock they owned, but only if the banks they owned included a member bank of the Federal Reserve System. As a result, only a fraction of the known bank holding companies were touched, and even they were touched mildly.† The act placed no prohibition on the formation of such group-banking syndicates. Nor did it subject bank holding companies to the prohibitions against mixing banking with nonbanking businesses.[45] It thus left wide open the two primary reasons for forming such holding companies: to evade state branching laws and to evade restrictions on bank entry into nonbanking business.

Under this permissive regulatory climate, bank holding companies grew significantly in size and number, particularly in the Western and Midwestern states where unit banking was most firmly rooted in state law.[46] As of December 31, 1954, the 114 bank holding companies identified by the Federal Reserve Board owned 452 banks with 861 branches and total deposits in excess of $23 billion. Although some of these bank holding companies were large conglomerates or small family firms owning only one bank, the more common pattern was the holding company in control of several banks. For example, the Northwest Bancorporation operated 72 banks with 22 branches located in seven states; the Equity and Morris Plan Corporation operated 10 banks with 19 branches located in four states and the District of Columbia; the massive Transamerica Corporation operated 47 banks with 167 branches located in five states. Most of these banking groups

---

ing greater service to every corner of the city and its environs, had come to bless the Detroit area. Within a matter of only a few months both the Guardian and the Detroit Bankers—two gigantic Detroit holding company groups of banks—began to totter. In 1932 the vast financial empire lay in ruins, 297 controlled banks and branch offices, $785 million in deposits— the scars of which disaster still mar the lives of millions of people."[43]

† As of December 31, 1954, for example, only 18 of the 114 bank holding companies identified by the Fed were registered under the 1933 act's provisions.[44]

in turn owned an array of nonbanking businesses. Transamerica, for example, controlled a far-flung empire of corporations engaged in life, fire, automobile, and marine insurance; oil and gas; fish canning and processing; frozen foods; castings; forge equipment; kitchen tools; and agricultural equipment.[47]

The Bank Holding Company Act of 1956: Restraint or License?

The growth of bank holding companies during this period did not proceed without challenge. On the contrary, bills designed to regulate bank holding companies more severely than did the 1933 law were introduced at every session of Congress between 1933 and 1955.[48] Support for these measures came primarily from smaller bankers wedded to the unit-banking principle and hence was most pronounced in the House, where these smaller bankers have traditionally enjoyed the most strength. Consistent support also came from the Federal Reserve Board. As Federal Reserve Board Chairman William McChesney Martin, Jr., explained, the Fed was convinced that the provisions of the 1933 Banking Act had "proved entirely inadequate to deal with the special problems presented by bank holding companies," particularly the problems of potential monopolization of credit facilities in a particular area and the destruction of the principle of separating banking from unrelated businesses.[49]

Not until 1956, however, did this support for further restrictions on bank holding companies bear fruit. Two factors seem to have made the difference. First, the postwar period witnessed a renewed spurt in bank holding company growth. Between 1949 and 1955, for example, the deposits of the fifteen leading bank holding companies increased at twice the rate achieved by all commercial banks.[50] Second, in a landmark decision, the Supreme Court handed the Federal Reserve Board a defeat in the famous *Transamerica* case, the first legal challenge the Board had initiated under the Clayton Act.[51] This decision left Transamerica free not only to continue the ownership of forty-six banks in five states, but also to acquire additional banks in these states or any other. In the process, it strengthened the determination of opponents of bank holding companies to seek a legislative solution to this problem.

What emerged from the legislative mill, not unexpectedly, was a mixed blend of provisions, some strong, some weak. Under the 1956 Bank Holding Company Act, all holding companies owning two or more banks were required to register with the Federal Reserve Board, file annual reports, and submit to examination. The act gave the Board strong controls over the future expansion of such holding companies by requiring advance Board approval of any new holding company formations as well as of any acquisitions by existing bank holding companies of 5 percent or more of the stock of any additional banks, and by specifying in Section 3(c) that the Board not give its approval unless, among other things, the proposed acquisition is "consistent with . . . the preservation of competition in the field of banking." In addition, the act contained fairly strict prohibitions on bank holding company acquisitions of nonbanking enterprises. According to the important Section 4(c) (8), bank holding companies could acquire only companies that were wholly engaged in activities of "a financial, fiduciary, or insurance nature" that the Federal Reserve Board determined to be *so closely related to the business of banking or of managing or controlling banks as to be proper incident thereto.*[52]

But the act also contained some mammoth loopholes. Most significant, as it turned out, was its definition of a bank holding company as one controlling *two or more banks*, thus completely exempting one-bank holding companies from regulation. At the time, this exemption made some sense: first, because most of the one-bank holding companies in existence at the time were either small, family-held corporations or large nonbanking corporations that owned relatively small banks; and second, because Congress' primary concern in the act was to avoid the further concentration of banking resources through multiple bank ownership.

However, this loophole eventually proved large enough for a third of the hundred largest banks in the nation to squeeze through into unregulated holding company operations. Indeed, Fed chairman Martin foresaw precisely such a development when he urged Congress to include one-bank holding companies under the 1956 law. Noted Martin:

> It seems clear that the potential abuses resulting from combination under single control easily exist in a case in which only one bank is involved. In fact, if the one controlled bank were a large bank, the holding company's interests in extensive nonbanking businesses might well lead to abuses even more serious than if the company controlled two or more very small banks. For these reasons, the Board would continue to urge that, whatever the percentage tests may be, the definition should be related to control of a single bank.[53]

A second major loophole in the 1956 act involved the definition of what constitutes holding company "control" of a bank. The definition ultimately adopted was 25 percent ownership of stock, even though effective control can frequently be attained with far less. As a consequence, any corporation controlling any number of banks with less than 25 percent of the bank's stock remained outside the reach of the act's regulations. Additional loopholes exempted partnerships or single individuals, labor unions and farm organizations that controlled banks as well as the possible use of trust investments to control banks.[54] Perhaps most significantly, however, the 1956 act transformed the holding company from a despised outcast into an "officially certified, fully licensed member of the nation's family of financial institutions."[55] Ironically, what began as an effort by independent bankers to remove the holding company from the banking scene ended up giving this hated institution legislative approval. As one commentator put it, "What some had hoped would be a death sentence has turned out to be a passport to the future."[56]

"The Pioneering Spirit"

The bankers lost no time setting sail with this passport in hand. As of May 7, 1958, 44 separate bank holding companies, accounting for 1,266 banking offices and $15 billion in assets (7 percent of commercial banking's total) had registered with the Fed. Ten years later, the number of registered bank holding company groups stood at 74, and their assets reached $50 billion, or 13 percent of banking's total.[57] This growth reflected the liberal interpretation the Federal Reserve Board put on Section 3(c) of the 1956 act, the section directing attention to the competitive consequences of holding company formation. Between 1956 and 1966, in fact, the Fed approved 85 percent of the requests presented to it for new holding companies or additional bank acquisitions by existing ones.[58] Moreover, under prodding from the Association of Registered Bank Holding Companies, the industry lobby group created in 1958, the Fed's *de facto* liberalization of the licensing criteria was made a formal part of the law. The Bank Holding Company Act Amendments of 1966 changed Section 3(c) to allow the Fed to ignore the anticompetitive consequences of a holding company formation or acquisition if these were somehow outweighed by the holding company's contribution to meeting the "convenience and needs" of the community (the same standard adopted in the Bank Merger Act Amendments of 1966).

Even more spectacular than the growth of registered bank holding companies, however, was the mammoth surge in one-bank holding companies, which had been exempted from the 1956 act. Between 1955 and the end of 1968, the number of one-bank holding companies jumped from 117 to 684, a sixfold increase. Even more important, the character of these firms changed radically, as the nation's banking giants began turning to the holding company form in the middle and late 1960s. No longer only small, family-held banking corporations, the ranks of one-bank holding companies had expanded by late 1968 to include 34 of the 100 largest commercial banks in the nation, including the top 6, and 9 of the top 12.[59] Thus, while the number of these institutions increased sixfold, the deposits under their control increased tenfold, from $11.6 billion in 1956 to $108.2 billion in 1968. By 1968, these unregistered bank holding companies accounted for 27.5 percent of all commercial bank deposits, twice as much as the registered bank holding companies.[60]

Why did the nation's bank barons turn to the bank holding company form so massively in the late 1960s? The immediate explanation is that the prospects for eliminating the one-bank holding company loophole in the 1956 law began to improve in the late 1960s, giving bankers a strong incentive to get on the bandwagon before the show was shut down—on the assumption that Congress would not have the nerve to make any regulations it adopted retroactive. Better to regroup at once and think about it later than to ponder the issue, only to find the way blocked once the time to act came.

The more basic explanation for the surge of holding-company formations by the nation's financial giants is understandably more complex, however. At heart, the holding-company form offered to the bank barons what it has always offered: a way to evade the law, this time the law forbidding bank entry into nonbanking businesses. What made this form of evasion so attractive in the late 1960s was a rather significant series of changes that had taken place in American commercial banking over the previous decade. Up through the mid-1950s, commercial banks in this country generally operated very much as they had in the past, passively accepting demand deposits and allocating the resulting balances into generally short-term loans and investments satisfying standard canons of safety.[61] The massive postwar growth of the savings and loan industry, however, awoke commercial bankers to the existence of formerly untapped sources of funds that could potentially be channeled into commercial-bank coffers. This awakening coincided with Federal Reserve System policies seeking to limit the growth of demand deposits by increasing reserve requirements in order to avoid inflation.[62] When the Fed eased restrictions on the interest rate commercial banks could pay on savings deposits, commercial banks began competing actively for the savers' dollar. They modernized buildings, opened new branches, and stressed the unique potential that monopolization of the checking-account business gave them to serve as "financial shopping centers," or "full-service banks" as the advertising slogans put it. The results were dramatic: between 1950 and 1968, the proportion of all commercial-bank deposits accounted for by time and savings deposits rose from 30 percent to 50 percent.[63] In addition, banks began competing for funds in other ways, such as by issuing certificates of deposit for sale in the capital markets and borrowing so-called Eurodollars. All of these efforts at attracting funds were successful, but they brought with them an "embarrassment of riches." Having attracted larger deposits, bankers faced the problem of how to put them to work profitably. Traditional loans would not do because, unlike demand deposits, on which the banks pay no interest, the new forms of deposits cost the banks money. Consequently, the bankers had to find more lucrative investments. They began moving into such areas as leasing, bond underwriting, mortgage services, factoring, credit cards, travel-bureau services, insurance, and numerous others.

The problem was that the law placed limits on this expansionism. As one bank consultant described the situation in 1968:

> The tremendous inflow of money into commercial banks was a form of energy. Used properly, as bankers came to realize, this energy would be income producing. The traditional structure of banking, however, placed limits on the use of these funds. *The banking history of the last several years is characterized by the breaking or bending of these traditional barriers.*[64]

The one-bank holding company form of organization provided the perfect solution to this dilemma—at least from the bankers' perspective. It allowed bankers to acquire not only "bank-related" businesses like mortgage-banking or credit-card firms, but also more exotic enterprises as well. The 684 one-bank holding companies in existence as of December 31, 1968, for example, owned, among other things, 40 farms, 161 real-estate firms, 8 retail merchandising stores, 6 petroleum producers or manufacturers, 4 building-material and farm-equipment outlets, and even 4 educational institutions.[65] No longer mere money-changers, such financial Goliaths as the First National City Bank's holding company could begin advertising in the *New York Times*: "Whatever you want from the years ahead—whether as businessman or consumer—at least one of the subsidiary companies of First National City Corporation can probably help you."[66] Quite clearly, the dike separating banking from commerce had sprung a giant leak.*

The bank regulatory authorities, except the Federal Reserve Board, generally viewed this development with little concern. The Comptroller of the Currency, in fact, was positively rhapsodic, and wrote glowingly of the "need to encourage the pioneering spirit" represented by bank-holding-company expansionism.[67] The chairman of the Federal Deposit Insurance Corporation was only slightly less enthusiastic, hailing the bank holding company as a sign of the "willingness to innovate" on the part of banks.[68]

For those on the other side of the barrier between banking and commerce, however, the deluge in prospect was chilling indeed.

---

* In addition, the bank holding company afforded bankers a way to tap additional sources of funds and thus outmaneuver their other depository institution competitors. In the first place, by enabling commercial banks to offer customers a host of services under one roof, the holding company arrangement promised to bring in additional customers and increase the incentive for customers to switch their savings accounts to the bank as well. Even more important, since holding company stock tended to sell at a higher price-to-earnings ratio than bank stock itself, banks that had formed holding companies were able to generate capital more easily in the stock markets, and could do so without worrying about restrictions placed on direct bank efforts to generate capital through stock sales. The holding company device thus offered bankers a way around the restrictions against raising interest rates to attract capital away from savings banks.

From their perspective, bankers were operating with an unfair competitive advantage afforded them by government. After all, the commercial banks had a legal monopoly on demand deposits, which gave them a virtually free source of funds. In addition, they were buffered by entry barriers, deposit guarantees, a backup source of ready cash in the form of the Federal Reserve System, and a protective system of bank examinations. No banker was suggesting that local insurance agencies or computer-leasing firms be allowed to enter the banking business and offer checking-account services. Yet the bankers considered it appropriate, while still enjoying their governmentally provided array of protections, to demand the right to move into the business of insurance and computer leasing. Once in these new lines of business, the banks could begin squeezing out their once independent competitors—by refusing to extend loans to them (or providing cheaper loans to their subsidiaries in the same field), and by letting potential bank borrowers know that they might be well advised to do their business with the banks' subsidiaries.

The dramatic growth of one-bank holding companies organized around the nation's very largest banks thus threatened to produce some basic transformations in the structure of American enterprise. Wright Patman put the matter clearly in early 1969 when he wrote that the issue created by the rapid surge of bank holding companies "is not strictly a banking issue at all, or even an issue only involving the relationships among different segments of the financial community. It is, in essence, a question whose answer could shape the ultimate structure of the entire American economy for many years to come."[69]

INTO THE BRIAR PATCH ...
AND OUT AGAIN

With pressure mounting from insurance agents, leasing firms, data processors, and other competitors of bank-holding-company subsidiaries, Congress finally took up the question of closing the one-bank loophole in the 1956 Bank Holding Company Act. Like Br'er Rabbit, the bankers were thrown into the briar patch. But also like Br'er Rabbit, they escaped in the end. Here is the story.

A Finger in the Dike: House Action

Not surprisingly, the action began on the House side, with the issuance in February 1969 of a report on one-bank holding companies prepared by Patman's Banking Committee staff. Entitled *The Growth of Unregistered One Bank Holding Companies— Problems and Prospects*, the Patman staff report elaborately documented the rapid growth of one-bank holding companies and minutely detailed their characteristics and subsidiaries on a state-by-state and city-by-city basis, a format well suited to arousing congressional concern. Against the backdrop of this report, Patman introduced H.R. 6778, a bill designed to close the one-bank loophole in the 1956 act, strengthen the provisions in the act concerning the definition of ownership, and push a host of additional long-time Patman pet proposals in the process, including prohibitions on tie-ins (arrangements making the availability of credit contingent on use of other banking services) and on interlocking directorates among financial institutions.[70] Under the Patman bill, all bank holding companies would be covered whether they owned one bank or several. Thus, in one fell swoop, the whole array of loopholes in the 1956 act—for one-bank holding companies, and for partnerships, trust departments, labor unions, and farm organizations in control of banks—would be swept away. In addition, the Patman bill extended the coverage to include situations where organizations exercised effective control over banks with less than 25 percent of stock ownership, a not uncommon situation since many corporations are controlled by persons holding blocks of 5 percent or less of the corporation's shares.

Apart from these changes in coverage, however, the Patman proposal stuck quite close to the 1956 act. Like this act, the Patman bill forbade bank holding companies, as redefined, from engaging in nonbanking businesses, and continued the definition of such businesses incorporated in the important Section 4(c) (8) of the 1956 act—i.e., any businesses which are not "so closely related to the business of banking . . . as to be proper incident thereto." As in the 1956 act, moreover, the Federal Reserve Board would continue to administer this provision, since Patman had generally been pleased with the rather strict interpretation of this provision the Fed had been giving under the original act. H.R. 6778 also provided that existing one-bank holding companies already in possession of nonbanking businesses would be required to divest themselves of such businesses. This, again, conformed to the 1956 act, which had required a similar divestiture on the part of the multibank holding companies. Finally, Patman's bill contained two proposals that grew out of his long-time battle against bank concentration in general: a prohibition against tie-in arrangements for all FDIC-insured banks, whether in holding companies or not, and a prohibition on all interlocking directorates among financial institutions, with a corresponding requirement for public disclosure of securities holdings by bank trust departments.

Soon after the introduction of H.R. 6778 in February 1969, and with hearings scheduled for April, the administration introduced its own bill, H.R. 9335, in March. As President Nixon explained when the bill was introduced:

> Left unchecked, the trend toward the combining of banking and business could lead to the formation of a relatively small number of power centers dominating the American economy. This must not be permitted to happen; it would be bad for banking, bad for business, and bad for borrowers and consumers.[71]

The Nixon bill was largely the work of the Treasury Department, which was headed at the time by David M. Kennedy, formerly the chairman of the board of Chicago's Continental Illinois National Bank, a bank that had reorganized itself as a one-bank holding company at Kennedy's suggestion the same month the new secretary took over at Treasury.[72] The man Secretary Kennedy put in charge of drafting this legislation Charls E. Walker, came to Treasury directly from his post as chief executive officer of the American Bankers Association, the powerful lobbying arm of the banking industry. Not surprisingly, therefore, the administration bill, although acknowledging the need to close the one-bank loophole and thus rejecting the position of some of the more radical industry opponents of any regulation, was significantly weaker than the Patman bill. In fact, in several significant respects it was weaker than existing provisions of the 1956 act, whose loopholes it was supposed to close. A brief comparison of the five key features of these various proposals bears this out:

1. *Definition of permissible bank-related activities.* The most important issue in the whole legislative battle over regulation of one-bank holding companies concerned the definition of permissible subsidiary activities for those companies, since it was the fear of bank expansion into nonbanking activities that provided the major impulse behind the legislation. Section 4(c) (8) of the 1956 act, as we have seen, allowed bank-holding-company expansion only into those businesses that are "so closely related to the business of banking . . . as to be proper incident thereto." In administering this Section 4(c) (8) language, the Federal Reserve Board disappointed the bankers by sticking to the letter of the law, thus making the *multi*bank holding company route unattractive for expansion-minded banks. As Federal Reserve Board Chairman Martin noted in 1970, "On the basis of the language of the statute and its legislative history, the Board has interpreted the Section 4(c) (8) exemption to mean that there must be a direct and significant connection between the proposed activities of the company to be acquired and the business of banking."[73] Pleased by this interpretation, Patman retained the section's language in his bill and simply extended its coverage to one-bank holding companies.[74]

Through the change of a few words, however, the Nixon administration proposed to change the rules of the game entirely.

Under its version, the strict "closely related to" and "proper incident thereto" language was replaced by language allowing bank
holding companies—both one-bank *and* multibank—to acquire
any firm whose activities are "financial or related to finance in
nature or of a fiduciary or insurance nature and to be in the public
interest."[75] Though administration witnesses denied any intention to weaken the earlier standard,[76] it is hard to sustain any
other conclusion, given the Fed's strict interpretation of the earlier language. In fact, Congressman William Widnall, the ranking
minority member of the House Banking Committee and the sponsor of the administration bill, made this "perfectly clear." Speaking at the outset of House hearings on holding company legislation, Widnall noted:

> In my opinion the *major and fundamental differences* be-
> tween our bill [sic] is the manner in which we differ with
> respect to future permissible financially related activities
> under the holding company structure.
>
> In no uncertain terms my bill is intended to *permit evolu-
> tionary changes to occur* with regard to activities per-
> mitted. . . .
>
> To those of us who support such an approach, there is
> implicit in our support a *dissatisfaction with the manner in
> which the Federal Reserve Board has narrowly interpreted
> section 4(c) (8)* of the 1956 Bank Holding Company
> Act.[77]

Under the guise of plugging loopholes, in other words, the Nixon
administration was sounding a retreat from the 1956 act's prohibitions on mixing business and banking.

2. *Administration.* The second key point of difference between
the Patman and administration bills concerns the important matter of administration. The Patman bill adopted the administrative
procedure of the 1956 act for supervising bank holding company
acquisitions and activities. This procedure essentially gave the
Federal Reserve Board sole authority over holding company ac-

quisitions of nonbanking subsidiaries as well as over holding company acquisitions of additional banks, thus eliminating the potential for "competition in laxity" inherent in the traditional three-part federal bank-regulation structure. In contrast, the Nixon bill proposed an elaborate *troika* approach, under which the Fed would retain jurisdiction over holding company acquisitions of banks, but jurisdiction over acquisitions of other businesses under Section 4(c) (8) would be split among the three regulatory authorities, the Fed (for state member banks), the Comptroller of the Currency (for national banks), and the FDIC (for state nonmember insured banks).[78] Although the Nixon bill required these three authorities to develop a single set of standards to guide their decisions, the potentials for weakening the prohibitions of the 1956 act were obvious, particularly given the Comptroller's publicly proclaimed eagerness to "encourage the pioneering spirit" by fostering bank-holding-company imperialism, and the similar predisposition on the part of the chairman of the Federal Deposit Insurance Corporation.[79] Not only would these two help ensure a laxer set of standards, but also, by interpreting these standards more liberally for the holding companies under their jurisdictions, they could whipsaw the Fed into following suit.

3. *Grandfather clause.* Like the original 1956 act, the Patman bill would require existing one-bank holding companies to divest themselves of all nonbank businesses declared illegal for them to operate. The administration bill, on the contrary, contained a "grandfather clause" permitting one-bank holding companies already in existence to retain all nonbanking subsidiaries acquired before July 1, 1968.[80] Even though this date preceded the period when most of the largest bank holding companies were formed, the concept of a grandfather clause would inevitably threaten the whole regulatory fabric of the act, for it would lead to powerful pressures to allow *all* holding companies—and, indeed all banks —to engage in the activities permitted by those firms fortuitous enough to have been "grandfathered in."

4. *Tie-in and interlock protections.* The Patman bill proposed to strengthen the procompetition features of the 1956 bill by outlawing tie-in arrangements and interlocking directorates for all federally insured banks. The Nixon bill made no mention of interlocks and restricted the prohibitions on tie-ins to bank holding companies instead of all federally insured banks.[81]

5. *Coverage.* Finally, the two bills differed on the extent of coverage proposed. The 1956 act covered only companies that owned 25 percent or more of a bank's stock, and even then exempted—in addition to companies owning only one bank—all cases where banks were owned by a partnership, a bank trust department, a labor union, or a farm organization. Patman's bill proposed to extend coverage to companies that, in the opinion of the Fed, effectively controlled a bank even without 25 percent stock ownership, and to drop *all* the exemptions. The administration bill would extend coverage to companies controlling banks without holding 25 percent of their stock, but stopped short of eliminating the exemptions for labor unions and farm organizations.

With these two bills in the hopper, the issue was thus joined and the major controversies clearly outlined. During April and early May, the full House Banking Committee held seventeen days of hearings, producing a printed record about 1,600 pages in length. It was Patman's intent to use these hearings to create a legislative atmosphere conducive to closing the one-bank loophole by vigorously documenting the harmful consequences likely to flow from existing trends. The first day of testimony, for example, featured academicians who detailed the dangers of not regulating all holding companies, and thus gave a ring of objectivity to the Patman legislative effort. In addition, the witness list was studded with representatives of the numerous industry groups that stood to lose if bank holding companies continued their unchecked advance: travel agents, insurance agents, data processors, courier services, and others—a broad cross-section of the middle-class small businessmen who dominated the service industries into which bank holding companies were expanding. Typical of the group was O. G. Grueninger, an Indianapolis travel agent, who told the committee:

> While I am not afraid of business competition, I feel that the unique position a bank enjoys makes it such an unfair competitor that the rapid expansion of bank travel bureaus threatens the continued existence of independent travel agencies such as mine. And this is not an unfounded fear. In Indianapolis, Indiana, during the past year alone, three independent travel agencies have closed. Three out of nine. Meanwhile, a large Indianapolis bank that has just achieved holding company status has installed new travel agencies in three additional branches (up from one previously) in the short span of only three months. It is difficult to believe that there is economic justification in such a saturation technique. Indeed, if only from a feeling of competitive necessity, other area banks may try to match their competitor's expansion and coverage. Needless to say, such action by banks, whatever their motivation, works to the detriment of the independent travel agent.[82]

Also included were representatives of the Independent Bankers Association, an organization representing some 6,500 smaller banks in forty states and vehemently opposed to the bank-holding-company concept as a threat to the tradition of independent unit banking and dispersed financial power.[83] The hearings thus presented a powerful case for regulation. As the staff member in charge of the hearings explained to us, "We were trying to create a public climate in which no one could vote against us. We wanted to create a feeling of urgency and crisis."

While Patman and his allies on the committee enjoyed the support of the Independent Bankers Association and the numerous industry groups threatened by bank holding companies, they faced formidable opposition from the bank lobby, particularly the American Bankers Association. With a membership list including

98 percent of all commercial banks, a budget estimated at more than $6 million annually, a network of regional and state associations, and a complex array of policy-making "professional groups" and councils, the ABA is one of the most effective lobby groups in Washington.* The thirty-two lobbyists in the ABA's Government Relations Division sit astride one of the most impressive financial research operations and publicity machines anywhere; they also have at their command a powerful network of "contact bankers" who are on good terms with congressmen back home and who can be mobilized quickly through a well-organized system of mailings and telegrams whenever the legislative situation requires it. Coupled with the standard fare of campaign contributions from central offices, state affiliates, and individual local bankers, the result is an ominous level of clout.

In the case of the Bank Holding Company Act, however, the ABA initially faced a bit of a problem: its membership was split. Smaller bankers, some of them members of the Independent Bankers Association, favored vigorous regulation of bank holding companies since they feared they would become increasingly unable to compete with the burgeoning giant congeneric corporations. The largest commercial banks, as well as the larger conglomerates that had acquired banks, opposed *any* regulation of one-bank holding companies, even that outlined in the somewhat mild Nixon bill. The split within the ABA was so severe, in fact, that a group of large, conglomerate-owned one-bank holding companies split off from the ABA in 1968 and formed the Association of Corporate Owners of One Bank to fight potential regulation.[84]

---

* Based on interview with Charles McNeil, Director, Government Relations Division, American Bankers Association, Washington, D.C., July 24, 1972. Because we were unable to secure the actual budget of the ABA, the figure reported here is an estimate. It was computed conservatively by assuming an average salary *plus expenses* of $20,000 for the 32 members of the Government Relations Division of the ABA and multiplying the resulting total for this division by 10, since this division accounts for 10 percent of the entire budget.

This split among the bankers found reflection among the bank regulatory agencies as well. The Comptroller of the Currency and his first deputy generally lined up behind the largest banks in opposing any closing of the one-bank loophole.[85] The Federal Reserve Board, on the other hand, argued for strong Section 4(c) (8) language (defining permissible activities for bank holding companies) and opposed the *troika* approach to administering the bill as an invitation to confusion and laxness.[86] The Fed even offered its own 4(c) (8) language, outlining a "laundry list" of ten permissible kinds of businesses for bank holding companies, plus a catch-all category outlawing all activities not "functionally related" to banking (instead of the "closely related" language of the 1956 act and Patman bill, and the weaker "related" language of the Treasury version).[87] Since any departure from the "closely related" language of the existing law could only be seen as a weakening, in view of the Fed's past interpretation, this proposed "functionally related" language clearly signaled the Fed's preference for a compromise that would bring one-bank holding companies under regulation for the first time, but would also loosen the restrictions on permissible acts for all bank holding companies.

Not only were the bankers split; they were also apparently unprepared for the vigorous committee attack on holding companies. So, according to one observer, "the defense [for holding companies] had to be largely carried out by witnesses for the Treasury and the federal banking agencies,"[88] most notably Treasury Under-Secretary Charls Walker.

By mid-April 1969, however, the bankers had regrouped. Seeing the support Patman was generating through his hearings, the large bankers who had broken away to form the Association of Corporate Owners of One Bank decided that *some* regulation was inevitable. The group thus felt compelled to work through the ABA to make sure the weakest possible bill was passed.[89] On April 16, 1969, therefore, the ABA Executive Council, following extended deliberations by five ABA policy committees, adopted a compromise position that adhered closely to the views of the larger banks and holding-company advocates who pay the lion's share of the ABA dues. Their position closely resembled the administration's, an outcome that is understandable since the author of the administration bill, Charls Walker, had been in charge of forging a unified ABA position on bank holding companies before taking his post at Treasury. Thus, the ABA strongly endorsed the more flexible Section 4(c) (8) language of the administration bill and applauded the proposed dispersion of supervisory responsibility on the ground that it would encourage "administrative flexibility."[90] But the ABA went well beyond the administration bill in urging a February 17, 1969, "grandfather clause" date, elimination of any regulations of tie-ins or interlocking directorates, and a return to the 1956 act's 25 percent stock-ownership standard for coverage.[91] On May 6, 1969, as the House hearings neared an end, these ABA terms were duly flashed to "Contact Bankers for House Banking and Currency Committee Members," with instructions to "promptly contact your Congressman" and "in your words urge that he support our position."[92]

The Escape

From all indications, the bankers did their homework well, for once the scene shifted from the publicity-cloaked hearing chambers to the quiet of the markup sessions, the tide began to turn in the bankers' direction. Between the end of the hearings on May 9 and the start of executive sessions on June 24, Republican Congressman William Stanton of Ohio drafted a brief one-page version of the bill incorporating all of the ABA demands. Then, when the committee began its markup, ranking Republican William Widnall took advantage of an unusual parliamentary situation to introduce Stanton's bill as a "second substitute" (i.e., a substitute for a substitute amendment). Under House rules, a "second substitute," once approved, becomes part of a bill, without any further votes on the amendment or the first substitute. But Stanton's bill, though offered as a substitute for an amendment to only a section of the bill, was really designed to be a finished product that could stand on its own and replace the entire bill. The committee was thus faced with the necessity to vote on a substitute to its entire bill *before* it had had a chance to begin to debate its separate sections. In a crucial roll-call vote on June 26, it did just this, backing the Stanton-ABA bill, twenty to fifteen. Voting in favor was a solid conservative bloc of Republicans and southern Democrats, including Democrats Robert Stephens (Georgia), Nick Galifianakis (N.C.), Tom Gettys (S.C.), Tom Bevill (Ala.), and Charles Griffin (Miss.); and Republicans Widnall, Stanton, Florence Dwyer (N.J.), Albert Johnson (Pa.), Chester Mize (Kan.), Ben Blackburn (Ga.), Garry Brown (Mich.), Lawrence Williams (Pa.), J. Glenn Beall (Md.), Chalmers Wylie (Ohio), and, by proxy, Margaret Heckler (Mass.) and William Cowger (Ky.).

Patman voted for the revised bill on final passage in order to be in a position to manage it on the floor, but the damage had been done. Stanton's bill, which became the new version of H.R. 6778, was far more lenient than the administration's bill had been: it established a February 17, 1969, grandfather clause (instead of June 30, 1968); maintained the 1956 act's 25 percent stock-ownership standard for coverage; adopted the *troika* administrative setup, but required only a *majority* vote among the three regulatory agencies to establish administrative guidelines instead of the unanimous agreement required in the administration bill; and adopted the "functionally related" language of the Fed's version of Section 4(c) (8) along with a "public needs test" which authorized the regulators to permit otherwise prohibited bank holding company acquisitions whenever these promised to produce "benefits to the public" that were not outweighed by "adverse consequences."

The bankers, needless to say, were delirious with joy at their scuttling not only of Patman's bill but of the administration's as well. And they remembered their friends at election time. Congressman Stanton was particularly richly rewarded. For example, the Lake County National Bank of Painesville, Ohio, a subsidiary of the Society Corporation bank holding company, generated contributions from its president and chief executive officer, three directors, the chairman of the board, a trust officer, two former directors, and one former honorary chairman. Five directors of another Society Corporation subsidiary, the Western Reserve Bank of Lake County, North Madison, Ohio, also contributed. Financial giants in New York and San Francisco also sent money to reseat Stanton. Contributions came from First National City Bank's senior vice-president, three vice-presidents, one director, and a clerk. And the senior vice-chairman and director of San Francisco's Bank of America reached into his wallet for Stanton, too.[93] In the meantime, the ABA passed the word in an "Urgent-Action" telegram to "all contact bankers for the House of Representatives": urge your congressman "to pass H.R. 6778 as reported, without *amendments*."[94] For the rest, the ABA turned its attention to the Senate.

Black Friday: In the Briar Patch Again

But the struggle in the House was by no means over. Between the reversal in committee executive session in June and consideration on the House floor in November, Patman and his staff took the offensive to discredit the committee's bill.[95] Columnist Jack Anderson pilloried the bank lobby for its role in the executive-session reversal, and articles inspired by the Patman staff began appearing in numerous newspapers. In the meantime, the lobbyists for insurance and travel agencies, data processors, and other industry groups rolled into action, mobilizing their memberships to put pressure on congressmen. The National Association of Insurance Agents (NAIA) was particularly effective. As Congressman Stanton complained during floor debate on the holding company bill:

> In the last 48 hours I have received more telegrams from insurance agents in my district, asking me to support amendments, than I have ever received on any other legislation. I thought that the education lobbyists in this country

had superceded some of the labor union lobbyists for the questionable title of lobbyist no. 1. However, over the past few months, I am convinced that the NAIA holds this questionable title at the present.[96]

When the holding company bill that had been reported out of committee on June 26, 1969, reached the floor on November 5, the stage was set for some fireworks. With speed and precision, the bankers' handiwork was systematically dismantled. First to go was the February 17, 1969, "grandfather clause." On an amendment by Republican Chalmers Wylie, the House approved the Patman version requiring divestiture of all nonbanking subsidiaries acquired since 1956.[97] Next was the critical Section 4(c) (8). On a motion by Republican Ben Blackburn, the House adopted language that, instead of listing *permitted* activities, listed *prohibited* ones (insurance, data processing, accounting, leasing, travel services, and commingled investment trusts).[98] This "negative laundry list" was designed to make sure the regulatory agencies did not frustrate the intent of Congress in administering the nonbanking prohibitions. A complementary amendment by William Moorhead then restored the "closely related" language of the 1956 act. And so it went until the bill had been completely rewritten. The one major challenge, a motion to recommit the bill, attracted the votes of 125 members, 11 of them on the Banking Committee—including such "liberals" as Lud Ashley, Thomas Rees, and Richard Hanna, as well as Republicans Beall, Brock, Brown, Dwyer, Heckler, Mize, Stanton, and Widnall—but it was turned aside decisively by 245 congressmen. On the final vote, the House passed the amended and strengthened bill 352–24, with only six Banking Committee members (Ashley, Brock, Brown, Mize, Stanton, and Widnall) voting no.[99] Bankers have labeled that Friday, November 5, 1969, "Black Friday," the day they suffered one of their rare defeats.

The ABA and its supporters lost for several reasons. Most important was the sellout image that was generated by the ABA-inspired committee bill and the immense publicity campaigns launched by the anti-holding-company industry groups. Members consequently feared that recorded votes for the banks might offend insurance agents and tag the member forever as being in the bankers' pocket. By pushing for recorded votes on every amendment, therefore, advocates of strengthened regulations ensured their victory. As one committee staffer recalled:

> By the time the committee bill got to the floor, it stunk so badly that no one wanted to support it. There were a lot of guys just standing around waiting to see what was going to happen. Anybody who voted for the committee bill would be branded. This was our most effective weapon. We had created a sellout atmosphere. The banking industry people had overstepped themselves and bitten off more than they could chew. They just got too greedy. If they had been content with Charlie Walker's [the administration's] bill we never would have been as effective.[100]

Another crucial reason for the success of Patman's coalition was that it was bipartisan. Conservative Republicans Wylie and Blackburn offered the two most important amendments. The committee's counsel later revealed that the staff was largely responsible for this:

> We had to convince Patman to spread the amendments around so that we could create the impression that there was a broad coalition. Wylie and Blackburn were essential in that effort. I wish we had brought more amendments to the floor. We could have passed anything. We disemboweled the ABA on the floor.

Even in defeat, however, the bank lobby demonstrated its strength, for while few members wanted to go on record in favor of the bankers' bill, few wanted to go on record against it either. As a consequence, the votes on the amendments were minuscule: 63–34, 50–25, 31–28. The banking lobbyists were nevertheless stunned at the scope of their defeat. In the November 7 *American*

Banker, a representative of a Chicago bank holding company called the bill a "monster" and said there should be a "regrouping" of forces "to go to work on the Senate."

ANOTHER WAY OUT: THE SENATE

The bankers had reason to be confident about their prospects in the Senate. As we have seen, chairman John Sparkman of the Senate Banking Committee shared few of the antibank Populist sentiments of his House counterpart. In addition, the bankers enjoyed an extraordinary level of access to this committee. James B. Cash and Matthew Hale, chief Senate lobbyist and counsel, respectively, for the American Bankers Association, had both been high-ranking staff members of the Senate Banking Committee in the early 1960s. Donald Rodgers, Secretary of the Association of Registered Bank Holding Companies, which lobbied hard on the holding-company amendments, had served as assistant counsel for the same committee in the late 1950s. During the holding company battle, he retained as counsel for the association a former chief clerk of the Senate Banking Committee, John Yingling, who was also hired as a lobbyist for the First National City Bank, one of the largest of the newly formed one-bank holding companies. Finally, Lewis G. Odum, a man whose relationship with chairman Sparkman is said to be "like father and son" as a consequence of Odum's thirteen years of service as Sparkman's aide, the last two of them in the position of Senate Banking Committee staff director, turned up during the one-bank holding company struggle as a lobbyist for CIT Corporation, a giant conglomerate one-bank holding company.[101] Before leaving the committee to become a lawyer-lobbyist in 1969, moreover, Odum had recruited a young protege, Hugh Smith. In 1972 Smith quit the committee to join Odum in his law and lobbying practice. In between, he took the major responsibility on Sparkman's behalf for handling the one-bank holding company legislation in the Senate.

From all indications, the bankers made good use of these exceptional links to the Senate Banking Committee. The first sign was Sparkman's protracted delay in scheduling hearings. Despite the urgency voiced by administration officials when they introduced their legislation in March 1969, six months elapsed between House passage of the bill in November 1969 and the beginning of Senate committee hearings in mid-May 1970. When administration sources made it known that the President would veto any bill with a "laundry list," and then announced the President's intention to name a Commission on Financial Structure and Regulation in January 1970, the new strategy of the bankers became evident. Devised by Treasury Under-Secretary and former ABA official Charls Walker, who had masterminded the original banker strategy of seeking to weaken the 1956 act while claiming to be plugging its loopholes, the new strategy grew out of the defeat in the House and called for abandoning the legislative effort in the Ninety-first Congress, purportedly to allow a more comprehensive review of the entire structure of bank regulation. The holding-company lobbyists calculated that the debacle they suffered in the House was a product of a freakish combination of events that would not likely recur on a second round in the House, particularly if the second round could be delayed until after the 1972 election, during which the bankers could apply the curative medicine of campaign contributions to obstinate legislators.[102] A bill introduced by Senator William Proxmire calling for a presidential commission to study restructuring the administration and regulation of the credit industry (S.1225) provided a perfect "front" for this new strategy, though Proxmire's proposal carried with it stipulations forbidding the formation of new bank holding companies and prohibiting existing ones from the same activities outlawed by the 1956 act until the commission recommended some legislation. No such stipulations were attached to the commission plan announced by the President in January 1970.

By late spring 1970, this strategy of delay had proved to be bankrupt. Registered bank holding companies chafed under regulations that did not apply to their unregulated one-bank competitors. Insurance agents, data processors, and others bewailed the continued unregulated bank takeovers of their businesses. Internal administration forces, mostly from the Federal Reserve, continued to urge action. Finally, Patman applied his own form of pressure: he refused to schedule hearings on the Senate-passed Urban Mass Transit Assistance Act, and thus held hostage a piece of legislation important to one of chairman Sparkman's senior colleagues on the Banking committee, Harrison Williams.[103]

Thus, while Sparkman sat, the pressures mounted. Finally, on May 12, 1970, the Senate Banking Committee began hearings on the one-bank holding company issue. However, unlike the House hearings, which provided a forum for opponents of bank holding companies as well as proponents, the Senate hearings were devoted far more heavily to banking industry representatives or their supporters. Most of these spent their time seeking to portray the House-passed bill as a proposal to dissolve the American banking system. The president of the ABA, for example, told the senators that:

> Put bluntly, in the guise of attempting to define the business of holding companies, HR 6778 seeks to circumscribe the business of banking itself, in such fashion as to constitute, in our considered judgment, a most destructive measure.
>
> It is a bill shaped by those who apparently do not understand the nature of the banking business, abetted by those who seek to reduce or eliminate competition for their own advantage, and enacted in an atmosphere of turmoil and haste. It would constitute, in our opinion, bad legislation.[104]

Treasury Under-Secretary Charls Walker made it clear that the bankers were especially exercised about the so-called "negative laundry list" written into the House bill:

In basic substance, the original Patman bill and the administration bill were not all that far apart. We differed on grandfather clauses quite strongly. We thought there should be
one. He thought there shouldn't be one. We differed on the
regulatory agency. We wanted the troika approach, as it has
been dubbed, and some new language. But the House committee sort of struck down the middle here. . . . Unfortu-
nately, on the floor of the House, they went on to say that
certain activities are not functionally related to banking and
listed several areas. Not only do we believe that the setting
up of a list by the Congress is the wrong way to approach
this—you have agencies to administer these things—but this
has been dubbed the negative laundry list and we think it is
highly anticompetitive by keeping bank holding companies
out of areas that will benefit the consumer.[105]

Behind Closed Doors: The "Green Stamp Amendment"

After twelve days of hearings, the committee began executive
sessions on July 7 to prepare a bill. Since the sessions were secret,
and since the Senate committee typically decides issues by discussion without formal, roll-call votes, it is difficult to determine
definitely who stood where.* On the basis of public statements
and interviews with members and staffers, however, it is possible
to piece together what happened. In a word, the action again
gave substance to a point stressed by chief ABA lobbyist Charles
McNeil: the committee stage is where the bankers are most
effective.[106] Through Sparkman and staffer Hugh Smith, the
bankers were able to exert great influence over the two most
important strategic weapons in any markup session, the committee print (the working draft of the bill) and the "agenda" (the
schedule highlighting the major points at issue in a piece of legislation). Together, these two structure the debate in a markup

---

* We repeatedly asked for access to the transcripts of the Senate Banking
Committee executive sessions on the Bank Holding Company Act Amendments of 1970, but were repeatedly denied access by members of the committee and the staff. By contrast, House members and staffers provided
complete access to the markup session transcripts.

session and confer strategic advantages on one side or another—for example, by calling an "exemption" a "loophole" or by incorporating weak language in the print requiring advocates of stronger language to propose and pass numerous amendments.

In the case of the Bank Holding Company Act Amendments of 1970, the print and agenda prepared by staffer Smith were weighted overwhelmingly in the bankers' direction. In fact, the print differed substantially from *all* the formally introduced bills (the original Patman bill, the original administration bill, and the House-passed bill), and consistently in the bankers' direction: it provided a March 24, 1969, "grandfather clause"; weakened the 1956 act's Section 4(c)(8) by adopting the "functionally related" language and public benefits test; established a ten-year grace period for divestiture of nonbanking activities; allowed bank holding companies during this ten-year period to continue to acquire essentially any companies or engage in any activities they wished; totally eliminated the "tie-in" regulations of both the Patman and administration bills; and specified that a holding-company application to acquire a bank would be automatically approved if not otherwise acted on by the Federal Reserve Board within ninety-one days.[107]

If the print and agenda contributed to the committee's ultimate endorsement of a probank bill, however, they were not alone in producing this result, for this committee already leaned in the bankers' direction. Of the fifteen members, only Proxmire favored strong regulation of holding companies, although Edward Brooke was concerned about making the bill's anti-tie-in provisions even stronger. Republicans Wallace Bennett, John Tower, Charles Percy, Charles Goodell, and Bob Packwood all strongly supported the ABA. A former staff member recalled that "the bankers had Percy in the bag from the beginning. Goodell had to keep his tail covered since he was then up for reelection."[108] Liberals Edmund Muskie and Harold Hughes participated very little in committee activities on the issue. But Alan Cranston, Ernest Hollings, Thomas McIntyre, and Walter Mondale all consistently supported the banks' desires to expand, in Mondale's case as a consequence of the influence of the Minnesota Mining and Manufacturing (3M) Company, a major conglomerate bank holding company in his state.

The final committee version thus changed few of the probank provisions written into staffer Smith's committee print. It did make the divestiture and grace period five instead of ten years; it allowed parties aggrieved by bank holding company expansion to sue; and it reinstated the tie-in provisions, though in weakened form. But the rest remained, including the March 24, 1969, grandfather clause, which the committee admitted was intended to give "the holding company . . . maximum flexibility to engage in the grandfathered activities in whatever manner it desires, so long as it does not purchase an existing going concern."[109] The bill was thus quite palatable to the bank holding companies, for with the grandfather clause, the divestiture grace-period provisions, and liberal Section 4(c) (8) language, their activities would be restricted very little.

More than that, the bill as cleared by the Senate Banking Committee would still exempt an astounding 81 percent of all holding companies from even the weak regulation left intact by the rest of the bill. This incredible outcome was the result of an amendment offered by Harrison Williams, who was up for reelection the following November. Dubbed the "Green Stamp Amendment" because of its similarity to a proposal made at the Senate hearings by a representative of Sperry and Hutchinson (the conglomerate, one-bank holding company best known for its S & H Green Stamps), this amendment proposed to exclude from the bill's coverage all conglomerate bank holding companies* owning banks with less than $500 million in deposits and all other one-bank holding companies that involve banks with deposits less

---

* A "conglomerate bank holding company" is one in which a conglomerate primarily involved in nonbanking activities purchases a bank. It differs from the "congeneric" form, in which the bank itself is the major actor and acquires subsidiaries.

than $300 million. Altogether, 900 of the 1,116 bank holding companies in existence at the time would be exempted from the bill by this provision. And according to Senator Proxmire, it seemed as if lobbyists from every one of them descended on the committee during consideration of this amendment:

> In my thirteen years in the Senate, I have never witnessed a more intensive lobbying campaign on behalf of a special interest amendment. I use the term "special interest" deliberately because that is exactly what the conglomerate amendment is. . . .
>
> Lobbyists for the conglomerate amendment were practically falling over one another in an effort to get it into the bill. They swarmed around the committee offices like bees around honey. At one point, they became so bothersome that the staff literally had to lock its doors to keep them out.[110]

Along with the lobbying of the bank holding company giants and the ABA, the "inside work" of Sparkman and staffer Smith, and the predispositions and political circumstances of the members, this conglomerate lobbying put the finishing touches on the gutting of the bill. With the adoption of the Green Stamp Amendment, the bill exempted all but the largest bank holding companies, and treated even these so leniently that they could find the bill quite palatable indeed. Moreover, for the multibank holding companies, the bill was a positive improvement, since it relieved them of the stringent requirements of the 1956 act's Section 4(c) (8). The "Action Letter" dispatched to contact bankers for the Senate from the executive vice-president of the ABA on September 2, 1970, summarized the results perfectly: "The major objectives of banking were accomplished during consideration by the Senate Committee on Banking and Currency."[111]

While the lobbyists rejoiced, however, others expressed shock, including the respected independent banking-industry daily, the *American Banker*. In an editorial entitled "Complete Reversal of Purpose," the *American Banker* noted:

The version of the one-bank holding company bill delivered up by the Senate Banking Committee surprised almost everyone except the lobbyists for the conglomerates who engineered it. And well it might. For now that some of the shock has worn off, the Senate committee's bill can be discerned as a complete reversal of the primary purpose of one-bank holding company legislation [which was] to reaffirm the important line between commerce and finance which in the judgment of many leaders both inside the banking industry itself and among its regulatory officials was becoming dangerously blurred.[112]

Going Along to Get Along

Neither the *American Banker* nor the coalition of small business groups that had been so persuasive in the House managed to convince the Senate, however. With the solid backing of chairman Sparkman and a committee majority, the Senate Banking Committee version of the one-bank holding company act had easy sailing in the Senate. Senator Proxmire, the chief opponent of the committee bill, managed to win majority support for only one strengthening amendment—that returning the "grandfather" date from March 24, 1969, as specified in the committee bill, to the June 30, 1968, date proposed in the original Nixon bill. And even then only five Senate Banking Committee members voted for this move, compared to six against.*[113] What is more, when Proxmire tried to move the date back for conglomerate holding companies as well, he lost, thirty–forty-five.[114] In contrast, a Bennett amendment, pushed by the ABA,[115] which would circumscribe the activities prohibited by the tie-in regulations, passed overwhelmingly, sixty-two–fourteen.[116]

Perhaps the most crucial vote of all, however, came on a motion to delete the Green Stamp Amendment. Proxmire expected to

* The five committee members voting in favor of changing the cut-off to the earlier date were Hollings, McIntyre, Proxmire, Hughes, and Brooke. Voting no were Bennett, Cranston, Packwood, Sparkman, Tower, and Williams. Goodell, Muskie, Percy, and Mondale did not vote.

win this vote, but lost, thirty-four to thirty-seven, when three key votes he was counting on—Metcalf of Montana, Burdick of North Dakota, and McGovern of South Dakota—switched sides. The switching of these three votes provides an especially interesting case study of the reach of banker and conglomerate power, and the effectiveness of bank lobbying. According to one close observer, all three of these liberal Midwestern senators voted as they did because of pressure from the National Farmers Union, the liberally oriented farm organization, which had gotten itself in hock to a Denver bank in the early 1960s as a result of some bad investments made by its pension fund.[117] Thanks to NFU pension fund officer Charles F. Brann, a former secretary of agriculture who served on the board of directors of the Central Bank and Trust Company of Denver, a loan was arranged from Central Bank and Trust to save the NFU pension fund from bankruptcy. In June 1968, however, Central Bank and Trust was acquired by the D. H. Baldwin Company, a conglomerate which soon after organized itself as a conglomerate bank holding company called Baldwin-Central.[118] As the conglomerate bank holding company exemption neared a vote on the Senate floor, Baldwin-Central called up its favor from the NFU, and the NFU proceeded to exert pressure on the senators it could influence. As a result, the Green Stamp Amendment survived the floor test, and the bill, with the conglomerate amendment included, passed the Senate seventy-seven to one, with only Proxmire voting no. The stage was thus set for a classic Senate-House conference.

TEST OF WILINESS:
THE HOUSE-SENATE CONFERENCE

Though much neglected by outsiders, conference committees are crucial decision-making centers in Congress. They are also decision centers in which committee chairmen have the upper hand. Conference rules require that a bill must have the support not of a majority of the House and Senate conferees together, but of each house's conferees separately. Since the committee chairman selects the conferees for his side, he can thus importantly influence the likely outcome. In the holding company act conference, the bankers could be pleased by Sparkman's choices: Bennett, Tower, Williams, and Sparkman all supported the holding companies' positions; only Proxmire did not. Patman's appointees, by contrast, had an antibank majority of four to three (Patman, Barrett, Sullivan, and Reuss *versus* Widnall, Johnson, and Stanton).

As the date of the all-important conference approached, the American Bankers Association mobilized its contact-banker network for one last push. A special "Action Letter" was dispatched on November 6, 1970, to contact bankers in each of the conferees' districts with instructions to make "a final effort to *contact Conferees*," and to do so "in person . . . if at all possible." Key points to be stressed were itemized and a summary of arguments provided. For particularly troublesome conferees, the list of contact bankers was especially lengthy. Only five local bankers were designated to call on Senators Sparkman and Bennett and Representatives Stanton and Johnson. But the ABA asked no fewer than eleven prominent St. Louis bankers to call on Congresswoman Leonor Sullivan, and seventeen Wisconsin bankers to work on Senator Proxmire and Congressman Reuss.[119]

While the bankers and other industry groups lobbied heavily, Patman and his staff devised their own strategy. Their task was to find a way to eliminate the Green Stamp Amendment without having to compromise everything they cared about in the House version of the bill, particularly the Section 4(c) (8) language and the grandfather clause. Given the extremely weak bill passed by the Senate, however, they were in a disadvantageous bargaining position—exactly where the bankers had hoped to put them.

But the House conferees did have two important weapons. One was the conference agenda, the list of basic issues to be decided. The House staffer for this conference explained to us:

Hugh Smith and I were supposed to write [the agenda] together, but he played a minor role because he wasn't really interested. I wrote the drafts and he offered corrections. We put some important things in that agenda. The agenda structures the tradeoffs in conference; it all depends upon how you classify something. What we wanted to do was to put it all in front of them and embarrass them with those exemptions. You see, depending upon how the thing was presented the exemptions could be made to seem either beneficial or really nasty.

The second weapon of Patman and his allies was an exotic strategy for dealing with Senator Williams' Green Stamp Amendment. The Senate had fortuitously tacked on to its version of the holding company bill a noncontroversial provision for the coinage of 150 million commemorative Eisenhower dollars with a 40 percent silver content. Senator Wallace Bennett strongly favored this provision, since his home state, Utah, had a substantial silver industry. More important, the major contractor for the silver jacketing material used in the coins was a Massachusetts subsidiary of Englehart Industries, a corporation owned by William Englehart of Newark, New Jersey, who just happened to be a major contributor to the New Jersey Democratic Party and to Senator Harrison Williams, the sponsor of the Green Stamp Amendment. Several of the House committee staff informed Englehart's Washington representative that the House conferees would reject the commemorative-medal provision unless Englehart demanded that Williams stop pressing his Green Stamp Amendment; in exchange Englehart would contribute to Williams' campaign for reelection. Apparently the deal worked, for on the first day of the conference, Williams agreed to drop his support for the amendment, and it died.[120] A counsel for the House Banking Committee defended the staff's strategy:

Sure, we made a deal which made several million dollars in profit for Englehart. But what is so bad about that when compared with the long run damage done to the economy and the public interest by the conglomerate amendment which would allow those huge corporations to escape regulation?

But some members of Congress weren't so pleased with the Englehart-Williams agreement. Leonor Sullivan sarcastically labeled the deal a

> major concession to certain economic interests in this country whose interests in honoring the late President Eisenhower seemed to be secondary to the speculative operations of the silver futures market. We received a major enough concession from the Senate conferees on one very important feature of the Senate version of the one-bank holding company bill to persuade the House conferees in turn to go along with the Senate on the use of some defense stockpile silver for the somewhat frivolous purpose of turning out 150 million commemorative coins.[121]

With the Green Stamp Amendment out of the way, the horse-trading in conference could begin in earnest. From all indications, it was tooth and nail all the way. On the critical Section 4(c) (8) issue, Patman and his allies seized the initiative at the outset by offering to eliminate the "negative laundry list" of the House bill. "We did this for several reasons," House staffer Benet Gellman explained:

> Usually, a conference sits around and bickers for the first two days without getting anything done. First, we wanted to throw them [the Senate conferees] off, get them off balance, by offering to make such an important exchange at the outset. Second, we didn't want to have to compromise on parts of the laundry list. . . . This would probably have resulted in the industry with the most political muscle retaining some protected status while the rest would be sacrificed. The legislative history of such a move would be interpreted as a blank check for the holding companies to rush into those activities excluded from the final laundry list.[122]

In return, the Patman forces secured approval of Section 4(c) (8) language that was far closer to the House version than to the Senate version. Under the final conference bill, holding companies could acquire:

> shares of any company the activities of which the Board after due notice and opportunity for hearing, has determined to be *so closely related to banking or managing or controlling banks as to be proper incident thereto.*[123]

Moreover, the Fed was instructed to determine, in making its judgment, that the benefits to the public to be gained by any such bank expansion outweighed possible "adverse effects," including effects on competition.

Though stronger than the comparable Senate language, this final conference version of Section 4(c) (8) also differed from the original 1956 version. No longer was there any requirement that the activities permitted be "of a financial, fiduciary, or insurance nature," nor did the key phrase "the business of banking" survive:

1956 Act	*1970 Amendments*
. . . shares of any company *all of the* activities of which are or are to be of *financial, fiduciary, or insurance nature* and which the Board after due notice and hearing, and on the basis of the record made at such hearing, by order has determined to be so closely related to *the business of banking* or of managing or controlling banks as to be proper incident thereto.*	. . . shares of any company the activities of which the Board after due notice and opportunity for hearing, has determined to be so closely related to banking or managing or controlling banks as to be proper incident thereto.

* Italicized portions omitted in final 1970 Act version.

What these changes really meant, however, was up for grabs. Before the ink was dry on this compromise, the two sides began a dispute over whether it constituted a strengthening or weakening of the 1956 language. Patman and his allies argued in the House conference report that the new version established "a more difficult standard than that found in the present law," because it added the "public benefits test" to the existing requirements. Therefore, the House report noted somewhat wishfully,

> there may be circumstances where the board would turn down an application under the second test—the public benefits test—that it would have had to approve under the old test because the only significant element in that standard was the "closely related" one. Now both tests must be met.[124]

Equally eager to create some "legislative history" to support his own interpretation, chairman Sparkman argued on the Senate floor that the conference version conformed "in all major respects" to the objectives of the Senate bill, particularly by providing the Fed the flexibility it requested "in order to permit it to depart from past precedents and to permit expansion of bank and bank related activities which will be required in order to meet fully the rapidly expanding and varying financial needs of the economy of the Nation." The new language, Sparkman contended,

> frees the board of the restrictive precedents established under the present act. . . . It provides that permissible activities may be related to the business of banking generally rather than perpetuating the concept that such activities must be related to the specific business carried on by the subsidiary banks of the particular holding company involved.[125]

It seems clear that Sparkman's view was the more accurate one, given the Fed's strict interpretation of the 1956 act provision and the conference's deletion of two of the key phrases used by the Fed to support its earlier interpretations. At least the Fed has chosen to read the results this way, and its decisions since the passage of the 1970 act have substantially broadened the range of permissible bank-holding-company activities—though in a cautious way so as to avoid a court challenge that could reestablish the 1933 Banking Act's clear prohibition on mixing banking and other business.[126]

The conference committee reached a similar compromise on the "grandfather clause." House conferees accepted the concept of a grandfather clause and agreed to the June 30, 1968, date originally specified in the Nixon bill. But they managed to insert in the bill a requirement that within two years the Federal Reserve Board must review the holdings of all one-bank holding companies formed before that date that control banks with assets in excess of $60 million to determine whether these holdings comply with the requirements of the act and can be kept.[127] On the tie-in issue, the conferees accepted the Senate version, which regulated tie-ins but incorporated the ABA-sponsored amendment defining tie-ins to exclude such traditional bank practices as the correspondent system.

Thus revised in conference, the Bank Holding Company Act Amendments of 1970 passed the House by a vote of 365–4, with all members of the Banking Committee in support. In the Senate, it passed by voice vote after Proxmire, the lone opponent of the original Senate bill, gave his approval to the conference work. In the end, almost everyone pretended to be satisfied.

WHO WON? . . . AND WHAT'S NEXT?

The Bank Holding Company Act Amendments of 1970 thus closed the 1956 act's one-bank loophole, which had become so gaping with the emergence of the giant financial congenerics in the mid- and late 1960s. In doing so, however, it weakened the traditional prohibitions on mixing banking with commerce, which had been preserved in the 1956 statute. Assessing the gains and losses from this important legislative battle consequently requires a rather complicated calculus. On the one hand, the act made it clear that the newly formed giant one-bank holding companies would not be permitted to expand indiscriminately into any economic activity they chose, as had been the case previously. But, on the other hand, it gave these institutions the mandate they sought to become "financial shopping centers" with the authority to extend their reach well beyond traditional banking to embrace such activities as investment counseling, property leasing, bookkeeping, data processing, loan servicing, and some insurance. In the process, it opened these arenas for multibank holding companies as well, and laid the basis for a further weakening of the banking/commerce barrier. After all, when the First National City Corporation can offer its customers the opportunity to lease a Citibank-owned steamship fleet as part of its "closely related" banking business, what is left in the nonbanking category?

If the intention of the 1970 act was to halt the growth of bank holding companies or prevent their takeover of additional businesses, therefore, it was a failure. By 1972, in fact, the number of bank holding companies had grown to 1,500, controlling 2,469 banks and 58 percent of the total bank deposits in the nation[128] —compared to 684 bank holding companies controlling 40 percent of all deposits when the legislative effort that culminated in the 1970 act began in early 1969. Clearly the 1970 act has done little to dampen the expectations of bank holding company enthusiasts. "Let's face it," the public relations director of the Association of Registered Bank Holding Companies boasted,

> there is a trend toward the formation of bank holding companies by the aggressive, progressive banks. Compare them with other conglomerates. Look at General Mills. What would have happened to them if the law had forced them to restrict their growth to making flour and bread. They are now one of the largest corporations in America. The same is true of a bank holding company. It allows the bank to spread out and expand geographically. These regulations have allowed banks to meet the needs of twentieth-century America for the first time.[129]

What is more, by eliminating the competitive advantage one-bank holding companies formally had over multibank companies by virtue of being unregulated, the 1970 act has revived the danger the holding company phenomenon posed to competition *within* the banking industry. Holding-company enthusiasts make no secret of this potential. "We're going to go to this one-stop shopping center in finance, that's certain," Senator Wallace Bennett's staff aide on the Banking Committee told us. "This *does* raise a problem about competition, but that's the Justice Department's worry."[130]

The one-bank holding company battle thus left unresolved at least as many issues as it settled. It helped guarantee that Congress would continue to be faced with the difficult chore of trying to devise appropriate guidelines to protect the public stake in the organization and operations of the country's powerful banking system. Indeed, many of these issues are before Congress at this writing in the form of the recommendations of the President's Commission on Financial Structure and Regulation, which was appointed at the height of the holding company battle. With the departure of Sparkman as chairman of the Senate Banking Committee in January 1975 and the succession of Proxmire, there is reason to believe the outcome may be somewhat less congenial to commercial-bank expansionism than was the case in 1970. Yet the other elements of the 1970 experience—the strength of the banking lobby, the pull of campaign finance, the weakness of traditional staff research capabilities, and the general ambiguities of the legislative process—all remain intact. Until these change, the one step forward, two steps backward experience of 1970 is likely to recur.

4

Brick by Brick:
Housing and
Urban Policy

The history of housing legislation, all in all, makes no ethical sense, no economic sense, no social sense. But it makes sense in terms of the system needs of political bodies.
—Lawrence Friedman[1]

If the story of federal banking policy illustrates how a powerful industry group can effectively utilize public authority to insulate itself from competition, the story of federal housing and urban development policy illustrates how even well-intentioned social programs can be frustrated by the congressional need to generate support among key economic interests. For forty years now, the United States government has been actively involved in the provi-

146

sion of housing and urban development assistance, all of it premised on the goal of eliminating the suffering of the urban poor. In
1949 Congress explicitly committed itself to providing a "decent
home in a suitable living environment" for every American family. This goal was reaffirmed in 1968 and supplemented by a
specific congressional pledge to aid in the construction of 26 million units of new housing, 6 million of them for low-income families, over the next decade—a rate of new construction of 2.6
million units per year, compared to the average of 1.5 million
units per year built during the previous six years.

Despite these bold promises, widespread urban blight and serious shelter needs persist. Indeed, in few other areas of national
life have promise and performance diverged so sharply. To be
sure, as we shall see more fully below, federal policy has significantly improved the housing opportunities of a substantial portion
of the middle class. But its success in relieving the desperate
housing needs of the urban poor, or in reducing urban blight, has
been far more limited. The National Commission on Urban Problems (the Douglas Commission) reported in 1968, for example,
that at least 4 million urban families still lived in substandard and
overcrowded dwellings, an equal number in units so deteriorated
that they need constant repair, and another several million in
dwellings with serious code violations.[2] The National Advisory
Commission on Civil Disorders (the Kerner Commission)
pointed out that in 1960 two-thirds of the nation's nonwhite families living in central cities resided in neighborhoods marked by
substandard housing and general urban decay.[3] Large swaths of
deteriorating neighborhoods in virtually every major American
city tell the story clearly for anyone who cares to read it.

Even middle-class families have suffered, moreover, as housing
starts have lagged behind the formation of new families, and as
housing costs have skyrocketed. In 1968, the Douglas Commission estimated that the nation would have to construct 2 to 2¼
million new housing units per year just to "break the back of our
minimum housing needs by 1980."[4] Despite the commission's

advice and the passage of new federal legislation in 1968, however, housing starts remained below 1.5 million units in 1969 and
1970. They reached 2 million units in 1971 and a record 2.4
million in 1972, but began falling off precipitously again, so that
by 1974 the figure was back down to a seasonally adjusted annual
rate of 1.5 million units and still falling.[5] Thus, in the five years
following passage of the 1968 Housing Act, the nation approached the congressionally mandated minimum goal for annual
housing starts only once.

Were this performance an isolated occurrence, of course, it
would occasion little concern. But the sharp downturn in housing
construction, which has generated cries of pain from the home-
building industry throughout 1974, is but the most severe of six
such extended recessions that have struck this industry since
World War II, frustrating the effort to close the housing gap
bequeathed by fifteen years of Depression and war.[6] The result
has been a persistent shortage of housing, particularly low-income
housing. One revealing symptom of this situation is the increased
number of families forced to locate in mobile homes. In 1972, for
example, a quarter of all private housing starts were accounted
for by mobile homes, compared to only 8 percent a decade earlier. If we look at single-family dwellings only, the figures are
even more startling: mobile homes accounted for 44 percent of
all new single-family housing starts in 1972, compared to only 12
percent a decade earlier.[7]

BANKING AND BUILDING:
THE FINANCIAL CONNECTION

The single most important reason for the erratic pattern of housing construction and for the persistence of severe urban blight and
serious housing shortages is the nature of the nation's money
markets. Virtually everyone who buys a home must borrow
money to do so; the same is true of municipalities undertaking
capital improvements. As of 1972, in fact, residential mortgages

outstanding amounted to a staggering $423 billion, more than twice the value of all corporate bonds. State and local governments accounted for an additional $181 billion in debt.[8] As housing specialist George Sternlieb has noted, "It would be difficult to overestimate the importance of the terms and availability of financing to the residential real estate market."[9]

In seeking needed funds in the capital markets, however, home buyers and local governments are at a distinct competitive disadvantage compared to the other potential users of capital. With their limited yields, long maturities, relatively small dollar amounts, and traditionally limited "marketability" from one jurisdiction to another, home mortgages have little attraction to the men whose decisions determine the flow of credit in the economy. As one writer has put it, "The volume of mortgage credit is a sort of residual, in that home buyers can obtain only that volume of credit which remains after the more volatile and persistent demands of corporations have been satisfied."[10] When the Federal Reserve Board reduces the money supply to stabilize the economy, therefore, it is the housing and urban development sector that is most severely hurt. Corporate clients, after all, can pass along the costs of higher interest rates to their customers in the form of higher prices, but the home buyer must absorb them himself. And these costs are immense. Each 1 percent rise in interest rates on a thirty-year mortgage, for example, boosts the monthly payment by 12 percent.[11] Even with a 6.5 percent, thirty-year mortgage, the purchaser of a $30,000 home will ultimately pay $68,267 for his home: $30,000 to cover the principal and $38,267 as interest. If interest rates rise to 9 percent—as they already have—the same house will cost $86,900 by the time the buyer pays off his loan. In addition, the way banks set up repayment schedules means that interest charges eat up almost all of the money paid by the home buyer during the early years of his loan. During the first year of a thirty-year, $30,000 loan at 6.5 percent interest, for example, less than $30 of the $2,276 paid to the bank goes to retire the principal; the rest goes for interest. Not until well into the eighth year does the portion of each month's payment going to retire the principal equal the amount going to pay the interest charge.

Every time interest rates rise and money becomes tight, potential home buyers disappear from the market, and the solution of the nation's housing problems is further delayed. Because of the extreme sensitivity of the mortgage market to changes in interest rates, in fact, the housing industry typically shoulders a disproportionate share of the retrenchment that monetary authorities seek to produce by tightening the money supply. When the Fed raised interest rates in 1966 to counter the inflationary pressures unleashed by the Vietnam War buildup, for example, the result was a 47 percent drop in housing starts.[12] According to one estimate, the housing sector, which accounts for less than 4 percent of the GNP, bore 60 to 70 percent of the burden produced by this effort to cool the economy.[13] Indeed, it is the knowledge of this extreme sensitivity of the housing industry to fluctuations in interest rates that gives the monetary authorities confidence that they can effectively cool the economy down by tightening the money supply, and the six sharp drops in housing construction since World War II testify to the potency of their medicine. The result is to force the cities, the urban poor, and the builders to pay the penalty for failures elsewhere in the economy. The severe drop in housing construction that has produced economic distress in the building industry throughout 1974 is but the most recent—albeit one of the most dramatic—examples of the gross inequities that result.

If the operations of the private capital markets leave housing generally on the short end of the stick, they leave low-income housing with virtually no stick at all. When interest rates rise, low-income home buyers are the first to be forced out of the market. Even in the best of times low-income home buyers have difficulty securing loans: first, because their low incomes make them poorer credit risks; and second, because they typically can afford only *used* housing, which bankers usually do not consider as choice loan property.[14] As a consequence, large areas of American cities have been effectively cut off from mortgage capital, leaving owners little alternative but to abandon the structures. Perhaps more clearly than anything else, the resulting widespread abandonment of usable housing, which has reached epidemic proportions in dozens of American cities, symbolizes the social waste created by the existing system of allocating credit through private capital markets that are unresponsive to considerations of social need.[15]

Despite pretentions of "neutrality," in short, the operation of the American credit system systematically hurts those most in need of assistance. Even Federal Reserve Board chairman Arthur Burns conceded as much. "We at the Federal Reserve Board pursue a general credit policy," Burns admitted to the House Banking Committee in 1970, "but the general credit policy that we pursue has a selective effect in the marketplace. And some of the selective effects are unhappy."[16]

Nevertheless, the Fed has sternly resisted any suggestion that it bears some responsibility for this situation and should take corrective action. On the contrary, the Fed has argued that its role is simply to set the aggregate amount of credit in use, not to allocate it among different sectors of the economy. The bankers have been equally rigorous in proclaiming their innocence of any blame for the way credit markets shortchange the cities and low-income home buyers. "Bankers are only the instruments and not the originators of governmental anti-inflation policy," protested the American Bankers Association president to the House Banking Committee in 1970;[17] he conveniently ignored the critical role that banks play in allocating whatever credit is available among competing claimants and in insisting that the Fed not interfere with this prerogative.

With the money lords foreswearing responsibility for the consequences of their action, it has been up to Congress to backstop for the housing industry and the urban poor. Given the close tie between the housing and development problems of the cities and the operations of the banking system, it was only natural that the Banking committees should be given jurisdiction for the resulting federal programs. But if this fortuitous jurisdictional arrangement created the opportunity to cope with the nation's serious urban problems at their source, Congress has been slow to seize it. Instead it has gingerly avoided any infringement on the hallowed autonomy of the private money lords or the Fed, while busying itself concocting intricate indirect devices through which to offset some of the grosser evils this autonomy produces. The result is a kind of treadmill operation, as Congress diligently protects with one hand a system whose harmful consequences it spends much of its time alleviating with the other. A glance at the basic contours of federal housing and urban development policy should make this clear.

FEDERAL HOUSING AND URBAN DEVELOPMENT POLICY: AN OVERVIEW

The Legacy

Four basic programs have formed the core of federal housing and urban development policy. Taken together, they constitute a complex, cumbersome, and seriously inequitable package that displays all too clearly the difficulty Congress faces when trying to aid those in need without displeasing powerful producer groups eager to protect their interests. Let us look at each of these sets of programs in turn.

1. *Savings bank protection.* Although pleas for federal assistance to help improve the housing conditions of the urban poor had been heard at least since the end of the nineteenth century, it was not until the Great Depression that the federal government actively entered the housing policy arena.[18] What finally prompted federal action was the massive unemployment produced by the virtually total collapse of the construction and mortage-lending industries in the early 1930s. It was thus not the housing needs of the poor but

the employment-generating power of a vibrant construction industry that provided the rationale for federal involvement. This fact is reflected in the character of the housing-policy instruments, with their emphasis on new construction and their charitableness to the major producer groups in the housing and mortgage-lending fields.

The earliest beneficiary of this generosity was the savings and loan industry. Although only a fledgling at the time of the Depression,* the savings bank industry was the only sector of the financial system investing most of its assets in home mortgages. But it had great difficulty attracting funds because of general public wariness about financial institutions, competition from commercial banks, and the limits that investments in long-term mortgages placed on the interest rates savings banks could pay their depositors.† The Depression naturally intensified these already chronic industry problems, bringing the savings industry to the brink of collapse, and the home-building industry with it.

To remedy this situation, Congress brought the savings and loan industry securely under the federal government's protective wing. The first step was the creation, in 1932, of the Federal Home Loan Bank System, consisting of a network of regional federal home loan banks, and a Federal Home Loan Bank Board (FHLBB) authorized to make advances to savings banks temporarily short on funds and otherwise to protect the stability of the industry, much as the Federal Reserve System does for commercial banks.[20] The next year, Congress authorized the federal chartering of savings and loan associations, thus relieving the savings industry of total reliance on state charters and opening the

---

* As late as 1945, savings bank assets came to only $8.7 billion, less than 4 percent of the $242.3 billion in the hands of all financial intermediaries.[19]
† Because mortgages carry fixed interest rates and long terms, financial institutions with heavy mortgage investments do not profit as much from general rises in interest rates. As a consequence, they find it difficult to raise the amount they pay depositors. As interest rates rise in the economy, and savings bank customers find better uses for their money, a process known as "disintermediation"—the shifting of capital from one type of financial institution to another—occurs.

way for the same "competition in laxity" that characterizes regulation of commercial banks.* The third step came in 1934, when Congress further underwrote the savings and loan industry by extending deposit insurance to savings bank depositors, thus encouraging investor confidence and placing the credit of the United States government behind the industry. These measures, along with provisions in the Internal Revenue Code exempting savings banks from income taxes so long as they invest in home mortgages, constituted a powerful tool for industry self-regulation, for utilizing public authority to advance industry prosperity and recovery. With the creation of the FHLBB, in fact, the savings industry secured a powerful spokesman for its views within the administrative hierarchy of the federal government. And over the years, the FHLBB has performed its role well, pushing for reductions in the costs of deposit insurance, for expanded resources for bailing the savings industry out of difficulties, and for regulations to limit competition for the saver's dollars through legal limits on the interest rates commercial banks can pay depositors, prohibitions on issuance of high-yield government securities in denominations small enough to attract the typical saver, and limits on interest-rate competition among savings banks. One of the most successful of these efforts was the passage in 1966 of an interest-rate control law, followed by an administrative agreement between the FHLBB and the Federal Reserve Board to forbid commercial banks from paying more in interest on savings accounts than are paid by savings banks.

This array of federal protections provided an ample cushion for savings bank expansion, particularly in the period following World War II, when personal incomes and savings increased markedly. Between 1934 and 1972, the savings and loan industry mushroomed from a $6 billion pygmy to a $206 billion giant

---

* As the official savings and loan industry history euphemistically puts it, "The dual system, in fact, meant that state and federal associations could *compete in securing legislative and regulatory improvements to serve their communities better.*"[21]

controlling 15 percent of all financial-institution assets.[22] And as the savings bank industry grew, so did its investments in mortgages. As of 1972, in fact, savings banks accounted for 55 percent of the $346.2 billion in mortgage loans outstanding on one- to four-family nonfarm homes.[23]

2. *Mortgage guarantees.* To supplement the savings bank assistance programs in attracting capital into mortgage lending, Congress in 1934 enacted a second policy tool: a mortgage-guarantee program aimed at the far more substantial resources then under the control of commercial banks and insurance companies. Administered by the Federal Housing Administration, the mortgage-guarantee program is essentially a federally underwritten insurance policy designed to seduce banks into investing in home mortgages by having the government assume all the risk. Under the program, potential home buyers must still secure their home loans from local banks and pay interest, but if the loan and the borrower meet FHA criteria, FHA will insure the bank against loss in return for a monthly fee paid by the borrower.* FHA thus offered banks precleared mortgage applicants and risk-free investments, all in the hopes of attracting bank capital into mortgage lending. The only hitch was that the banks were obligated to lower their inflated charges for mortgage lending and otherwise liberalize loan terms.†

In 1938 these inducements were expanded with the creation of the Federal National Mortgage Association (FNMA), known

---

* FHA criteria specify maximum mortgage amounts and interest rates, and require that both the borrower and the property he is preparing to buy meet the standard of "economic soundness." The fee paid by the borrower is computed at the rate of one-half of one percent of the face amount of the loan each year.

† When FHA was first created, home mortgages typically carried maturities of only 10-12 years, required down payments of 40-50 percent, and frequently had interest charges in excess of 10 percent. FHA-guaranteed loans could extend 20 years, required only a 20 percent down payment, and carried a maximum interest rate of 5-5.5 percent. Over the years, the down payment and maturity provisions of the FHA program have been liberalized, but the interest rate limit has been steadily increased.[24]

affectionately as "Fannie Mae." FNMA was the answer to the
bankers' complaints that mortgage loans were still unattractive
investments because their long terms made it difficult for investors
to convert them back into cash when more profitable investments
came along. Eager to please, Congress created in FNMA a place
where approved lending institutions could unload their FHA-
guaranteed mortgages in return for cash raised by FNMA with
government backing in the open market. With the creation of
FNMA, the federal government thus agreed not only to protect
lenders against the risk of default on the original loans, but also
to protect them against the risk of losing out on more profitable
investments at some future date. FNMA thus completed the circle
of indirection by which the federal government undertook to bolster the housing industry: rather than borrow money in the market at the lower interest rates available to it and then lend the
proceeds out at below-market-interest rates to those in greatest
need, the federal government insured private banks against loss
on mortgage loans and then agreed to borrow in the market to
pay off the private bankers whenever they wanted to get out of the
mortgage business. And to add icing to the cake, the FNMA
charter specified that the original lender can continue to "service"
the loan and reap the profit this involves even after selling the
mortgage to FNMA.*

Not surprisingly, the loan-guarantee program proved immensely popular with bankers and builders, for it brought benefits
to the housing sector without limiting the autonomy of the financial institutions or placing the government in competition with
them. Over time, the loan-guarantee concept became the standard

---

* One of the more lucrative aspects of this loan servicing operation has to
do with "escrow accounts," the sums of money normally included in monthly
loan payments to cover the costs of property taxes and home insurance. Since
both taxes and insurance are paid only once a year, the servicing agent thus
accumulates a substantial amount of money during each year from each loan
it services, but typically pays no interest on this money. If the agent services
1,000 loans, for example, and has an average escrow balance of only $300
on each, this means that it has access to $300,000 of interest-free capital.

vehicle for government action in the housing field, and variations of the basic program were devised to meet a host of housing-related special purposes. In 1944, for example, a liberalized version of the basic FHA program was made available to returning veterans under the Veterans Administration to permit guarantees of mortgages with even lower down payments and longer terms than those provided by FHA. Other special-purpose guarantee programs, each with its own detailed eligibility requirements and unique benefits, were provided within FHA to cover: prefabricated housing (1947), cooperative-owned housing (1948); housing in Alaska and in the vicinity of military installations (1949); housing in "outlying areas" (1950); housing in disaster areas and for persons displaced by urban renewal (1954); trailer park sites (1955); housing for the elderly (1956); and nursing homes (1959). In addition, as interest rates and housing costs have increased, Congress has acceded to banker and builder requests to increase the maximum loan amount eligible for FHA guarantee, to permit higher interest rates on FHA-guaranteed loans, and to allow bankers to charge their FHA-covered borrowers "discount points" to make up the difference between what the bank can earn on an FHA-guaranteed loan and what it could earn on a loan not covered by the FHA interest ceiling.* In these ways, the federal government has made mortgage lending a far more profitable business for the banks.

3. *Public Housing.* The third basic component of federal housing policy is the public housing program, originally enacted in 1937 and expanded in 1949. Public housing was designed to make decent rental housing available to the urban poor at rates they could afford, and thus cope directly with the serious slum housing conditions afflicting most American cities. But because of

---

* "Discount points" are flat charges assessed on sellers (and typically passed on to buyers) at the time of closing of a home purchase deal. If the bank charges "two points," on a $30,000 loan, the buyer must pay $600 (2 percent of $30,000) to the bank merely for the privilege of securing the loan. The $600 is nonreturnable and is not applied to the loan. It is a direct, out-of-pocket cost to the buyer.

the stern opposition of the builders and bankers, who feared government competition, this goal had to be pursued indirectly. Rather than build housing itself, federal assistance is channeled through local housing agencies, which have full responsibility for selecting sites, setting eligibility requirements, and managing the projects. Federal assistance covers only the costs of construction, so that the local housing agencies must charge rents to cover maintenance and operating costs. The local agencies must also raise their own capital by issuing bonds for sale on the market. The federal government agrees to pay both the principal and interest on the bonds on behalf of the local agency, thus relieving it of the debt-service costs. In addition, as an inducement to investors, the federal government "insures" the bonds and exempts the interest from federal taxation. This indirect mode of federal assistance naturally pleases private financial institutions, which handle most of the local bond financing. But it means that the federal government loses out financially in two ways at once: by having to pay interest rates 50 to 100 percent higher than those available to it as a borrower, and by forgoing tax receipts on the interest paid to the private investors. As one critic has noted, "Public housing simply provides an additional way for private investors, most particularly commercial banks, to make profits with the state assuming the risk."[25]

4. *Urban Renewal.* The fourth major federal housing and urban development program is "urban renewal," or "slum clearance" as it was called prior to 1954. The urban renewal program, created by the 1949 Housing Act, was a response to the concern over widespread blight and deterioration in central cities, and to the realization that private enterprise could not (or would not) revitalize central-city areas on its own because of the high costs of urban land, the dispersed ownership of this land, and the need to deal with areas sizable enough to produce a permanent impact.[26] Urban renewal was thus designed to make revitalization profitable for private developers. This was to be accomplished by providing federal loans and grants to local renewal agencies to cover up to

two-thirds of the costs of acquiring blighted urban land, clearing it, installing needed public facilities, and selling the land to private developers at prices low enough to permit profitable development by the private sector. Through urban renewal, the federal government thus provides a kind of "reverse price support" program, allowing large-scale developers to secure valuable downtown real estate at below market prices. Although federal regulations stipulated that renewal projects had to be residential in character either before redevelopment or after, local renewal agencies were otherwise left to their own devices in deciding what to do where. Beginning in 1954 this was modified somewhat by a federal requirement that renewal plans be related explicitly to an overall "workable program" of community development for the city; federal planning assistance was provided to aid in the production of these programs.

In addition to the "workable program" requirement, numerous other modifications of the basic urban renewal package have been added over time. The most important of these was the 1954 change that converted the program from simple slum clearance to broader urban renewal through the inclusion of provisions allowing grants for neighborhood rehabilitation, and building-code-enforcement efforts. Other, more recent, changes have established relocation payments, citizen-participation vehicles, loans to cover administrative and relocation costs in addition to acquisition and clearance costs, and stipulations for preserving recreation space. In the process, urban renewal has become an increasingly powerful—if rather cumbersome—mechanism for utilizing public authority to make inner-city redevelopment economically attractive to private interests.[27]

5. *Tax and Highway Programs.* In addition to the explicit housing and urban development programs, the federal government heavily influences housing and urban development activity in several other ways. Two of the most important of these are the income tax system and federal transportation policies. Under the tax laws, homeowners can deduct from their taxable income the

cost of local property taxes and mortgage interest payments. In 1970 alone, these provisions cost the Treasury $5.2 billion, far more than any other federal housing program.[28] These sizable benefits provide a strong incentive toward home ownership.

Equally powerful has been the massive program of interstate highway construction undertaken by the federal government beginning in the mid-1950s. The interstate highways opened vast new areas on the periphery of major cities for urban development and thus greatly facilitated the massive population shift to suburbia characteristic of American urban life over the past two decades. At the same time, the interstates obliterated thousands upon thousands of units of central-city housing, typically low-income housing lying astride the interstate routes through major cities.

By the early 1960s, the federal government thus had in place a complex array of housing and urban development programs, some of them explicit and some disguised in tax and transportation policies. The fairest thing that can be said about these policies and programs is that they turned out to be a mixed blessing. On the one hand, the Home Loan Bank–FHA–VA–FNMA nexus managed to increase the volume of mortgage credit and to bring young families with moderate incomes and little savings into the housing market on a massive scale.[29] Throughout the 1940s and 1950s, the VA and FHA loan-guarantee programs accounted for 25 to 35 percent of all mortgages.[30] Even those not covered by federal loan guarantees benefited from the program, since the early success of FHA in demonstrating that home mortgages were reliable investments induced other lenders to liberalize their mortgage-lending terms.* At the same time, the support afforded the

---

* Between 1934 and 1972, for example, the average maturities on home mortgages increased from 11 to almost 27 years; down-payment requirements declined from 44 to 22 percent; and mortgage contracts were greatly simplified, permitting them to be sold in the money markets more easily and hence to attract the capital of investors hesitant to tie up their capital in 20 to 25-year non-transferable mortgages.[31]

savings and loan industry put this industry in an excellent position to capitalize on the surge in personal disposable income following World War II, and thus helped generate a sizable pool of capital for use in "conventional" (non-FHA) mortgage lending. The major result was that middle-class families took advantage of federal assistance to flee the cities in record numbers. Meanwhile, the urban renewal program made impressive progress in helping to revive the cores of numerous American cities—Boston, Philadelphia, New Haven, and Pittsburgh, to name a few.[32] Euphoric supporters pointed with pride to the expanded local property tax bases and general upgrading of downtown real estate attributable to the program.[33]

For all its accomplishments, however, the Home Loan Bank–FHA–VA–FNMA–public housing–urban renewal complex that formed the heart of federal housing and urban development policy was seriously flawed as a vehicle for solving America's urban problems. By financing a massive middle-class migration to the suburbs, federal housing policy contributed directly to what is now acknowledged as the nation's most serious urban dilemma: the isolation of the poor in central-city ghettos shut off from job and educational opportunities that are increasingly concentrated in the suburban ring. As housing specialist Bernard Frieden recently put it, "Our solution to the national housing problem has been creating a national urban problem."[34]

Nor was this an accidental by-product of federal policy. By acceding to banker demands to limit federal housing programs to measures that would bolster private financial institutions, and thus forgoing cheaper direct-loan or grant programs, Congress was essentially restricting program benefits to middle-class families with incomes sufficient to cover mortgage payments and denying federal assistance to the poor, who needed it most. FHA statutes even specified that loans accepted for FHA guarantees be "economically sound," a conservative standard that FHA officials, with banker and builder encouragement, interpreted to give a strong preference to new housing in the suburbs over the existing housing more commonly available to the poor in the urban core. Of the $27.7 billion of loan guarantees provided by FHA during its first twenty years, more than two-thirds covered loans for new construction.[35] Indeed, the "economic soundness" doctrine provided a ready excuse for FHA to turn its back on central-city areas and adopt a set of loan criteria exactly parallel to that of the private lending industry which constituted the agency's primary clients. "Over the years," a recent Department of Housing and Urban Development audit concedes, "FHA operated quite successfully as an insurer of mortgages closely tied in to the attitudes and postures of the homebuilding and mortgage banking industries."[36] "FHA was not originally concerned with the special housing needs of disadvantaged persons," noted another HUD report in 1966. "FHA's regular programs of assistance for new sales housing tended over the years to be concentrated in suburban areas, skipping over older central city areas or the graying areas around them."[37] It should come as no surprise to learn, therefore, that less than 11 percent of all FHA loan guarantees made prior to 1965 had gone to the 40 percent of all families earning less than $6,000 annually.[38] As of 1960, in fact, the median income of FHA beneficiaries was $8,256—almost triple the official poverty-level income for a family of four.* In short, FHA has historically been insuring banks against loss on relatively safe loans to upwardly mobile middle-class whites from whom the banks collect the near equivalent of market-interest rates plus compensatory "discount points," while neglecting the far more serious needs of more risky borrowers. While this conservatism has made the agency one of the more profitable enterprises of the U.S. government and earned it the support of builders and bankers, it has yielded far more questionable returns for the cities.†

* By 1970, the FHA median had risen to $13,608—50 percent above the national median income.[39]
† As of 1970, FHA had accumulated $1.5 billion in reserves against outstanding loan guarantees, and had invested over $1 billion of this sum in

In theory, a vibrant public housing program might have compensated for these shortcomings in the banker- and builder-oriented loan-guarantee program. But the public housing program was hardly vibrant. Some of the key housing interest groups—in particular, the builders and realtors—vehemently opposed the program, arguing that it placed the government in competition with private industry in the housing field and thus constituted a step on the road to socialism. These views were shared by Republican conservatives, who came to power under the Eisenhower administration and quickly poured additional cold water on the hopes of public housing enthusiasts. Although the 1949 Housing Act called for an infusion of funds sufficient to construct close to a million units of public housing by 1955, therefore, the opposition reduced this infusion to a trickle, and the indirect mode of federal assistance coupled with rising borrowing costs reduced the actual amount available even further. As a result, the goal of 1 million units by 1955 was not even half fulfilled ten years later. In addition, by giving local governments veto power over the location of public housing projects, Congress severely restricted the sites available, and ultimately forced local public housing agencies to rely extensively on tenement-type projects that conserve land and capital but trap the poor in suffocating, unlivable structures conducive to crime and delinquency. Equally troubling have been the rigid and punitive eligibility requirements built into the system, such as the requirement that no one be permitted in public housing who can afford to pay rents within 20 percent of the lowest cost of privately owned housing available in the vicinity. Moreover, as rising operating costs have forced local agencies to raise rents, public housing has taken an increasing bite out of the meager incomes of its occupants, leaving precious little for non-shelter expenses such as food, health care, and clothing.

For all its inadequacies and insufficiencies, however, at least

securities that earned the federal Treasury a 5.7 percent annual yield. So cautiously had FHA been run, in other words, that it has emerged as a not insubstantial money-maker for the federal government.[40]

public housing has provided some benefits to at least 600,000 of the poor. Nothing of the sort can be said of urban renewal. In the process of reviving the commercial cores of American cities, urban renewal has destroyed low-income housing on a massive scale, replacing it with, if anything, housing for middle- and upper-income groups whom urban renewal officials were seeking to attract back to the cities. Although, as we have seen, the 1949 Housing Act specified that renewal areas had to be predominantly residential in character either before renewal or after, the fact that control was left essentially in the hands of local powers-that-be meant that, in city after city, commercial interests were able to take advantage of federal largesse to obliterate troublesome low-income neighborhoods and replace them with lucrative commercial structures. When the National Commission on Urban Problems investigated the damage in 1967, it discovered that the federally funded urban renewal program had destroyed approximately 400,000 units of low- and moderate-income housing and had constructed only 41,580 such units in their place.[41] The costs of urban renewal, in other words, were falling most severely on the central-city poor.

As if the inequities built into the explicit federal housing programs were not sufficient, moreover, those embodied in the federal tax system are even more glaring. The $5.2 billion in tax deductions provided to homeowners in 1970, for example, was five times the $1.1 billion invested in low-income housing that same year. And most of the benefits of this "tax subsidy" accrue to middle- and upper-income families, because fewer of the poor own their homes and because the size of the tax write-off increases with the value of the home. The income tax write-offs for local property taxes and mortgage interest rates are thus the largest federal housing programs, at least in dollar terms. And, like most of the other elements in federal housing policy, they deliver most of their benefits to those who need them least.

Housing in the 1960s: The Great Fumble

By the early 1960s, these flaws in federal housing and urban development policy were becoming increasingly apparent, especially as protests, culminating in a wave of urban rioting, focused national attention on the plight of the central-city poor. At the same time, the existing policy tools were proving inadequate to meet the production and asset-expansion goals of the builders and savings bankers. The whole structure of federal housing policy, as we have seen, relied exclusively on a complex system of enticements and payoffs to the private money managers. The ultimate decisions about how much capital went into housing thus remained in private hands, where they had always been. The problem was that the value of the enticements provided by the federal government was steadily declining, as bankers grew accustomed to them and as the disparity between interest rates allowed on FHA loans and those on alternative investment opportunities steadily increased. The four cyclical declines in housing production between World War II and 1960 had already demonstrated this vulnerability, but the general rise in interest rates and the increased bank aggressiveness that took place in the 1960s made it even clearer. One symptom was the sharp drop in utilization of FHA and VA loan guarantees: while 41 percent of all private, nonfarm housing starts were covered by FHA and VA insurance in 1955, in 1965 the figure was only 17 percent.[42] In addition, as commercial banks began competing more aggressively for savings and investing them, through bank holding companies and other devices, in higher-yield, nonmortgage investments, the flow of new savings into savings banks began declining—reversing a twenty-year period of expansion. Tied as they were to long-term mortgages with fixed, and relatively low, yields, the savings banks found it hard to raise the interest paid to savers and thus compete effectively for deposits. When the Federal Reserve Board tightened the money supply sharply in 1966 in an attempt to counteract the inflationary pressures unleashed by the Vietnam War, the impact on the savings industry, and ultimately on housing construction, was disastrous. In fact, by 1971, the special President's Commission on Financial Structure and Regulation (the Hunt Commission) was reporting that "without changes in their operations, there is serious question about the ability of deposit thrift institutions to survive."[43]

The situation in the 1960s, in short, bore strong resemblance to that in the 1930s, as social-welfare concerns coalesced with industry difficulties to generate pressures for new federal initiatives in housing. And as in the 1930s, Congress responded with a flurry of activity. In the Housing Act of 1961, for example, Congress greatly expanded FHA's program of guarantees on rehabilitation loans, made special provisions to insure more liberal loans for low-income housing (by relaxing the "economic soundness" doctrine), and established a new program of below-market-interest-rate loans to sponsors of low-income rental housing projects (the 221[d] [3] program).* In the wake of the first wave of urban rioting, Congress in 1965 enacted an experimental program of "rent subsidies" under which the poor could live in rental properties at below-market rentals, with the federal government making up the difference to the landlord. That same year, Congress finally responded to presidential pressures to elevate the old Housing and Home Finance Agency responsible for federal housing and urban development programs into full cabinet status as the Department of Housing and Urban Development. In addition, it made some significant changes in the public housing program, authorizing public housing authorities to acquire and rehabilitate *existing* housing for use in local public housing programs. A year later, the FHA "economic soundness" doctrine was substantially rescinded, and an elaborate, experimental program of federal assistance to specially selected central-city neighborhoods (the Model Cities program) was launched. Two years later, Congress was back at

---

* Under the 221(d)(3) program, FNMA was authorized to purchase FHA-insured below-market-interest-rate loans from lending institutions at par—i.e., at prices computed as if the loan bore market interest rates.

the drawing boards again, and in the massive 1968 Housing and Urban Development Act established yet another tier of federal housing programs—this time a scheme for allowing low-income families, or sponsors of rental projects to be occupied by such families, to secure bank loans on which the federal government pays much of the interest, thus substantially reducing the cost to the low-income family (the 235 and 236 programs).

During this same period, efforts were made to reorient the urban renewal program by providing more relocation assistance, by introducing citizen-participation mechanisms, and by making loan and grant funds available on a far more substantial basis for rehabilitation and building-code enforcement designed to end urban renewal's traditional single-minded focus on demolition and clearance. In addition, a host of new programs was inaugurated to help cope with the serious problem of urban sprawl—which earlier federal policy had encouraged. These measures included FHA permission to insure land development and "new community" loans; grants for purchase of open space, water and sewer construction, advance acquisition of land for public facilities, and urban beautification; and, in 1970, a program of federal subsidies to developers of "new towns" as well as the establishment of a federal commitment to formulate a comprehensive urban growth policy.

For all their inventiveness, however, the new programs of the 1960s did little to break the policy mold inherited from the 1930s. The long-standing conflict between the social-welfare and industry-promotion goals of federal housing policy thus persisted, producing a continuing residue of ambivalence and schizophrenia that was reflected in growing program complexity. New programs were piled on top of old ones and then severely circumscribed by limited funding and rigid eligibility limits designed to prevent government from competing with private interests.* While Congress

---

* The rent supplement program is an excellent example of this. Limited in funds, it was also hampered by a set of congressionally inspired regulations that rendered it largely unworkable. These regulations stipulated that a

moved steadily toward ever-more-explicit subsidies for low-income housing, it also turned a receptive ear toward industry groups clamoring for special favors, frequently under the guise of helping the poor. Thus the maximum interest rates and mortgage amounts on FHA-insured mortgages were steadily increased; the proportion of urban renewal funds that could go for *non*residential projects expanded; and a new law setting ceilings on the interest rates savings banks could pay depositors was adopted and quickly followed by an administrative arrangement setting commercial banks' interest rates on savings accounts below those paid by savings banks.* And in the Emergency Home Finance Act of 1970, Congress provided a new subsidy to the savings bankers in the form of $250 million worth of cut-rate loans that savings and loan associations could then invest in mortgages at a profit.

Even the low-income housing subsidy programs that became an increasingly large part of federal housing policy in the 1960s showed evidence of the dead hand of the past in the form of complex, indirect subsidy forms geared as much—if not more—to the needs of the builders and lenders as to those of the poor in whose name they were justified. Nothing illustrates this better than the Housing Act of 1968, the act that Lyndon Johnson christened the "Magna Carta to liberate our cities," and that established the wildest subsidy scheme of them all, the now infamous 235 and 236 programs.

Created to meet a congressionally mandated goal of 6 million units of new low-income housing by 1978, the 235 and 236 programs established what amounts to a "price support" program for

---

tenant could not receive a supplement greater than 70 percent of the rent (the original idea was to prevent the poor from paying over 25 percent of their income in rent), set dollar limits on construction costs for eligible tenants, set dollar limits on rents, and limited the amenities that could be included in projects covered by rent supplements.

* Under Regulation Q, in effect since the 1930s, the interest rates paid by commercial banks on their savings deposits were already controlled by the federal bank regulatory authorities. The new arrangement pegged the commercial bank rate to the new savings bank rate regulations.

mortgage lenders. Here's how it worked. Under the 235 program, a low- or moderate-income family—defined by the law as a family earning less than 135 percent of the income limits set for public housing eligibility in each locale—can purchase a home on a long-term, FHA-guaranteed mortgage at prevailing interest rates, but make monthly payments to the lender as if the mortgage carried an interest rate as low as 1 percent. The federal government makes up the difference to the private lender. The 236 program applies the same concept to the financing of multiunit rental housing. In both programs the banker is free to charge what the traffic will bear. As interest rates rise, so does the federal subsidy for each unit of subsidized housing. In this way, builders are guaranteed a market for their products when interest rates rise and nonsubsidized home buyers disappear from the market; but they achieve this without infringing on the power of bankers and the Federal Reserve to control the nation's credit system. Indeed, everyone comes out ahead—except the public, which, under the guise of aiding the poor, must pay off the bankers.

What makes this especially painful is the fact that this form of subsidy is probably the most costly way to achieve the desired result, even though it may appear less costly—since the subsidy payments are stretched out over the term of the loan. For example, the cost of subsidizing the interest on a $15,000, thirty-three-year home mortgage from 8.5 percent down to 3.5 percent is $29,028.[44] The government could thus come out ahead if it made a cash *gift* to the borrower of the original $15,000 and cut the banker out altogether; and it could come out even better, without reducing the benefits to the poor, if it borrowed the money itself at 4 or 5 percent and made direct loans at the same 3.5 percent interest. In one project described before the Subcommittee on Housing for the Elderly of the Senate Special Committee on the Aging, the federal government committed itself to paying $8,138,520 under the 236 program for a 211-unit housing project in Biloxi, Mississippi, which it could have purchased for only $2,415,600—one-third as much—under the Section 202 direct-loan program Congress had created in 1959 to finance housing for the aged but which it replaced in 1968 with 236.[45] The difference results from the fact that under the direct-loan program the government borrows money at 5 percent and lends it out at 3 percent, whereas under 236 it sends the sponsors to a private lender to whom they must pay 8.5 percent interest; then the government subsidizes the difference between what the banker charges and what the loan would cost if it bore an interest rate of 2 or 3 percent.* Table 17 summarizes these computations for the Biloxi project, and also shows the added construction financing cost required under the 236 program. The figures show the almost criminal waste in federal housing policies, which pump grossly disproportionate subsidies into the hands of the financiers to achieve a stingy dribble of benefits for the urban poor.† It is no wonder, then, that in the Ninety-second and Ninety-third Con-

---

* Opinions differ as to why this particular subsidy route was chosen, but two explanations are prominent. One points to perennial banker opposition to direct government loan programs, which place the federal government in competition with private financial institutions. The other focuses on the accounting system adopted by the federal government in 1968 which played directly into bankers' hands by counting the full face value of any government loan as a regular budget expenditure the year the loan is made, even though the borrower is expected to pay back the loan in full with interest over time. This accounting quirk made a direct loan approach seem politically unacceptable, since it would have created a massive—if illusory—immediate budget impact. The accounting procedure thus provided a ready excuse for taking the bankers' preferred route.

† In addition to the benefits already mentioned, investors in 236 projects reap rewards in the form of tax deductions. Under the 1969 Tax Reform Act, Congress opened two loopholes to induce private investors to sink their capital in 236 projects. The first are the so-called "recapture provisions," under which an investor can generate large tax losses to offset high-bracket regular income by depreciating low-income housing projects rapidly, but then still have the taxable gain (difference between net sales price and depreciated value) from the sale of the project taxed at the lower capital-gains rate. The only limitation on this loophole is that a portion of the excess depreciation claimed as a result of using accelerated depreciation can be taxed as ordinary income (i.e., "recaptured"), but the amount subject to recapture decreases 1 percent a month beginning after 20 months so that the amount recaptured falls to zero after 10 years [IRC Sec. 1250 (a)(1)(C) (ii)]. Under these provisions, for an investment of $1,000, an investor can

TABLE 17.

Santa Maria Del Mar, Biloxi, Miss., FHA Project 065–44803
(SH–MISS–05) 211 Dwellings; Initial Loan Closing 4/28/70

"202" program 3% interest; 50 years		"236" program 8½% interest; 40 years
$2,687,900	Construction costs, including architectural & engineering fees	$2,687,900
212,500	Title recording, land consultant, insurance, legal, organizational	212,500
61,000 16 months at 3%	Interest during construction	189,267 16 months at 8½%
45,750 6 months at 3%	Interest during development on entire mortgage loan amount	—0—
3,000	Preliminary expenses	—0—
39,850	Project contingency	—0—
—0—	0.5% mortgage insurance (2 years)	33,400
—0—	0.3% examination	10,020
—0—	0.5% inspection	16,700
—0—	2% financing	66,800
—0—	2% Ampo (amount to make project operational)	66,800
—0—	1.75% FNMA/GNMA fee	58,450
$3,050,000	Total mortgage loan amount	$3,340,000 (rounded down from $3,341,837)

Cost to government to repay
$3,050,000 at 5%* over 50 years

Annual interest subsidy $203,463 for 40 years would total $8,138,520 over life of project. (This subsidy based on actual $3,250,000 "conversion" mortgage loan.)

Principal	$3,050,000
Interest	5,258,200
	$8,308,200

Repayment to government
$3,050,000 at 3% over 50 years

Principal	$3,050,000
Interest	2,842,600
	$5,892,600

$2,415,600

Net cost to government	$8,138,520
	− 2,415,600
Excess cost of 236 program over 202	$5,722,920

* Interest paid by government: 1969—4½%; 1970—4⅞%; 1971—5½%.

gresses the Banking committees were back at work, producing in the 1974 Housing Act still another new instrument for providing improved housing for the poor.*

Working steadily for almost four decades, the Banking committees in Congress have produced a rich harvest of ingenious programs, each designed to ameliorate a major failing of the market mechanism affecting the cities without fundamentally changing that mechanism. But while each separate authority may be a gem of legislative inventiveness, together they represent an administrative nightmare and a serious distortion of equitable social priorities. FHA alone, for example, administers fifty separate loan-guarantee programs, each with its own eligibility requirements and special provisions. The most recent *Basic Compilation of Authorities on Housing and Urban Development* published annually by the House Banking Committee now runs to 1,105 pages of text and is still growing. Had Rube Goldberg turned his hand to

---

gain tax advantages in excess of $2,000 over 10 years above and beyond any appreciation in the value of the investment itself.

The second loophole picks up where the "recapture" provision leaves off. Called the "rollover provision," this second loophole permits the owner of a low-income 236 (or 221[d][3]) project to escape completely from taxation on the gain realized through the sale of such property if he sells the project to a tenant organization and then reinvests in another similar project [IRC Sec. 1039]. Since the major profits to be gained from these projects are the tax benefits derived from accelerated depreciation, this provision provides an avenue for an investor to sell out a project after he has reaped all the tax benefits he can from it (after the value of the project is fully depreciated) and move on to another project without immediate tax consequences. Since investors consequently have only short-term (10-year) interests in the projects, however, they are likely to concern themselves very little with the project's quality or durability. So substantial have these tax advantages been that investors throughout the country have clamored to get a "piece of the action," and shares of limited-partnership, low-income housing corporations now trade on the regular stock exchanges. The title of a January 1972 *Journal of Taxation* article summarizes the situation well: "Low Income Housing (F.H.A. 236) Programs: One of the Few Tax Shelter Opportunities Left."

* For details, see pp. 240–308.

fashioning legislation instead of weird mechanical contraptions, he could hardly have surpassed what the Banking committees have done in the housing and urban development sphere. Indeed, so cumbersome has this mechanism become that the National Association of Home Builders (NAHB) sells a "Pocket Guide to Low-Income Housing Programs" to its members, with the suggestion: "You can't be a player in the low-income housing game without knowing the numbers—the FHA and other agency section numbers which refer to the various rental and for-sale housing programs."[46] In the opinion of many housing lobbyists, most legislators even on the Banking committees do not know which program is which, but few are as honest about it as Congressman Ben Blackburn, who told a witness before the House Banking Committee in 1970, "I must confess I have been on the committee for 3 years and I still don't know the numbers of the programs we kick around."[47] Even George Romney, a man who built an impressive career as a manager of large, complex institutions, had to admit defeat before the chaos that confronted him in the housing field. In a speech to the National Association of Home Builders in January 1973, as he prepared to leave office after four disastrous years as secretary of the Department of Housing and Urban Development, Romney explained:

> It became crystal clear by 1970 that the patchwork, year-by-year addition of programs over a period of more than three decades had created a statutory and administrative monstrosity that could not possibly yield results even with the wisest and most professional management systems.[48]

Instead of opting for direct mechanisms to solve the nation's housing and urban problems, Congress persists in concocting weird, Rube Goldberg-type devices. As housing specialist Lawrence Friedman put it:

> Housing and urban development has become an empire of little gimmicks and bailiwicks, programs and subprograms, a bewildering, baffling congeries of devices, many of them

motivated by the hope that the market can somehow be
galvanized cheaply into life.[49]

Programs are adopted with little thought about their long-run
effects.* Even John Sparkman, the father of virtually every major
federal housing program over the past two and one half decades,
was willing to concede his frustration as the 1969 credit squeeze
sent housing starts plummeting again in 1970. Moaned Sparkman
on the Senate floor:

> At the peak of our affluence, we are unable to build homes
> that the vast bulk of our people can afford. We have to
> resort to subsidies and to artificially contrived market de-
> vices to wean capital away from more lucrative but less
> essential uses into one of the basic needs of our society—
> decent housing.[51]

What is the explanation of this peculiar pattern of federal housing policies? In particular, to what extent are the Banking committees and Congress generally responsible?

Part of the answer, certainly, lies in the sheer complexity of the
subject matter. Urban development is a dynamic process, only
barely understood and not easily controlled by public policy, at
least not without basic changes in the way economic life is organized in this country. The pattern of urban housing is as much a
product of the pattern of income distribution, the nature of employment opportunities, and the character of the transportation
system as it is of explicit housing practices and policies. And even
if we knew how to manipulate these various elements in the
proper sequence to produce more desirable outcomes, there
would remain the problem of implementing this wisdom through a
governmental structure that disperses control over the various
policy tools among several layers of government and among numerous decision-makers at each level.

* Brookings Institution economist Henry Aaron, for example, recently chastised Congress for enacting federal housing programs "without clear understanding of their probable effects and without clearly defined standards
governing the quality of housing and related services to be provided."[50]

Though the complexity of the subject and of the decision-making structure is part of the answer, however, it is only part. There is little evidence, after all, that the content of policy has been very sensitive to improvements in understanding. In relative terms, the organizational framework for the formulation of housing policy in Congress looks reasonably sound. Though not in control of such crucial policy tools as the interstate highway program, or welfare policy, or income tax provisions, the Banking committees do have under their jurisdiction a surprisingly wide range of urban programs as well as the regulation of the financial system whose operations play so important a role in perpetuating the nation's basic urban ills. Significant solutions are thus organizationally within the committees' reach. Moreover, both committees have delegated responsibility for housing policy development to semiautonomous subcommittees equipped with their own budgets and staffs. These two subcommittees are the only legislative subcommittees in Congress with responsibility over the full range of programs of an entire cabinet-level department. What is more, among their members are the most senior legislators of their respective parent committees, a situation that guarantees support for subcommittee decisions at the full committee level. The stage is thus set about as well as anywhere for coherent policy formulation. Indeed, the very way in which housing legislation is handled —namely, in massive, omnibus bills touching on the full range of federal housing policy—would seem designed to facilitate this result. Yet, as we have seen, the programs that emerge from these committees are as incoherent and disorganized as any in Congress, demonstrating little overall sense of direction and responding piecemeal—and often contradictorily—to problems that require more comprehensive solutions. How can we explain this apparent paradox? A more detailed look at those responsible for making housing policy in Congress and at the political pressures brought to bear on them should provide some important clues.

THE CONGRESSIONAL CAST

Responsibility for the formulation of housing and urban development policy in Congress rests primarily with four subcommittees: the Housing subcommittees of the House and Senate Banking committees and the subcommittees on HUD expenditures of the House and Senate Appropriations committees. All of these subcommittees, naturally, must secure approval for their proposals from their respective parent committees, but all enjoy a considerable degree of autonomy and the capability to dominate the policy debate. This is particularly true of the two Appropriations subcommittees, due to the traditions of specialization and decentralization in the appropriations process.[52] But it is also true on the legislative side, where such autonomy is more unique. The Housing subcommittees of the Banking committees were created in the early 1950s in an effort to establish a locus of urban-policy expertise in the Congress and hence a place where key urban and housing lobby groups could focus their fire. Their formation reflected, at least in part, the dissatisfaction of urban-oriented legislators at the rural dominance in the Banking committees and the need to "end-run" Banking committee chairmen on both House and Senate sides who had only minimal interest in the newly enlarged urban policy responsibilities of the Banking committees. These subcommittees, initially established on a temporary basis, quickly laid claim to permanent budgets and staff hiring privileges and have fought successfully over the years to retain the autonomy such resources bring with them.

As we shall see more fully below, the handling of housing policy through this decentralized structure has both advantages and disadvantages. On the one hand, it facilitates the development of expertise in a field desperately in need of it (though this advantage is less in evidence on the appropriations side, since the two Appropriations subcommittees responsible for HUD expenditures also have jurisdiction over space, science, and veterans affairs expenditures). On the other hand, this specialization artificially segments the policy process, divorcing housing policy from the financial policy questions with which it is intimately related and thus sacrificing the great opportunity that location of responsibility for housing issues within the Banking committees potentially provides. Whether the advantages outweigh the disadvantages, however, the composition and styles of these subcommittees clearly play an important part in shaping policy, and therefore deserve attention.

Membership

Given the obvious relevance of the work of the Housing subcommittees and the related Appropriations subcommittees to the problems of the cities, one might expect to find these subcommittees heavily dominated by urban legislators. Yet this has traditionally not been the case. In both House and Senate, and in both authorization and appropriations arenas, urban—and particularly central-city*—legislators have historically been fairly evenly matched against rural and small town ones, albeit less so on the Housing subcommittees than on the parent committees.

Though mitigated somewhat by the impact of reapportionment, this historical pattern was still in evidence in the Ninety-second Congress, and continued—though in significantly modified form —into the Ninety-third. On the Senate side, as Chapter 2 notes, the Housing subcommittee contained all fifteen members of the full committee. Although the committee displayed a general liberal orientation, however, only eight of its members represented states with larger than average metropolitan populations, and three of these—Tower of Texas, Bennett of Utah, and Roth of Delaware— were ideological conservatives generally hostile to enlarged governmental responsibilities in social welfare areas like housing (see Table 13, Chapter 2). The Senate Banking Committee (and its

---

* The use of the terms "urban" and "central city" follows census usage here. An area is classified urban if it contains 2,500 or more persons and is incorporated. A "central city" is a city of 50,000 or more that forms the hub of a Standard Metropolitan Statistical Area.

Housing subcommittee) in the Ninety-second Congress can thus be thought of as composed of four separate "blocs" so far as urban legislation is concerned: a group of four "urban liberals," a group of four urban conservatives, a group of three nonurban liberals, and a group of four nonurban conservatives (see Table 18). The difficulty of forging strong housing and urban development legislation geared to the social-welfare concerns of the central-city poor thus becomes clear. The four urban liberals must, at a minimum, secure the support of the three nonurban liberals on the committee and then attract in addition at least one urban conservative or nonurban conservative vote. In practice, chairman Sparkman has provided this pivotal vote, but has typically held out for program packages that can win the endorsement of the urban conservative bloc as well. Though Senate Banking Committee measures typically come to the floor with ringing endorsements from all quarters, this should not obscure the serious compromise of purpose that the structure of committee "support blocs" requires as a condition of reporting legislation to the floor in the first place. This is especially true in view of the fact that at least two of the "urban liberals"— Williams of New Jersey and Cranston of California—represent states whose urban populations are overwhelmingly *suburban* (both are more than 55 percent suburban, compared to the national average of 35 percent). Since central-city and suburban interests frequently diverge,[53] this situation adds an additional strain to the effort to forge progressive and equitable housing and urban development policy.

In the Ninety-third Congress, the pattern of decision-making within the Senate Housing Subcommittee changed significantly. Dissatisfied with the cumbersomeness of a fifteen-member "subcommittee," Sparkman reorganized the committee's subcommittee structure and established a smaller, nine-member Housing Subcommittee. On this newly reorganized subcommittee, the liberals have a five-four edge, since several conservatives, both urban and nonurban, were not seated (see Table 19). But this edge remains slim and is vulnerable to threatened defections on

TABLE 18.

Ideology and Constituency Base of Senate Housing
Subcommittee Membership, 92nd Congress

Group and members	Percent urban (U.S. Av. = 73%)	Percent metro.* (U.S. Av. = 68%)	Group ratings 1972			
			ADA	COPE	ACA	Conservative Coalition
A. *Urban† liberals*	87	84	*84*	*95*	*10*	*12*
Williams (D., N.J.)	89	77	85	100	5	8
Cranston (D., Cal.)	91	93	90	100	5	7
Stevenson (D., Ill.)	83	80	80	89	10	10
Brooke (R., Mass.)	85	85	80	90	19	21
B. *Urban conservatives*	76	75	*14*	*10*	*82*	*74*
Tower (R., Texas)	75	74	0	0	94	72
Bennett (R., Utah)	80	78	5	11	90	85
Roth (R., Del.)	72	70	25	10	73	82
Taft (R., Ohio)	75	78	25	20	70	58
C. *Nonurban‡ liberals*	62	47	*68*	*83*	*17*	*16*
Proxmire (D., Wis).	64	58	75	70	18	15
Mondale (D., Minn.)	66	57	95	90	0	2
McIntyre (D., N.H.)	56	27	35	88	33	30
D. *Nonurban conservatives*	60	53	*15*	*13*	*71*	*62*
Sparkman (D., Ala.)	58	52	0	10	80	69
Gambrel (D., Ga.)	55	50	15	0	60	64
Packwood (R., Ore.)	67	61	45	40	55	61
Brock (R., Tenn.)	59	49	0	0	88	75

* Percent metro = percent in Standard Metropolitan Statistical Area.
† Urban = state with above average urban population.
‡ Nonurban = state with below average urban population.
SOURCES: Population figures from U.S., Bureau of Census, *Congressional District Data Book*, 93rd Congress. ADA, COPE, and ACA ratings are from *Congressional Quarterly Weekly Report*, Dec. 9, 1973, p. 113. Conservative coalition rankings are from *Congressional Quarterly Weekly Report*, Nov. 18, 1972, pp. 3026–3027. The figures shown are the percentage of votes in 1971 and 1972 cast with the "conservative coalition" when it operated.

TABLE 19.

Ideology and Constituency Base of Senate
Housing Subcommittee Membership, 93rd Congress

Group and Members	Percent metro* (U.S. Av. = 68%)	Group Ratings, 1973		
		ADA	COPE	ACA
A. Urban liberals	83.6	80	88	6
Williams (D., N.J.)	76.9	80	91	0
Cranston (D., Cal.)	92.7	85	90	8
Stevenson (D., Ill.)	80.1	85	82	7
Brooke (D., Mass.)	84.7	70	89	8
B. Urban conservatives	75.6	13	28	76
Tower (R., Tex.)	73.5	0	18	92
Taft (R., Ohio)	77.7	25	38	60
C. Nonurban liberals	57.6	85	82	28
Proxmire (D., Wis.)	57.6	85	82	28
D. Nonurban conservatives	56.7	30	45	41
Sparkman (D., Ala.)	52.3	10	70	46
Packwood (D., Ore.)	61.2	50	20	36

* Percent metro = percent in Standard Metropolitan Statistical Area.
SOURCE: Population figures from U.S., Bureau of Census, *Congressional District Data Book*, 93rd Congress. Group ratings from *Congressional Quarterly Weekly Report*, Dec. 9, 1973, p. 113.

the part of senators like Cranston, whose constituency is far more concerned with the suburban part of the urban policy dilemma, and whose own background in the building and land-development business inclines him in a similar direction.

The same difficulties that confront urban-oriented legislators in the Senate Housing Subcommittee are present in the House Housing Subcommittee, but they are complicated by the less liberal orientation of the full Banking Committee. As noted in Chapter 2, the House Banking Committee in the Ninety-second Congress was more liberal—as measured in terms of members' floor votes —than the House as a whole, though still less liberal than its counterpart on the Senate side. The Housing Subcommittee is, in turn, more liberal than its parent committee. Membership in the subcommittee is determined by seniority, which northern, urban legislators have developed over the past decade. Thus, of the eleven most senior Democrats on the House Banking Committee in the Ninety-second Congress, all but two could be classed as "urban liberals," and one of these two was chairman Wright Patman, a maverick on anyone's scale. Eight of these urban liberals held seats on the committee's Housing Subcommittee, giving them, along with one Republican liberal, a potential majority of nine to six (see Table 20).

But urban liberal dominance in the House Housing Subcommittee is not complete. At least three of the "urban liberals" really represent suburban constituencies far more similar to those represented by the Republicans on the subcommittee than to the big-city districts represented by the liberal Democrats. These three included Margaret Heckler of Massachusetts, who is a Republican and therefore inclined to vote with her party cohorts in the subcommittee. To the extent that issues break along central city *versus* suburban or small-town lines, therefore, the central-city liberals were outnumbered during the Ninety-second Congress by nine to six. Furthermore, their position remained the same or weakened slightly in the Ninety-third Congress, when arch-conservative John Rousselot replaced moderate Florence Dwyer on the Republican side, and Orange County, California, Democrat Richard Hanna replaced Newark, New Jersey, Democrat Joseph Minish.

If urban programs have a difficult time in the legislative subcommittees, however, they face an even more formidable challenge in the Appropriations subcommittees. In both House and Senate, the Appropriations subcommittees responsible for HUD appropriations also handle appropriations for a disparate array of programs, including the National Aeronautics and Space Administration, the Selective Service System, the Veterans Administration, and the Securities and Exchange Commission. This curious situation is a throwback to the days when HUD was, like these other agencies, a sub-cabinet-level independent office. What it

TABLE 20.
Ideology and Constituency Base of House
Housing Subcommittee Membership, 93rd Congress

| Group and Members | Nature of District | | | Interest group ratings, 1972 | | | |
	Percent central city	Percent sub-urban	Percent metro*	ADA	COPE	ACA	Con-servative Coali-tion
A. *Urban liberals*	71.8	25.7	95.5	76	82	12	17
Barrett (D., Penn.)	100.0	—	100.0	81	100	5	14
Sullivan (D., Mo.)	87.7	12.3	100.0	38	100	25	29
Ashley (D., Ohio)	82.5	17.5	100.0	88	100	14	15
Moorhead (D., Pa.)	100.0	—	100.0	94	100	0	8
St. Germain (D., R.I.)	30.8	69.2	83.4	75	91	5	17
Gonzales (D., Tex.)	92.0	8.0	100.0	56	100	26	34
Reuss (D., Wis.)	100.0	—	100.0	100	82	4	5
Minish (D. N.J.)	33.9	66.1	100.0	88	91	14	10
Heckler (R., Mass.)	19.1	58.5	75.6	63	56	12	24
B. *Urban conservatives*	9.9	78.2	88.0	14	36	61	52
Widnall (R., N. J.)	—	100.0	100.0	19	36	59	62
Brown (R., Mich.)	18.0	44.7	62.3	13	19	64	69
Stanton (R., Ohio)	—	80.7	78.8	19	30	52	25
Blackburn (R., Ga.)	31.4	65.4	96.1	0	18	100	75
Dwyer (R., N.J.)	—	100.0	100.0	19	75	29	27
C. *Nonurban liberals*	—	—	—	—	—	—	—
None	—	—	—	—	—	—	—
D. *Nonurban conserv.*	12.7	11.9	34.6	6	11	61	68
Stephens (D., Ga.)	12.7	11.9	35.2	6	11	61	68

* Percent metro = percent in Standard Metropolitan Statistical Areas.
SOURCES: Population figures from U.S., Bureau of Census, *Congressional District Data Book*, 93rd Congress. ADA, COPE and ACA ratings are from *Congressional Quarterly Weekly Report*, Dec. 9, 1973, p. 113. Conservative coalition rankings are from *Congressional Quarterly Weekly Report*, Nov. 18, 1972, pp. 3026–3027. The figures shown are the percent of votes in 1971 and 1972 cast with the "conservative coalition" when it operated.

means, however, is that members are attracted to these subcommittees for reasons completely unrelated to HUD and its urban programs. In fact, this mixture of responsibilities has attracted a group of legislators downright hostile to urban programs, particularly urban programs with a social-welfare flavor. On the House side, where this antipathy is most decisive because of the traditional primacy the House enjoys in the appropriations process, it is most in evidence. Of the ten members of the House Appropriations Committee's Subcommittee on HUD-Space-Science-Veterans Affairs in the Ninety-second Congress, only three could generously be classed as urban liberals, but only by including members from such relatively small metropolises as Springfield, Massachusetts (163,000), and Fort Wayne, Indiana (178,000); and counting as liberal a legislator (Robert N. Giaimo [D., Conn.]) with an ADA rating as low as 31 in 1972. For the rest, the subcommittee is dominated by conservatives, most of them from rural districts. As Table 21 shows, this situation worsened in the Ninety-third Congress, as the subcommittee balance shifted from a six-to-four conservative majority to a seven-to-four conservative majority.

In the Senate, nonurban elements also dominate the Appropriations subcommittee responsible for housing and urban development programs, though somewhat less so than in the House. In the Ninety-second Congress, for example, only four of the eleven members hailed from states with urban populations at or above the national average (see Table 20). In ideological terms, conservatives enjoyed a six-to-five edge. In the Ninety-third Congress, several urban liberals joined the subcommittee and several nonurban conservatives departed, leaving a fairly secure urban and liberal majority in control. But the new liberal majority on the Senate HUD Appropriations Subcommittee must still contend with their entrenched, conservative, nonurban counterparts on the House side.

Leadership and Operating Style

The disparate and ideologically diverse membership of the key subcommittees responsible for housing and urban development policy naturally places a high premium on the art of compromise. And fortunately for the internal cohesion of the subcommittees,

TABLE 21.

Ideology and Constituency Base of House and Senate
HUD–Space Science–Veterans Appropriations Subcommittee Membership,
92nd and 93rd Congresses

	House		Senate	
Group	92nd Cong.	93rd Cong.	92nd Cong.	93rd Cong.
Urban liberals	Boland (D., Mass.) Roush (D., Ind.) Giaimo (D., Conn.)	Boland (D., Mass.) Roush (D., Ind.) Tiernan (D., R.I.) Giaimo (D., Conn.)	Pastore (D., R.I.) Case (R., N.J.) Percy (R., Ill.)	Pastore (D., R.I.) Inouye (D., Ha.) Bayh (D., Ind.) Mathias (R., Md.) Case (R., N.J.) Brooke (R., Mass.)
Urban conservatives	McDade (R., Pa.) Dawson (R., Cal.)	McDade (R., Pa.)	Allott (R., Colo.)	Fong (R., Ha.)
Nonurban liberals	Talcott (R., Cal.)		Magnuson (D., Wash.) Mansfield (D., Mont.)	Proxmire (D., Wis.) Mansfield (D., Mont.) Chiles (D., Fla.)
Nonurban conservatives	Evins (D., Tenn.) Shipley (D., Ill.) Pryor (D., Ark.) Jonas (R., N.C.)	Evins (D., Tenn.) Shipley (D., Ill.) Chappell (D., Fla.) Talcott (D., Cal.) Scherle (R., Ia.) Ruth (R., N.C.)	Ellender (D., La.) Stennis (D., Miss.) McGee (D., Wyo.) Smith (R., Me.) Hruska (R., Neb.)	Stennis (D., Miss.) Stevens (R., Ala.)

they have been blessed with chairmen who are past masters at this art. In the Senate the Housing Subcommittee has been in the hands of John Sparkman since its creation. As indicated above, Sparkman has made a religion of moderation during his long Senate career. Though rooted in southern conservatism, he has functioned as a gatekeeper on reform, willing to put his stamp of approval on new ideas when the pressure for them becomes compelling, but moderating and muffling change in the process. While paying close attention to "constituency work," Sparkman thus takes a Burkean view of his role as a legislator, supporting proposals for which he feels the time is ripe even when his constituents might object. "I have never been guided solely by what I thought was the prevailing opinion of my constituency," he explained to us.[54] Sparkman's style in the Housing Subcommittee is to listen until all positions have been stated and debated, and then to sum up the "consensus" as he sees it, taking special care to accommodate conservative and Republican perspectives on legislation in an effort, as he sees it, to ensure passage on the Senate floor. "We try to make all our legislation as nonpartisan as possible," Sparkman explained. "I never take a bill to the floor unless I'm sure it will pass."[55] Given his considerable prestige and skill at judging the mood of Congress, Sparkman's "consensus" normally prevails, usually without any voting.

While this style contributes to internal committee harmony, however, it does little to give direction on the substance of policy. For this Sparkman relies on his committee colleagues, and, indirectly, on the private interest groups and administrative agencies with the greatest stakes in committee deliberations. Both of these alternatives are imperfect, however: the latter because it surrenders to others the policy initiative that is rightfully Congress' and the former because other members have taken rather limited interest in Housing Subcommittee business. Second-ranking Democrat Proxmire, for example, focuses on defense spending and general economic policy through his posts as chairman of the Senate Appropriations Subcommittee on Foreign Operations and chairman of the Joint Economic Committee. Third-ranking Williams is preoccupied with his responsibilities as chairman of the Senate Committee on Labor and Public Welfare. Fourth-ranking McIntyre, from rural New Hampshire, is not only busy elsewhere, but disinterested. Not until we get to fifth-ranking Mondale, in fact, do we find a senator who took an active, leadership role in the framing of housing policy in the Ninety-second Congress; but when the Ninety-third Congress convened, Mondale too departed, surrendering his fifth-ranking position on the Banking Committee for an eight-ranking slot on the Senate Finance Committee.

In an effort to stimulate greater member interest in subcommittee business, Sparkman has endeavored to parcel out policy areas among them. Williams was thus encouraged to specialize on urban mass transit and given relatively free rein to formulate legislation in this area. The same has been done for Stevenson in the area of urban planning assistance, and Brooke in public housing. But nowhere is there forceful leadership in fitting all the separate pieces together. As one subcommittee staffer complained, "I think we're spinning our wheels on this subcommittee. We don't have a sense of going anywhere."[56]

The same compromise style of leadership operates in the House subcommittee as well. Until 1966, the Housing Subcommittee in the House was the property of Albert Rains, an Alabama Democrat cut in the mold of John Sparkman. Since that time, the chairman has been William Barrett, a disarming South Philadelphia politician of the old school whose main claim to fame prior to his elevation to the Housing Subcommittee chairmanship was his practice of traveling back to Philadelphia each day for ward heeler-type "confessionals" with his lower-middle-class constituents in a small storefront office—a practice he continues to this day. Barrett is a kindly, self-effacing man, but hardly a dynamic leader brimming with new ideas and creative innovations. As one lobbyist explained, "Ashley [fifth-ranking Democrat Thomas Ludlow Ashley] and Sullivan [second-ranking Democrat Leonor Sullivan of St. Louis] know about housing, but

Barrett does not. This presents a delicate tactical problem for us. We can't go behind Barrett's back, so we try to keep lines of communication open while dealing mainly with others."[57]

What Barrett does possess amply is humility and a canny political sense, a knack for seeing the grounds for potential compromise, and the personality to smooth ruffled feathers and soothe ill feelings. One indication of his skill has been his handling of efforts by full-committee chairman Wright Patman to reduce the Housing Subcommittee's autonomy. Patman is not a member of the Housing Subcommittee and is jealous of its special position. This jealousy seems to be rooted in two factors: the first is procedural and reflects the anxiety of an activist-innovator chairman that an important range of policy within his committee's jurisdiction lies outside his immediate control; the second is more substantive and reflects Patman's view that the autonomy of the Housing Subcommittee constitutes a set of blinders that blocks housing policy questions off from the financial and monetary policy issues that lie behind them, and thus leads to inadequate Band-Aid solutions to basic problems. Patman has made frequent efforts to draw the link between the way the financial system operates and the persistent problems the housing sector encounters. For example, when housing construction plummeted in 1969 for the fifth time since World War II, Patman proposed to deal with the situation directly, by requiring pension funds and commercial banks to invest a portion of their assets in low-interest mortgages (H.R. 15402), by establishing a direct government loan program to make low-income housing and community development loans (H.R. 14639), and by restructuring the Federal Reserve System to force it to make additional capital available for housing (H.R. 11). As Patman pointed out when introducing this legislation, the persistence of low-income housing shortages and continual fluctuations in housing construction demonstrated structural shortcomings in the mortgage credit system that could not be papered over by more partial solutions and indirect expedients and hence raised "questions about our housing economy that can no longer be ignored"[58] (implying that the Housing Subcommittee was ignoring them).

Patman has tried several times to clip the subcommittee's wings. At the start of the Ninety-second Congress, for example, he proposed that Housing Subcommittee funds be channeled through the full-committee budget. Failing in that, he suggested that the subcommittee be split in two and a separate subcommittee on mass transit be created. This proposal won the support of several of the younger urban legislators on the committee like Edward Koch of New York City and Parren Mitchell of Baltimore, who felt frustrated at being frozen out by the seniority system from participation on the Housing Subcommittee, the Banking Committee subcommittee with greatest relevance to their constituents.

Because of a long-standing, close relationship with Patman, Barrett's first response to these initiatives was conciliatory. Even after his senior subcommittee colleagues convinced Barrett to resist Patman's threatened encroachments, Barrett has remained a loyal Patman supporter on the full committee, thus easing some of the tension that might otherwise exist between them.* In the case of the mass transit subcommittee idea, Barrett ultimately acquiesced when he realized the threat posed to the Housing Subcommittee itself by continued frustration on the part of the younger urban members of the full committee.†

---

* One good example of Barrett's practice of lining up behind Patman occurred in the summer of 1972 when Patman introduced as an amendment to the 1972 housing bill then under consideration in executive sessions his pet proposal to require the General Accounting Office to audit the Federal Reserve System. Even though this provision promised to add additional controversy to the already controversial subcommittee bill, and hence delay enactment, Barrett sided with Patman against Republican objections that the federal audit proposal was out of order in a housing bill.

† One other factor responsible for Barrett's acquiescence was the developing consensus on the Bolling House Reform Committee that urban mass transit should be taken from the Banking Committee and vested in a transportation-oriented committee like Public Works. As it turned out, this was one of the few reform proposals proposed by the Bolling Committee that was accepted.

On substantive matters within the subcommittee as well, Barrett plays a deferential, supportive role. Fortunately for him, member interest on the House side is somewhat stronger than it is in the Senate, no doubt because House members serve on fewer committees and have fewer demands on their time. In recent years a group of younger committee members led by Congressman Ashley of Toledo has moved into the policy leadership vacuum left by Barrett and, to a large extent, by Sparkman. Ashley has emerged, in fact, as a major critic of traditional federal housing policy, arguing that it fails to reflect any coherent urban growth policy. "The whole housing delivery system has broken down," Ashley observed. "We have to reexamine the whole structure of federal programs in this area."[59] Ashley began this process in 1968, when he secured permission from Patman to conduct a series of hearings on urban growth policy, hearings that ultimately led, in 1970, to legislation authorizing a program of federal assistance to "new town" developers and requiring preparation of an urban growth policy report by the administration every two years.[60] Then, in 1970, Ashley was instrumental in launching the Housing Subcommittee on an independent inquiry into federal housing and urban development policy, as the subcommittee split into three study panels, each with its own chairman, and discussed papers prepared by outside consultants.*[61] Rather than fight these initiatives, Barrett has supported them, seeing in renewed subcommittee vigor a vicarious means to expand his own prestige. As one subcommittee staffer explained:

> Barrett is willing to allow other members to play a key role on the subcommittee. He relies heavily on Ashley for community development matters, St. Germain for mass transit, and Sullivan for settlement costs. Barrett feels his influence has increased as a consequence.[62]

---

* For more detailed discussion, see pp. 272–297.

The Omnibus Approach and the Politics of Confusion

But innovations such as have been occurring in the House sub-committee have not altered in any fundamental way the traditional process by which housing policy is made in Congress. This process has, by and large, relegated Congress to a reactive role, sniping at minuscule portions of particular programs while failing almost completely to consider the whole. In making housing and urban development policy, in fact, the Banking committees and their Housing subcommittees have operated very much like wholesale dry goods distributors. Each legislative season they receive several truckloads of legislative proposals from various manufacturers—HUD, the special interests, and assorted colleagues—which they unpack, examine briefly, and then systematically repackage in bundles containing just enough of each manufacturer's product line to guarantee that manufacturer's assistance in the ultimate promotion and sale of the product on the floor of Congress. That the repackaged bundle has no coherence or stylistic unity is understandable. Indeed, only rarely will it contain the right mix of sizes for the ultimate consumers, since the consumers can more easily be convinced to accept what is available than the producers can be convinced to rework what they have made.

Housing bills thus tend to be massive pieces of omnibus legislation containing literally hundreds of program modifications and new authorities. The 1972 housing bill, for example, ran 229 pages in length and included 10 separate titles with 136 separate sections. The title on "Miscellaneous Provisions" alone contained 27 sections, covering everything from the establishment of a public-facility loan-guarantee program to the waiver of the planning requirement under the 1965 water and sewer program.

Since a housing bill is always big enough for another bright idea or client demand, this approach naturally facilitates compromise, but it also effectively muffles serious debate. In the "you-scratch-my-back-I'll-scratch yours" spirit embodied in omnibus housing bills, the name of the game is conflict-avoidance. The sheer complexity of the resulting legislation makes a sham of congressional floor debate and thus robs the public of possibly its only open forum for a frank and thorough discussion about the content of the legislation. Indeed, considering its size and complexity, this legislation has been handled with surprising dispatch on the floor, especially in the Senate, which prides itself on its role as the nation's debating society. The massive 1972 Housing Act, for example, cleared the Senate after less than one afternoon of debate without any real discussion of its basic provisions, and by a vote of eighty to one.

Nor is consideration of this complex legislation significantly more meaningful at the committee or subcommittee stages. This is particularly true in the Senate, where members rely extensively on staff to resolve basic issues in the legislation *prior* to markup sessions and then work from predigested agendas that abstract the few remaining issues during the markups. "We try to keep the issues to a minimum to the members," explained Carl A. S. Coan, staff director of the Senate's Housing Subcommittee. "We kick it around here at the staff level to iron out the issues."[63] The result, however, as the staff director of the full Senate Banking Committee conceded, is that "many members don't know what's in the bill."[64]

Although House members rely less extensively on staff and tend to examine the legislation more completely themselves, the omnibus bills have similar effects there as well. As chairman Patman recently noted, such bills "def[y] thorough understanding by members of the House" and lead to markup sessions characterized by "inadequate debate, and a steadily mounting frustration and impatience on the part of Committee members."[65] "This is the most carelessly passed legislation I've ever seen," noted *New York Times* correspondent John Herbers.[66] Even the House's Housing Subcommittee conceded the point. "The enactment of housing and urban development legislation proceeded at an extraordinary pace throughout the 1960s," it noted in a recent report. But

> the processes by which that legislation was enacted . . . changed very little. Virtually every year, the Executive Branch submitted proposals to expand or modify existing programs and to add new ones. These proposals, for the most part, tended to deal piecemeal with the numerous problems resulting from rapid social change. Congressional hearings on these and other proposals generally produced witnesses for the same organizations year after year, organizations which, quite properly, presented often familiar institutional viewpoints. After varying intervals, legislation was reported by Committees, passed by the two houses of Congress, and eventually signed into law (often concurrently with the development of new proposals to be submitted within a few months). Although the process can appear orderly and deliberate, in fact, it consumes inordinately long periods of time without the compensating benefit of increased concentration and analysis. . . . It affords neither the analytical framework needed to deal comprehensively with the increasingly complex and interrelated problems of housing and urban development, nor an effective method for evaluating the effectiveness of existing programs and policies. As a result, the Congress continues to lose, to the Executive Branch, the initiative needed to deal effectively with housing and urban development problems.[67]

Why, then, does reliance on this procedure persist? One reason is the time pressure on members. "Packaging housing matters in omnibus bills gets us out of a lot of work," explained Carl Coan. "Otherwise we couldn't get the members to meetings."[68] Equally important are the pressures on staff time. The Senate Housing Subcommittee has five professional staff members, only two of whom, in the Ninety-second Congress, had extensive experience in the housing field (Carl Coan and Robert Malakoff). On the

House side, the Housing Subcommittee employs six professionals. In contrast, HUD and the private lobbies maintain large research and "legislative liaison" staffs generating reams of material supporting their policy positions. Faced with a yearly avalanche of new proposals from the administration and the private lobbies, the subcommittee staffs have their hands full just figuring out what is being proposed and explaining it to the members. What is more, as we noted in Chapter 2, considerable staff time is absorbed in constituency "case work," especially in the Senate, where both Sparkman and ranking Republican Tower make heavy demands on staff director Coan and minority counsel Skiles to handle problems that constituents in their respective states encounter with HUD. The result is to leave the staff no time to explore alternative policy approaches or to undertake serious policy analyses on their own. "They're so overwhelmed they can't think far ahead at all," is the way one insider put it.[69] Until the experience with "study panels" in the House, moreover, there was little stimulus from the members, let alone from the chairmen, to push them in this direction. Rather, the staff has been confined to a "broker" role, gathering proposals from the key lobbies, shuttling among them to work out differences and formulate compromises acceptable to the members, and then packaging the results in giant omnibus bills. As a consequence, the policy arena comes to be a "closed corporation," as one Senate staffer put it.[70] "Housing policy is formulated within a narrow range of acceptability by a small group of experts and technicians," another close staff observer pointed out. "The perceived possibilities are very narrowly construed; and the result is a lot of incremental tinkering, which is just what technicians are good for."[71]

This mode of staff operation is virtually institutionalized, moreover, in the pattern of staff recruitment; for the subcommittees draw their staffs from many of the same outside groups from which they draw their legislative proposals. As the staff director of the Housing Subcommittee in the House observed, the actors in the housing policy process tend to "make the circuit" among the key decision centers: Congress, HUD, and the lobbies. The staff directors of both the full Senate Banking Committee and its Housing Subcommittee, for example, are both recruits from HUD's predecessor, the Housing and Home Finance Agency. In the case of the latter, Carl A. S. Coan, additional ties have been created through family connections. During the late 1960s, Coan's son—Carl A. S. Coan, Jr.—served in the HUD General Counsel's office, where he was responsible for formulating HUD's legislative program and presenting it to Congress. Since 1969, the younger Coan has been performing the identical function for the National Association of Home Builders, the major special-interest group with which his father's subcommittee must deal.

Nor does the game of musical chairs stop there. The elder Coan was originally recruited to the Senate Housing Subcommittee by one Joseph McMurray, father of the current staff director of the House Housing Subcommittee and a member of the Federal Home Loan Bank Board, the agency responsible for overseeing the savings and loan industry. Both the Mortgage Bankers Association and the National Association of Home Builders have former employees on the staff of the House Banking Committee, the latter on the Housing Subcommittee. In 1973 this subcommittee hired as its counsel the man who had replaced Carl Coan, Jr., at HUD in 1969, Ray James.

Since omnibus housing bills require the complex juggling of proposals from numerous outside interests, and hence a great deal of close work with these interests, this intimate pattern of recruitment facilitates their formulation and makes the whole procedure seem natural and benign. In the process, however, it narrows the range of debate and restricts the array of options taken seriously, while leaving the Congress defenseless against the persistent pressures of special pleaders.

Perhaps the most important reason for adherence to the omnibus approach to housing policy, and for the diffuseness and frequent irrationality of the policy that results, however, is the immense influence that the major private lobby and administrative actors wield in this policy sphere. "Until very recently," one House Banking Committee staffer pointed out, "the committee never saw the 'people' on housing, only the lobbyists. Most of the housing laws have been written by the special interests."[72] A staff member on the Senate side concurred: "The Housing subcommittees define their problem as how to satisfy the special interest constituencies they face rather than how to formulate the best policies to deal with the pressing issues of housing and urban development."[73] The omnibus approach facilitates this process. The special interests recognize they can gain more by burying their pet proposals in massive housing bills than they can by having these proposals stand alone. "Our legislation doesn't go anywhere unless it's on a housing bill," a United States Savings and Loan League (USS&LL) lobbyist conceded.[74] Modest social-welfare advances can thus be purchased legislatively only by incorporating them into large omnibus housing bills containing a heavy admixture of special-interest legislation. For example, according to Congressman William Moorhead, committee liberals have consistently resisted extending FHA authority three to five years into the future because this authority was part of the "bait" they used to ensure home-builder and mortgage-banker concurrence in continuing the public housing program.[75] Writing housing legislation under these circumstances thus becomes a kind of balancing act, an act that Sparkman and Rains, and now Barrett, have transformed into an art. The problem is that it forces policy into the mold set by the structure of the interest group pressure system organized to influence Congress on housing policy. To understand the peculiar shape of federal housing and urban development policy, therefore, it is necessary to look beyond the Congressional actors and look in detail at the peculiar shape of the pressure system within which they operate and to which they respond.

THE SUPPORTING CAST: THE BANKERS,
BUILDERS, BROKERS, AND BUREAUCRATS

Perhaps the most important fact about the politics of housing has been the absence of broad-based, majority support. From its origins in the tenement-house movement of the late nineteenth century, the push for federal involvement in urban housing and slum clearance has always centered in a relatively small band of reformers and social welfare advocates. Despite the fervor of their pleas, federal involvement in housing and urban development still had to await the Great Depression, when the ranks of the reformers were suddenly swelled by builders, construction workers, mortgage lenders, and real estate brokers—all of whom finally saw some virtue in government intervention, but all of whom evaluated that virtue in terms of its contribution to the viability of their respective industries. That the policy that emerged was pegged to the needs of these industries, and that it aimed at the broad middle group of American households instead of at the very poorest, should therefore come as no surprise. As Lawrence Friedman has written, "To enact a law requires more than passion. Social legislation usually demands some sort of coalition of political forces, cemented together by an appeal to material or other vital interests of some numerous powerful group."[76]

In the absence of any broad-based, organized support for federal policies to save the cities and help the poor, even the most conscientious legislative advocates of such policies have felt compelled to turn for support to those private interest groups with a strong nonwelfare stake in housing policy and to appeal as well to the growing public bureaucracy with a vested interest in keeping these programs alive. The historical conservative-rural bias built into the structure of congressional representation—particularly in the House—has further deepened this dependence, for only by demonstrating private-interest support and relying on nonradical indirect approaches has federal housing policy sur-

vived ingrained congressional opposition to urban-focused social
welfare measures.

During the 1960s, this general political climate for housing and
urban legislation seemed to be changing. The old coalition of
labor and urban reform elements, which had organized the
National Housing Conference and which had sustained the public
housing program during the dark days of the Eisenhower administration, received important new support from the developing civil
rights forces and from a newly vibrant coalition of urban chief
executives. Indeed, some analysts professed to see a powerful
"urban lobby" emerging on the national political scene composed
of labor, civil rights organizations, professional planners, urban
consultants, academics, and city government officials—all of
them interacting within a relatively small number of national organizations like the National League of Cities/U.S. Conference of
Mayors, the National Association of Housing and Redevelopment
Officials, and the Urban League.[77] During the Great Society era,
this network of specialists produced political miracles, enacting
the poverty program, creating HUD, establishing the Model Cities
program, and passing the important 1968 Housing Act, which set
an explicit goal for low-income housing production and established two new programs to implement it (235 and 236). There
was about it all a sense of invincibility that gave rise to the belief
that public-interest lobbies would henceforth call the shots on
federal urban legislation.

But hard analysis compels a different conclusion. The sad fact
is that the newly emerging and much-touted "urban lobby" altered the underlying logic of the politics of urban policy very
little. In the first place, the so-called public-interest and liberal
lobbies behaved very much like the private interests they were
seeking to unseat. The mayors wanted more money for the urban
poor, but they wanted it channeled through city hall. The unions
supported housing for the poor, but they insisted on retention of
provisions requiring payment of "prevailing wage rates" on federal housing projects (the Davis-Bacon law) and on adherence to

existing local building codes, even though both of these increased housing costs and thus reduced the benefits available to the poor. As for civil rights forces, committee insiders complain about their inactivity. "They haven't caught on to the fact that there's a lot of action here," complained one House Banking Committee staffer.

Even had they done so, however, there is reason to question whether Congress would have responded differently. As Robert Wood, the first undersecretary of HUD and a key figure in the network of urban "brain-trusters" who came into prominence in the 1960s, pointed out recently, Lyndon Johnson was trying to enact urban legislation in the absence of a public consensus, what Wood calls "the necessary majority."[78] Johnson consequently had to pay a price. In particular, the legislation had to be handled as quickly and quietly as possible, lest it awaken the slumbering giant of popular resentment against social-welfare policies for the central-city poor. And the easiest way to accomplish this was through active appeasement of the special interests. Is HUD to reorient federal housing policies to focus on the central-city poor instead of the suburban middle class? Then the FHA bureaucracy must be put in charge of the new task, lest its opposition torpedo the whole undertaking by arousing popular attention and mobilizing public antagonism. Is more low-income housing to be made available through public subsidies? Then interest subsidies must be used to avoid opposition from the bankers, and new construction stressed to appease the builders. The 1968 Housing Act, taken by many as the crowning achievement of the public-interest "urban lobby," can also be viewed as an even more important victory for the special interests—extending to the housing sphere the same protections earlier provided to agriculture and defense, and capping it all off with such elaborate protestations about the virtues of private enterprise and the need to rely on it that one wonders why there was a need for the act in the first place.

In short, even for members of Congress eager to promote housing for the poor, not to mention for those eager mainly to be reelected, the path of prudence in the housing sphere was as clearly marked in the 1960s as in the 1930s: Frame housing policy to please at least the major organized private interests and strategically placed bureaucrats, since it will rarely engage the attention, let alone the support, of anyone else. In the process, however, even those most hostile to special-interest dominance in other spheres of policy willingly accept it in the housing sphere. In practice, this gives immense influence in the politics of housing to four key sets of actors: the bankers, the builders, the real estate brokers, and the bureaucrats in HUD and the local agencies it funds.

The Bankers

No single group has so strategic a role in the housing policy drama as do the bankers, for they control the resource most desperately needed by the other actors: mortgage capital. That federal housing policy has taken the form of ever-more-desperate efforts to seduce the bankers into helping the cities and the poor is in large measure a reflection of the skill with which the bankers have handled this role. In particular, the bankers have consistently and effectively mobilized their economic and political power to insist on one crucial point: that federal efforts to assist the housing sector operate *through* the existing financial institutions instead of around them. They thus played an important part in the decision in the mid-1930s to scrap the New Deal's experimental Home Owners' Loan Corporation, a low-interest, direct government loan program replaced by FHA.[79] They repeated this performance in 1968, when an experimental below-market-interest-rate program for housing the poor (the 221[d][3] program) was eliminated in favor of the interest-subsidy approach (the 235 and 236 programs) on grounds that interest subsidies would "encourage private lenders to participate."[80] The bankers also argued for rigid, and generally low, income limits on the subsidy programs lest lower middle-class families taste the benefits of the interest subsidy and refuse to pay the higher interest fees charged by the banks. Middle-income groups should be allowed to depend on private enterprise for their housing needs, the bankers contended, even though, with rising interest rates, this meant trouble for the home-building industry.[81] The 1971 Policy Statement of the Mortgage Bankers Association summarizes the banking community's position toward federal housing assistance:

> In coping with the housing needs of the poor, adhere to the following principles: (a) every possible opportunity should be provided for the *expansion of private markets*; (b) government aid should be clearly *supplemental to private action* and should not compete with, displace, nor interfere with the development of private markets; (c) in extending assistance to the needy, government should *work through the instrumentalities of the private market*; and (d) direct aid should be provided in a manner that will permit its *curtailment* as the recipients improve their earning capacity.[82]

While all types of financial institutions share this forceful opposition to direct government loans and to subsidy devices that cut into the existing bank clientele, they differ on several significant aspects of housing and housing-related policy. To speak of "the bankers" as a group, therefore, is to ignore one of the most crucial aspects of the politics of housing: the existence of conflicts among the several types of financial institutions. The United States, as we have seen, has an exceedingly complex financial structure consisting of commercial banks; an array of savings institutions (savings and loan associations, mutual savings banks, life insurance companies, pension funds, and credit unions); a set of specialized "borrowing intermediaries" that tap pools of savings for use in corporate finance (investment bankers), mortgage lending (mortgage bankers), or consumer finance (finance companies); and numerous "government intermediaries" like Fannie Mae, the Federal Reserve Board, and the Federal Home Loan Bank Board.[83]

For a variety of legal and historical reasons, these various types of financial institutions specialize in different types of transactions. For example, commercial banks, which control about half of the $1.6 trillion of assets in private financial institutions,[84] channel only about 15 percent of their assets into residential mortgages,[85] most of this in FHA- or VA-guarantee mortgages. By contrast, savings and loan associations, which control only 15 percent of all bank assets, invest almost exclusively in residential mortgages, typically "conventional" mortgages, i.e., those not covered by FHA or VA guarantees.* Mortgages bankers, finally, resemble savings banks in dealing exclusively in real estate mortgages, but resemble commercial banks in restricting much of their activity to government guaranteed mortgages.

The differences in the character of their businesses naturally affect the way these institutions view government efforts to assist housing. And this is particularly true in view of the fact that the supply of savings, and hence of investment capital, available in the economy is relatively fixed at any given moment. Mortgages can claim a larger share of the available capital, therefore, only if some other sector reduces its share. But, as we have already seen, mortgages are at a distinct disadvantage in this competition for capital. The crucial policy decision, therefore, is the extent to which the government should intervene to assist mortgage lenders to compete for funds, and, if so, how. Given the significant differences among financial institutions in the extent to which they rely on mortgage lending, it is not surprising to find that there are great differences in their positions on this issue.

The commercial banks, pension funds, insurance companies, and investment bankers—all of whom have numerous other, and frequently more profitable, investment opportunities than residential mortgages—have little concern over the plight of the residential-mortgage market. These powerful institutions enjoy the advantages of a defensive pose in the formulation of housing policy. They can stand above the battle but still determine its

* As of 1973, therefore, commercial banks accounted for only 14 percent of all mortgage loans outstanding and savings banks for 58 percent.

basic contours by shooting down proposals for structural change. For while these institutions have relatively little to gain from federal housing policy, they have much to lose. In particular, they can lose the luxury of ignoring the nation's housing and urban development needs, a luxury that brings them handsome profits from their alternative investments in such ventures as corporate mergers and land speculation.

Whenever proposals surface to tap the vast resources of the commercial banks, pension funds, or insurance companies for low-income housing and urban development, or to employ the credit-creating powers of the Federal Reserve System to the same end, the big guns roll into action. Typically, the American Bankers Association, with its impressive research capability and far-flung "contact banker" network, leads the attack, and the Federal Reserve Board brings up the rear. Over the years, this combination has been more than sufficient to squelch proposals for structural reform that would interfere with private market dictation of capital flows or require the use of monetary policy to promote particular economic and social priority programs.

While the commercial banks, insurance companies, and pension funds can afford an attitude of "benign neglect" toward the mortgage market and the politics of housing, the savings banks find themselves in the thick of the fray, for they rely almost exclusively on the mortgage market for their livelihood. Savings banks are in direct competition with commercial banks for savings deposits, but are limited in the use of these assets to investments in residential mortgages. Anything that reduces the attractiveness of mortgages or limits the savings available to mortgage-lending institutions thus arouses the ire of the savings associations. But the savings banks cannot afford a purely defensive posture because the long-term nature of their investments makes it difficult for them to compete effectively for deposits. While espousing the virtues of private enterprise, therefore, they are not above appealing to Uncle Sam to provide by law what the market fails to give them by right. As one S & L spokesman put it in

1970, "The home mortgage market cannot survive in a highly competitive, completely 'free' money market."[86] Hence, the savings banks have turned repeatedly to government to help make the market less competitive.

To aid in this effort, the savings banks support impressive lobby activities in Washington. The most important of these, clearly, is the United States Savings and Loan League, which represents the burgeoning savings and loan industry, already a major beneficiary of governmental intervention in mortgage finance.* As the S & L industry has grown in size, so has the power and influence of the League. "Commercial banks used to have a monopoly on a lot of issues up here," Senate Banking Committee minority counsel John Evans explained to us. "But that was before the S & Ls became so effective. Now I don't know any member on this committee who is anti-S & L."[87] Part of the source of S & L influence, Evans explained, is congressional sympathy for the difficult box in which savings institutions have found themselves during the past decade because of the need to pay ever-higher interest rates to attract savings deposits while depending for their income on interest from loans made at lower interest rates many years ago. Even Wright Patman, the nemesis of the banking community generally, has a warm spot in his heart for the S & Ls as a consequence of this situation. "The S & Ls are the underdogs of the financial world," Patman explained to us. "The commercial banks are brutal to them."[88] But Patman's softness toward the S & Ls is the product of an earlier time, when the industry was not the mammoth giant it is today. As U.S. Conference of Mayors executive John Gunther pointed out:

> Mr. Patman hates banks, but he loves S & Ls. He thinks there's a difference and there probably was in the 1940s. But

* The other major voice of the savings industry is the Association of Mutual Savings Banks. Mutual savings banks differ from savings and loan associations in terms of their ownership structure, permissible asset composition, and legal organization. Mutual banks are largely concentrated in the northeastern states.

with regard to urban policy, banks and S & Ls are virtually
identical. Their policy is to channel all urban programs
through the existing banking system.[89]

Whether justified or not, however, the Savings and Loan
League hardly relies exclusively on the sympathy of legislators. It
also orchestrates a broad-based and coherent lobbying effort. According to chief League lobbyist Stephen Slipher, three crucial
elements—information, financial assistance, and grass-roots political clout—form the core of this effort.[90] Information flows pro-
fusely from the impressive research operation that the League's
$3-million-per-year budget helps support. Through a series of pol-
icy committees and a Legislative Council representing the "leadership of the business," moreover, this information is packaged in
policy statements carrying the weight of collective industry judg-
ments. Like the commercial banks' Federal Reserve Board, the
savings and loans also have an official mouthpiece inside the government in the Federal Home Loan Bank Board, which can dress
in sophisticated technical language and give the symbolic stamp
of official approval to proposals that might otherwise appear to be
mere special-interest pleading. That the FHLBB and the League
regularly support the same proposals is no accident, of course.
"It's more a natural meeting of the minds than a prearranged
thing," explained League lobbyist Slipher—and well it might be,
since the board is wired into the savings and loan industry from
top to bottom.*

To ensure a receptive audience for its views in Congress, the
savings and loan industry provides more tangible benefits to
members of Congress as well. At the top of the list are campaign
contributions. In preparation for the 1972 elections, for example,
the industry's campaign finance committee, SPEC (Savings Polit-

---

* The Federal Home Loan Bank Board consists of three members appointed
by the president with Senate approval. Traditionally, however, the president
has also needed the approval of the League as well. In turn, the board and
the Federal Home Loan Bank System, which it supervises, rely on the
savings and loan banks for their entire budget. In addition, there is an 18-
member statutory Advisory Council, two-thirds of whose members are chosen

ical Education Committee), amassed a war chest of at least $100,000, $65,000 of which had been spent by the end of May according to records submitted to the clerk of the U.S. House of Representatives.[91] Unlike the American Bankers Association, which ran into trouble in 1970 by sending unsolicited contributions to several congressmen, who returned them after some adverse publicity, the League, according to lobbyist Stephen Slipher, "follows the principle that a girl can only dance with someone who asks her, and therefore makes campaign contributions only to members of Congress who solicit them."[92] If this is so, then a lot of Banking Committee members have been soliciting dances from the savings and loan industry, including Congressmen Patman, Widnall, Barrett, Johnson, Moorhead, Gettys, Rees, Brown, and Blackburn, and Senators Sparkman, Muskie, Tower, Mondale, Proxmire, Percy, and Brooke.

In addition to campaign contributions, the savings industry buys access for its views as well through payment of speaking fees to congressmen, and occasionally by naming congressmen to the boards of directors of local savings banks. In 1972, for example, various savings and loan industry groups contributed indirectly to Senator John Sparkman's tough reelection campaign by paying a total of $5,500 to hear the powerful chairman of the Senate Banking Committee address various industry powwows. Other Banking Committee members who reaped rewards from the savings industry banquet circuit in 1972 included Senator Taft and Representatives Brown, St. Germain, Hanna, Ashley, Johnson, Patman, and Blackburn.[93] The appointment of congressmen to S & L boards of directors or the provision of favorable investment opportunities in S & L stock as a way to soften Congress up for

---

by the boards of the regional banks, which are in turn owned wholly by the member S & Ls. As if this were not sufficient to ensure industry dominance of the board, an additional advisory body, the Conference of Federal Home Loan Bank Presidents, was also provided for. In the Federal Home Loan Bank Board and its affiliated network of regional banks, in short, the League and the savings industry generally have important allies within the governmental bureaucracy.

industry views has also been used, but generally on a more limited and cautious scale. According to Slipher, such tactics have "never been significant in our legislative plan. We've never found it productive."[94] But others claim that local savings banks have traditionally made skillful use of this tool.[95]

While information and financial contributions create the potential for influence, they are not sufficient by themselves. The clincher is the third element: the demonstration of political clout back home, in each member's district. And, next to the ABA, the League has one of the most effective "local contact" systems in the business. With only 4,800 members, the League can maintain close contact with its membership, especially since each S & L belongs to the League directly, instead of through a tier of state organizations. With numerous S & Ls in each member's district, moreover, the League can easily create the appearance of a groundswell of local business concern on matters of importance to the industry. "Before we go up to the Hill on something," Slipher explains, "we try to pave the way by making sure that every member of the Banking Committee has at least a couple of letters from S & L guys back home."[96]

Coupled with its "motherhood and apple pie" image as the promoter of the virtues of saving and home ownership, this careful nurturing of political support by the League has brought ample rewards to the savings industry. Among other things, Congress has bestowed special tax advantages, an agency to protect S & L liquidity, a federal deposit guarantee system, and a regulation that limits the interest commercial banks can pay on savings accounts and thus keeps the commercial banks from siphoning savings away from the S & Ls. On the administrative side, Congress first created, in the FHLBB, an official voice for the industry, and then, under League pressure, extricated it in the 1950s from the clutches of the Housing and Home Finance Agency in which it was originally lodged. "We thought the S & Ls deserved a separate voice in the government," explained lobbyist Slipher. "This is a protocol-minded town and S & Ls did not like being the stepchild of a housing agency."[97] Nothing demonstrates the political power of the S & L industry more clearly than the success with which it has fended off efforts to reincorporate the FHLBB into the housing bureaucracy over the past decade and a half—for example, during the formation of the new cabinet-level Department of Housing and Urban Development in 1965 and more recently in the Nixon administration's proposed executive shakeup.

Compared to the ABA and the U.S. Savings and Loan League, the Mortgage Bankers Association is the "weak sister" of the banking lobby groups, largely because it has not had to be anything else. As middlemen in the mortgage-lending system, mortgage bankers care only that enough capital be available for mortgage finance, regardless of whether it accumulates in the hands of savings banks, pension funds, insurance companies, or even commercial banks. Therefore, while the savings banks continuously appeal to Congress for help in increasing their deposits, the mortgage bankers can take the high ground of free-market orthodoxy and oppose all forms of favoritism to one set of financial institutions over another.

The mortgage bankers do have an important stake in federal housing policy, of course, since they originate the bulk of FHA-guaranteed mortgages, the only mortgages really marketable on a mass basis nationwide. The mortgage bankers' stakes are thus different from those of the savings banks which keep the bulk of their assets in conventional loans. For example, mortgage bankers favor increasing the loan amounts and interest limits on FHA loans while savings banks prefer to keep them low to preserve a sphere for their own activity.

To protect its members' unique stakes in this arena, the MBA maintains a Washington office with a staff of sixty-eight persons and an annual budget of $2.5 million. Much of this staff is occupied in operating the "correspondent system," the mechanism by which mortgage bankers transfer funds among financial institutions. The MBA is thus different from ABA or the USS&LL in that it performs a business function for its members, who include the full array of participants in the correspondent network: insurance companies, commercial banks, savings banks, and some lawyers and brokers, as well as about eight hundred mortgage bankers *per se.*

Although its diversity complicates lobbying action, the MBA has developed an effective lobbying operation as well. "We want to feed at the federal trough, too," the MBA's legislative counsel explained to us.[98] To do so, MBA executive director Oliver Jones pointed out, "We decided we have to be convincing and helpful." The organization thus has two full-time lobbyists on Capitol Hill and two to three people "on their feet in the HUD building every day" to work on the thousands of legislative and administrative details that arise under the FHA programs.[99] At the same time, it has reached into its members' pockets for campaign contributions and honoraria payments. Recipients of MBA campaign largesse over the past two years, for example, have included Banking committee members Towers, Sparkman, and Mondale in the Senate, and Hanna, Moorhead, Minish, and Hanley in the House.[100] In 1972 the MBA ranked sixth among all special-interest groups in honoraria payments to senators.[101] Finally, for the past several years, the MBA has been in the enviable position of having its former legislative counsel serving on the minority staff of the House Banking Committee. All in all, MBA Executive Director Jones put it modestly, "We're just beginning to operate well on the Hill."[102]

Because the various bank lobbies haggle among themselves, Congress finds it easy to delude itself into thinking that merely by settling the disputes among the financial warlords it is adequately and judiciously serving the public interest. "One reason for the good oversight over the financial institutions," Senator Wallace Bennett's staff aide on the Senate Banking Committee confidently asserted, "is the competition among these institutions. Each one is so interested in getting a leg up on the other that we can just sit back and serve as the adjudicator."[103] The problem with this view is that it overlooks the broad area of agreement shared by these institutions, and the absence of consumer representation powerful enough to challenge the banking-community consensus. The result, therefore, is to leave the financiers with a hammerhold on mortgage-credit policy, despite the disagreements among them about the details of that policy.

One recent illustration occurred in 1970, when Congress passed the Emergency Home Finance Act. This act grew out of the severe credit crunch that developed in 1969 and sent the housing and savings industries into a tailspin. With the builders, savings bankers, and construction unions pressing for relief, Wright Patman and Leonor Sullivan introduced four proposals calling for some basic reforms in the underlying structure of American capital markets, including the creation of a new Home Owners Loan Corporation to make direct loans to home buyers and thus provide a mechanism for what Sullivan called "government yardsticking of what a fair rate of return should be."*[104] The bankers vigorously opposed any such fundamental reform,

---

* The proposed Home Owners Mortgage Loan Corporation would receive $10 billion out of the regular federal budget for mortgage loans to moderate income home buyers at interest rates not to exceed 6.5 percent. The bill would thus put the federal government in direct competition with the private mortgage lenders when interest rates rose above 6.5 percent. In addition to the Home Owners Loan Corporation idea, three others were also introduced, all by Patman. The first (H.R. 14639) would create a National Development Bank to make low-interest loans for housing and community development projects out of a pool of capital built up from the sale of securities issued by the bank. By requiring the Treasury to purchase up to $3 billion of Development Bank securities when requested, the proposal would provide a permanent source of new capital for socially needed community development efforts without having to rely on the politically uncertain appropriations process the way the Sullivan proposal did. The second proposal (H.R. 15402) went even beyond this by stipulating that large pension funds, which control over $80 billion in assets, be required to invest a portion of their assets in government-guaranteed low- and moderate-income home mortgages. The logic behind this proposal was the view that since these pension funds reap handsome tax advantages from their peculiar status, they should provide some social benefits as a *quid pro quo*—particularly if the benefits could be provided at no real risk to the pension assets thanks to the government loan guarantee. H.R. 15402 also explicitly author-

and they received solid support from the Federal Reserve Board. The battle was joined when the FHLBB proposed a compromise plan, a wild scheme for pumping additional capital into the savings industry by providing a subsidy to the FHLBB to reduce the interest it charged member savings banks on "advances."[105] Congress thus had before it a choice between another Rube Goldberg subsidy to the bankers and a more fundamental reform of the existing home finance system. With the bankers lined up so clearly against the reform option the issue was not long in doubt, especially since even William Proxmire, the one Senate Banking Committee member whose views on banking are closest to Patman's, failed to provide support. Noted Proxmire, "I have a lot of sympathy with these [Patman-Sullivan] proposals, but I also believe we ought to try first to work within our existing financial institutions."[106] After considerable maneuvering and a temporary victory for the Patman-Sullivan proposals in the House Housing Subcommittee, therefore, Congress adopted the FHLBB savings bank subsidy scheme. It took advantage of the situation to respond as well to a long-standing savings industry request for a government-supported "secondary mortgage market" for *conventional* mortgages to complement what FNMA provided for FHA and VA loans. "We have now ended up—after six months of intensive effort—with a bill which subsidizes the savings and loans, but does virtually nothing for the average American family," complained Congresswoman Sullivan at the end of the voting. "This has been a tragic waste of everyone's time, for the bill is now an empty shell."[107]

---

ized the Federal Reserve to purchase obligations issued by federal housing agencies like Fannie Mae or FHLBB in order to pump additional capital into mortgage lending during credit squeezes. Finally, the fourth measure (H.R. 11) proposed a restructuring of the Federal Reserve System to increase its responsiveness to overall national social and economic goals by reducing the terms of Federal Reserve Board Governors, opening the system to GAO audit, eliminating the crucial bank-dominated Open Market Committee that largely shapes Fed monetary policy, and requiring that the Fed justify its actions explicitly to Congress.

The Builders

If the bankers, particularly the commercial bankers, are the Dutch Uncles of the housing policy drama, perennially critical of proposals to interfere with the credit system, the builders play the role of the reformed sinner who has discovered how to make virtue pay. For decades the builders have been the mainstay of federal housing policy, actively supporting the tortured federal effort to stimulate housing construction without interfering with private enterprise. The Federal Housing Administration has thus been the darling of the home builders even more than of the bankers, for the agency's reliance on private builders, its preference for new construction, and its resulting subsidization of the postwar suburban building boom were the answers to the building industry's dreams. (When Lyndon Johnson proposed the creation of HUD in 1965, therefore, the home builders, through their national organization, insisted that one of the assistant secretaries be designated FHA commissioner and that FHA remain intact in the new department.) By contrast, the builders have looked askance at programs that siphoned precious housing funds into existing housing in the central city, or, like public housing, put government in competition with private home builders. The prevailing mix of federal housing policies, with its heavy emphasis on production, thus perfectly reflected the builders' preferences.

When these policies came under severe attack in the early 1960s, however, the home builders got religion. Instead of opposing federal housing subsidies for the poor, as in the past, the builders emerged in the mid-1960s as active promoters of such schemes. Part of this conversion may have reflected a sense of moral obligation, but if so, it was powerfully assisted by a growing realization that the conventional FHA mechanism was losing its punch and that stronger medicine would be needed to prime the home-building pump in the tight-money period of the 1960s and 1970s. During the twenty years from 1935 to 1954, for example, FHA insured 3.76 million homes, or almost 23 percent of the

16.6 million that were built. This proportion began to decline, however, falling to 18–19 percent in the late 1950s and to 13–14 percent by the mid-1960s.[108] Coupled with the pressure the Vietnam War buildup was beginning to exert on interest rates, and hence on the availability of mortgage capital, this decline in the attractiveness of FHA made the builders more receptive than ever to new devices to protect their industry from the vagaries of overall monetary policy. The riot-sparked search then under way for new ways to house the urban poor on a massive scale could thus not have occurred at a more opportune time from the perspective of the home builders. The result was a dramatic conversion, as the home builders decided to join the very liberal groups they had fought for the past twenty-five years over public housing, and to support a massive expansion of housing subsidies for the poor.

But the builders were not so carried away with fervor for the poor that they neglected to condition their support for low-income housing subsidies on the acceptance of a subsidy mechanism that would maximize profits for their industry. In practice, this meant maximum discretion for the private builder (that is, avoiding reliance on local public housing agencies), lax eligibility standards to permit servicing the "better off" among the poor, priority for new construction over rehabilitation or investment in existing housing, reliance on the FHA administrative structure with which the builders were familiar, and insulation from the impact of rising interest rates.

The 235 and 236 programs authorized by the 1968 Housing Act thus fit the builders' specifications with rare precision. They provided sizable subsidies to allow private builders, operating with private financing, to build housing that would be privately owned. FHA was to administer both, and was clearly instructed not to fritter away subsidy resources on existing housing.* Only the adoption of income limits for the programs violated the build-

---

* The House report on the bill, for example, argued that "In order to achieve the substantial increase in the number of dwellings available to low and moderate income families that is sorely needed, the committee ex-

ers' blueprint, which had called for only indirect income limits in order to assure a "massive building and marketing program," and "volume results."[110] Yet the income limits adopted were not so rigid as to displease the builders completely, and Congress obliged them further by specifying a detailed target figure for housing construction over the coming decade that was 60–70 percent *above* that achieved in the previous decade. The home builders thus emerged from the 1968 legislative session with a handsome payoff for their good works on behalf of the poor. Were there any doubts on this score, the 1969 credit squeeze put them to rest, for as rising interest rates cut into conventionally financed housing, the new FHA subsidy programs took up much of the slack, insulating the builders in part from what might have been an even more serious depression. In fact, thanks largely to 235 and 236, FHA units accounted for 30 percent of all privately owned nonfarm housing starts in 1970, two and a half times the average for the mid-1960s.[111]

That the 1968 Housing Act, not to mention earlier measures, adhered so closely to home-builder wishes was not, of course, an accident. For the builders maintain what is generally regarded as one of the most effective lobby operations in Washington—the National Association of Home Builders. With its 51,000 members and $4.5 million budget, the NAHB has a combination of assets few other pressure groups can rival. In the first place, its members are generally closely keyed in to the local political structures on which members of Congress must build their careers, so that virtually every member has a builder back home with whom he is on friendly terms. This is especially true in the South, the Southwest, and the West, the fastest-growing regions of the country, where home-builder strength is particularly great. The NAHB can thus count among its "special friends" such powerful allies as Banking Committee members John Sparkman and John Tower in

pects that assistance under this new program will be oriented toward new or substantially rehabilitated units."[109]

the Senate, and Robert Stephens, Richard Hanna, Wright Patman, and, until his retirement in 1966, Albert Rains in the House. Like the "farm bloc," in short, the home builders have strength where it really counts in Congress and can therefore forge unbeatable coalitions of southern conservatives and northern liberals for its prohousing programs.

But the NAHB does not depend on friendship alone to win votes. It also maintains an impressive staff operation in Washington to generate the information its friends need to present the builders' views effectively and to interpret these views to other congressmen. "Highly qualified and well-paid," is the way the respected *National Journal* described the NAHB staff in a profile on the organization in 1971[112]—and with good reason. The home builders long ago recognized the need to attract competent staff to service Congress' desperate need for information. Its executive director, Nathaniel Rogg, is a skilled economist with close personal ties to such governmental higher-ups as former Federal Reserve Board chairman William McChesney Martin, Jr. NAHB's six vice-presidents also bring to the organization a combination of technical knowledge and extensive political contacts with key decision-makers in Congress and the agencies built up over long experience in Washington housing policy circles. The NAHB's most recent coup, for example, was the hiring in 1969 of Carl A. S. Coan, Jr., former assistant general counsel for legislative policy coordination at HUD and the son of the staff director of Sparkman's Housing Subcommittee in the Senate. Such an attractive package of skills and contacts is hard to come by. Also on the NAHB's payroll is Burton Wood, a former congressional aide, who served as director of congressional liaison for FHA between 1961 and 1969 before joining the NAHB as vice-president for legislative relations in 1969.[113] Not only does the NAHB buy the services of former top government officials, however, it also dispatches some of its own people to HUD and the Congress in return. Burton Wood, for example, spent seven years as an NAHB lobbyist before going to FHA's legislative liaison office in

1961. George Gross, Housing Subcommittee counsel in the House, also did a stint as a Home Builders lobbyist. And, most interesting of all in this game of musical chairs, the man President Nixon named to the all-important post of HUD assistant secretary for Housing Production-FHA Commissioner in 1969, Eugene A. Gulledge, was serving at the time as president of NAHB (and was a member of the Federal Savings and Loan Advisory Council). So enmeshed is the NAHB with the public decision-making apparatus dealing with housing, in fact, that the distinction between public and private is all but obliterated. As a result, the question "What do the home builders think?" becomes a kind of instinctive response to any proposed change in housing law. During executive sessions of the House Housing Subcommittee on the 1972 Housing Act, when Representative Leonor Sullivan proposed a series of consumer provisions to protect home buyers against shoddy construction, for example, subcommittee chairman William Barrett instinctively proposed deferring a vote "until we can check this with the builders."[114] No such provisions were even proposed in the Senate. As one Senate Banking Committee staffer explained, "When the senators want to know what the consumer needs in housing, they generally turn to the Home Builders or to HUD."[115]

In addition to a well-oiled local contact system and a skilled staff, the Home Builders also make ample use of the ubiquitous instrument of campaign contributions. Given the paucity of national records, and the builders' preference for letting local affiliates handle much of the campaign money, tracing builder contributions is difficult. Yet records filed with the appropriate officers in the House and Senate by the Builders Political Action Committee (BIPAC) leave little doubt about builder generosity to their friends. Sparkman alone received $3,700 in campaign funds from BIPAC in 1972, in addition to a $1,500 honarium for an NAHB speech. John Tower also scored big with the home builders, as did chairman Patman and ranking minority member Widnall on the House side. Other recipients of BIPAC largesse in preparation for the 1972 elections were Senators Taft, Mondale, Percy, and Brooke, and Representatives Hanna, Annunzio, Johnson, Moorhead, and Minish—all of them Banking committee members.

What gives the builders an added edge, finally, is their ability to disguise their profit-seeking manipulation of public authority under the protective cover of a carefully nurtured "good guy" image. "The goals of our industry are the goals of most Americans," lobbyist Carl Coan, Jr., explained innocently. "We're for housing."[116] As one House staff member put it, "The builders think of themselves as doing God's work, and they try not to let the members forget it."[117] For congressmen inclined to support the home builders anyway, it is comforting to know they are on the side of the angels, the side of the family and the homestead.

NAHB efforts to influence the content of the 1972 Housing Act provide a revealing insight into how the lobby mobilizes its resources and how they pay off. This bill proposed a major rewrite and simplification of the entire corpus of federal housing law. Though the Home Builders generally got their way in the HUD and Senate versions of the bill, they encountered a "runaway" subcommittee in the House, for reasons we will examine more fully below. To correct the damage, the NAHB lobbyists had to take the initiative. After prevailing on chairman Patman to review the subcommittee bill in full committee, the Home Builders prepared a packet of some thirty-four amendments to change the objectionable features in the subcommittee's bill. Each proposed amendment was typed on a blank sheet of paper with no evidence of its origins in the Home Builders' offices. NAHB lobbyists then parceled these proposed amendments out to friendly legislators to be introduced on cue during full-committee executive sessions. At the same time, local home builders were instructed to turn on the heat. On sixteen out of the thirty-four proposed amendments, the Home Builders were able to reverse the subcommittee majority's decision. If we consider major substantive changes only, the Home Builder record is even more impressive. On ten out of fifteen such proposed amendments, the committee majority sided with the Home Builders against its own Subcommittee on Housing. These included such significant changes as the weakening of proposed consumer protections against shoddy construction, the elimination of a program of federal assistance to state development corporations, a reduction in the share of subsidy funds allowed for existing housing from 40 percent to 30 percent, and the easing of a subcommittee measure requiring local government approval before any subsidized housing projects are constructed.

The NAHB is not alone, however, in representing the interests of the residential construction industry before Congress. In recent years several additional lobby organizations have also appeared on the scene, including the Home Manufacturers Association, the Council of Housing Producers, and the Mobile Home Manufacturers Association. These organizations tend to represent the larger, corporate interests increasingly involved in the housing industry and focus their attention on stimulating federal subsidies for experiments with mass-produced housing and federal intervention to simplify and liberalize contradictory local building codes that interfere with the expansion of industrialized housing. On both of these points they differ from the NAHB, which tends to give greater voice to the smaller-scale builder operating in only a limited geographical region and using traditional building techniques. Although the size and effectiveness of the NAHB gives it a decided edge in any showdown, these other groups have managed to penetrate the policy process for their limited purpose measures as well, not the least by utilizing the standard technique of hiring lobbyists well known to the insiders of the housing policy subsystem. For example, the Council of Housing Producers, representing fourteen of the largest producers of housing in the nation, retains as its Washington lobbyist Philip Brownstein, FHA commissioner during the mid-1960s and still a member of the board of directors of FNMA. The Home Manufacturers Association follows suit, retaining as its Washington lobbyist Milton

Semer, a former Senate Banking Committee staffer who served as the general counsel of the Housing and Home Finance Agency during the early 1960s and then as a special presidential adviser on housing.[118]

The Brokers

Despite some family quarrels, however, the various builder organizations have far more in common than they have separating them. As a consequence, the only real effective counterweight to the NAHB in the determination of federal housing policy has come from the National Association of Real Estate Boards (NAREB), the organization from which the builders broke away in 1942 to form the NAHB. Like the builders, the real estate brokers have a deep interest in cheap money for mortgage loans, tax breaks for homeowners, and minimum governmental intervention in the real estate market. But unlike the builders, they are more concerned with the 63.4 million units of housing in the existing stock than the 1.2 to 2.0 million new units added each year. They have thus resisted the new-construction bias of federal housing policies, particularly as reflected in the costly subsidy programs of the 1960s. "The home builders consider it a cardinal sin to subsidize a person in an existing house," complained NAREB lobbyist John Williamson."[119]

What bothers the brokers is not simply that the builders are getting all the gravy, but also that by allowing poorer families to buy new houses, the subsidy programs reduce the demand for lower-priced existing housing and hence cut into broker profits. In testimony before the Senate Banking Committee in 1970, for example, the chairman of NAREB's special lobbying arm, the Realtors' Washington Committee, blasted HUD for the "new-production" focus the agency had given the 235 subsidy programs, claiming it had resulted in a "depressed market for modestly priced existing homes." "In redirecting the program into one which now contemplates as its major objective the resurrection of the Nation's depressed home building industry," the realtors' representative charged, "the Department has succeeded in making subsidy benefits . . . an even more serious threat to the lower priced housing market than prevailing high interest rates."[120]

Because of their middleman role in the real estate market and their primary focus on the existing housing stock, the realtors need to make fewer demands on government than the production-oriented builders. "We have to measure our gains by what we have prevented from happening," NAREB lobbyist Williamson told us.* It is perhaps a sign of the times, however, that a trade group with such limited avowed demands should nevertheless feel compelled to maintain so elaborate a lobby operation. For, though less extensive than NAHB's, NAREB's lobby arm is still an impressive apparatus. John Williamson, NAREB's chief lobbyist, prides himself on being the "dean" of the special-interest lobbyists dealing with housing, a central figure in the intimate network of acquaintances in Congress, HUD, and the other lobby groups that really shape federal housing policy.[122] Like the other special-interest groups, NAREB supports its Washington staff with several echelons of linebackers. The first echelon consists of a Washington-based research operation supplemented by an elaborate network of "institutes" and "committees" and by about 150 full-time staffers in the organization's central office in Chicago. The second echelon is the Realtors' Washington Committee, an 80-person body responsible for devising NAREB policy on pending or proposed legislation and for mobilizing pressure on members of Congress. "We try to include people with good contacts with the Banking committee members on the Realtors' Washington Committee whenever we can," Williamson explained.[123] The same logic inspires the realtors' final defense line as well: the 1,600 local boards which form the base of the NAREB pyramid. These boards operate much like medieval guilds, setting eligibility

---

* One recent example of NAREB success was the defeat of the Land Use Policy Act in 1972 and again in 1974. This act was designed to provide federal assistance to states for more comprehensive and thorough land-use planning, and was vigorously opposed by the realtors.[121]

standards and administering licensing tests to potential realtors, and thus controlling entry into the real estate business. The local boards naturally serve effectively as political instrumentalities as well. Leaving nothing to chance, however, the Washington Committee asks the local boards to develop "contact lists" designating local realtors who are "close" to the district's congressman or senator, and who can therefore be rolled into action when the Washington staff gives the word. "Congressmen are more concerned about what prominent realtors back home are thinking than what we tell them," NAREB lobbyist Williamson conceded, "so we spend a lot of time keeping the local network humming."[124]

To maintain this entire apparatus in smooth operating order, NAREB also lubricates it liberally with campaign contributions. The Real Estate Political Education Committee operating out of Chicago does the centralized campaign-financing work, but normally dispenses contributions through the local boards, where they are harder to trace.[125] The Washington staff restricts its own financial activity to the purchase of tickets for "testimonials" on behalf of members of Congress. "I prefer to be invited to the testimonials," explains lobbyist Williamson. "That means they're asking us for money. It's too embarrassing the other way." Apparently the real estate lobbyists are a congenial group, for they had the privilege of attending thirty to thirty-five testimonials during the first six months of 1972 alone, purchasing four or five tickets to each at $100 apiece.

Along with the builders, therefore, the real estate brokers constitute a sizable barrier that housing and urban development legislation must clear on its way to passage. For the most part, NAREB's role has been conservative, reflecting the free-enterprise orthodoxy that dominates the ideological outlook of its membership.* For example, NAREB has formed the backbone of the special-interest opposition to public housing and during the

---

* As lobbyist Williamson explained, "I have to tell our membership over and over that we have a managed economy and always will."[126]

1960s exacted its pound of flesh in housing legislation by insisting on rigid and frequently punitive eligibility requirements in low-income housing programs to guard against too heavy a reliance on public intervention to house the poor. For these same reasons, NAREB has typically had more influence in the House than in the Senate, because of the traditionally greater dominance in the House of a small-town conservative outlook akin to that of the leaders of NAREB. That many of the liberal housing reform innovations of the 1960s failed to progress beyond the experimental stage can thus be attributed in substantial measure to the influence of NAREB in the politics of housing, and particularly to the success of this organization in mobilizing preexisting ideological hostility to social-welfare legislation.

The Bureaucrats

While for the builders, the brokers, and even the bankers, concern about federal housing policy is but one among a number of crucial concerns, for at least one set of major actors in the drama it is the whole show. The sixteen thousand bureaucrats in the Department of Housing and Urban Development and the eight thousand officials in local housing and redevelopment agencies across the nation who administer the public housing and urban renewal programs are full-time participants in the politics of federal housing policy. Indeed, their ability to concentrate on the details of federal housing policy exceeds that of any of the other actors, including Congress, with the result that they are in a position to maintain the initiative in the whole policy-making process.

According to popular mythology, to be sure, ours is a government of separation of powers, of neatly demarcated legislative, executive, and judicial institutions and functions. But in the housing sphere at least, something closer to a parliamentary system is at work, with the legislative institutions responding to the executive ones up and down the line. "HUD has a hammerhold on the legislative process in housing," one Senate staffer observed.[127] HUD writes virtually all the housing legislation, leads off the testimony, comments on all amendments, attends all the committee executive sessions, and then helps the staff write up the "committee's" report. During congressional consideration of the 1972 Housing Act, for example, HUD assistant general counsel Ray James, who drafted the book-length legislative package HUD presented to Congress, became a kind of super staff aide to the Banking committees, taking up quarters in the anteroom outside the committee chambers during executive sessions to give technical advice, and then sitting down with the staff after the sessions to draft legislative language. According to the Senate Housing Subcommittee's minority counsel, "Ray James wrote most of the committee report on the 1972 Housing Act, particularly the section explaining Title I, which consolidated and reorganized the whole package of federal housing policies. The staff then reviewed what Ray wrote."[128] That it might be inappropriate for the agency charged by Congress with administering a law to draft not only the law itself but even the report specifying how *Congress* intended to have the law implemented apparently bothered nobody. But, then, why should it, since it has been standard procedure for years? Indeed, as long-time HHFA, and later HUD, associate legislative counsel Hilbert Fefferman conceded, "There have been years when the committees' reports have been written from start to finish by Ashley Foard [HUD's general counsel until 1972] and myself."[129] Explained Fefferman:

> There are really not a whole lot of people working on these bills. All the hundreds of pages of bills, reports, committee hearings, position papers, and committee agendas are actually produced by about fifteen people who have been in this business for years. When we're all sitting around the table at midnight working out the details of a bill or report language, you hardly know who's from Congress and who's from HUD. We may not have a parliamentary system in formal terms, but we do informally.[130]

This does not mean that Congress plays no autonomous role in formulating housing policy, of course, only that its role has traditionally been limited to making mid-course corrections rather than setting the basic trajectory.

The reasons for this are not hard to discern. In the first place, HUD controls a reservoir of technical talent and program information that far exceeds the meager resources available to the House and Senate Banking committees. The committees can occasionally raise searching questions, but they usually have little way to verify the responses and are easily overwhelmed by HUD technical objections to legislative proposals. Most legislative proposals consequently originate with the relevant HUD program officers, or are at least cleared by them if proposed by others. The very nature of housing law, with its excessive detail and incredible complexity, contributes to this, for it puts a premium on the technical expertise HUD so clearly monopolizes. Few members even read the housing laws, so that unless the staff catches something, or an interest group raises an objection, HUD pretty much has its way. A HUD staff document detailing internal department procedures for legislation portrays the resulting pattern of committee dependence all too clearly:

> The Department provides the Congressional committees with all possible technical assistance in connection with legislation. During periods of active Congressional consideration of housing and urban development legislation, staff members of the committees and subcommittees are in almost daily contact with the Department's lawyers, requesting drafts of bills or of perfecting amendments, explanatory materials, and background data. The Department's lawyers also often *prepare draft language for inclusion in subcommittee and committee reports.* Much of this work represents drafting of legislation and related materials that reflect the position of the Department and the Administration.[131]

As one Senate Banking Committee staff member said, "HUD has a tremendous research capability. The key is to know the questions to ask and to review HUD work carefully and critically, but we rarely have the time or the inclination to do that."[132]

Supplementing HUD's clear technical superiority is an elaborate Congressional Relations operation designed to win friends for the agency on the Hill. The Congressional Relations people are "HUD's lobbyists," assistant general counsel Ray James noted. They handle all congressional inquiries directed to HUD and, in return, seek to persuade legislators to support HUD legislation and appropriations. For members of the Banking committees, particularly those on the House side, the resulting relationships with HUD can be quite important, for the HUD programs are the only real "gravy" programs these committees have. Access to water and sewer grants, urban renewal funding and subsequent administrative followup, open-space program approvals, and the chance to get a piece of the action on 235 and 236 housing all constitute important rewards that an urban congressman can hope to secure by virtue of his position on the committees overseeing the operations of HUD. To make political capital out of their committee assignments, therefore, Banking committee members must obligate themselves to the HUD Congressional Relations people. And, according to Jack Woolley, director of HUD's Congressional Relations operation, most Banking committee members take the bait, since the Congressional Relations Division averages four times as much traffic from Banking Committee members as from other legislators.[133] Not surprisingly, HUD treats these requests with tender loving care. For example, Woolley noted, "HUD has done everything it is capable of doing for Lud Ashley," one of the House Banking Committee's more prominent housing specialists.[134] The same is true for John Sparkman, who channels a heavy load of "case work" to HUD through Housing Subcommittee staff director Carl A. S. Coan, Sr. "Of course, I don't mind at all, that's what I'm here for," Woolley adds cagily.

Although members of HUD's General Counsel's Office, which is charged with getting HUD's legislative package through Congress, may despair that "we don't bribe the legislators enough,"[135] it seems clear that HUD activity of this sort significantly affects

congressional decision-making on housing policy, albeit sometimes in unexpected ways. According to Representative William
Moorhead of Pennsylvania, for example, member interest in securing benefits from HUD sometimes delays handling of HUD
legislation. "One reason for slow going on housing legislation,"
Moorhead noted, "is that committee members not on the Housing
Subcommittee have no clout with HUD on behalf of their constituents if they merely rubber stamp the subcommittee bill."[136]

A third important source of HUD influence flows from the
personnel exchanges that bind the agency to Congress and the
lobbies. HUD or its predecessor agency, HHFA, has provided the
formative socialization experience for virtually every major actor
in the politics of federal housing. The staff directors of both the
Senate Banking Committee and its Housing Subcommittee, for
example, are progeny of HHFA whom Sparkman brought over to
Congress in the middle-to-late 1950s. Three of the five staff members of the Housing Subcommittee in the House also came from
HUD. Nor is this extraordinary network of alumni restricted to
congressional committee staffs; the agency has also trained many
of the key lobbyists and prominent real estate lawyers active in
the field. "HUD's General Counsel's Office is just like the Internal
Revenue Service," one Home Builder lobbyist told us. "The law
firms and lobbies rely on it to train their personnel. After all, why
should they pay for the training when the government can do
it?"[137] The NAHB, as we have seen, has been an especially
active recruiter of HUD trainees. Virtually the entire Home
Builder lobbyist team consists of former HUD employees, some
—like Wood and Coan—drawn from the top echelons. Philip
Brownstein, who represented the FHA before the Banking committees in his role as FHA commissioner until 1968, now represents the Council of Housing Producers before the same committees. Even the "public-interest" lobbies draw on former HHFA
personnel. For example, Nathaniel Keith, chairman of the National Housing Conference, a pro-public-housing coalition of
labor and liberal groups created in the late 1930s, worked for

FHA between 1940 and 1953, long enough to write a substantial portion of the congressional committee reports on the landmark 1949 Housing Act. Since then he has earned his living as a consultant to cities on HUD programs, while lobbying Congress as chairman of the Housing Conference on these same programs.[138]

In the politics of housing, in other words, all roads lead back to HUD. To be sure, this does not automatically give HUD a prior claim on its alumni's allegiance, but it does suggest a frightening uniformity in outlook born of common experience. More than that, it highlights the symbiotic relationship that binds the actors in the housing drama to HUD and stifles criticism of the agency or its programs. The plain fact is that the whole circle of decision-makers—in HUD, on the committee staffs, and in the lobbies—share a heavy stake in the perpetuation of the existing HUD programs in which they have made such heavy investments of time and energy. "Our only function is to deal with FHA for both our members and the committees," a Home Builders lobbyist explained. "We've spent a long time learning the ropes in these programs and we're not about to throw that away. Without FHA, we're out of a job."[139] At the very least, the common background in HUD or HHFA shared by so extraordinary a number of the key housing policy decision-makers produces a kind of institutionalized myopia that buffers the bureaucracy from criticism and restricts reform to marginal tinkering. Out of it all, the agency retains friends and gains power.

Were the bureaucracy merely a neutral instrument unquestioningly implementing policies devised in accordance with the public's best interests, this HUD influence would be a matter of less serious concern. But the bureaucrats in HUD, like those elsewhere, habitually view the public's interests through glasses heavily colored by considerations of agency survival and growth. Not How can the public best be served? but How can the public best be served in a way that enhances the agency? comes to be the question that dominates all others. And since agency survival and growth is ensured to the extent that support can be found from powerful outside friends, the tendency is to transform the bureaucracy into an agent of the powerful interest groups in the field.

This common pattern has been exaggerated in the case of HUD because HUD has historically been not one agency but several, each with its own programs, its own favored clients, and its own view about how to save the cities. HUD grew, after all, out of the old Housing and Home Finance Agency, which included the Federal Housing Administration, the Urban Renewal Administration, the Public Housing Administration, and several other indigestible parts—each of which nurtured a set of supportive relationships with outside client groups and lobbied against the others for a larger share of whatever urban or housing-related monies Congress might appropriate. FHA has traditionally enjoyed a clear advantage in this intrabureaucratic jockeying for position thanks to the firm foundation of support it has nurtured with the NAHB and the mortgage lenders, both of whom, as we have seen, are firmly plugged in to the congressional power structures on the Banking committees. Both the public housing and urban renewal branches of HUD, and of HHFA before it, have had to look farther afield for allies, and have had to contend in addition with an ideological climate in the Congress that is generally hostile to their activities. To cope with this situation, they have developed supporting relationships with a coalition of self-styled public-interest groups such as architects and planners, with the northern urban wing of the Democratic Party, and with semipublic professional organizations.

At the center of this coalition is the National Association of Housing and Redevelopment Officials (NAHRO), the association representing the employees of local public housing and urban renewal agencies, as well as others professionally involved in the work of urban redevelopment.* NAHRO got its start in the 1930s as the representative of local groups involved in slum-

---

* According to its own description, the NAHRO membership "comprises the official and unofficial leadership in both public and private sectors for programs of community development and housing action."[140]

improvement programs and as an advocate of federal involvement in housing the urban poor. With the adoption and expansion of federal public housing and urban renewal activities that relied on local public agency professionals for their implementation, the organization gained a solid membership base and important new strength, emerging in the 1960s as "the professional home for policy-makers, administrators, program professionals, and technicians who deal daily with the planning, development, and management of housing for low- and moderate-income families and with the initiation and accomplishment of community development programs through urban renewal, rehabilitation, housing code enforcement, and 'new town' development."[141] In addition to its professional service activities, NAHRO maintains an elaborate research capacity that draws on the day-to-day experience of its membership and brings it to bear on the formulation of housing and urban development policy at both the congressional and administrative levels through a system of policy councils and legislative liaison agents. As NAHRO staff director Mary Nenno explained, "Our chief asset is our knowledge and expertise."[142] NAHRO has managed, in the process, to establish itself as the research arm of the urban liberal representatives in Congress, providing the detailed staff work that the lack of time and paucity of committee staff make it impossible to do within Congress. For example, it was largely NAHRO's handiwork that found legislative expression in the Section 117 Concentrated Code Enforcement Program and the Section 312 Direct Rehabilitation Loan Program incorporated in the housing acts of 1964 and 1965. NAHRO also claims credit for the formulation of a simplified urban renewal procedure incorporated in the 1968 Housing Act, and for fifteen additional "technical amendments" adopted in the 1969 and 1970 housing acts. Most important, as we shall see, it was NAHRO that formulated the Democratic alternative to the Nixon administration's community development revenue sharing package, which became a part of the 1972 housing bill and which was ultimately enacted in the 1974 Housing and Community Development Act.

While NAHRO has provided an important counterweight to the private lobbies, however, it has not been a wholly disinterested one. Like the private lobbies, NAHRO has strong institutional stakes in particular approaches to the solution of housing and community development problems. For example, it is wedded institutionally to the public housing program and to the principle that housing for the poor should be channeled through local public housing agencies. When the rent supplement program was proposed in 1965, therefore, NAHRO vigorously opposed it, since it was designed to work through private landlords and thus totally bypass the agencies in which NAHRO's members work. By the same token, NAHRO has a strong stake in the continuation of urban renewal, and particularly in routing urban renewal funds through local urban renewal agencies rather than directly through city hall. Although the organization has been surprisingly willing to explore different alternatives, there is no denying, as staff director Nenno conceded, that such alternatives create some "tension" within the organization.[143] To the extent that legislators rely solely on NAHRO to formulate program ideas different from those served up by the private lobbies, therefore, they still remain firmly inside the existing, organizationally conditioned mix of approaches inherited from the past.

The public housing and urban renewal forces within HUD also receive support from the nation's mayors, who are organized nationally in the U.S. Conference of Mayors (representing the larger cities) and the National League of Cities (representing the moderate-sized and smaller cities). Historically, the mayors have enjoyed substantial influence within the presidential (northern, urban) wing of the Democratic Party,[144] which they have used to sustain and expand public housing and urban renewal activities against the entrenched congressional and special-interest opposition. During the 1960s, the League and Conference became increasingly effective on the legislative side, successfully translating increased press attention to urban ills into a political resource for influencing publicity-conscious legislators by staging elaborate "media events" in congressional committee chambers that allowed obscure congressmen to bask in the reflected light of such stellar performers as Mayor John Lindsay of New York City.

One measure of the effectiveness of these efforts was the mayors' success in securing congressional approval for the creation of the Department of Housing and Urban Development in 1965. Compared to the Housing and Home Finance Agency which it replaced, HUD offered a stronger institutional voice for the cities at the highest levels of the federal government. More importantly, it promised to increase the role of the mayors and their liberal-labor allies in the formulation of federal urban policy by subjecting the traditionally dominant FHA bureaucracy within HHFA to strong, department-wide policy leadership exercised through the secretary's office.

The creation of HUD did not solve the problem of internal administrative fragmentation within HUD, however, for the mayors were forced to come to terms with the other constituents of the agency in order to secure congressional support for the reorganization. And all of these conditioned their support on protection of the institutional integrity and autonomy of their particular satrapies within the bureaucracy. Thus, the savings and loan industry, as we have seen, resisted efforts to reincorporate the Federal Home Loan Bank Board into the HUD orbit. By the same token, the NAHB insisted that FHA remain intact and that one of the HUD assistant secretaries be designated FHA commissioner. When Congress authorized the new 235 and 236 housing subsidy programs in 1968, moreover, the NAHB saw to it that FHA got the action, despite the feelings of many that the agency was ill-suited to administer an avowedly social welfare program.

Thus when Romney took command of HUD in 1969, he found an agency still splintered internally, and with its separate parts firmly entrenched with outside lobbies and their friends in Congress. As Romney later described it, "In 1969, the Department was a top-heavy, uncoordinated, bureaucratic conglomerate, with each part nearly autonomous, replete with confusing red tape, lengthy processing, and inefficiency."[145] "You can call it what you will," Romney told the members of the House Appropriations Committee in 1970. "It was nothing but a series of competing bureaucracies or fiefdoms."[146]

While moving to streamline the agency, moreover, Romney accentuated some of the long-standing internal agency strains, most notably significantly tipping the balance in the agency toward the home-builder–FHA complex. Taking his cue from the 1968 Housing Act's stress on the need for more new housing, particularly for low- and moderate-income families, Romney undertook to recast HUD in the image of an automobile assembly line geared to maximum production. To the glee of the home builders, Romney announced to a congressional appropriations subcommittee soon after he took office, "As I see it, the role of the Department of Housing and Urban Development emerges about like this: First, we're charged with stimulating housing production. . . ."[147] The selection of former NAHB president Eugene Gulledge for the new post of FHA commissioner–assistant secretary for housing production symbolized this probuilder production focus well. Explained Romney, "Our national goal is housing production, so—quite naturally—we chose a man who knows every angle of the business of producing housing."[148]

The peculiar shape and character of federal housing and urban development policy is thus a reflection of the highly structured web of special-interest and executive-branch pressures at work on Congress in this sphere. Theoretically, of course, the competition among these special interests could lead to sound policy overall. But this would require a level of leadership, member independence, and staff capacity that is nowhere in evidence. What happens instead is that the Banking committees and their Housing subcommittees traditionally serve as mere clearinghouses for special-interest proposals, which they lump together in unwieldy, omnibus legislative packages and sell to the nation as urban "policy."

The absence of broad-based citizen support for more comprehensive, equitable, and far-sighted policy gives the committees a ready defense for this easy identification of the public interest with the interests of the key housing lobby groups. That federal housing policies are inefficient, inequitable, and special-interest-oriented is, according to this view, small price to pay for the fact that they exist at all. Moreover, the lobby groups have successfully rationalized their special-interest proposals by shrouding them in lofty social-welfare terms that capitalize on the "motherhood" character of housing. To hear the National Association of Home Builders tell it, for example, the pursuit of profit is a secondary goal compared to the organization's dedication to the "task of satisfying a fundamental need of our society—the task of providing, through the American system of free enterprise in cooperation with constructive governmental policies and attitudes, a good home in a good environment for every American family."[149] James V. Allen, chairman of the Mortgage Finance Committee of the Home Manufacturers Association, was even more lyrical as he movingly wrapped the warm blanket of family life around the entire construction industry during testimony before the House Banking Committee in 1970. "Places we live in are close to the land," Allen told the enraptured congressmen:

> Life inside these dwellings is intimate and filled with all the qualities of human existence—sometimes good, sometimes bad. *The hundreds of thousands of people who make up the housing industry take on these characteristics.* All of us feel a closeness to the land, and an intimacy with family life that has always been a part of civilization.[150]

As one House Banking Committee staff member put it:

> The lobby groups do not think of themselves as serving narrow private interests, of course. The builders in particular

think of themselves as doing God's work. And liberal legislators have been content to vote for any housing legislation
on the grounds that it was a liberal program that earned
them good marks with the ADA.[151]

The result, however, is a "hear-no-evil, see-no-evil" atmosphere
that stifles criticism and solidifies the status quo.

THE OVERSIGHT OVERSIGHT

Perhaps no better evidence of the pernicious consequences of this
atmosphere is available than the dismal performance of the Housing subcommittees in the area of oversight. The subcommittees
were created in the early 1950s primarily to investigate a growing
scandal in one of FHA's housing programs.[152] Since then, continued funding has customarily been justified in terms of the
subcommittees' role as investigators and overseers of federal
housing and urban development programs. For example, in his
request for Housing Subcommittee funds for the second session of
the Ninety-first Congress, Senator Sparkman asserted that "members of the Banking and Currency Committee are very much
cognizant of their responsibilities in the area of oversight and in
order to perform these functions properly, the funds requested by
this resolution are necessary."[153] Despite this rhetoric, however,
the subcommittees have almost totally ignored the oversight function, unless we count as oversight the handling of constituent
complaints and the hit-or-miss questioning of administration officials during the periodic hearings on administration legislative
packages.

This failing has been particularly marked on the Senate side.
To be sure, the Senate's Housing Subcommittee publishes an annual *Progress Report on Federal Housing Programs*, but this report is more in the nature of a promotional booklet describing the
various HUD programs and detailing the level of activity in each
during the preceding year than it is an analysis of what the programs are accomplishing. So far as the latter is concerned, the

Senate committee has completely avoided the question. During the past ten years at least, while enacting program after program in rapid succession, the Senate Housing Subcommittee has not paused to evaluate, in any systematic fashion, what they all add up to.

Until late in 1970, the same criticism applied to the Housing Subcommittee on the House side. In that year the subcommittee divided itself into three study panels of five members each to examine some of the persistent, underlying issues in the housing and urban development field and to assess the way existing programs were affecting them. Although the panel format provided a novel opportunity to step back from the rush of legislative business and take a broader look at developing urban problems (see page 272), as an oversight mechanism the panels had some serious drawbacks. In the first place, they completely avoided the subject of housing finance and mortgage credit, on the ground that the passage of the Emergency Home Finance Act of 1970 and the lack of time made this discussion unnecessary.[154] The most fundamental issue in the whole housing scene was thus not treated. In the second place, there was no systematic, analytical core to the panel undertaking, no effort to formulate a solid framework for a serious evaluation of what federal programs were doing. The schedule alone makes this clear. The panels were organized in October and expert papers scheduled for delivery by early 1971. With only a couple of months to do their work, the experts had no chance to conduct new research or undertake even partial program evaluations. Even within these constraints, the subcommittee conspicuously avoided inviting experts with radical perspectives on the nation's housing problems, so that the alternatives presented were themselves rather narrowly defined. While a refreshing and thoroughly laudable departure from previous routines and an excellent antidote for total reliance on industry perspectives, the panels did not provide the opportunity for the thorough evaluation and oversight effort that the subcommittee itself acknowledged was necessary.

These oversight weaknesses in both House and Senate might have gone unnoticed, as they had in the past, were it not for a serious scandal in federal low-income housing programs that surfaced during the latter part of the Ninety-first Congress and continued into the Ninety-second. Throughout the 1960s, as we have seen, FHA was subjected to a host of legislative and administrative mandates designed to alter its long-standing preoccupation with suburban, middle-class housing and focus its attention on the housing problems of the central-city poor. In 1961, for example, Congress converted the Section 221(d) (2) program, under which existing FHA "economic soundness" standards were waived and persons displaced by urban renewal could get FHA guaranteed loans with down payments of only $200, into a program available to low-income families outside urban renewal areas as well. This was followed in 1966 by a blanket waiver of the "economic soundness" doctrine for housing in riot areas, so long as the housing could be judged an "acceptable risk" (Section 302, Demonstration Cities and Metropolitan Development Act of 1966). In 1967, FHA commissioner Philip Brownstein called on FHA local offices to take advantage of this liberalization, and to stop rejecting projects "simply because it involves poor people, or because it is in a portion of the city you have been accustomed to rejecting or redlining for old-fashioned, arbitrary reasons."[155] Then, in 1968, Congress vastly expanded FHA's role as a provider of housing for low- and moderate-income persons by adopting the 235 and 236 interest-subsidy programs and by providing an even more general waiver of the strict "economic soundness" doctrine, this time for all low-income housing, whether in riot areas or not (Section 237, Housing and Urban Development Act of 1968). These provisions became the cornerstone of the substantial effort launched by newly installed HUD secretary Romney to stimulate greater housing construction, particularly as the administration's anti-inflation tight-money policy dried up conventional mortgage capital in 1969 and left the subsidy programs as one of the few remaining sources of housing financing.

Faced with these clear policy signals from on high, local FHA offices waded boldly into the low-income housing markets across the country. The problem, however, was that they persisted in adhering to standard operating procedures that took no account of the special needs of their new clients. The result, in city after city, was that they became central actors—sometimes consciously —in a massive con game worked on the central-city poor. With FHA in the market, local real estate speculators began buying up central-city slum properties, making cosmetic repairs, securing inflated FHA appraisals that would justify mortgages two and three times what the properties were worth, and then unloading the property to the unsuspecting poor, who were offered their own home for a down payment as low as $200 (the speculator sometimes even paid the down payment) and monthly mortgage payments frequently below the cost of rents in the area. Because FHA was guaranteeing the loan, mortgage bankers were willing to wink at the inflated assessments. The speculators were thus able to double and triple their original investments and the banks to benefit from higher mortgage amounts without risk of loss. But as the cosmetic repairs began peeling away, the new low-income homeowners found that their newly purchased homes were unlivable hovels, with patched-over holes in the floors and inoperative plumbing. As repair bills mounted, the poor had little choice but to abandon their houses. The result, by the late 1960s and early 1970s, was to leave the Department of Housing and Urban Development in possession of immense quantities of slum housing in city after city. In Philadelphia between January 1968 and June 1971, for example, FHA foreclosed on 2,848 homes, a loss of $40 million in one city.[156] The situation in Detroit was even more severe: 7,574 units representing over $100 million in losses in FHA's default inventory by April 1, 1972.[157] By 1972, Secretary Romney was acknowledging that HUD might own 240,000 defaulted slum houses within the next few years, and other estimates ranged as high as 390,000—enough to house over a million people.[158] In addition to these problems with the ownership programs, other difficulties were being encountered in the low-income rental project programs (the 221[d][3] and 236 programs). For one thing, project sponsors were making a practice of "low-balling," that is, incorporating unrealistically low estimates of project costs and projected rentals in project prospectuses in order to secure FHA approval, and then coming back after the projects were completed requesting FHA approval of higher rents.[159] In addition, there was mounting evidence that project sponsors, originally attracted to the low-income rental projects by the unusually lucrative tax dodge they provided, were failing to build livable structures capable of surviving beyond the eight to ten years during which the maximum tax benefits would be derived. According to *New York Times* correspondent John Herbers, who made a nationwide tour of 236 projects in 1971, "They are building junk."[160] At any rate, by March 31, 1971, 26 percent of all 236 mortgages were already in default.[161]

These developments did not go unnoticed in Congress. Patman's staff on the House Banking Committee picked up hints of the emerging scandal from newspaper stories and citizen complaints as early as the summer of 1970 and secured permission from Patman to look further into the matter. By the end of the summer, a collection of the complaints received by the committee, as well as a brief staff study of administrative problems with the 235 program in Washington, were transmitted to HUD for response. When this response proved unsatisfactory, Patman secured full-committee approval for a wider staff study of the 235 program alone, a study that was completed in December and issued on January 6, 1971.[162] That same day, Secretary Romney issued a complete denial, branding the report "inaccurate, misleading, and very incomplete." Eight days later, however, Romney was forced to concede that only the latter of these charges still held, as he acknowledged to the press that "it is apparent that abuses are more prevalent than had previously been evident."[163]

Despite what was now acknowledged to be a major scandal brewing in the programs they were responsible for overseeing, however, the Housing subcommittees in both House and Senate took no action. Aside from securing some pious promises from Romney that "something was being done" to tighten program administration, the subcommittees preferred to turn the other cheek. Accordingly, they launched no investigations, conducted no special oversight hearings, undertook no staff studies. In fact, were it not for Representative John S. Monagan (D., Conn.), chairman of the Legal and Monetary Affairs Subcommittee of the House Government Operations Committee, and Senator Philip Hart (D., Mich.), chairman of the Monopoly and Antitrust Sub-committee of the Senate Judiciary Committee—both of whom launched investigations in 1971—there is reason to believe that the full story of the low-income housing scandals might have remained as well concealed as the Watergate story almost was, even though the full story turned out to be far worse than even Romney conceded in 1971.[164]

Why did the Housing subcommittees neglect to follow up the lead Patman uncovered? Why did they pursue the coverup route instead of pursuing the oversight responsibilities they claimed in their own funding requests? Subcommittee chairmen Sparkman and Barrett claimed lack of time was the reason, and committee staffers concurred.[165] "I used to have more time for oversight before," Senate Housing Subcommittee staff director Coan explained, "but I don't anymore."[166] "There's no time to conduct oversight when there's a staff of only three guys and we have to work year-round on massive housing bills," agreed Housing Sub-committee staff counsel George Gross on the House side.[167]

While this argument clearly has substantial merit, particularly in view of the fact that the Housing Subcommittee in the House was in the middle of its study panel deliberations and both sub-committees had just received massive administration housing bills to consider when the scandal stories broke, it is also only part of the story. After all, the Senate subcommittee did find time in 1971 to undertake a special study of international housing pro-grams sponsored by federal agencies and to arrange two sets of hearings supportive of HUD and its clients in their struggle with the Office of Management and Budget over budget levels and impoundments.¹⁶⁸ Moreover, the House subcommittee's panels, though billed as an evaluation of HUD effectiveness, conspicuously avoided any mention of the problems with the low-income programs.

Far more persuasive as an explanation of the oversight oversight is the "hear-no-evil" atmosphere growing out of the subcommittees' political stake in FHA's good name. Both chairman Sparkman and ranking minority member Tower in the Senate faced reelection campaigns in 1972 that could be hurt by disclosures of fraud and ineptitude in the programs they had jointly done so much to enact in 1968. And even liberals could find reason to pretend the scandals did not exist, on the ground that support for low-income housing subsidies was too tenuous to risk undue disclosure of program failures. Congressman Moorhead was candid on this point: "The reason the subcommittee refused to do oversight on these programs," he pointed out, "is that it was proposed by opponents of the programs."¹⁶⁹ Full-committee chairman Patman's efforts were thus not welcomed by his committee's own Housing Subcommittee. "Patman saw this as an opportunity to grab the limelight," complained one Housing Subcommittee staffer. "He's always been hostile to the 235 program." The fact that the low-income subsidy programs had become the darling of the home builders, thanks to their important contribution in sustaining housing construction during the 1969–1970 credit crunch, undoubtedly contributed to the subcommittees' behavior.*¹⁷⁰ With such strong industry support for the first major federal housing initiative in two decades with even a mild social-welfare orientation, most subcommittee members apparently felt it was better

* In an effort to defend the subsidy programs against their critics, the NAHB hired the Real Estate Research Corporation of Chicago to conduct a complete evaluation. In essence, this report concluded that the 235 and 236 subsidy programs were basically sound, and that any difficulties were the result of poor administration and hence could be remedied.

not to rock the boat than to carry out the subcommittees' legally mandated oversight functions.* Indeed, not until the Nixon administration budget cutters seized upon the scandals to justify a freeze on all subsidized housing expenditures in January of 1973 did the Senate's Housing Subcommittee open oversight hearings. But by this point the purpose of these oversight hearings, as Senator Sparkman explained it, was not to conduct another critical inquiry into program failures, but to accent the positive, to provide a forum where the "serious charges" leveled against these programs—including those leveled by the administration itself—could "be answered."[171]

This sensitivity to the perceived fragileness of the political balance underlying federal housing programs also helps to explain what happens in the initial passage of housing and urban development legislation. For it is this same defensiveness, this same sense of beleaguerment in the face of conservative opposition that continually induces liberals on the Banking committees to lean over backward to secure industry support for their housing and urban development measures, and that consequently gives these measures their peculiar shape. The effort to formulate a housing and urban development bill in the Ninety-second Congress reveals this clearly.

HOUSING AND URBAN POLICY IN THE NINETY-SECOND CONGRESS

The Ninety-second Congress turned out to be important in the history of federal housing policy not because of any legislation it produced, but because of the lesson it taught about the limits of congressional independence. At issue in this Congress were several immensely significant pieces of legislation, including a proposed consolidation and simplification of the entire corpus of

---

* One of the few known exceptions to this statement was Senator Adlai Stevenson III (D., Ill.), who pressed Sparkman to launch an inquiry into the subsidy programs early in the 92nd Congress.

accumulated law governing FHA subsidized and unsubsidized housing programs; the Nixon administration's proposal for replacing categorical grant programs for community development activities with a comprehensive program of "community development revenue sharing"; a streamlining of public housing law; a program of operating subsidies for urban mass transit; a new program of federal urban planning assistance; and a host of smaller measures covering everything from consumer protections in home buying to modifications in the rules governing the real estate lending powers of commercial banks and savings and loan associations. But despite lengthy hearings in both House and Senate, and markup sessions that, at least in the House, broke all previous records for length, none of these measures passed. They therefore remained on the agenda in January 1973 when the Ninety-third Congress convened and became the subject of another round of lengthy Housing Subcommittee and Banking Committee hearings and executive sessions that consumed much of 1973 and 1974 before culminating in the passage of the important Housing and Urban Development Act of 1974.

What happened to the Ninety-second Congress' housing legislation? Why, after so elaborate a process of committee consideration, did it ultimately fail? And what, if anything, does this experience suggest about the politics of housing in general, and about the ultimate shape that the 1974 Housing Act took in particular?

To answer these questions, we will focus particularly on the two most important pieces of housing legislation under scrutiny in the Ninety-second Congress: the housing consolidation and community development revenue sharing proposals. Even so, the account must necessarily be incomplete because of the massiveness and technical complexity of these proposals and the resulting impossibility of capturing, within the limited space available here, the full political dynamics that went into their formulation over the four years they were under active consideration. Nevertheless, it is possible to examine the basic contours of this political process and thus to explore the informative insights they provide into the politics of federal housing policy.*

Executive Initiative

As has traditionally been the case, the two major housing and urban development proposals considered in the Ninety-second Congress originated in the executive branch. Within this branch, however, the two proposals had quite different origins. The first, the proposal to consolidate the close to fifty separate authorities governing FHA's various subsidized and unsubsidized housing programs, was largely the work of newly installed HUD Secretary George Romney.[172] Romney, a former Michigan governor and automobile executive, came to HUD committed to transforming the agency into a more efficient promoter of housing construction. From this perspective, the existing mix of FHA housing programs, with their varying eligibility requirements, their diverse subsidy formulae, their different definitions of income, and their separate legislative bases, seemed an important obstacle in the way of maximum utilization of FHA programs. Accordingly, Romney instructed HUD's general counsel's office to prepare a revision of the basic National Housing Act that would simplify the FHA program structure and thus encourage greater use of FHA programs—both subsidized and unsubsidized—by private developers. "The first major goal of the legislation," Romney pointed out in unveiling the proposal in mid-1970, "is to improve the capacity of our housing programs to stimulate the production of a large volume of dwelling units."[173]

Although the lengthy bill that emerged from this revision completely reorganized FHA's programs, however, it barely altered the content of those programs. Rather, what the bill proposed was

---

* Although the political dynamics behind selected provisions of particular housing bills have been analyzed in the literature, there is not, to my knowledge, a single account of the full range of compromises involved in an *entire* bill. As a result, the true character of the politics of housing and urban policy has remained somewhat obscure. The account that follows seeks to remedy this long-standing deficiency, at least in part.

a regrouping of FHA's numerous single-purpose programs under four broad categories—subsidized, nonsubsidized, single-family, and multi-family[174]—and the application to each of a common set of definitions and regulations. For example, instead of setting statutory dollar limits on the maximum size of FHA mortgages allowed under each separate program, as was done in existing law, the new proposal would peg the maximum mortgage amount to the cost of producing a "prototype" unit of housing in each locale. Under the consolidation proposal, therefore, mortgages on all subsidized units would be required to be within 110 percent of the prototype cost in the area, while mortgages on nonsubsidized units could not exceed 200 percent of the prototype cost.[175] This scheme would thus introduce a new flexibility into the FHA system by allowing maximum mortgage limits to rise as housing prices rise and by adapting mortgage limits to the very significant regional variations in housing costs around the country. In the process, it promised to enable FHA to survive in the business its employees traditionally preferred: assisting home builders and mortgage lenders in providing homes for the mostly white, suburbanizing middle class.

In addition to standardizing maximum mortgage amounts, the bill also proposed a new system for determining eligibility under the housing subsidy programs. Under existing law, each program operated under a different set of eligibility requirements and defined "income" differently for purposes of computing eligibility. Public housing, for example, established income limits on the basis of the lowest rents at which unassisted housing was available in substantial supply in a community. The Section 221(d) (3) program, in contrast, geared its eligibility requirements to the local median income, but made fewer exemptions in defining income than did the public housing law. The Section 235 and 236 programs operated under two sets of eligibility criteria, one set at 135 percent of prevailing public housing limits and one geared to the 221(d) (3) limits in the area. However, the definitions of income under 235 and 236 were different in significant ways from those in these other programs.[176]*

The new bill proposed to replace this hodgepodge of separate limits with a single uniform one: participation in the subsidized programs would be open to all families earning less than the median income in their area, except that 80 percent of the participants would have to earn less than 80 percent of this figure. In calculating income, the bill proposed to consider all income, and thus to eliminate all the detailed exemptions written into the existing law for each separate program. Nevertheless, the use of median income—or even 80 percent of the median—as the eligibility limit for the subsidy programs meant that these programs would be available to moderate-income families as well as to the very poor, and that this would be true of *all* the subsidy programs. The great danger in this was that these programs could come to focus even more on the moderate-income families to the exclusion of the poor, since a greater volume of housing construction can be stimulated by distributing the available pool of funds among moderate-income families, who need less subsidy per unit of housing, than among poor families.

A third basic change proposed by the Romney consolidation bill was the establishment of a uniform system for calculating the subsidy amount available to each family participating in an FHA subsidy program. Here, too, existing law presented a jumble of arrangements: subsidization of all construction costs in public housing (which was not covered by the consolidation law), subsidization of up to all but 1 percent of the mortgage costs under the section 235 and 236 programs, subsidization of up to all but 3 percent of the mortgage costs under the 221(d)(3) program of below-market-interest-rate loans, and subsidization of the difference between market rents and 25 percent of family income in the

---

* Differences in the definitions of income for deciding eligibility included such issues as whether to count the earnings of minor children, whether to permit deductions for dependents, and whether to count food stamps.

rent supplement program. The proposed consolidation bill would replace these varied provisions with a single subsidy formula under which a family would pay *either* 20 percent of its first $3,500 of income plus 25 percent of any income in excess of $3,500, *or* what a home or apartment would cost if it had been purchased (or constructed) with a mortgage bearing only 1 percent interest, whichever is *higher*. As Romney recognized, however, this formula still would not make housing assistance available to families in the $3,500 to $5,000 income range, since the acceleration in housing costs meant that these families could not afford the housing cost based on the assumption of a 1 percent mortgage without paying far more than 25 percent of their income for housing.[177] Accordingly, separate provision was made in the consolidation bill for a "deeper subsidy" for some families, although sharp objections from the President's Office of Management and Budget limited these provisions.[178] In particular, the deep-subsidy provisions incorporated in the bill cleared by OMB would provide additional aid up to 60 percent of the monthly home-ownership costs for the subsidized home-ownership programs (primarily the old 235 program), and up to the full mortgage costs (instead of up to all but 1 percent) for the subsidized rental programs; but the amounts allocated for these deeper subsidies were restricted to 20 percent of the funds available to the home-ownership program and 36 percent of those available to the rental program.[179] In other words, the subsidy programs were to go primarily to the "deserving poor," those with incomes in excess of $5,000, leaving a considerably smaller share for the really poor. In this way the programs could produce the most new construction for the available money.

In addition to these three basic provisions, the consolidation bill also proposed a host of other changes designed to standardize cost-certification procedures, application requirements, premiums and fees, down-payment requirements, and numerous other matters. While leaving the basic substance of the existing programs intact, therefore, the consolidation bill proposed significant changes in the administrative arrangements surrounding them, in the level of assistance provided, and in the patterns of access.

While the housing consolidation proposal originated with HUD Secretary Romney and encountered objections in the President's Office of Management and Budget, the community development revenue sharing proposal traveled the opposite route within the executive branch, beginning with the President and OMB and encountering stiff opposition within the HUD bureaucracy. Announced by the President in a special message on urban development in March 1971, the community development revenue sharing package was part of Nixon's plan for dismantling the existing patchwork system of narrow-purpose grants-in-aid to states and local governments and moving toward a system of general grants to state and local governments (*"general* revenue sharing") supplemented by a series of additional grants in designated but broadly defined substantive areas such as health, education, and community development (*"special* revenue sharing"). By tying federal funds to designated policy areas, but without specifying the particular program activities to be funded within those areas, the administration argued, it could encourage more efficient use of federal money without completely surrendering the national government's priority-setting function. In addition, by eliminating complex application requirements and distributing funds according to an automatic formula, the administration spokesmen claimed that special revenue sharing would get federal funds to where they were most needed, rather than to where the skills of grantsmanship were most in evidence. Under the administration's community development plan, therefore, existing special purpose grant-in-aid programs for urban renewal, open-space land purchase, code-enforcement grants, rehabilitation loans and grants, neighborhood facilities, and Model Cities would be combined into a single pool of funds, 80 percent of which would be distributed automatically (i.e., without the need for a proposal) to units of general local government (i.e., city halls instead of urban renewal agencies) according to a "need" formula reflecting the population, poverty, amount of overcrowded housing, and extent of housing deficiencies in the area, and 20 percent of which would be available to the secretary of HUD for distribution to small communities and for allocation to communities that received more under the previous grant-in-aid system than they would under the new formula system of distribution (the so-called "hold harmless" provision).

From the point of view of the HUD bureaucracy and its client groups, particularly in the urban renewal area, several features of this plan were profoundly troubling. In the first place, by lumping urban renewal—the largest HUD community development activity—together with open space, water and sewer, and other suburban-oriented programs and leaving it to local officials to decide what use to make of the funds, revenue sharing raised the possibility of diverting to other uses a substantial share of the central-city-oriented urban renewal and slum clearance funds it had taken two decades of political struggle to generate. The community development program could thus become a massive water and sewer program that would divert funds from central-city uses and channel them into suburban uses instead. In the second place, by making funds available directly to city halls, the administration plan threatened to bypass the local renewal agencies with which the HUD bureaucracy had customarily dealt. In the third place, by distributing the funds according to an automatic formula with no requirement for detailed proposals or HUD review of the uses of the money, the plan promised to reduce significantly the role of the HUD bureaucracy and hence the size of the staff necessary. Finally, by allocating funds according to a strict "need" formula, revenue sharing promised to shift funds away from communities that had traditionally been active participants in urban renewal programs toward those that had neglected their community development problems and lacked the technical capabilities to deal with them. To be sure, the provision allowing the HUD secretary to use a portion of the 20 percent of all community development funds left in his discretionary fund for "hold-harmless" purposes promised some protection for the cities with the most extensive involvement in urban renewal activities, but only over the short term. Most of these cities would ultimately lose funds.

Although efforts were made in lengthy sessions with OMB officials to alter some of these features,[180] the OMB–White House view prevailed in most cases, and the HUD bureaucrats and their interest-group allies were forced to appeal their case to Congress.

In addition to these two rather substantial proposals for reorganizing HUD's housing and community development programs, the Ninety-second Congress had before it almost fifty other housing and urban development bills, covering such matters as urban mass transit, regulation of mortgage settlement costs, housing for the elderly, the creation of a National Institute of Building Sciences to develop national building-material standards, and numerous technical, special-interest amendments such as a request from the U.S. Savings and Loan League to liberalize the real estate lending powers of savings and loan banks. Although the housing consolidation and community development proposals dominated the session, therefore, these other provisions were available to help structure the incentives on behalf of passage of whatever bills the committees recommended.

The Housing subcommittees of the House and Senate Banking committees pursued two somewhat different courses in responding to these administration initiatives. In the Senate, the Housing Subcommittee proceeded according to what has become the traditional method, touching base, largely at the staff level, with the established poles of interest-group pressure and fashioning a series of workable compromises satisfactory to these groups and congenial to the ideological predispositions of the committee's diverse membership. In the House, the Housing Subcommittee struck out during the Ninety-second Congress on a significantly new route designed, so its sponsors claimed, to escape special-interest and executive dominance and reequip Congress to exert legislative initiative in this area. The history of the 1972 housing bill thus affords a rare opportunity to assess the virtues of two significantly different approaches to congressional policy-making on the same pieces of legislation. How did these approaches differ? And what were the results?

The Senate: The Politics of Accommodation

In the Senate, the handling of the 1972 housing bill resembled the handling of every major housing bill of the previous two decades. In practice, this meant that much of the burden of fashioning a response to the administration's initiatives fell to Carl A. S. Coan, Sr., the staff director of the Senate's Housing Subcommittee. Coan, a man in his early sixties, has been actively involved in the politics of housing and urban policy since 1957, when he left the old Public Housing Administration and joined the Senate Banking Committee staff as research director. As staff director since 1961, Coan has played a pivotal role on Sparkman's behalf in packaging the massive housing and urban development bills enacted into law with such regularity during the 1960s and early 1970s. Urbane, immensely knowledgeable, and low-keyed, Coan has generally provided the crucial link between the generally liberal, urban groups affected by federal housing and urban development policy and the generally conservative, rural senator who has chaired the Senate's Housing Subcommittee since its inception. As one Senate staffer observed, "Coan is in a difficult position working for Sparkman because he is more liberal than his boss." According to most accounts, however, he has handled this role with immense skill, coordinating action on the numerous housing and urban development measures submitted to Congress each session and cuing Sparkman to the range of opinion and the acceptable middle ground on each. "Carl has been in the field with Sparkman long enough to know how he thinks," explained one Senate Banking staffer. "He therefore anticipates Sparkman's reactions and adjusts proposals to fit them." The key to Coan's success has thus been his skill at clothing liberal proposals in conservative wrappers, at pursuing liberal goals through conservative means. In practice, this has been accomplished through an elaborate clearance process under which the subcommittee and its staff perform essentially as "brokers," taking administration proposals and running them past key outside support groups until satisfactory compromises have been worked out among the parties, usually at the staff level.

In supervising this activity, Coan operates with considerable autonomy. This is largely a function of the heavy outside demands on subcommittee members (including Sparkman) and partly a function of the traditionally autonomous position of the Housing Subcommittee within the Banking Committee. "We fight for autonomy all the time," Coan pointed out. Indeed, when Sparkman became full-committee chairman in 1967, Coan argued for retention of the subcommittee's autonomy in order to guarantee his own ability to operate freely, without having to check with full-committee staffers.[181]

In practice, however, Coan's autonomy is rather narrowly confined. The sheer bulk of the workload exercises a powerful constraint, making it all but impossible to do anything but just barely stay on top of the legislation under consideration and keep tabs on general developments in the field. The pattern of staff organization works in the same direction. Though nominally in charge of four staff professionals, Coan really has authority over only two because of Sparkman's practice of parceling out subcommittee staff slots to interested colleagues. As a result, Coan must negotiate, maneuver, and persuade in order to get his own staff to work on the projects he assigns. Finally, subcommittee autonomy is limited by the tightly structured network of interest groups and pressures that define the political context within which housing policy is made.

In the case of the 1972 Housing Act, these constraints, and the mode of subcommittee operation that reflects and contributes to them, managed to transform what might have been a rather basic restructuring of federal housing and urban programs into a far more limited—and, in some respects, backsliding—set of reforms. An examination of the handling of the two major housing and urban programs before the Banking Committee in the Ninety-second Congress should make this clear.

Housing Consolidation. The housing consolidation proposal (S. 3639) began its course through the Congress in March of 1970, during the second session of the Ninety-first Congress—a year earlier than the community development revenue sharing proposal. At the time, the Senate Banking Committee was hard at work on the emergency home finance bill and an urban mass transit bill. Therefore, although Secretary Romney made a special plea for action within six months, it was not until late July that hearings could begin on the consolidation measure.

What quickly became apparent in these hearings was that support for S. 3639, the administration bill, was considerably less than enthusiastic among the key housing lobby groups. In the first place, because the bill had essentially been written singlehandedly by HUD assistant general counsel Ray James without active consultation with the loybbists,[182] there was considerable confusion about what the bill actually contained. What is more, the heavy workload taxing the key actors on the subcommittee staff and in the lobby groups during the 1970 session made it exceedingly difficult for them to find out as thoroughly as they felt necessary. Not only had the urban mass transit and emergency home finance acts just been cleared, but proposals were also pending to launch a new program of assistance to developers of new towns, to mandate the formulation of a national urban growth policy, and to fund an emergency community facilities program. Under the circumstances, a bill that would totally rewrite the statutory guidelines for all existing FHA programs could not be pushed through quickly without great danger to all concerned.

The numerous "technical" imperfections that various groups began to discover with the bill only intensified this reluctance to act without time for detailed study. The mayors, for example, discovered that the simplified subsidy payment schedule outlined in the bill (20 percent of income up to $3,500 and 25 percent of that in excess of $3,500) would increase rents for a substantial number of persons now in the subsidy programs.[183] The home builders criticized the "prototype" cost feature presented in the bill because the prototypes that were to provide the basis for computing maximum mortgage amounts in both subsidized and unsubsidized housing programs, as well as in public housing, were to be only "of modest design but of a quality consistent with property and design standards acceptable in the area" (Title I, 3-b). The builders considered this too vague and pushed for specification of additional permissible cost items such as basic amenities and heavy-duty construction. In addition, the NAHB attacked the bill's failure to set a clear maximum on the amount of subsidy funds that could be diverted to *existing* housing and thus taken away from the task of stimulating construction. Such a provision had been placed in the original 1968 law, but left out of the administration bill. Finally, the NAHB questioned the use of the 80 percent of median income figure as the basic income limit for the subsidy programs, on the ground that this would leave many moderate-income families out of the new-home market.[184]

On all of these points the home builders had the support of NAHRO[185] and the unions.[186] They were vigorously opposed, however, by the realtors, who argued that the income limits in the administration bill were too high, and that subsidy benefits would consequently be diverted from the poor to middle-income families in a misguided effort to use the housing-subsidy program to support the home-building industry. Asked the realtors' representative rhetorically, "Is our national policy going to be to increase production or to house poor people?"[187]

Aside from the confusion about what was in the bill and the detailed substantive objections, there was also considerable skepticism about the timing of the proposed change. 1970 was a bad year for housing. With credit tight, housing starts were sharply down. But in this constricted market, the new subsidized-housing programs launched by the 1968 Housing Act were doing yeoman's service in keeping the home-building industry alive during the squeeze. Even the NAHB, whose membership stood to gain the most from a streamlining of FHA procedures, therefore expressed skepticism about changing horses in midstream. Explained the NAHB president, "The FHA programs, especially those for low- and moderate-income families, have been the mainstays of the production we have had. It is for this reason that our members look with some apprehension upon any proposal which would so completely rework the ground with which they are so familiar."[188]

Given these numerous objections, the Senate committee decided after the hearings to delay action on the consolidation measure until the Ninety-second Congress convened in January 1971. This meant that the Housing Subcommittee had a golden opportunity to undertake the thorough review of federal housing policy that most observers conceded was necessary, but that the administration bill hardly began. In a sense, the bill merely unlocked Pandora's box. It was now up to Congress to decide whether to lift the lid and deal forthrightly with the confusion that lay within. At least one witness during the hearings urged such an approach. AFL–CIO research director Nathaniel Goldfinger called the subcommittee's attention to the fact that "the bill has the appearance of action without the substance." According to Goldfinger, the key to solving the nation's housing problems was to alter the operation of the capital markets in order to introduce new sources of funds into the mortgage market. But, as Goldfinger charged, "instead of new programs and new money, we see only sophisticated financial gimmickry aimed at extracting higher interest rates from homeseekers."[189] It was therefore up to the Housing Subcommittee to seize the initiative.

What happened instead was that the Senate's Housing Subcommittee acted according to standard operating procedure. Neither chairman Sparkman nor ranking Republican Tower had much stomach for a thoroughgoing program reassessment, particularly since the main lobbies, except the realtors, were pleased with the existing system. During the latter part of 1971 and early 1972, therefore, Coan busied himself with the traditional chore of transmitting perfecting amendments between the lobbyists and HUD, as HUD undertook a revision of the original submission. "Most of the feedback from the private interests to the General Counsel's Office came via the committee staffs," recalled the prime author of the HUD bill.[190] In this process, the NAHB had a particular advantage, since its former president was the FHA commissioner, its chief congressional lobbyist was Coan's son, and its members had close ties to both Sparkman and Tower back home. When the administration resubmitted its bill in June 1971, therefore, it showed clear evidence of the home builders' influence. For example, the new proposal (S. 2049) raised the income limits on the subsidy programs from 80 percent of the median income to 100 percent, thus increasing the pool of moderate-income families eligible for assistance and increasing the number of homes that could be built with the existing subsidy funds. The revised bill also set an upper limit on the proportion of subsidy funds that could go for existing housing and directed the HUD secretary, in computing prototype costs, to take account of such factors as "the extra durability required by economical maintenance of assisted housing," the "provision of amenities," and "good design."

The only serious alternative to the administration bill that was considered by the subcommittee was the so-called Brooke-Mondale bill introduced late in the summer of 1971, after the hearings on the consolidation bill and close to fifty other measures (including the community development revenue sharing proposal) were over. The origins of this alternative bill are significant. When the housing consolidation bill first reached Congress, Coan managed to secure help in processing it from subcommittee staffer Alexander Hewes, a young attorney serving as Senator Edward Brooke's personal staff aide on the Housing Subcommittee. Brooke, the Senate's only black, was the subcommittee's most ardent champion of housing assistance for the poor and the author of the so-called Brooke Amendment of 1969, which forbade public housing authorities from charging tenants more than 25 percent of their income for rent. Brooke was thus the natural candidate to pick up the ball for the subcommittee in reviewing the administration's consolidation proposal. Consequently, Hewes soon found himself with the chore of analyzing the administration's massive bill and deciding what alternatives might be proposed to it.

As a novice to the field, Hewes naturally had to seek assistance from those in the know. He therefore solicited ideas from all of the major housing lobby groups and then, by his own account, "beat the bushes searching for new ideas."[191] What quickly became apparent, however, was an important truth about the politics of federal housing policy: there are really few groups that can deliver the legislative goods when it gets down to the wire.

In the case of the housing consolidation proposal, it was NAHRO that came through for Hewes, and it was thus NAHRO's position that came to be the only substantial alternative to the administration proposal that was considered. NAHRO had long ago learned how to make itself felt in the legislative process. "We don't do lobbying for votes," explained NAHRO staff director Mary Nenno, "but we know how receptive congressional committees and their staffs are to proposals that are well thought out and researched. They have no independent mechanism for getting information; they either have to rely on the administration or people like us."[192] Accordingly, NAHRO maintains a permanent system of study committees and "policy congresses" to generate legislative proposals for submission when the time is ripe. In 1970, with the Nixon administration consolidation proposal on the horizon, NAHRO had formed a study committee on housing consolidation, which was ready with a policy statement by late December 1970, when Hewes approached the group.[193] NAHRO was concerned that the public housing program, which was the bread and butter of its members, was fast becoming a dumping ground for the most disadvantaged segments of the population, while the private subsidy programs—particularly the Section 235 and 236 programs—were skimming off the relatively better-off among the poor. With the Brooke Amendment on the books and tenant incomes holding steady or declining while project costs were rising, many local housing authorities found themselves in serious financial straits, especially since the Nixon administration had impounded $75 million in operating-subsidy funds intended to help local agencies recoup some of the rent losses caused by the Brooke Amendment.

To cope with this crisis, NAHRO proposed to liberate the public housing program from some of the restrictions under which it labored and permit it to compete with the private subsidy programs in seeking a full range of income groups as tenants. This was to be achieved by merging into one comprehensive program not only the FHA programs, as was done in the administration bill, but the public housing program as well. Under the merged program, the same basic financing mechanisms would persist as before—i.e., interest subsidies under the FHA programs and tax-exempt bonds under public housing. But the "continued occupancy limit" in public housing, under which local housing agencies must evict tenants who earn more than the basic eligibility limit, would be rescinded, and both public housing agencies and sponsors of FHA-subsidized projects would be permitted to rent to anyone earning less than the median income at initial occupancy. In this way public housing agencies could increase their rental revenues. At the same time, the NAHRO proposal would require that at least 20 percent of the units in both public housing and subsidized FHA programs be reserved for the poor, so that the private projects, too, would be required to service the lower-income groups. However, extra "deep" subsidies would be made available to both public housing and FHA private sponsors to make up the income lost by renting to these lower-income families. Finally, the proposal called for public housing projects to pay local real estate taxes for the first time, and proposed a system of federal "incentive grants" to local governments to induce them to accept subsidized housing more readily.[194]

The NAHRO scheme thus went well beyond the administration proposal, yet it was clearly of the same genre. The basic program elements would remain the same: public housing built by local public agencies and interest subsidies. The major change would be to allow public housing to serve moderate-income groups for the first time and to require sponsors of FHA subsidized housing projects to serve a segment of the lower-income population in one-fifth of their units. In addition, the proposal called for federal operating subsidies to 236-type projects to enable them to accommodate these lower-income families without charging them more than 25 percent of their income in rent.

This was the only solid alternative Hewes uncovered in his brief research, and it was the one he proposed that Brooke endorse. Senator Walter Mondale, another Banking committee liberal, was getting a similar message through his own staff aide, Gary Stenson. Like Brooke, Mondale was a natural target for NAHRO. He had sponsored, with Charles Percy, the provision in the 1968 Housing Act that established the 235 and 236 programs. More importantly, Mondale's former legislative aide, John McGuire, was NAHRO's research director, responsible for formulating NAHRO policy positions and transmitting them to Congress. By early 1971 Hewes, Stenson, and McGuire were working as a team, refining NAHRO's policy goals and pressing them on the HUD drafters of the revised consolidation bill.[195] NAHRO had thus succeeded in "capturing" the two most likely exponents of basic reform in the housing subsidy system and mobilized them behind a set of reforms that left the prevailing mechanisms of federal housing policy essentially intact and that approached the problems of the poor from the perspective of the administrators. In the process, the opportunity that the administration proposal seemed to create for a thorough rethinking and debate on the whole pattern of federal housing policy was substantially lost.

But even the modest alterations proposed by NAHRO proved too much for OMB to accept. During the intra-administration deliberations that preceded introduction of the revised consolidation bill in June 1971, OMB sternly opposed any "deeper" subsidies in the assisted housing programs, even if this meant either that occupancy would effectively be limited to those with incomes over $6,000 or that tenants would have to pay more than 25 percent of their income for rent.[196] What is more, there was considerable skepticism in HUD about the wisdom of merging FHA with public housing, so that this portion of the NAHRO proposal was also omitted in the administration bill. The battle then shifted to the Housing Subcommittee.

Because of HUD opposition, NAHRO could count on no Republican support on the subcommittee, except for Brooke. On the Democratic side, Sparkman, too, was a question mark. He clearly preferred private subsidy schemes over public housing, and therefore viewed the merger of the two programs quite skeptically. The fact that the Brooke-Mondale bill was introduced late, after the hearings were nearly over, provided a ready excuse for Sparkman to dismiss it on the ground that the key lobby groups never got a chance to review it properly in regular hearings. The tardy submission also meant that the proposal would not have the benefit of visible public support and that it would be left to the technicians in closed executive sessions, precisely the arena where HUD operated best.

By the time the Senate Housing Subcommittee convened for executive sessions on February 3, 1972, the idea of completely merging the FHA and public housing subsidy programs was all but dead. So far as the housing consolidation bill was concerned, in fact, only one major issue remained to be settled between supporters of the Brooke-Mondale (NAHRO) bill and supporters of S. 2049, the administration bill. This was the critical question of how deep the subsidy should be on the 235 and 236 programs, and consequently what income group could be served by the programs without exacting an excessive share of family income.

Under S. 2049, at least 80 percent of all units in a multifamily project would pay a minimum rent computed to be at least sufficient to cover the cost of a 1 percent mortgage. For *up to* 20 percent of all units, however, HUD would be authorized to make additional assistance payments to reduce this minimum rent by 70 percent, i.e., down to 30 percent of the basic rent (Sec. 502[f][2]). Thus, for example, on a typical unit that would have a market rental of $229 per month, the minimum rent required for at least 80 percent of the units would be $132 per month. The special deeper subsidy provisions would reduce this to $40 per month for up to 20 percent of the units. But any family with an income below $2,000 could not afford to pay this sum without spending over 25 percent of its income for housing. In contrast, the Brooke-Mondale bill would *require* that *at least* 20 percent of the units in each subsidized project be reserved for those in need of a deeper subsidy, and set this subsidy at a rate sufficient to absorb not only full debt-service costs but also all operating costs except utilities.* Under this approach, therefore, families with incomes as low as $1,000 per year could afford to live in subsidized projects without having to pay more than 25 percent of their income for housing. In addition, the Brooke-Mondale bill proposed a program of operating subsidies to assist sponsors in meeting cost increases not under their control. The bill thus promised considerably higher subsidy expenditures for the very poor than did the administration bill, first, because it *required* that 20 percent of the units in each project be reserved for the poor instead of simply *allowing* it; and second, because it offered a larger subsidy for these families.

When OMB made it clear to Romney that the bill would be vetoed if it passed with this provision,[197] the heat was on to

---

* The Brooke-Mondale substitute also proposed a maximum subsidy covering the full interest and principal (instead of all but 1 percent) on the home-ownership program, set a maximum limit of 25 percent of income on rents in the rental programs, and proposed a system of operating subsidies to cover the difference between revenues and costs on rental projects.

eliminate it. With the home builders also opposed to it, Sparkman and staff director Coan followed suit and used their positions to structure the debate against the provision. The agenda prepared for the subcommittee's markup session, an agenda Coan allowed HUD's Ray James to write in large part, provides the best example of the subtlety with which this was done: it referred to the Brooke-Mondale deep-subsidy proposal as the "open-ended subsidy," a misleading term that was calculated to trigger conservative opposition.[198]

Despite the pressures, Brooke and Mondale proved persuasive in the executive sessions, thanks in substantial measure to the data their staff aides were able to feed them about existing experience under the 236 program. Almost all of this data, which demonstrated that only moderate-income families could afford subsidized housing and that the poor were being forced to pay well over 30 percent of their income for subsidized units, was generated by NAHRO researchers, typed on NAHRO typewriters, and run off on NAHRO mimeographs. Such is the independence of Congress when it seeks to escape, even minimally, executive-branch dominance.

Before Brooke and Mondale could cap their victory, however, Romney put the screws on Brooke one final time, making a special trip to Brooke's Capitol Hill office and appealing for a compromise to save the bill from likely presidential veto.[199] The result was the insertion of a provision giving the secretary of HUD the power to reduce the requirement that 20 percent of the units in each subsidized project be reserved for the very poor whenever necessary "to assure the economic viability of the project" (Sec. 502[f] [2] [A]). In addition, the committee report on the bill, written largely by HUD officials, set a tone quite hostile to the intent of the Brooke-Mondale bill. Explaining the significance of the revised act, the report laid primary stress on its contribution to making FHA programs "more efficient producers of a large volume of housing," a goal that cannot be achieved so readily when the subsidy monies are being used for the poor.[200]

Except for the operating-subsidy and deep-subsidy features, few items in the bill were actively debated, either in the executive sessions or on the Senate floor once the bill was introduced for debate on March 2, 1972. On the assurance of Chairman Spark-man that this was "a bill worked out through extensive hearings and . . . quite extensive consideration in executive sessions," the Senate cleared the entire bill, eighty to one, without even once debating seriously the merits of the current structure of federal housing aids. What ultimately emerged from the Senate in March 1972, therefore, was a housing consolidation bill almost identical to the one the administration had introduced a year earlier, and a set of programs virtually unchanged from what existed before. Whatever opportunity the consolidation proposal offered to take a comprehensive, analytical look at the whole array of federal hous-ing programs was thus all but completely lost on the Senate Hous-ing Subcommittee. Only Banking Committee conservative Bill Brock even raised the issue. Berating the committee for its failure to break out of the approaches of the past, Brock alone opposed the bill on the floor, saying, "I vote 'No' today not so much in disagreement with those of my colleagues who support this bill be-cause they see no present alternative, but in dismay with our inability to seek those alternatives."[201]

Community Development. If the Senate's Housing Subcommit-tee functioned largely as a broker between HUD and the special interests in the handling of the housing consolidation legislation, it institutionalized this role in the handling of the community development legislation. The Nixon administration's proposal for community development revenue sharing was built squarely on the emerging consensus among those involved in federal urban renewal and community development efforts about the need for consolidating the existing special-purpose grant-in-aid programs. Longstanding complaints about delays in processing applications, about the excessive premium placed on grantsmanship, and about the rigidities inevitably built into a system that earmarked funds for narrowly defined special purposes provided the basic impetus for the proposal. The proposal thus posed a serious challenge to the historic link between urban politicians and the Democratic Party by placing a Republican president squarely behind an idea with strong support among the nation's mayors. But the Nixon White House put a special Republican twist on this basic idea by proposing to distribute community development funds automatically in the future according to a simple formula, by eliminating the community-participation features developed over the years in the urban renewal program, and by downplaying the role of the urban renewal agencies traditionally involved in local community development efforts. The proposal thus threatened to undermine the role of the Congress in setting priorities for the expenditure of federal community development monies, and seemed likely to disrupt the existing network of agencies and actors immersed in the ongoing business of urban renewal in cities across the country.

As the first special revenue sharing package to reach Congress, the community development legislation thus represented an important test of the Democratic majority in Congress, and of the coalition of urban groups that has provided the basic support for federal urban programs since the 1930s. The task for these groups was to fashion an alternative proposal that would preserve the desirable streamlining features of the Nixon bill and accommodate the interests of the Congress and the urban lobby, but still stand a chance of securing needed presidential support.

The responsibility for managing this task in the Senate fell naturally to Carl Coan, but Coan relied extensively on the community development establishment outside Congress for help. Early in 1970, in fact, with the administration bill in the offing, Coan organized a small, private task force that met over lunch for a period of months to formulate an alternative community development proposal. Participating in these sessions were representatives of the key groups involved in the community development business: Robert Maffin of NAHRO; Albert Walsh, the administrator of New York City's Housing and Development Administration and a frequent NAHRO spokesman; David Garrison, lobbyist for the National League of Cities; John Evans of the AFL–CIO; David Stahl, deputy mayor of Chicago; Ralph Taylor and Howard Moskoff, both former HUD officials in the Johnson administration now working for real estate development firms; Hugh Mields, of the prestigious Washington consulting firm of Linton, Mields and Coston; and Henry Schechter and Norman Beckman of the Library of Congress.[202] This was, to be sure, hardly a representative group. What it did was to bring together the organizations that would ultimately play the largest role in lobbying any proposed community development legislation and allow them to write their own bill, so that unseemly conflicts could be avoided in the open glare of Senate testimony and debate.

Within this task force, moreover, the initiative ultimately went to those with the resources and the interest to do the necessary staff backup work. In practice, this meant that NAHRO carried the ball. As in the case of the housing consolidation bill, NAHRO established its own internal study committee on community development legislation in 1970 and began formulating a proposal different from the one then under discussion in the executive branch. Given its membership base in local renewal agencies, NAHRO opposed the idea of distributing community development funds to cities on the basis of population, poverty, and housing conditions instead of on the basis of past involvement in urban renewal and related community development activities. Although this opposition was justified in terms of the need to recognize "the importance of experience, expertise, and capacity to perform and absorb this money in an efficient manner,"[203] it also reflected a fear that a need formula would ultimately shift resources away from cities where NAHRO's members were concentrated. By the same token, NAHRO questioned the automatic character of the revenue sharing approach, since it provided no way to prevent the channeling of funds away from traditional urban renewal-type activities and into activities in which NAHRO's membership had little stake. Instead, NAHRO endorsed the so-called "block-grant approach," which was favored by Democratic Party leaders and which would differ from special revenue sharing by tying the expenditure of funds to more detailed congressionally defined purposes and by requiring an application spelling out how the city's proposed activities would advance these purposes.* In addition, NAHRO took issue with the Nixon administration intention to channel community development monies directly to the mayors, bypassing the local renewal agencies that handled all urban renewal funds under the existing system. Finally, NAHRO was eager to link the community development programs together with federal low-income housing programs for the first time, so that renewal agencies could count on federal commitments to make funds available for low-income replacement housing for those displaced by slum clearance activities.

The Coan task force provided the perfect vehicle for translating NAHRO's proposals into legislation, especially since the participants were basically in agreement with NAHRO's overall orientation. Throughout much of 1970 and into 1971, therefore, the task force worked out the details of the basic NAHRO proposal, discussing which programs would be consolidated, how funds would be distributed, what the application and review process should look like, what activities would be eligible for assistance, and how the transition from the current system to the new one would be handled. All parties were agreed, however, that a "block-grant approach" rather than a revenue-sharing approach was necessary to ensure local adherence to general national priorities in the

---

* In truth, the administration bill was itself a form of block-grant proposal, since it combined numerous categorical programs into a block-grant program. However, in the course of the debate, the terms "block grant" and "special revenue sharing" took on special meanings to emphasize the difference between the Democratic proposal (the block-grant approach), which retained an application requirement and a clear set of congressionally devised priorities for the use of CD monies, and the administration proposal (the revenue sharing approach), which would dispense with the application requirement and distribute CD funds by means of an automatic formula and with far fewer constraints on permissible uses.

spending of community development funds. When it became apparent in late April 1971 that the administration's proposal did indeed incorporate too few safeguards, the Senate's legislative drafting service was enlisted to reduce the task force ideas to legislative form.

The resulting bill, S. 2333, sponsored by Senator Sparkman and formally introduced on July 22, 1971, clearly reflected these origins. In the first place, unlike the administration bill (S. 1618), which proposed to distribute community development (CD) funds according to an automatic "need formula," the Sparkman bill would distribute them on the basis of past experience: 75 percent of all community development funds would be reserved for localities already conducting two or more types of community development activities, and the funds would be distributed among these localities according to a "basic grant entitlement" computed by averaging the amount received by the locality for community development over any three of the previous five years and then adding 15 percent for the first year of the new program, 30 percent for the second year, and 45 percent for the third. By guaranteeing not only existing funding levels but also future increments, this approach obviously benefited current recipients of community development assistance, precisely the places with the greatest NAHRO membership and with chief executives most likely to take an interest in the lobbying activities of the National League of Cities/U.S. Conference of Mayors. S. 2333 also differed from S. 1618 in several other ways congenial to these same groups:

1. It made local renewal agencies eligible recipients of funds, instead of restricting eligibility to units of general local government.

2. It extended the list of activities eligible for CD assistance, but specified more clearly that these activities must be in support of the slum clearance, blight removal, and low-income housing production efforts traditionally defined as national priorities. It thus sought to avoid the possibility opened by the administration

bill that CD funds would be diverted away from the inner cities and into massive, community-wide public works programs.

3. It would require local communities to submit plans for the expenditure of the CD funds to ensure that these national priorities would be followed and traditional commitments honored.

4. It proposed $2.5 billion in expenditures for fiscal year 1973, compared to $2 billion in the administration bill, and called for three-year authorizations and two-year appropriations, so that HUD could make two-year contracts with localities in an effort to guarantee continuity of programs over time.

5. It required the secretary of HUD to "set aside" funds for the level of subsidized housing construction called for in the local CD plan approved by HUD, and thus provided a link between the community development and housing assistance programs.

6. It required HUD to act on local community development plans within ninety days, by noting that any plan not acted upon before that time would be automatically approved.

7. It eliminated the provision in S. 1618 that would require cities with populations below fifty thousand located outside metropolitan areas to receive their community development funds through the rural development revenue sharing package, which would operate through the Department of Agriculture and the states.

8. It made the "establishment and maintenance of viable urban communities as social, economic, and political entities," a basic goal of national policy for the first time, thus going beyond the "decent home in a suitable living environment" goal of the 1949 act.

While it differed from the administration's community development revenue sharing proposal in several important respects, however, S. 2333 also shared with this proposal one fundamental feature: it would eliminate most of the statutory safeguards those affected most severely by urban renewal—especially the central-city poor—had managed to insert in the law during many years of struggle. These included the requirement that no more than 35 percent of all urban renewal funds be spent on nonresidential projects (42 U.S.C. 1460[c]); that each unit of low-income housing destroyed be replaced by a new one if the vacancy rate in a locality was low (42 U.S.C. 1455[h]); that citizen groups be permitted to participate actively and effectively in Model Cities and urban renewal decision-making through such vehicles as "project area committees"; and that cities develop and implement "workable programs" as a condition for eligibility for urban renewal assistance (42 U.S.C. 1451), a provision HUD had begun using effectively in the late 1960s and early 1970s to induce local communities to expand the supply of low- and moderate-income housing, to provide relocation assistance to families displaced by urban renewal, and to increase citizen participation in urban renewal planning.[204]

To be sure, the administration bill was more brutal than S. 2333 in emasculating these protections. It made no special provision at all for community participation in the formulation and implementation of community development plans, leaving the central-city poor to the tender mercies of local political structures historically more responsive to the needs of downtown commercial constituents than to those of the poor and minority groups. In addition, as we have seen, the administration bill did not even tie CD assistance to the solution of central-city blight and housing deterioration, opening the way for diversion of the funds into suburban public works projects.

But if S. 1618 reflected the interests of suburban groups eager to use federal largesse to finance general community development investments, S. 2333 moved part way in the same direction and reflected as well the eagerness of the urban renewal establishment to escape the troublesome restrictions placed on redevelopment activities by the urban poor. All that S. 2333 required regarding citizen participation, for example, was a certification that the local agency "has afforded an adequate opportunity for public hearings with respect to any acquisition and disposition of private land included in the proposed development activities" (Sec.

7[d] [2] [A]). Meanwhile, the bill gave the local governing body veto power over the community development plan, a provision that promised to open the program to pressures from politically potent interests hostile to the needs of the central-city poor. The program streamlining advocated in both S. 1618 and S. 2333 was thus a euphemism for emasculating the limitations placed by the traditional victims of urban renewal on local government action, proving again that one man's red tape is another's safeguard. Given the origins of these proposals, however, this outcome is not surprising.

When the Senate's Housing Subcommittee conducted its hearings on pending housing and urban development legislation in early August and mid-September 1971, the Sparkman bill was greeted with a resounding chorus of support from the key lobby groups involved in community development work, most of whom could easily testify that the bill accorded with the policy positions of their organizations—for the very good reason that they had written the bill.* In addition, the bill enjoyed the support of the Democratic leadership in Congress, which was already on record in opposition to the administration's proposed automatic formula approach to special revenue sharing because it denied Congress a sufficient say on federal spending priorities. Solicitor General Elmer B. Staats concurred in this view, charging that "S. 1618 does not provide for adequate accountability to either the executive branch [or] the Congress for the spending of Federal tax revenues."[206] The only sour note permitted to intrude into the proceedings, aside from that of Romney, came from an OEO

---

* Mayor Alioto of San Francisco, speaking on behalf of the National League of Cities and the U.S. Conference of Mayors, thus noted that "the policy positions of both the League and the Conference [adopted in June 1971] are essentially identical in their support for the basic elements of S. 2333." By the same token, Robert Maffin of NAHRO pointed out, not surprisingly, that "S. 2333 is generally consistent with the position the National Association of Housing and Redevelopment Officials have taken over the past year in developing proposals for a comprehensive community development program and a comprehensive housing assistance program."[205]

lawyer who documented the crucial safeguards for the poor that both S. 2333 and S. 1618 proposed to eliminate and pointed out that "the community development proposals before the Subcommittee, while they promise relief from the rigid categorical limitations of the past, threaten to undercut the limited protections now available to ensure responsiveness of the federal programs to the needs of minority communities and the poor."[207]

Between September 1971 and early February 1972, when the subcommittee markup sessions began, Coan worked closely with HUD officials and with subcommittee staffer Win Skiles, ranking Republican Senator John Tower's aide on the Housing Subcommittee, to try to resolve the differences between the two bills. Although Coan and the outside lobbies had done their homework well in orchestrating a groundswell of support for S. 2333, the administration was ultimately able to recoup some of the lost ground thanks to the threat of a presidential veto, Sparkman's penchant for compromise and conciliation, and the fact that both Sparkman and Tower came from states whose local governments would probably gain more from the "need"-based distribution formula in the administration bill than from the experience-based formula in S. 2333. The basic compromise struck in the executive sessions in early February 1972, therefore, was to retain the formal application requirement of S. 2333 but to adopt the distribution formula of the administration bill, with only two modifications: a specific legislative guarantee that communities would receive at least as much under the new system as they had under the old, and a limitation on the increase in funds a community with little past record of involvement in community development activities could receive during the early years of the new system.* The subcommittee accepted the HUD position that units

* Under the Senate's bill, 75 percent of all CD funds would be distributed among metropolitan areas according to the size of population, the degree of poverty (counted twice), the extent of housing overcrowding, and the level of recent program experience. The same formula would be used to distribute funds among governments in the metropolitan area, except that: (1) any metropolitan city of 50,000 or more persons would be guaranteed a level

of general local government should have primary responsibility for CD funds, but accommodated the NAHRO position by authorizing local governments to delegate this responsibility to local renewal agencies. On the insistence of OMB, the subcommittee dropped the provision requiring HUD to set aside funds to honor subsidized-housing commitments outlined in local CD plans.

On the question of citizen participation and other statutory safeguards for the victims of urban renewal, the subcommittee ended up with wording only slightly stronger than in the administration and task-force bills. Subcommittee liberals like Mondale and Brooke urged a significant strengthening of these provisions, including statutory provisions to equip the poor with the technical assistance to participate more meaningfully in community development planning. Conservatives like Tower and Brock, on the other hand, vigorously opposed such provisions, pointing to the troublesome experience with community participation in the OEO and Model Cities programs, and endorsing the administration view that full responsibility should be vested in locally elected officials. Eager to avoid a floor fight that might blow the issue open and lead to really stringent community participation requirements, the League of Cities/Conference of Mayors proposed a compromise that ultimately won subcommittee approval. Under it, communities were required to certify that they had afforded "adequate opportunity for citizen participation in the development of the annual application" and that they had provided for "the meaningful involvement of the residents of areas in which community development activities are to be concentrated in the planning and execution of these activities." How this was to be done, however, was left purposefully vague so that community groups could not claim statutory authority for any particular

---

of funding at least as large as that under existing programs; and (2) whenever a city's basic formula entitlement exceeded its recent program experience by more than 35 percent, the secretary of HUD could withhold a portion of this excess to allow a slower phase-in. In all cases, however, applications would still be required to secure the allocated funds.

community participation mode. The committee report underlined this point, noting that the committee had "agreed that there is no single, commonly-understood definition" of community participation. The report stated, "The Committee concluded it would be unwise for it to frame a single model for citizen participation; but instead decided that program objectives would be better served by relying on local governments to develop acceptable models of citizen participation."[208] What this meant, as Senator Robert Taft noted in the "individual views" he added to the committee report, was that " 'citizen participation' is defined so generally that whatever participation best suits the local power structure or the most vocal minority interest in the area could be deemed acceptable."[209] In the process, an important safeguard for minority groups and the poor in the community development process was seriously weakened, though not as mortally as in the original bills.

The compromise language averted a floor fight when the bill came up for consideration on March 2 and 3, 1972. Indeed, like the housing consolidation legislation, the community development provisions of the 1972 bill cleared the Senate with scarcely a whimper of floor debate, thanks to the bipartisan push organized by Tower and Sparkman. So effectively had they worked out the necessary clearances and lined up votes behind their compromises, in fact, that the only substantive debates on the Senate floor during consideration of the 1972 Housing Act concerned the bill's proposal for mass transit operating subsidies and an amendment introduced by Jacob Javits calling for a special program of neighborhood rehabilitation grants. The housing consolidation and community development block-grant proposals that formed the core of the bill sailed through unchallenged and undebated. In the process, Congress placed its stamp of approval on a bill whose basic substance was shaped by the urban renewal–mayoral establishment, with concessions to the suburban-focused Republican administration, a bill that promised to eliminate much of the confusion in federal community development programs, but at the price of eliminating some vital safeguards for the poor and diverting funds away from communities historically involved in urban renewal.

The House: The Struggle to Innovate

Like the Senate, the House's Housing Subcommittee received the administration's housing consolidation measure in March of 1970, conducted hearings in the summer of 1970, and postponed consideration of the measure until the Ninety-second Congress in view of the extraordinarily heavy workload already on the agenda for the 1970 session. Unlike the Senate, however, the House's Housing Subcommittee resolved to take advantage of this postponement to break out of the traditional, executive- and special-interest-dominated mode of formulating housing policy by organizing its three study panels in October 1970, one each on Housing Production, Housing Demand, and Developing a Suitable Living Environment. The idea for these panels originated with subcommittee staffers Gerald McMurray and George Gross, who had become disenchanted with the traditional method of housing policy formulation, a method that left the subcommittees and their staffs in purely reactive roles and that had produced an irrational mix of programs geared to no overall, coherent policy goals. McMurray and Gross were burdened by fewer intimate attachments to the key housing lobby groups than were their counterparts in the Senate, even though Gross had spent three years in HUD's legislative liaison office, a year as an NAHB lobbyist, and two years working for the New England Regional Commission before joining the subcommittee staff in 1969; and McMurray was the son of FHLBB member and long-time housing specialist Joseph McMurray.

Most important, these staffers had the support of an influential group of subcommittee activists seeking to establish their dominance in housing policy formation. These included fifth-ranking Democrat Thomas "Lud" Ashley, who took the lead in the late 1960s in pushing for a national urban growth policy to give structure and order to federal urban policies; third-ranking Democrat Leonor Sullivan, who had recently conducted an inquiry into shoddy real estate lending practices[210] and was increasingly concerned about the absence of consumer protections in the housing field; and sixth-ranking William Moorhead, a former college roommate and long-time friend of Ashley's with considerable interest and experience in urban renewal matters. Ashley had emerged in the 1960s as an advocate of greater subcommittee autonomy in the formation of housing policy. What is more, through his ardent championship of what became Title VII of the 1970 Housing Act, which charged the federal government with the responsibility of developing a national urban growth policy and established a new program of assistance to developers of large-scale "new towns," Ashley established close ties with the planning, architectural, academic, and large-scale developer groups and thereby acquired some independence from the traditional housing special-interest groups.[211]

For these subcommittee activists and the staffers allied with them, the panels were seen as an opportunity to expose subcommittee members to ideas not filtered through the distorting prism of special-interest perspectives, at least not the same perspectives as had captured these programs in the past. "They did not want and were not receptive to input from those of us in the housing and urban lobby," confirmed NAHRO's Mary Nenno, "we were shut out of it."[212] Subcommittee chairman William Barrett, as we have seen, was happy to accommodate the "Young Turks" on his subcommittee on the assumption that their activism would enhance his own prestige. As for the Republicans, they viewed the panels as an implicit challenge to "liberal" housing programs with which they had grown increasingly disenchanted.[213]

The panels began their work in late 1970.

Thirty-six expert papers were commissioned, mostly from academics and "think tank" types to avoid capture of the discussion by the special interests that dominate the regular legislative hearing process. In addition, several investigative field trips were arranged. With this as background, the panels then met separately in the spring of 1971 to formulate recommendations and prepare a report. From all indications, subcommittee members found the experience helpful and informative; attendance was high and the discussion lively.[214] Most important, the panels provided an opportunity for subcommittee activists like Ashley, and the staffers allied with them, to expose the more conservative subcommittee members to some novel ideas. What emerged by June 1971 was a set of panel recommendations and a staff report that, while hardly radical, as we have seen, went considerably beyond what the traditional actors were serving up, and hence what the normal hearing process would have produced.

In the first place, the panels challenged the traditional production focus of federal housing policies, the emphasis on program activities geared to stimulating the construction of new housing. Pointing to the loss of 6 million housing units and the abandonment of hundreds of thousands of others during the 1960s, the panel report argued that "exclusive emphasis on those governmental actions which tend to stimulate housing production is not sufficient [to provide housing for low- and moderate-income families]. If total housing production requirements for such families are not to reach impossible proportions, there must be much greater emphasis and expenditure of effort on the preservation and maintenance of the existing housing supply."[215] In particular, the panel report recommended: (1) the creation of an Urban Homestead Loan Program, under which resident owners of existing two-to-six-unit structures in still viable neighborhoods could secure insured loans to refinance their mortgages and make improvements; (2) a Neighborhood Preservation Assistance Program, under which federal grants would be made available to local governments to finance 90 percent of the costs of improving public facilities in designated neighborhood preservation areas; and (3) an expansion of the national housing goals and of the Annual Housing Report specified in the 1968 Housing Act to include attention to the existing housing stock as well as new production. Along the same lines, the panels encouraged a shift from production subsidies to income subsidies directed at the consumers of housing through an expansion of the housing allowance experiments*[216] and focused attention as well on the need to lower housing costs through such devices as a federal program to aggregate housing purchases in order to provide a market for more efficient, large-scale housing producers, and the creation of a National Institute of Building Sciences to facilitate the introduction of new housing technology now barred by local building codes.

The panels also departed from tradition by laying far greater stress on the growth policy implications of existing federal housing and urban development programs. This was most clearly evident in the proposal of Ashley's panel to "restructure the basic delivery system of Federal housing assistance" in order to break the suburban exclusion of low-income groups and thereby "increase the access of the occupants [of low- and moderate-income housing] to employment opportunities, and . . . reduce the concentration of lower income families in the central city."[217] This was to be achieved by channeling all housing subsidy monies—whether for public housing, 235, 236, rent supplement, or rural housing programs—through metropolitan or state housing agencies, which would formulate plans detailing how much subsidized housing was needed, and where it was to be built. The plans would be required to scatter low-income housing in suburban communities, instead of concentrating it in central-city areas. As an incentive to outlying communities, grants totaling as much as $3,000 per unit would be made available to local governments

---

* The housing allowance experiment, authorized by Congress in 1970, is designed to test the effect of giving housing subsidies directly to families in need, instead of channeling funds through complex producer subsidy schemes like the 235 and 236 programs. This "demand-side" approach has been opposed by the producer groups for years on the ground that it will fail to stimulate the high level of new construction these groups favor. The original authorization was $20 million for two years. The panel report recommended raising this to $75 million over three years.

that accepted subsidized housing. This housing-assistance block-grant system was tied to a companion community development block-grant proposal that emerged from the subcommittee panel chaired by Moorhead and that was quite similar to what ultimately emerged from the Senate several months later except that the House panel's plan would deny community development monies to any community not covered by an approved metropolitan housing agency plan for subsidized housing.* The panels also recommended three other devices geared to rationalizing urban growth policy and facilitating the dispersion of low-income populations:

1. A program of federal financial assistance to stimulate the creation of state *urban development corporations*, which could organize and construct integrated, comprehensive urban renewal and subsidized housing projects on the scale needed.

2. An Urban Development Bank authorized to extend credit to local governments at reduced rates in order to lower capital improvement costs and provide capital to local governments during periods of tight money.

3. A new program of planning and management assistance designed to equip states and local governments to formulate metropolitan-wide housing and urban growth plans and put them into effect.

The third area in which the panels introduced a novel perspective into the housing policy debate concerned the subject of consumer protection. As the panel report put it, "All renters and homeowners, and particularly those of subsidized housing, deserve more protection and education from the Federal housing

---

* It was the House's Housing Subcommittee panels that first came up with the "entitlements" idea that was ultimately incorporated in the Senate bill. Under this plan local communities would be "entitled" to a certain share of CD funds through a distribution formula based on need (as defined by population, poverty, and housing conditions) but would still have to submit proposals outlining uses of the funds to claim their "entitlements." The Senate-passed bill differed, however, in incorporating past experience with CD programs into the entitlement formula.

agencies, which traditionally have dealt primarily with lenders and builders."[218] The report recommended the creation of a Homeowners Bureau in HUD to provide education and counseling to participants in FHA's subsidized home-ownership programs; the formation of a management counseling staff to train and assist management personnel operating federally subsidized, rental housing projects; and the appointment of a "housing ombudsman" within the office of the secretary of HUD to "function within the councils of HUD solely in the interest of the occupants of Federally-assisted housing."[219] Like the focus on existing housing, this concern for consumer protection challenged the headlong production focus of existing programs. Noted the panel report, "The great emphasis on volume production that has developed tends to relegate management questions to a minor role before construction is approved. *There is an urgent need to move in the other direction, to increase the management role at the inception of project development.*"[220]

After completion of the panel report, the Housing Subcommittee staff proceeded to translate the recommendations into legislative form. The resulting bill, H.R. 9688, was introduced on July 8, 1971, and contained nine separate titles, embodying, respectively: (1) the proposal to expand the national housing goals to emphasize preservation of existing housing and attention to housing costs; (2) the neighborhood preservation and urban homestead proposals; (3) the proposals for HUD counseling and management assistance and a housing ombudsman within HUD; (4) the expanded housing allowance experiment; (5) the metropolitan housing agency and housing block-grant idea; (6) the subcommittee's community development block-grant proposal; (7) the proposal for federal aid to state and metropolitan development agencies; (8) the urban development bank proposal; and (9) the program of federal planning and management assistance to state and local governments.

On two of these titles, community development (Title VI) and planning assistance (Title IX), the subcommittee bill strongly resembled the administration's own community development proposal (H.R. 8853), except that the subcommittee's community development plan was a "block-grant" system requiring formal applications for funds and hence federal review of the use of the funds, while the administration's bill adopted the "revenue sharing" approach with far fewer strings to enforce federal priorities. In addition, the subcommittee endorsed the housing consolidation concept proposed in the revised housing consolidation bill (H.R. 9331) that the administration introduced in June 1971, but it indicated in the panel report an intention to amend the proposal to make it "conform to the recommendations made by the panels."[221] For the rest, however, the subcommittee bill plowed some significant new ground. But it soon became apparent that the bankers, builders, and bureaucrats—if not the real estate brokers—found much of this ground thoroughly unproductive.

The Counterattack. It was during the hearings that began in early August and extended, after a break, into mid-September 1971 that the housing lobby and the administration got their chance to react to the panels' work as reflected in H.R. 9688. Not unexpectedly, given the bill's stress on existing housing and its provision in Title V for local government participation in decisions about where subsidized housing should be built, the realtors' representatives were rhapsodic, praising the bill as the "first in many years" to come to grips with basic housing and community development problems. The great strength of this bill, noted the NAREB spokesman, "lies in its penetration and exposure of weaknesses in the conventional wisdom that has motivated most of our urban assistance programs."[222] Planners, architects, academics, and large-scale developers testifying at the hearings also supported the subcommittee's innovations. HUD's Romney was generally supportive as well. The subcommittee had, after all, endorsed HUD's consolidation bill. What is more, it had incorporated into its community development plan the need-based distribution formula endorsed by HUD instead of the experience-based formula proposed by the mayors and NAHRO and incorporated in the Senate's bill, although the subcommittee bill's application and review provisions were criticized by Romney.[223] Perhaps most significantly, Romney gave a significant boost to Ashley's metropolitan housing agency scheme embodied in Title V of H.R. 9688. The suburb-cracking aspects of this scheme meshed nicely with Romney's own efforts to open suburban communities to low-income housing, efforts that he pursued during his tenure at HUD—to the dismay of the White House— through threats to deny HUD water and sewer aid to suburban communities refusing low-income housing and through the formulation of site-selection criteria that would give priority in distributing housing subsidy funds to projects located outside the central-city core.[224] Though questioning the mechanics of the Title V proposal, therefore, Romney warmly supported its "main thrust," noting, "I don't really believe that we are going to get an adequate approach to meeting the housing need in the metropolitan areas until we can bring about a consideration on a metropolitan basis of how the housing needs of that whole area can be best met, and be best met in terms of all the considerations that enter into it."[225]

But the traditional lobby groups reacted negatively. Title V, the housing block-grant proposal, was the main point of contention. Although Ashley viewed it as a way to open the suburbs to low-income housing through the use of "incentive" payments and the threat of denial of CD funds, the housing lobby viewed it as a threat to the production goals of the subsidy programs. The home builders were particularly vehement on this point. According to the NAHB president, by channeling all housing subsidy funds through metropolitan housing agencies, which would be required to formulate plans for the amount and location of low-income housing, Title V "would, in many cases, place complete control of HUD subsidy programs into the hands of the very same officials who now use zoning, land use controls, and other devices to defeat the production of low- and moderate-income housing."[226] The result, he argued, would be to *restrict*, not expand, the dispersal of low-income housing to the suburbs, and, in the process, "add greatly to the difficulties of both homebuilders and HUD in achieving the *housing production goals* with which HUD is now charged."[227] In addition, the NAHB was unsympathetic to the "market aggregation" concept embodied in Title V, the notion that metropolitan housing agencies could package large enough orders for housing to make reliance on industrialized housing technology feasible. Trumpeted the NAHB, "We represent the organized homebuilding industry of the United States [and] we state unequivocally that this theory of 'market aggregation' by or through a governmental agency is unsound, unrealistic in terms of the facts with respect to housing production and, if enacted, that it would be greatly disruptive and discriminatory in its impact on housing production."[228] The NAHB was even doubtful about the administration's consolidation bill for fear it might "disrupt processing within the HUD programs." As the group's president pointed out, "We think it is important to stress that the present HUD programs are working well and, under them, the industry is achieving housing production levels which are setting new records."[229] The fact that the subsidy programs were increasingly serving only the upper-income groups eligible for assistance—the median income of Section 235 participants stood at $6,200 in 1970—was far less important to the builders' representatives, preoccupied as they were with the demonstrated pump-priming power of the 1968 subsidy schemes. Bold new approaches like those embodied in Title V, therefore, fell on unsympathetic ears.

Nor were the home builders any more enthusiastic about the program of federal assistance to state and metropolitan development corporations proposed in Title VII of the subcommittee bill. Like the Title V provisions, the development-corporation idea represented an effort to get beyond the piecemeal, fragmented development process characteristic of American urban areas, in this case through the promotion of agencies capable of larger-scale, better-planned developments.* To the builders, however, these development corporations represented "creeping socialism" corrosive of private enterprise. "Frankly," explained the NAHB president, "we believe the Federal Government has no business using its funds to create public building and development companies which necessarily would operate in competition with developers and builders in private business."[231]

If the vigorous opposition of the builders might have been expected, that of the other elements of the generally liberal housing and urban lobby was probably not. Yet, aside from the AFL–CIO, which expressed special support for Title V's intention to make housing for low-income groups available where jobs are located,[232] and the American Institute of Planners, which urged even more severe sanctions than those embodied in Title V for communities that refuse their "fair share" of subsidized housing,[233] the main organized urban-interest groups reacted coolly to the subcommittee's innovations. The National League of Cities/ U.S. Conference of Mayors, for example, praised the "laudable goals" of the Title V proposal, but argued that its problems outweighed its merits. What troubled the mayors was a contradictory set of fears: on the one hand, a fear that the proposal would allow suburban communities to siphon off part of the limited housing subsidy funds that would otherwise go to the central cities; and, on the other hand, a fear that the metropolitan housing authorities would be so dominated by antipoor suburban interests that they would refuse low-income housing completely (which would, of course, leave all of the metropolitan area's share for the central city). Explained the mayors' representative:

> I cannot afford to give up some of the housing dollars that I now hope to receive in order that they may be allocated to a suburb instead. What guarantee is there that those dollars will still be used to house low-income people? If low-income units are built, is there any chance at all that any of the low-

---

* As we have seen, this idea grew out of the Moorhead panel and reflected as well the views of Ashley.[230]

income families living in the central city will be eligible to
use the units?[234]

NAHRO, too, was full of "serious reservations" about Title V.
It argued, first, that the title's proposal to allocate housing funds
among metropolitan regions according to a need-based formula
would not work because of the inadequacies of census data; second, that the metropolitan agencies authorized to make housing
plans might "fail to guarantee adequate representation of the center city and its poor"; third, that combining all housing subsidy
funds into one bundle might divert money from public housing
(the bread-and-butter of NAHRO's membership); and fourth,
that the whole plan would impede low-income housing construction rather than facilitate it.[235] Complained New York's Housing
and Development Administrator, Albert Walsh, on behalf of
NAHRO:

> I beat my head against the wall all day every day trying to
> build housing. And I have a great concern about having to
> go to another agency and saying, please, may I build this
> project. And the metropolitan agency says, no, you have got
> too much housing in Harlem already. And I say, but the
> people of Harlem desperately need housing, and I can't wait
> for you to build it in Scarsdale, because I don't think it is
> going to happen. That is what it comes down to.[236]

Neither of these major public-interest groups provided much
support for the other controversial features of the subcommittee
bill, either. On the community development provisions, both the
mayors and the redevelopment officials endorsed the block-grant
approach of H.R. 9688, but objected to the proposed formula
distribution of funds.[237] And neither had kind words for the subcommittee's efforts to link the housing and community development programs together for the first time through a proposal in
the panel report giving the HUD secretary authority to deny
community development funds to communities that balk at participation in metropolitan housing agencies, or that refuse to pro-

vide low-income housing to families employed in the community, as the community development title (Title VI) of H.R. 9688 put this requirement. More seriously, neither defended the urban development bank or state and metropolitan development corporation proposals, which were vigorously opposed by powerful private lobbies and by congressional conservatives.[238] As a consequence, the subcommittee liberals and staffers who formed the backbone of the panel experiment quickly found themselves isolated and on the defensive *vis-à-vis* the traditional housing lobby. There was, in fact, a certain "We'll-show-you-you-can't-do-without-us" quality in the response the subcommittee proposals received. "The main problem with the House process was the lack of opportunity it provided for everyone to participate in the formulation stage," explained NAHRO's Mary Nenno. "We like Mr. Ashley. He's one of the most progressive up there. If we had been able to get in sooner, we could have headed off a lot of problems."[239]

What made this isolation especially serious was the thinness of the support for the liberal-activists' proposals within the subcommittee itself. The sentiment among Republicans and conservative Democrats on the subcommittee, and in the House as a whole, ran strongly against federal efforts to open the suburbs to low-income housing. Ranking Republican Widnall, for example, expressed strong opposition to HUD's use of water and sewer grants to force small suburban communities to accept such housing,[240] and moves were afoot to place an absolute prohibition on construction of subsidized housing, even by private builders, unless specifically approved by the relevant local government. As the scandals in the subsidy programs unfolded during 1971, moreover, conservative hostility to these programs only increased, and several liberals began to sour on them as well.[241] Under the best of circumstances, Ashley and his allies would have had a difficult time selling their proposals to tie housing and community development assistance to an urban growth policy designed to increase housing opportunities for the poor in the suburbs, where the jobs are. Against the united opposition of the builders, the mayors, and the redevelopment officials, this task became downright impossible.

Backlash: The Subcommittee Markup. When the Housing Subcommittee finally got down to markup sessions on the major legislative proposals before it on March 7, 1972, following a series of post-hearing field trips, the panel initiatives took a rather severe beating. On the very first day of markup sessions, a battle erupted over the extent to which CD funds should be conditioned on acceptance of low- and moderate-income housing. The issue arose over the question whether to include HUD's water and sewer program in the community development block-grant package or leave it separate. The water and sewer program was one of the favorites of small suburban and rural communities, which received most of its benefits. Conservative Democrat Robert Stephens of Georgia, with Widnall's support, argued that the program should be kept separate so that these communities would not be forced to take low-income housing as a condition of getting water and sewer aid. Ashley objected strongly: "If we are saying it doesn't matter what type of community you are or what you are doing in the way of efforts to accommodate families of low or moderate income, I would be obliged to vote against the whole concept of revenue sharing."[242] Noting that liberals Reuss and Moorhead were absent and that the rural-suburban interests were in ascendance, subcommittee chairman Barrett managed to defer a vote on the water and sewer issue. But to no avail; when the issue came up again two days later, Ashley's was still a minority position. Operating behind closed doors, the subcommittee members took issue with Ashley and gave vent to their racial and class prejudices, as illustrated in the following exchange:

> *Ashley*: What you are saying, of course, is that these funds can be used for an all-white, upper middle class community that makes no provisions for families of low- and moderate-income.

Blackburn: You are talking about my constituency.

Stephens: We have gotten a lot of votes from that category.

Ashley: I don't give a damn about the votes.

Stephens: You have got to pass a bill. I don't give a damn
about the votes either, unless voting for a piece
of legislation.

Ashley: Not on that basis.[243]

In short order the water and sewer program was taken out of the
community development package.

Although the subcommittee's Democratic majority was able to
hold out against Republican efforts to gut other provisions in the
community development proposal that would direct CD funds
toward activities supportive of improved low- and moderate-
income housing—chiefly the application requirement and a
funding formula based partly on past community development
activity—the vote on the water and sewer issue made it clear
that the more ambitious panel recommendations were in deep
trouble. This was particularly true of Ashley's Title V housing
block-grant proposal. The title was eliminated from the bill early
in the executive sessions, thanks in substantial measure to builder
opposition and Romney's refusal to push the proposal.[244] Eager
to resuscitate the idea, Ashley revised it and reintroduced it as a
demonstration program to be tried in only ten areas, and even
there without the sanction of denials of CD funds to communities
refusing to participate, and without the incentive grants opposed
by HUD budgeters. But with the builders still opposed, the proposal failed even in this watered-down form by a six–six vote—
with Republicans Stanton and Heckler joining Democrats Barrett,
Ashley, Reuss, and Stephens in support; and Democrats Gonzalez, St. Germain, and Minish joining Republicans Brown,
Blackburn, and Widnall in opposition.[245]

If the builders rejoiced at the defeat of Title V, however, it
could not have been for long. Miffed at the poor treatment accorded his proposal, Ashley struck upon a bold strategy. He

threw his weight behind the one measure before the Ninety-second Congress that was most despised by the NAHB: a proposal introduced by Banking Committee Republican Bill Archer, a conservative from Texas, to require local government approval for all 236 projects prior to construction. This proposal promised to sharply reduce the amount of subsidized rental housing constructed, especially in the suburbs. Ashley amended this to add 235 (home ownership) projects as well, and the measure was inserted in the revised subcommittee bill by voice vote. Explained Ashley, "I did it to get the home builders so frightened that they would come around to support my metropolitan housing authority idea as a reasonable compromise."[246]

This was only the beginning of the grief the subcommittee piled on the home builders. For, when they reached the housing consolidation title, subcommittee members gave vent to the frustrations that had been building during the previous two years over the failures of the subsidy schemes devised in 1968. In a series of moves, liberals like Ashley and Sullivan sided with subcommittee conservatives in support of what was esentially the banker and realtor—as opposed to the builder and bureaucrat—position on the subsidy programs. This involved, in the first place, reducing the maximum mortgage amounts allowed on FHA subsidized and unsubsidized loans to force the builders to focus on lower-income groups.* In addition, the maximum income limit for participation in the subsidized housing programs was reduced from the 100 percent of median income figure proposed in the administration bill to 80 percent, as proposed by the realtors and mortgage bankers, who were eager to restrict the coverage of the subsidy programs and thus keep the maximum number of people in the private real estate and mortgage markets. This had the effect of limiting the eligibility for subsidy aid to those in greatest

---

* The Senate bill, following the revised HUD bill, had set the maximum mortgage amount on subsidized housing at 120 percent of local prototype costs, and on unsubsidized housing at 200 percent. The House's Housing Subcommittee lowered these to 110 percent and 180 percent, respectively.

need, but simultaneously left a large pool of moderate-income families priced out of the housing market thanks to rising interest rates and housing costs. To compensate for this, Sullivan introduced a proposal for direct government loans at 6.5 percent interest to moderate-income families. After surviving an initial vote, however, this radical proposal ultimately failed, since it ran headlong into administration opposition and posed too serious a challenge to the existing financial structure.* But the reduced income limits remained.

The third major change the subcommittee made in the housing consolidation proposal was to increase the allocation of subsidy funds permitted to go for existing, as opposed to new, housing from 30 percent to 40 percent. This move reflected one of the central themes of the panel deliberations, which stressed the importance of the existing housing stock as a pool of decent, low-cost housing for the poor. Explained Ashley, "We may possibly have travelled rather heavily in the direction of new housing as distinguished from existing housing and I would like to make that clear to some people, including HUD and the home builders."[248]

Finally, at the behest of Sullivan, who expressed concern that "the present laws do not give enough protection to the buyer of housing although there are plenty of protections for the lenders and the builders,"[249] the subcommittee adopted a series of consumer protections in housing. Most important was a provision requiring builders to provide warranties on new and rehabilitated homes covered by FHA- or VA-guaranteed mortgages. As originally formulated, Sullivan's proposal called for only one-year warranties, but Ben Blackburn suggested raising this to five, and subcommittee liberals, recalling the recent housing scandals, were inclined to go part of the way. When Barrett proposed checking this with the builders prior to voting, St. Germain objected that

---

* In the subcommittee debate over this Home Owners Loan Fund title, William Stanton, the ABA spokesman on the Holding Company Act, led the opposition. Asked Stanton facetiously at one point in the debate, "Why don't we just take over the S and Ls?"[247]

"that is like asking the criminal if he likes the sentence he is getting," and Blackburn and Sullivan pushed for a vote. The result was insertion of a requirement for three-year warranties on all new, and one-year warranties on all rehabilitated, housing covered by FHA or VA guarantees. In addition, the subcommittee adopted a provision directing the secretary of HUD to set maximum limits on the "settlement costs" charged to buyers for title fees and other legal work required in purchasing a home. These provisions, originally proposed by Chairman Patman in a bill that sought to regulate kickbacks and other inside deals in real estate as well, were reviewed in public hearings in early February 1972, and became Title IX of the subcommittee bill, though in slightly weakened form.

The subcommittee's solicitude for the consumers of federal housing and urban programs was not boundless, however. Its treatment of the community participation features of the community development title, and of public housing tenants, indicate the limits of its concern. On the community participation issue, the subcommittee adopted language considerably weaker than that in the Senate bill, despite the fact that witnesses such as former HUD Secretary Robert C. Weaver criticized the subcommittee's H.R. 9688 during the public hearings on precisely this point.[250] In the House subcommittee, in contrast to the Senate, no one spoke up for special provisions to equip citizens' groups to participate effectively in CD planning and execution. On the contrary, even liberals scorned the idea. "I don't know if we should write this in the bill," noted Sullivan, "but they should be made aware, they should have their voices heard, but they should not be on the voting end of this kind of thing . . . they should have no voting rights on the developments that occur."[251] Henry Gonzalez, a Mexican-American representing the barrios of San Antonio and the only minority group representative on the subcommittee, was equally vehement in opposing strong community participation, despite the views of the community he was purporting to represent. "The significant thing is to make sure the Congress doesn't intend this to be interpreted that citizen groups can substitute themselves for the legal governmental units elected by the people," argued Gonzalez.[252] As a consequence, the sub-committee bill required only that local communities provide citi-zens affected by CD activities with "adequate information," and that they hold public hearings to "obtain [their] views." Such was the representation afforded the poor on the Housing Sub-committee.

When it turned its attention to the public housing program, moreover, the subcommittee bore down even more heavily on the poor than it had on the builders, going so far as to intrude on local landlord-tenant law by imposing a provision in public hous-ing leases requiring eviction of any tenant whose rent becomes past due by sixty days. On this provision as well, Gonzalez joined Sullivan and the conservatives against the liberal Democrats, prompting Barrett to query Gonzalez, "Do you know what you voted aye on?"[253] The subcommittee also overturned the Brooke Amendment by setting a federal minimum rent in public housing, and attacked the notion of giving public housing participants a voice in project management. Only the strong support of Barrett, Moorhead, and Reuss, in fact, managed to protect the public housing program from even more Draconian measures. Under the circumstances, the deep-subsidy provisions embraced by Brooke and Mondale in the Senate went nowhere in the House.

What emerged from the House's Housing Subcommittee after two months of arduous executive sessions was a bill that diverged significantly from the tasty morsel served up for the housing lobby groups by the Senate Banking Committee. To be sure, the result-ing bill contained few of the controversial innovations proposed by the panels. Gone were the metropolitan housing agencies, the housing block grants, the stimuli to market aggregation, and the urban development bank. All that remained of the novel panel recommendations, in fact, were the neighborhood preservation and state development corporation provisions, and the latter in somewhat weakened form. In addition, to the dismay of HUD, the subcommittee endorsed the basics of the Senate version of the community development proposal, except that it omitted the water and sewer program, made no reference to local redevelopment agencies as permissible recipients of CD funds, and limited the kinds of noncash contributions that would count toward the 10 percent of CD costs the bill required local governments to shoulder.* Finally, the bill did endorse the fundamentals of HUD's proposed housing consolidation measure, including extension and enlargement of the interest-subsidy programs.

But the subcommittee measure also contained some bitter pills for the key lobby groups to swallow. It defied the builders on mortgage limits, eligibility limits, the division of subsidy funds between new and existing housing, the warranty provisions, and, most important, the requirement of local government approval of all subsidized-housing construction. It also displeased the public housing officials and tenant groups thanks to its harsh treatment of the public housing program. The bill therefore presented a serious dilemma for the housing lobby. Both HUD and the mayors were eager for a bill, HUD because of the consolidation provisions and the mayors because of the community development provisions, which met the mayors' specifications in both House and Senate versions. The White House and OMB, however, remained vehemently opposed to the block-grant approach to community development revenue sharing, with its hold-harmless provisions, its application requirement, and its detailed statement of purposes. The builders, for their part, viewed the House subcommittee bill as worse than no bill at all, because of the local government approval provision. Attention therefore turned to the full House Banking Committee to see if the cat unleashed by the Housing Subcommittee could be put back in the bag.

---

* On the water and sewer and local redevelopment agency issues, the subcommittee was endorsing positions pushed by HUD. On the local share requirement, however, it was challenging the administration view, which argued against a local share requirement completely.

Into the Bag and Out Again: The Full Committee Stage. The disarray within the housing lobby provided Patman with a perfect opportunity to fish in troubled waters, and thus to demonstrate to the Housing Subcommittee that its autonomy was not without limits. Responding to builder pressure, Patman took the unusual step of scheduling public hearings on the housing bill before the full committee in early June. He noted wryly, "I can't recall a time when a housing bill has been the target for so much criticism and pressure from private sector industries which it directly affects. The fact that the bill is being attacked from every direction leads me to assume that Chairman Barrett and his subcommittee must have done something right."[254]

This situation posed particular difficulties for HUD's George Romney, whose task it was to overcome administration objections to the modified block-grant approach to CD funding embodied in the subcommittee bill in order to rescue the bill from likely defeat and thus salvage his pet proposal for consolidating HUD's confused housing programs. The provision in the subcommittee bill calling for prior local government approval of all subsidized housing construction illustrates Romney's dilemma well; for, though it ran counter to Romney's own avowed goal of promoting low-income housing in the suburbs and seriously threatened the production goals of the home builders, it conformed all too well to the "new federalism" rhetoric of the Nixon administration, with its emphasis on local government control. With the builders threatening to torpedo the whole bill if this provision remained, Romney thus had the unenviable chore of persuading administration higher-ups to oppose a provision that seemed to express the essence of one of their dominant domestic policy themes.

Romney's solution was to emphasize the similarities between the subcommittee bill and the original administration proposals and to secure OMB approval to accept language in the committee's report on the bill in lieu of changes in the bill itself to protect the administration's position on such matters as the proposed application requirement for CD funding and the operation of the CD

funding formula.* In the case of the provision for local government approval of subsidized housing, Romney's carefully crafted
statement to the committee on June 13, 1972 turned the administration's argument on its head by portraying this requirement as
a federal imposition rather than a source of local self-government.
Noted Romney, this requirement placed the federal government
in the position of "dictating to local governments in very specific
terms the way in which they must make their local housing
decisions," and therefore had to be opposed.[255] Through such
artful dodges, Romney managed to keep administration forces
behind his pet bill.

The National League of Cities/U.S. Conference of Mayors also
soft-pedaled their objections to the bill, emphasizing instead that
"the [Ninety-second] Congress is coming to its final days and it is
very important to us in the cities that we get a bill from the
committee and to the House floor before adjournment."[256] The
builders and housing and redevelopment officials were far less
gentle, however. NAHB president Stanley Waranch, for example,
expressed "deep distress" and "alarm" over provisions in the subcommittee bill for local government approval of subsidy housing,
three-year warranties, reduced maximum mortgage amounts, channeling up to 40 percent of subsidy funds into existing housing, a
low subsidized housing eligibility limit, and aid for state development corporations. Waranch cautioned, "We believe it is absolutely essential that these provisions be dropped or sharply
modified by this Committee before it reports out a housing bill
this year."[257] By the same token, NAHRO representative Albert
Walsh bewailed the "many serious defects" in the subcommittee
bill, and proposed twenty-one "essential" amendments without
which "the bill would not be workable and could actually do

* In the case of the application requirement, for instance, Romney first
noted administration opposition but then pointed out that "At a minimum,
it would be helpful if your committee made it clear either in the bill *or the
committee report* that Federal processing of the application should involve
review only of matters—and these should be few—required by the act to
be set forth in the application." (Emphasis added.)

serious damage to our current efforts."[258] Opposition also poured in from bar associations and title companies over the settlement cost provisions (Title IX), and from welfare and tenant groups over the provisions that raised rents in public housing and authorized evictions.

While the lobbyists worked behind the scenes, the full committee began markup sessions in early July. It quickly became apparent that Chairman Patman had his own hidden agenda. Rather than taking up the bill by sections and debating only those to which amendments were proposed, Patman insisted on having the 270-page bill read line by line, requesting clarification and amplification and inviting amendments as he went. As a consequence, progress was torturously slow. After three weeks of work, in fact, the committee had still not finished Title I of the bill—the housing consolidation provisions—and the prospect of adjournment in November without a bill began to loom large. As Patman explained to us, "HUD has that housing bill. They got ahold of Bill Barrett and put whatever they wanted into it. That's a recodification. That can be a dangerous thing. I'm going to find out what's in it."[259]

While Patman deliberated and delayed, everyone else tried to figure out what he was doing. "Nobody ever knows what Patman is up to," complained Conference of Mayors executive John Gunther. "Nobody can talk to him, which is a tragedy."[260] "Patman marches to his own music," concurred a high HUD official. "He doesn't tell Romney. He doesn't tell Barrett. Reading Patman is impossible. After thirty years I can't figure him out at all." So frustrated did the bill's supporters on the Housing Subcommittee become, in fact, that they leaked the story of what was going on in the secret markup sessions to Evans and Novak, who dutifully wrote an article depicting Patman as a typical, obdurate southern conservative manipulating the powers of his office to pigeonhole liberal legislation.[261] Gunther, for his part, speculated that Patman was responding to pressures from Texas public housing and urban renewal officials, who stood to lose from the community development title's proposal to channel CD funds through the mayors' offices.

However, far more plausible explanations of Patman's behavior are available. In the first place, foe of the commercial banks that he is, Patman was opposed to the interest subsidy approach which the subcommittee bill—following the HUD housing consolidation proposal—perpetuated as the main vehicle for housing the poor. By his own account, Patman supported this approach in 1968 chiefly as a personal favor to fellow Texan Lyndon Johnson, whose portrait, inscribed with the advice LBJ's father gave him on his election to Congress—"If you want to vote right, vote with Wright"—adorns Patman's office wall. But the scandals in the subsidy programs, plus their increasing cost as market interest rates rose, deepened Patman's suspicions and strengthened his resolve to push a direct-loan approach instead. The subcommittee's willingness to continue supporting the interest subsidy approach, and its refusal to back Sullivan's Home Owners Loan Fund, therefore turned Patman against the bill. In addition, Patman staffers Jake Lewis and Paul Nelson saw delay on this bill as a way to repay the mayors' organizations for their failure to support Patman's 1970 proposal to create a National Development Bank empowered to extend credit for inner-city housing, urban community facilities financing, and small business. According to Lewis, the Conference and League are "too timid" and are unwilling to oppose the banks, even when it will help the cities.[262] The mayors' failure to support even the modest urban development bank proposal offered in the original subcommittee bill (H.R. 9688) and the resulting defeat of this proposal in the subcommittee markups merely strengthened these sentiments. A third reason for Patman's behavior on the housing bill during the summer of 1972 was his eagerness to secure approval of a package of consumer protections against financial manipulations in real estate transactions that he had introduced late in 1971 (H.R. 93337). The major proposal in this package—the regulation of settlement costs—had been accepted by the Housing Subcommittee, but several other features—including a prohibition on interlocking relationships between financial institutions and real estate businesses, a requirement that banks pay interest on escrow balances, and a strict prohibition against having officers of lending institutions serve as attorneys for persons applying to the institutions for residential loans—failed in subcommittee. Moreover, the settlement-cost provision itself was in danger in full committee thanks to extensive lobbying by lawyers and title companies, and Patman was eager to use his position to muster builder and HUD support for this provision. Finally, Patman had some additional, less relevant, pet proposals he wanted to push as well, including a long-standing effort to audit the Federal Reserve System (see Chapter 2) and authorization for subpoena power for his staff to look into the Watergate burglary.

All of this made for high drama in the committee. When the Evans and Novak article appeared, for example, Patman decided to open the executive sessions to the public, giving observers a revealing look at the limited knowledge most of the committee's thirty-eight members brought to the task of evaluating this complex piece of legislation. "We knew it was bad, but we never thought it was this bad," remarked one lobbyist who watched the proceedings. Midway through the consideration of the public housing title, with few Republicans in attendance because it was the day before the Republican National Convention began, Patman introduced an amendment authorizing the General Accounting Office to audit the Federal Reserve. When Republican Garry Brown challenged the germaneness of the amendment on a point of order, Barrett, on cue, provided a tongue-in-cheek rejoinder, noting that "the gentleman's purpose in offering the amendment is obviously to make more money available for the mortgage market." By a sixteen to seven roll call vote, Patman finally got his audit.

Once the Federal Reserve audit amendment passed, in fact, Patman picked up the pace, and on September 19, following a late August recess, the Banking Committee disgorged H.R.

16704, its massive 314-page housing bill. H.R. 16704, as cleared by the committee, showed the influence of steadyhanded lobby pressure in an atmosphere characterized by confusion and doubt. Purged from the bill were several of the nasties attacked by the key special interests, including the three-year warranty, the assistance program for state development corporations, the 40 percent allowance for existing housing, the entire settlement-cost title, the restriction of CD funds to city halls instead of local redevelopment agencies, and the local matching requirement in community development. Nevertheless, in preparing the report to accompany the bill, the subcommittee staff put a good face on the measure, noting the "increased and widespread dissatisfaction with both the substantive aspects of Federal housing and urban development programs and the administration of specific programs," but claiming the bill as "an important first step" in implementing a critically needed national growth policy and in signaling "a shift in congressional expectations concerning the role of FHA from that of a lender- and builder-oriented agency to one closely involved with protection of the homebuyer and renter of FHA-financed properties."[263]

But it was all in vain. The bill still contained the requirement for local government approval of subsidized housing projects, low maximum mortgage amounts, and low income limits for the subsidy programs. As a result, the builders and NAHRO were cool toward the proposal, thus neutralizing two of the main props traditionally supporting federal housing legislation. As Congressman Moorhead explained, "The old coalition we've pieced together to pass previous omnibus housing bills seems to be forming *against* this one. We haven't been able to structure the pay-offs well enough."[264] With the settlement-cost regulations out, and the interest subsidies in, moreover, Patman had little enthusiasm for the bill, even though it now embodied his federal audit measure as well as a modest, experimental direct-loan program. Altogether, in fact, twenty-two members expressed dissatisfaction with the bill in supplementary or dissenting views. What is more, with only a few weeks left to go in the Ninety-second Congress, the prospects for working out the needed compromises on the floor seemed dim. It was no great surprise, therefore, when the Rules Committee on September 27, 1972, voted to refuse to schedule H.R. 16704 for floor debate. The bill that began amid such high hopes for basic reform during the panel deliberations of 1971 thus came to a crashing end, even in mongrelized form, twelve months later, the victim of powerful, special-interest cross-currents and extensive political demagoguery.

POSTSCRIPT:
THE HOUSING AND COMMUNITY
DEVELOPMENT ACT OF 1974

The failure of the 1972 Housing Act, and particularly of the panel innovations, demonstrates the impotence of congressional reformers in the absence of either administration or special-interest support. In the Ninety-third Congress, it became apparent that this lesson had been thoroughly reabsorbed by the key housing policy activists in both the House and Senate Banking committees. But by the time the Banking committees began work on a replacement for the defeated 1972 bill, the whole political climate surrounding federal housing and urban policy had changed dramatically. In particular, on January 5, 1973, the Nixon administration peremptorily halted all future commitments under the subsidized housing programs, impounding the substantial sums Congress had appropriated. Though justified publicly in terms of program "failure" and coupled with a promise of a six-month review of all housing programs, the moratorium also reflected the budget-cutting, anti-inflation sentiments then in the ascendance in the administration. From this perspective, the housing subsidies, which allowed low- and moderate-income families to purchase homes even during periods of tight money, were really working too well, insulating the housing sector from the effects of rising interest rates and thus keeping it from playing its traditional role as the absorber of whatever economic slowdown is needed to keep the economy in equilibrium. By halting these subsidies, the administration was thus throwing the building industry and moderate-income families back onto the tender mercies of the private capital markets.

In addition, on September 19, 1973, nine months after the moratorium began, the President issued a highly critical statement on federal housing policy based on the housing study the administration had launched at the time the moratorium was announced. Three indictments of previous federal efforts to house the poor formed the heart of the President's message. The first was an attack on the poor design and accelerating costs of public housing, an attack that echoed a long-standing Republican Party position. The second was a criticism of the inequities in the subsidy programs, inequities that arose from the confusion in eligibility requirements and from the fact that the newer programs (especially 235 and 236) were frequently providing better homes to those earning $5,000 to $6,000 than were occupied by, or available to, nonsubsidized families earning $7,000 to $8,000—a situation that was generating considerable political heat. The third charge was an attack on the purported wastefulness in the existing approach which, as the President's statement put it, "concentrates on the most expensive means of housing the poor, new buildings, and ignores the potential for using good existing housing."[265]

Behind all of these indictments, moreover, was a fundamental criticism of the whole production orientation of federal housing programs. Noted Nixon's statement, "The main flaw . . . in the old approach is its underlying assumption that the basic problem of the poor is a lack of housing rather than a lack of income. Instead of treating the root cause of the problem—the inability to pay for housing—the Government has been attacking the symptom. We have been helping the builders directly and the poor only indirectly, rather than providing assistance directly to low income families."[266] To remedy this, Nixon proposed a shift from production subsidies to a direct cash assistance—or housing allowance—program, but only after more experimentation with the housing allowance concept. In the meantime, Nixon proposed a wholly new approach to housing construction assistance as well. This approach would build basically on the so-called Section 23 leasing program, under which local public housing agencies were authorized to rent privately owned apartment units on behalf of eligible families and contract with the owners to pay part of the rent. Under the September 1973 proposal, HUD would deal directly with the owners or developers of apartment complexes (eliminating the role of the local public housing agencies) and arrange to pay the developer the difference between the fair market rent and a special rent for units made available to low-income families in these complexes.

In political terms, this dramatic reversal of administration policy severed the warm relationship that had developed with the home builders during the production-oriented Romney years at HUD. Some hint of this change was already apparent in the lack of discipline displayed by House Banking Committee Republicans in offering numerous amendments that helped delay consideration of the 1972 housing bill during the summer of 1972. But the announcement of the moratorium and the replacement of Romney as HUD secretary early in 1973 made the breach patently obvious. Since the subsidy programs were all that had kept the housing industry from serious depression in the tight credit period of 1969–1970, the home builders were, as they put it, "seriously disturbed,"[267] especially since a new period of credit stringency was already developing. They were joined, moreover, by the housing and redevelopment officials organized in NAHRO, and by the mayors, both of whom were already on record in opposition to the administration on its approach to the community development legislation. The result was a complete square-off between the administration and these key elements of the housing and urban development lobby on both the housing and community development measures.

These groups found a receptive audience in the Senate Banking Committee and its newly reorganized, nine-member Housing Subcommittee. The Subcommittee had a clear liberal majority composed of Democrats Proxmire, Williams, Cranston, and Stevenson, Republican Brooke, and, to a lesser extent, Republican Taft. In addition, both Sparkman and Tower were long-standing friends of the home builders, while staff director Coan was tied to the NAHB by close family connections. The Senate Banking Committee therefore took up the cause of the housing lobby with vigor. In early April 1973 it conducted a series of "oversight hearings" designed, among other things, to provide a forum to lambast the Republican administration for its shutdown of housing subsidy programs. Most importantly, when it got down to writing a replacement for the 1972 housing bill, following hearings in July and the introduction of the administration's new housing proposals in September, the Senate Housing Subcommittee gave full vent to the housing lobby's position. What emerged from the Senate Banking Committee in February 1974, therefore, was a bill (S. 3066) that diverged widely from the administration's proposals.

In the housing area, for example, the Senate subcommittee bill, which was ratified by the full committee and the Senate with few changes, defied the administration's moratorium by authorizing substantial funding increases for the 235, 236, and traditional public housing programs during fiscal years 1975 and 1976.* The subcommittee did incorporate the administration's proposed leased housing program, but limited the funding to $880 million instead of the $1.08 billion requested, and stressed that "primary responsibility for carrying out the leasing program should be vested in public housing agencies,"[269] instead of in HUD and local developers as proposed in the administration proposal. In addition, the Senate bill committed the secretary of HUD to reserve housing subsidy funds, "to the extent feasible," to meet

---

* The increases for the two fiscal years would equal $120 million for 235, $380 million for 236, $365 million for traditional public housing, and $210 million for public housing operating subsidies.[268]

the housing objectives in approved community development applications, thus tying the housing and community development programs together.

In the community development area, the Senate subcommittee was even more brutal to the administration's position. Not only did it reject the no-strings-attached revenue sharing approach in favor of "block grants" as it had in 1972, but it also totally rejected reliance on a "need formula" for distributing the funds. A key factor in this rejection was the position of Senator Robert Taft, who defected from the administration when he became convinced, as he noted in the committee's report, that "no formula which was presented to the Committee seemed to match my sense of relative community needs any better than the funding distribution under the past programs."[270] Accordingly, the subcommittee bill, which was eventually approved by the full committee and the Senate, proposed to distribute CD funds almost exclusively on the basis of past involvement in HUD programs. Under this bill, 75 percent of CD funds were reserved for metropolitan areas, and were then to be distributed within these areas to cities with an "entitlement" based on previous program involvement (the "hold-harmless" amount, but with a provision for annual increments), and then to communities without an entitlement on the basis of applications submitted to HUD. The system thus guaranteed to keep funds flowing to the very places that had received them in the past, so long as an application outlining a program of activities aimed at relieving blight and serving community development needs was submitted to HUD. In addition, however, the Senate Housing Subcommittee also imposed far more stringent limits on the activities eligible for CD assistance than were proposed by the administration or included in the Senate's 1972 bill. In particular, to avoid siphoning CD funds off into general public works activities, the subcommittee imposed a flat prohibition against use of more than 20 percent of the CD funds a community receives for "activities which are not intended to be of direct and significant benefit to families of low or moderate income or to areas which are blighted or deteriorating," unless the HUD secretary certifies a community must do so "to meet urgent community needs" (Sec. 308[b][1]). The subcommittee also prohibited devoting more than 20 percent of CD funds to so-called "software" or public service programs like training, crime prevention, child care, health, or welfare, so that the funds could be reserved for the more traditional bricks-and-mortar urban renewal activities. Both of these prohibitions catered to the wishes of the redevelopment establishment, which feared that the administration's community development proposals would divert funds from traditional urban renewal activities and work a particular hardship on those cities most deeply involved in urban renewal programs.

The Senate committee's bill thus tried to guarantee that CD funds would be reserved for relief of the acute problems of central city blight and that they would flow uninterruptedly to those cities that had already demonstrated a determination to deal with these problems.

Despite their opposition to most of the key feaures of S. 3066, administration forces did not press their case during consideration of the bill on the Senate floor in early March 1974, recognizing, as Senate Banking Committee Republicans Tower, Brock, and Packwood noted in supplementary views filed with the bill, that an "item by item debate of the many issues presented by a measure of this complexity" was a "near impossibility."[271] The strategy, clearly, was to recoup the losses in the House and then force the Senate Committee to compromise in conference. Accordingly, few objections were offered on the Senate floor, and S. 3066 cleared the Senate virtually unscathed on March 11, 1974 by a vote of seventy-six to eleven.

As it turned out, the administration's confidence about prospects in the House were well founded. In the first place, the liberal Democrats on the House Banking Committee generally hailed from central-city areas more likely to be aided by efforts to preserve existing housing than from those to build new housing in the suburbs. In the second place, the activist elements on the

House Housing Subcommittee—particularly Ashley—recognized the need to work with the administration if they wanted to pursue, in the face of home builder opposition, the federal growth policy measures they favored. Third, House members generally were apparently feeling the heat from constituents on the inequities of the subsidy programs. Tied more closely to such constituent pressures, and generally more conservative than senators, the House members turned on the housing subsidy measures with zeal. As one House Banking Committee member sized up the situation, "I just don't think that the old programs as they are presently constituted can get through Congress."[272] Finally, and most decisively, the administration made it clear it would veto any bill that extended the existing housing subsidy programs or that diverged too widely from its own community development measure. In addition, it made clear its intention to sit on the already appropriated housing subsidy funds until Congress acted.

Despite the plea of NAHRO representatives, who pointed out that "close dancing is coming back,"[273] therefore, the House Banking Committee's Housing Subcommittee moved further away from the housing lobby to embrace key elements of the administration's position during the extensive markup sessions that stretched from February 5 until April 30, 1974. In particular, the subcommittee eliminated new funding for the 235 and 236 programs, restricted new funding for traditional public housing to $50 million, and shifted almost the entire federal housing assistance effort to the administration's proposed Section 23 leased housing program, for which it authorized $1.014 billion for fiscal years 1975 and 1976. In addition, the subcommittee expressed its continued displeasure at the public housing program by establishing a minimum rent for public housing tenants computed at 10 percent of gross income. All that liberal elements managed to salvage, in fact, was a provision keeping the 235 and 236 programs "on the books" in case the new program failed. In addition, Ashley obtained administration acquiescence to his "housing block grant" concept, under which housing subsidy funds would be distributed through metropolitan agencies charged with encouraging the spread of low-income housing in the suburbs. But, as it appeared in the subcommittee bill (H.R. 14490), this concept was badly mauled; gone was any reference to metropolitan housing agencies, the intellectual heart of the original idea. Instead, housing funds would be distributed by the HUD secretary to *local units of government*, and the local governments would then be obligated to spend them according to a local "housing assistance plan." All that remained of the original scheme, therefore, was a mild incentive for localities to formulate housing assistance plans, since only communities that had such plans could refuse low-income housing and communities without such plans could not qualify for community development funds. Whether this would open up suburbs to low-income housing, however, remained open to serious doubt. For the rest, however, the House bill was a clear step backward from the viewpoint of efforts to house the urban poor.

The House's Housing Subcommittee, working under the effective bipartisan leadership of Ashley and Brown, also walked the extra mile toward the administration position on the community development measure. While sticking to a block-grant approach (i.e., an application requirement), the subcommittee adopted a need-based, formula distribution system. Although communities receiving more under the existing categorical programs than would be provided under the formula were protected by a "hold-harmless" provision, the bill followed administration wishes by proposing to phase out this protection after three years. As critics would quickly point out, the result would be to cut back severely on community development funds for some hundred cities that had historically been the most active participants in urban renewal and model cities programs. The subcommittee bill also made "urban counties" eligible for CD funds, thus opening the possibility that central cities might lose such funds to the suburbs. The bill also eliminated the local matching requirement on CD funds and left the list of eligible CD activities unencumbered by specific prohibitions of the sort embodied in the Senate bill. All the administration was forced to concede in return for this tailoring of the bill to its specifications was the requirement that applicants for CD funds must formulate a housing assistance plan specifying the kind and general location of assisted housing needed in the community. With this move, the subcommittee linked the federal government's housing and community development measures far more intimately than had been done in the past and thus fulfilled a long-standing Ashley goal. But it did not require the administration to provide the housing funds called for in approved local CD plans, as was proposed in the Senate bill.

Against the vigorous opposition of full-committee liberals like Parren Mitchell and Edward Koch, who argued that the subcommittee bill would take funds away from the central cities most actively involved in slum clearance and kill federal efforts to house the poor, the bill survived full-committee executive sessions in late May and early June virtually intact, thanks largely to the insistence of sponsors Barrett and Ashley that any major amendments would jeopardize a carefully constructed series of compromises formed with HUD and thus trigger a presidential veto. Since the House was scheduled to take up the Nixon impeachment question in early August, and since the expectation was that the impeachment process would occupy Congress for the remainder of the session, Ashley and Barrett argued convincingly that major amendments would prevent passage of any bill in the Ninety-third Congress. As opponents pointed out afterward, "Throughout the markup sessions of the full committee, the single thread of thought that was consistently uttered by the proponents of the bill was that this was the best we could do in light of the threat of a Presidential veto."[274] As it turned out, with all existing housing programs stalled because of the administration's impoundment of funds, this threat was sufficient to win a full-committee majority over to support of the subcommittee bill. The same magical formula worked on the floor of the House, as the Housing Subcommittee bill—renumbered H.R. 15361 to incorporate minor changes added in the full committee—cleared the House on June 20, 1974 by a vote of 351 to 25. Only one substantive amendment, rein-stating the old Section 202 direct-loan program for rental projects for the elderly, squeezed through. By contrast, a proposal to rein-state the 235 and 236 programs—the darlings of the home builders —and to provide $1,140 million for them over the next three years, failed decisively; and opponents of the CD funding formula did not even bother to offer an amendment, pinning their hopes on the Senate conference to turn around the bill passed by the House.

With impeachment talk heating up, the question then became whether H.R. 15361 could be married to the Senate's much dif-ferent S. 3066, particularly in the limited time available before the House was scheduled to take up impeachment. For three weeks, Senate conferees held out. But then in early August, on the eve of the impeachment vote in the House Judiciary Committee, and facing the prospect of lengthy impeachment hearings, they finally conceded, accepting the House version on virtually every one of the key housing and community development items at issue. All that the Senate was able to rescue from its approach in fact, were a commitment to extend the life of the 235 and 236 programs through fiscal 1976, but at drastically reduced funding levels; a reduction of the minimum public housing rent proposed in the House bill from 10 percent of gross income to 5 percent; an agree-ment to review the workings of the formula for distributing CD funds after three years; and a stipulation that local communities give "maximum feasible priority" in spending these funds to activi-ties of direct benefit to low-income families or to blighted or deter-iorating areas.

For the rest, however, the resulting bill was a rebuff to the housing lobby that had played so prominent a role in framing the Senate bill. The home builders, for example, while managing to liberalize down-payment requirements on the traditional FHA loan guarantee programs, lost the 235 and 236 programs, the lushest housing subsidies Congress ever enacted. In their place, the bill substituted the administration-backed leased housing pro-posal, which was supposed to generate 400,000 units of new rental housing, but which would inevitably require an extended start-up period and involved considerable uncertainty. By the same token, the mayors and redevelopment officials, while pleased by the scrapping of the categorical assistance programs, lost the battle to protect the cities most active in slum clearance work from severe budgetary cuts under the new community development program. According to the conference bill, community development funds would henceforth be distributed to municipalities on the basis of need, defined in terms of population, housing overcrowding, and the extent of poverty; and cities that had managed to secure funds under the urban renewal, model cities, and other categorical programs in excess of their formula amount would have only three years of continued operation at existing funding levels before being phased down to their formula shares. Finally, the bill virtually ended all future commitments to build additional units of public housing, despite lengthy waiting lists for public housing in almost every major city in the nation. For crucial segments of the housing lobby, in other words, about all that could be said about this bill was that it was better than no bill at all, but only marginally so.

Although Nixon resigned two days after the conferees reached their agreement, eliminating much of the urgency for quick action that had produced the Senate capitulation, the conference report remained intact and easily cleared both House and Senate by August 15. A week later, newly installed President Gerald Ford affixed his signature to the first major piece of housing and urban legislation since 1968, the Housing and Community Development Act of 1974. Though four years of struggle to formulate a new approach to federal housing and urban policy thereby came to an end, the result for the housing lobby was more a temporary ceasefire than a permanent peace. "HUD wants to halt all new Government-sponsored construction eventually," liberal Democrat Pete Stark noted on the House floor. "With that as their stated goal, this bill takes on a more important function—it is the finger in the dike to keep HUD subsidizing new housing."[275] The only question that remained unanswered was when conditions would become ripe to build the dike anew.

Rebuilding the Dike:
The Emergency Middle Income Housing Act of 1975

Fortunately for the housing lobby, the answer to this question was not long in coming, for in the November 1974 congressional elections these urban-oriented interests amassed significant new strength, especially in the House. Moreover, with housing production at a thirty-year low, thanks to the prevailing high interest rates and the suspension of the housing subsidy programs, the builders and mortgage merchants were in a position to revive their most telling argument from the 1930s: that aid for their industries was essential for national economic revival. The stage was thus set for bold efforts to repair the damage created by the Nixon administration's moratorium on housing subsidy programs and the subsequent 1974 Housing Act.

One of the first steps in this direction was the ouster of Wright Patman as chairman of the House Banking Committee, for Patman's dilatory handling of the 1972 housing bill, his philosophical opposition to many forms of mortgage finance subsidies, and his status as a maverick "outsider" in the House made him a questionable ally in the work that lay ahead. In quick order, the House Committee under newly installed Chairman Henry Reuss then changed its name from Banking and Currency to Banking, Currency, *and Housing*; and set to work rebuilding the partly dismantled governmental protections designed to shelter the now depressed home construction and finance industries.

But the House committee did not restrict itself to mere reconstruction. Freed by the depression in the building industry from any need to justify their work in terms of the housing needs of the poor, committee members also built anew, passing what must certainly be one of the great boondoggles of all time. Styled the Emergency Middle Income Housing Act of 1975, the bill that cleared the House Banking Committee on March 14, and the full

House seven days later, took the interest subsidy approach that the discredited 235 and 236 programs had formerly made available only to lower-income families and extended it to the broad middle class. Under the scheme, the federal government would be obligated to pay banks a subsidy sufficient to bring mortgage interest rates down to 6 or 7 percent for all home buyers whose earnings fell within 120 percent of the median income in their locality (i.e., for families with yearly earnings of up to $13,500–$17,000). For those home buyers wanting the 6 percent rate, the subsidy would last six years. For those willing to settle for 7 percent, it would last the life of the mortgage. Whatever the choice, the plan would make interest subsidies available to 60–70 percent of the American population and thus fulfill the long-standing builder dream to insulate the housing industry completely from the vagaries of fluctuating interest rates—and do so without the bothersome need to rely on low-income people. To guarantee this result, moreover, the bill stipulated that at least 70 percent of the subsidy funds would be reserved for mortgages on *new* homes.

As in the 1930s, therefore, the economic pump-priming functions of the home building industry took precedence over the shelter needs of the poor and the neighborhood development needs of the cities in the formulation of federal housing and urban policy. With a price tag conservatively estimated at $12 billion, however, the new dispensation made the authors of the 1934 Housing Act, which had established the FHA loan guarantee program, look like timid, unimaginative pikers. Only the nagging opposition of administration critics, who pointed to the inflationary implications of the proposed new scheme, spoiled the fun; but these critics could muster only 106 votes in opposition to the bill on the House floor, well below the 259 cast in its favor.

This same constellation of forces that enabled the home builders to recoup their 1974 losses in the House operated as well in the Senate. Within three weeks of passage of the House bill, therefore, the Senate Banking Committee cleared a companion measure, which incorporated the middle-income interest subsidy program

5

Cowboys Who Lasso Themselves: The Battle Against Inflation

For at least a decade now, congressmen have been complaining about the usurpation of their rightful powers by an insatiable executive branch which, when given an inch of rope by a trusting Congress, has cleverly stretched it, formed a lasso, and tied all the members up. After realizing what it surrendered in the 1964 Gulf of Tonkin Resolution, which Presidents Johnson and Nixon used to conduct the war in Vietnam, Congress surely could have been expected to maintain a jealous hold on its remaining powers. But the story of the way Congress responded to the problem of infla-

NOTE: This chapter benefited greatly from the research assistance of Michael Massey, who also prepared a preliminary draft.

311

tion in the early 1970s illustrates how limited that body's learning powers are, and how adept the members are at lassoing themselves and surrendering to executive power.

Beginning in the latter 1960s the United States economy entered a period of serious inflation and general economic disruption, as the demands of the Vietnam War competed with consumer demands generally to force prices upward at an accelerating pace. During the early years of this inflationary surge, President Lyndon Johnson pretended it did not exist, arguing persistently that the nation's economy could provide guns and butter simultaneously with only minor disruptions. By the time Richard Nixon took office in 1969, the inflationary fires were burning brightly. But free-market ideologue that he was, Nixon was hardly the man to tackle the inflation problem directly. Throughout the 1968 campaign, in fact, he eschewed any form of controls on wages, prices, or interest rates, and espoused instead an orthodox position calling for reduced government spending and restrictive monetary policy.* The key economic advisers Nixon brought to Washington with him—George Schultz, Her-

---

* A "restrictive monetary policy" is one that seeks to limit the amount of money in circulation. This is achieved by having the Federal Reserve sell securities or require larger "reserves" to be held by member banks. This set of policy prescriptions was premised on the "demand-pull" theory of inflation, which attributes price rises to excessive government deficit spending that encourages a too-rapid expansion of the money supply and thus leads to an excess of demand over the available supply of goods in the economy. The cure for inflation, according to this view, is to reduce government spending and contract the money supply while making efforts to increase the supply of goods through such devices as investment tax credits.

A contrary view sees inflation as a product of "cost-push" factors such as rapidly rising corporate profits, excessive wage increases, or oligopolistic price control. The cure for inflation, according to this view, is to impose direct controls on wages and prices, especially in the major industries.

Since most inflationary episodes involve both demand-pull and cost-push factors, however, even adherents of the demand-pull school of thought sometimes favor temporary wage and price controls, if only to dampen the harmful and self-defeating "inflationary psychology" until the more traditional policy tools can work their effects. In cases of particularly virulent price inflation, moreover, there is often a strong possibility that the level of money

bert Stein, and Arthur Burns—reflected these predispositions; and with the elevation of Burns to the chairmanship of the Federal Reserve Board in late 1969, the stage was set for a test of the orthodox faith in monetary policy as an antidote to inflation.

Within eighteen months of Nixon's inauguration, the bankruptcy of this approach had become apparent. The administration's policies did manage to slow economic growth, produce a near depression in the housing industry, and throw thousands of workers out of jobs—but they did not reduce the rate of price inflation. By early summer 1970, Democratic economist Walter Heller was talking in amazement of Nixon's success at producing a new economic phenomenon which Heller christened "stagflation": the simultaneous existence of stagnation and inflation. In late May, Democratic Party chairman Lawrence O'Brien hailed the achievement as the creation of a new branch of economics: Nixonomics. The Joint Economic Committee in Congress, meanwhile, issued a report in late March urging greater presidential activism in restraining wage and price increases, and even the committee's Republicans agreed that new wage-price action was needed.[1]

Nevertheless, Nixon held firm to his faltering "game plan." In a special radio address on economic policy on June 17, 1970, the President emphatically ruled out wage-price controls, claiming that they "would lead to rationing, black marketing, total federal bureaucratic domination and would never get at the real causes of inflation." Promised Nixon:

> I will not take this nation down the road of wage-and-price controls, however politically expedient they may seem. They only postpone a day of reckoning, and in so doing they rob every American of an important part of his freedom.[2]

---

supply contraction needed to control the inflation may be so great as to produce a severe over-reaction, sending the economy into a recession. Under such circumstances, direct wage and price action may be needed to complement the monetary policy tools. It was precisely this question that was at issue in the early years of Nixon's first term.

Given this presidential obduracy in the face of a clearly failing policy, Congress had a rare opportunity to seize the initiative. What is more, since the most commonly discussed alternative to the President's policy was some form of wage and price controls, the responsibility for taking advantage of this opportunity fell squarely on the Banking committees, which, under both House and Senate rules, have jurisdiction over all matters relating to "control of prices of commodities, rents, or services."[3] Instead of taking the initiative and putting Congress in control of economic policy, however, the House and Senate Banking committees played political games, enacting legislation that merely shifted the monkey onto the President's back again, but with a sweeping delegation of power. Only after the President accepted the challenge did the members realize how much authority they had surrendered. But by then it was too late.

THE FIRST INCH

The inch of rope that grew into a huge lasso was given in the form of a nongermane title appended to the 1970 extension to the Defense Production Act of 1950. The Defense Production Act originated as a mechanism to assure sufficient resources for defense needs during the Korean War by, among other things, establishing defense procurement priorities, authorizing the stockpiling of crucial resources, and protecting contractors supplying defense needs against claims for breaching other contracts. Since its creation, the act had become an essential part of government defense procurement policy and was regularly extended every two years.

In the Senate Banking Committee, the Defense Production Act extension was handled routinely in 1970, except for an intense debate over a proposal offered by Defense Department critic William Proxmire to impose a uniform cost-accounting system on defense contractors.* The extension bill (S. 3302), with Proxmire's

---

* Proxmire's proposal reflected his conviction that the Defense Department was losing millions of dollars on cost-plus-fixed-fee contracts because of the

cost-accounting feature included, was reported out by the Senate Banking Committee on May 21 and cleared the Senate on July 9, 1970—all without any mention of wage and price controls,

Not so in the House. With the November 1970 midterm elections fast approaching, and with Nixon publicly blaming the spendthrift ways of the Democratic majority in Congress for the continued inflation, House Democrats decided to counterattack, but in a peculiar fashion. They proposed to immerse the President in authority, to supply him with more than ample power to control the inflationary surge, and thus to shift the blame clearly back to the Republicans if the President continued to refuse to act. Accordingly, in late May, House Banking Committee chairman Patman, claiming to speak for the "overwhelming majority" of the Banking Committee, wrote the President offering "to give you any tools which you feel are needed to bring the current economic situation under control."[4] As a sign of earnestness, moreover, Patman and Henry Reuss, one of the Banking Committee's foremost economic experts, introduced a brief rider to the Defense Production Act extension bill (H.R. 17880) scheduled for committee hearings in June. The rider, which appeared as Title II of the bill and was called the Economic Stabilization Act of 1970, was a disarmingly simple and straightforward proposal giving the president wide-ranging authority to "issue such orders and regulations as he may deem appropriate to stabilize prices, rents, wages, and salaries at levels not less than those prevailing on May 25, 1970" and to make whatever adjustments are necessary "to prevent gross inequities." Though scheduled to expire at the end of February 1971, this title would nevertheless give President Nixon more power over economic decision-making than any other peacetime president, and with virtually no congressional controls, no procedural safeguards, no legislatively mandated standards, and no provision for appeal or even public scrutiny.

---

cost-accounting practices of contractors. He therefore proposed to give the General Accounting Office, an arm of the Congress, authority to establish a uniform cost-accounting system and to police it.

Since the President was not asking for this authority—indeed had categorically rejected it in his June 17 speech on the eve of Banking Committee hearings on H.R. 17880—it is hard to sustain any other conclusion than that the Banking Committee Democrats were engaged in a game of political one-upmanship, especially since Title II did not *require* the President to freeze wages and prices, but merely *authorized* him to do so. To be sure, Henry Reuss professed to see the Title II authority as part of a larger economic package. He therefore stressed the temporary character of Title II's vast grant of authority, noting that "it is envisaged that any action to be taken by the President under it would be short-term action, typically for the two or three months in which permanent wage-price-income guideposts and policies are being worked out."[5] But since the President's June 17 speech made it clear no such permanent guideposts and policies were anticipated, aside from a vague promise of periodic "inflation alerts," this argument is not persuasive. What is more, although the Democrats could justifiably argue that Congress could not *administer* a wage-price control program on its own even if it mandated one, and that therefore presidential concurrence was needed, the sweeping language of Title II made even this argument suspect. Patman therefore provided a better clue to what the Democrats were up to when he suggested that the purpose of Title II was "to educate the President to the fact that there is an economic crisis and that people want action." Noted Patman, "All of us want to make sure that the President has all the possible tools to deal with the economic crisis that is before us." Title II was needed, he argued, to "shore the President up, to give him some more muscle, some more will to do something meaningful— something besides more boards and commissions."[6] The idea, in short, was to put the President on the spot, to place squarely on his shoulders the politically unpopular chore of imposing wage and price controls while relieving the Democrats of any responsibility for the state of the economy in anticipation of the upcoming November 1970 elections.

As United Auto Workers President Leonard Woodcock pointed out, however, Title II was really an "idle gesture" since the President's June 17 speech disavowing any intention to invoke controls made the authority granted in this title "somewhat academic." What Congress should do, Woodcock urged, was to take direct action to control prices itself, instead of waiting around for the President to act.[7] Banking Committee Republicans drove this point home as they sought to wiggle out of the political predicament they found themselves in by adopting the disingenuous tactic of challenging the Democrats to impose a wage and price freeze themselves if they thought it was so necessary. Republican Congressman Gary Brown of Michigan, for example, charged that Title II of H.R. 17880 should be renamed "The Domestic Gulf of Tonkin Resolution" because of the incredibly free hand it proposed to give the President on the economic front.[8] Conservative Republican Ben Blackburn of Georgia was equally scornful of the Democrats' apparent opportunism, asking one witness at the hearings whether he thought

> Congress [would get] the best of both worlds, if we grant the authority but do not direct the President to use that authority, then in the event inflation is not curbed we can criticize the President very freely by arguing that he should have used the power. On the other hand, if the President does manage to curb inflation using present policies then the Congress can forget that as a political issue. I think Congress has more responsibility than to say "We are going to give you the power, but we are really not suggesting that you use it."[9]

But the Democratic majority on the Banking Committee would have none of this, and reported H.R. 17880, complete with Title II's wage-price control authority, by a straight party vote on July 27, 1970. Three days later, amid Republican charges of "devious Democratic demagoguery" and a Republican suggestion that the bill be rechristened the "Election Year Squeezeplay,"[10] H.R. 17880 was scheduled for debate on the House floor. There, both sides played their respective roles to completion. The Republicans, though opposed to controls, offered two amendments that would have imposed them, but with Congress (i.e., the Democrats) bearing the responsibility. Thus Garry Brown proposed to amend Title II by creating a special legislative committee authorized to decide when a wage and price freeze should be imposed. Brown, who confessed that he balked at any controls, claimed that he "disliked even more the failure of this Congress, of the House of Representatives, to face up to its responsibilities when it has the vehicle to do so through my amendment which will permit it to accept the responsibility to retain the authority for the imposition of wage and price controls."[11] And Ben Blackburn, another foe of controls, proposed changing the language of Title II to impose a freeze immediately instead of leaving it up to the President. Both of these amendments were easily turned aside, however. Throughout the debate, the advocates of controls insisted that the President, not the Congress, should have the responsibility for imposing them. Of all the Democrats clamoring for wage and price stabilization authority, in fact, only Jonathan Bingham of New York actually supported their direct implementation by Congress. Rather than criticize the President for his inaction on the economic front, Bingham argued, Congress should establish an independent board of economic experts to impose a freeze and monitor it.[12] Such bold initiatives found little support, however, and amid the grand posturing and harsh partisan rhetoric, H.R. 17880 cleared the House unchanged by a vote of 257 to 19, as most Republicans chose not to go on record opposing the bill for fear their Democratic opponents would use it against them. Noted Republican Chalmers Wylie of Ohio, whose amendment to strike Title II from the bill was handily defeated, "This is the season when it becomes more and more difficult to separate fact from fiction."[13]

This separation was apparently equally difficult for the House-Senate conference committee to maintain, for Senate conferees accepted Title II even though the Senate bill had contained no comparable provision. The Senate as a whole then approved this decision in a hasty voice vote on August 13. Two days later, President Nixon signed the bill, but noted that he would have vetoed it were it not for the fact that continuation of the defense production authority was crucial to the defense effort. The political gamesmanship prevalent throughout the consideration of the bill continued to the last minute, as the President first observed that "wage price controls simply do not fit the economic conditions which exist today," but then chastised Congress for failing to "face up to its responsibilities and make such controls mandatory" if it really thought them necessary.[14]

While the President and Congress passed the buck back and forth, "stagflation" continued unabated. During 1970 alone, the consumer price index climbed 6 percent, on top of earlier increases of 5.4 percent in 1969 and 4.2 percent in 1968. By the end of the year, 6 percent of the labor force—5.4 million persons —were unemployed, a one-third increase over the previous year.[15] In response, the congressional Democratic leaders publicly urged the President to impose an immediate thirty- to sixty-day wage and price freeze.[16] But the congressional leadership remained unwilling to take such action itself. The most they could muster was a one-month extension of the wage and price control authority (scheduled to expire in February 1971), which was attached as a rider to a Small Business Administration bill in the House in late November and ratified by the Senate on December 10, 1970.[17] For the rest, political temerity and rising frustration were the order of the day. Having given the President a substantial length of rope, the Congress waited patiently for the President to tie them up.

ADJUSTING THE LASSO

They did not have long to wait. Already by late 1970, voices were being heard from within the Nixon administration calling for greater wage-price action by the President. The opposition of

Treasury Secretary David Kennedy to the dominant White House view on wage and price controls was well known to Washington insiders,[18] and in December 1970 Federal Reserve Board Chairman Burns added his voice by urging creation of a wage and price review board to mobilize public pressure against inflationary increases.[19] Although the President held firm to his free-market orthodoxy in his Economic Report to Congress on February 1, 1971—vowing that "I do not intend to impose wage and price controls which would substitute new, growing, and more vexatious problems for the problems of inflation. Neither do I intend to rely on an elaborate facade that seems to be wage and price control but is not"[20]—as the failure of the existing policy became increasingly apparent, some breaks in the armor soon appeared. Most important, when the House Banking Committee took up the question of extending the wage-price authority again in late February 1971, newly appointed Treasury Secretary John Connally testified that the administration was now ready to accept the standby authority to set up wage-price controls, even as he protested that "we do not believe that a network of general wage-price controls is needed at this time, nor do we believe that the American people would long stand for such regimentation, *under present circumstances.*"[21] The day Connally testified, Nixon took his biggest step on the wage-price front to date by forcing a program of wage constraint on the construction industry through a suspension of the Davis-Bacon Act, the act that requires contractors on federally sponsored construction projects to pay "prevailing" (typically union-negotiated) wages. One month later, on March 29, 1971, Nixon formally invoked the Stabilization Act authority for the first time, issuing an executive order establishing a special board empowered to hold wage increases in the construction industry down to the averages of previous years, and a second board to develop criteria for judging construction industry price and profit levels.

The reaction to these moves among advocates of wage-price controls on Capitol Hill was, surprisingly enough, one of outrage.

Senator Proxmire, for example, claimed that "the authority was never intended to single out a particular group of wage earners without stabilizing the cost of living as a whole."[22] Appearing before Proxmire's subcommittee on April 7, 1971, Congressman Reuss made a similar point. "I still, for the life of me, cannot figure out whether the President was, in fact, using this law in his arrangement with the building and construction trades unions," Reuss objected. "If he was, however, I believe it was a misuse of the law under the very clear legislative history when this bill went through the House. It was not to be used against just one industry or one segment of industry."[23] Yet the act itself said nothing of this sort. Congress was beginning to feel the rope it had put around its neck.

Even at this point, however, there was room to escape. The wage-price control authority was scheduled to expire on March 31, 1971.* Congress thus had another crack at reconsidering the vast power it had granted the President under the guise of taking the initiative in economic policy. Yet, despite the fact that there was now some evidence the President might use this authority, and use it in ways the congressional advocates of controls disapproved, the stabilization act was extended again almost unchanged, and this time for a year.

As before, the House led the way. It began hearings on February 23, the day the administration announced its suspension of the Davis-Bacon Act and its voluntary program of wage-price constraint in the construction industry, but well before the President's March 29 executive order establishing a formal wage-price stabilization program for the construction industry. On March 5, the committee reported a bill (H.R. 4246) to extend the sweeping standby wage-price stabilization authority two full years, until March 31, 1973, and provide $20 million for the administration of controls in the event the President invoked them. Because the

---

* As we have seen, the authority was originally scheduled to expire on February 28, 1971, but had been extended in mid-December, 1970, for another 30 days, to March 31, 1971.

administration had indicated its willingness to accept the standby authority, the debate lacked the partisan acrimony that character- ized the 1970 discussion, although Democratic sponsors of the original measure did not let the occasion pass without requiring administration forces to eat some of their words. Moreover, some Republicans still had their doubts. Ranking Banking Committee Republican William Widnall conceded on the House floor that "This authority remains . . . in my opinion, a partisan political gimmick."[24] His colleague, Gary Brown, even sought to reintro- duce an amendment he offered in 1970 deleting the presidential standby authority altogether and vesting the responsibility for imposing wage and price controls in a special congressional com- mittee; but his amendment was turned aside when Patman raised a point of order protesting that it had not followed proper proce- dure. Nevertheless, Brown used the opportunity to warn his col- leagues:

> The situation today is little different from . . . last year. The fact the administration may have changed somewhat its po- sition of outright opposition to such standby authority to one of "accepting" the provisions of H.R. 4246 should make more doubtful the desirability of passage of such standby authority. . . . The willingness of the administration to ac- cept the standby wage-price authority this year . . . should prompt fears in many about the unnecessary or improper use of the broad discretionary authority of the President.[25]

This warning echoed one issued by Federal Reserve Board Chairman Arthur Burns less than a month earlier. Testifying before the Joint Economic Committee in February 1971, Burns said of the Economic Stabilization Act authority: "You are giving too much power to the President under this legislation. You are giving the President virtually dictatorial power."[26] Nevertheless, the House voted by an overwhelming 382 to 19 to extend for another two years the sweeping and uncluttered stabilization authority it had first granted the President in August 1970. The only limitation it imposed was a provision inserted at the behest of Democrat William Moorhead during Banking Committee markup sessions that stipulated the control authority would expire six months after the President first invoked it, so that Congress could at least review the situation. For the rest, the authority remained as broad and unrestrained as in the original version.

The Senate moved somewhat more cautiously, although—as it turned out—no more forcefully, in extending the stabilization authority. On March 4, 1971, it passed a temporary two-month extension of the control power, while preparations were made to commence hearings on March 29 before the Banking Committee's Subcommittee on Financial Institutions, chaired by William Proxmire. The day these hearings began—which also turned out to be the day the President invoked the stabilization act with respect to the construction industry—the House concurred in this temporary extension, but not before rejecting an amendment offered by Henry Reuss to forbid imposition of wage-price controls on a single industry like construction. If Congress were to retake the ball of economic authority that it had dropped at the President's feet and that the President now seemed determined to run with in the wrong direction, therefore, it was now up to the Senate to take the lead.

But the Senate did not. With the administration now firmly committed to extension of the standby control authority, Senate Republicans generally fell into line. As for the Democrats, they were effectively locked in. After stressing the need for wage and price controls for more than a year, they could hardly reverse course now that the President was beginning to take some of their advice. Proxmire, the main Senate advocate of control authority in 1970, typified this dilemma. After pushing the Stabilization Act so vigorously in 1970, he felt compelled to endorse its extension in 1971, even while confessing at the start of the hearings that "I have grave reservations about giving this broad grant of authority to the President, particularly if it can be used in a discriminatory fashion."[27] Proxmire sought to reconcile himself to this dilemma by proposing a very limited extension of the authority. Instead of the two-year extension proposed by the administration,[28] Proxmire's bill (S. 1201) would extend the authority only an additional four months, from June 1 to October 1, 1971. But any thoughts of limiting the "broad grant of authority" the act gave the President ran headlong into administration arguments about the need for "flexibility"—arguments that echoed the case the Democrats had made in July 1970 when pushing the original Stabilization Act through Congress over Republican opposition.* What is more, Proxmire was constrained by his eagerness to win administration support for a proposal that he had packaged together with the stabilization-authority extension in S. 1201: a plan to channel credit into socially important sectors of the economy such as housing, small business, urban and rural poverty areas, and state and local government by authorizing the Federal Reserve Board to vary the reserve requirements of member banks to encourage investment in these sectors, particularly during tight-money periods.† Most of the discussion in the Senate hearings, in fact, focused on this latter proposal.

The bill that emerged from the Senate Banking Committee on April 29, 1971, therefore, diverged little from the Economic Stabilization Act of 1970. The committee bill did retain the October 1, 1971, cutoff date proposed by Proxmire, but this was altered on the Senate floor when the members approved, by voice vote, a Tower amendment to extend the President's standby authority through April 30, 1972. The one substantial change incorporated in the Senate bill was a provision prohibiting the President from applying wage and price controls to a single industry, but even this provision was seriously watered down by a giant loophole allowing the President to apply such selective controls if he de-

* Ranking Banking Committee Republican John Tower made this point forcefully while questioning Representative Henry Reuss when the latter appeared before Proxmire's subcommittee on April 7, 1971.[29]
† "Reserve requirements" are the nonearning assets banks are required to hold in their coffers as reserves against potential withdrawals.

termined that wages and prices in some industry had increased at a rate grossly disproportionate to that in the rest of the economy. Nevertheless, the price of inclusion of even this pallid restriction was the defeat of Proxmire's variable reserve requirement proposal, which the Federal Reserve Board, the Treasury Department, and the commercial bankers had all opposed during the hearings. When Republican Bob Packwood proposed an amendment on the Senate floor that would prohibit presidential imposition of controls without a concurrent resolution by Congress, on the ground that Congress must "reassert its powers in the field of wage and price controls," it was Proxmire who led the attack against the amendment.[30]

So despite the administration's reiteration that it would not impose general wage and price controls, and although most committee members thought the administration had already used the control authority in an improper manner, the Senate Banking Committee and its parent body went along with yet another extension of the broad control authority, passing S. 1201 by sixty-seven to four on May 3. Two days later, the House approved the Senate amendments, dropping the earlier House provision that would have terminated control authority six months after they were first invoked (which would have been September 29, 1971, since the administration had imposed controls on the construction industry March 29) and adding the mild Senate provision prohibiting single-industry controls in the absence of a showing of grossly disproportionate wage or price movement. On May 18, 1971, the President put the seal on this congressional abdication of power by signing the control-authority extension into law.

TIGHTENING THE NOOSE

Three months later, following a steady worsening of economic conditions, President Nixon surprised the nation, and the Congress, by invoking the Stabilization Act authority. He imposed a ninety-day freeze on all nonagricultural wages and prices and announced a dramatic New Economic Policy complete with an historic devaluation of the dollar and proposals for massive tax cuts for industry. To oversee this New Economic Policy and plan for the post-freeze Phase II of the program, the President created the Cost of Living Council, composed of the secretaries of Agriculture, Commerce, Labor, and Treasury; the director of the Office of Management and Budget; the chairman of the Council of Economic Advisers; the director of the Office of Emergency Preparedness; the President's Special Assistant for Consumer Affairs; and the chairman of the Federal Reserve Board as an adviser.[31]

Then, on October 7, 1971, the President unveiled Phase II of his New Economic Policy, a comprehensive stabilization program covering prices, rents, wages, and salaries for as long as the Economic Stabilization Act of 1970 remained in effect. Phase II would be administered by the Cost of Living Council and by two new entities created by the October 15, 1971, executive order that implemented the administration's new scheme: first, a Pay Board composed of fifteen members representing business, organized labor, and the general public; and second, a Price Commission composed of seven members, all from the general public. As the October 15 executive order explained:

> The Cost of Living Council will establish broad stabilization goals for the Nation, and the Pay Board and Price Commission, acting through their respective Chairmen, will prescribe specific standards, criteria, and regulations, and make rulings and decisions aimed at carrying out these goals.[32]

The congressional response to these executive initiatives was generally supportive, but the main congressional advocates of controls reacted like jilted lovers, as they came to realize the vast authority they had given the President and the meager control they retained themselves. Critics particularly attacked four features of the stabilization program: its failure to cover agricultural products, which had contributed so heavily to the ongoing inflation; its failure to control interest rates; its failure to freeze profit

levels; and its failure to make provision for wage increases negotiated prior to the freeze but not scheduled to go into effect until
after its imposition. As the operation of the stabilization program
unfolded, moreover, additional complaints surfaced to the effect
that the Cost of Living Council was soft on price increases while
bearing down on wage hikes.[33] Within three weeks of the imposition of the freeze, Democrat Henry Reuss was complaining on the
House floor that "We Democrats . . . gave the President good
meat and potatoes to make a nourishing stew. He has taken the
good ingredients, but covered them with a chocolate sauce that
makes the whole thing an inedible mess."[34] A week later William
Proxmire was confessing his "embarrassment" at having sponsored the 1970 act in the Senate. Proxmire bewailed that the
Economic Stabilization Act had given the President "unprecedented power to control wages and prices with virtually no congressional standards or criteria on how the authority should be
used and no legal safeguards for affected parties." Quoting from a
statement by economist Arthur Miller, Proxmire lamented that
"Congress gave away not only the ball game, but the entire ball
park."[35] During an appearance on William Buckley's television
program *Firing Line* a week later, Proxmire conceded that the
1970 act had been left deliberately broad to "put the President on
the spot," but he vowed to impose the will of Congress more
forcefully on the shape of Phase II.[36]

Given the scope of the authority granted the President in the
Stabilization Act, however, the opportunity for doing this had
already been lost. Patman did convene four days of "oversight"
hearings in early October to provide a forum for critics of the
administration's handling of the freeze and an occasion for congressional forces to make some input into the organization of the
post-freeze Phase II controls.[37] But the administration announced its Phase II plan before Patman's hearings were even
completed. As the Pay Board–Price Commission–Cost of Living
Council apparatus went into operation, establishing guidelines,
issuing pronouncements, and generating rulings, Congress could

only look on impotently. The three agencies were not even subject to the congressional oversight mechanisms since the members were presidential appointees not requiring Senate confirmation and therefore able to resist congressional requests to testify. In fact, they were not even made subject to the Administrative Procedures Act, which sets minimum due-process restrictions on administrative decision-making, including provisions for public access and reporting.

The administration did offer Congress an opportunity to put its imprint on Phase II in late October 1971, when Nixon submitted a bill requesting a further one-year extension of the Stabilization Act beyond its scheduled April 30, 1972, termination. Though six months remained under the Stabilization Act authority, the administration was eager to secure an extension immediately so there would be no doubt about its ability to enforce its edicts and keep them in effect. And, although convinced that the 1970 Stabilization Act provided sufficient authority to establish Phase II,[38] the administration wanted a number of additional provisions to clarify its powers and put Congress on record as endorsing the new structure so as to avoid legal entanglements later on. Thus the bill that the administration transmitted to Congress on October 19 (H.R. 11309 in the House and S. 2712 in the Senate) proposed seven crucial elaborations on the basic authority first granted in 1970: (1) it proposed to beef up the enforcement powers by giving the Phase II bodies subpoena power and adding civil penalties of $2,500 per violation to the $5,000 criminal penalties already provided in the law; (2) it exempted the new structure from the Administrative Procedures Act, allegedly to avoid great delay, and gave appointees to the new boards immunity from conflict-of-interest statutes; (3) it established a special judicial structure for appeals from Pay Board or Price Commission decisions involving the federal district courts and a specially created Temporary Emergency Court of Appeals; (4) it stipulated that only the Justice Department, and not individual citizens, could bring criminal proceedings and other enforcement actions against Phase II offenders; (5) it deleted the provision attached to the stabilization legislation in May prohibiting imposition of controls on a single industry unless wages and prices were "grossly disproportionate"; (6) it proposed to have the Congress ratify all actions taken under Phase I so as to squelch any legal challenges arising from the Phase I controls; and (7) it requested standby authority to control interest rates and dividends as well as wages, prices, rents, and salaries. Furthermore, the bill made no effort to give statutory standing to the Pay Board, Price Commission, or Cost of Living Council, thus restricting congressional authority over them.

Not surprisingly, many of these provisions stimulated vigorous opposition. Representatives of organized labor were particularly hostile, chastising the administration proposal for its "disturbingly expansive conception of executive power."[39] What irked the union leaders was the growing realization that Nixon's stabilization program was taking a heavier toll on labor than on management, thanks to the absence of controls on profits or interest rates, the provision of an investment tax credit for corporations, and the greater ease with which price changes, as opposed to wage increases, can go undetected. The absence of a requirement for Senate confirmation of Pay Board and Price Commission members, the lack of sufficient due-process provisions, the failure to provide consumers standing to enforce the Phase II rulings by bringing suits against offenders, and the move to secure *post-hoc* congressional ratification of all Phase I decisions all seemed to suggest, as the AFL–CIO's representative put it, that Phase II really constituted "an elaborate smoke screen to justify wage regulation alone."[40] Consumer advocate Ralph Nader was even more pointed in his criticisms, terming Phase II, and the legislative proposal accompanying it "the most radical proposal made by any U.S. President in the twentieth century" because it proposed to delegate vast power over the economy not just to the President, but through him to a set of agencies with nebulous legal structure (H.R. 11309 made no mention of the Cost of

Living Council, Pay Board, or Price Commission) and manned by a majority of nongovernmental employees who were to be exempt from conflict-of-interest statutes as well as from the Administrative Procedures Act.[41]

Given these fundamental objections, the early advocates of standby presidential stabilization authority in Congress began groping for ways to control the monster they had created and loosen the rope it had fixed around their necks. Henry Reuss, for example, suggested subjecting Wage Board and Price Commission members to Senate confirmation and making provision for formal administrative review of their decisions.[42] Patman insisted that the administration subject interest rates to controls as well as prices, wages, rents, and salaries.[43] And Proxmire questioned the wisdom of acceding to the administration request for an immediate further extension of the stabilization authority, arguing it would be preferable to force the administration to return to Congress after two or three months of experience under Phase II. Complained Proxmire, "Now we are really buying a pig in a poke . . . we have delegated an enormous amount of power to the President; he, in turn, has given almost all of it to these two boards, neither of whom are elected by anybody, none of the members of which are confirmed by the Senate."[44]

In pressing their case, however, critics of the President's proposals faced an uphill battle. Nixon was still riding a wave of public euphoria as a result of his decision finally to take bold, direct action against inflation. Under these circumstances, few legislators could afford to vote against the President for fear the vote would be widely construed—and certainly portrayed by the administration—as a vote in favor of inflation. What is more, the prevailing sentiment stressed the need to give the President flexibility and to avoid the creation of a cumbersome stabilization bureaucracy that would quickly become mired in red tape. This sentiment worked against proposals for greater procedural safeguards in the exercise of the control authority. Finally, Congress found itself in a difficult tactical situation because the Phase II structure was already in place and beginning its operation when Congress took up the extension and amendment legislation; any delay to weigh alternative structures and generate political support for them would simply provide more time for the existing structure to establish precedents and formulate standards that would be increasingly difficult to change later on.

Under these circumstances, the administration's Democratic critics, who had also been the main advocates of the broad authority the President was now using, did surprisingly well in the marathon executive sessions and floor debates that took place in both House and Senate during November and early December 1971. For example, in the Senate Banking Committee, which completed its work on the bill on November 20, Proxmire, working closely with liberal Democrats Williams, Mondale, Stevenson, and Cranston, managed to insert provisions to (1) authorize consumers to sue for triple damages (three times the amount of the overcharge) or $1000 in cases of violation of stabilization orders; (2) require confirmation of newly appointed members of the stabilization bodies in the future; (3) exempt wages of persons earning less than the minimum wage or the poverty level from stabilization controls; (4) require approval of retroactive pay increases in cases where contracts had been negotiated prior to imposition of the August 15 freeze, unless they were "unreasonably inconsistent" with Pay Board guidelines; and (5) establish a set of general standards for wage-price guidelines—namely, that the guidelines be "fair and equitable," that they prevent "gross inequities" and windfall profits, that they take account of changes in productivity and cost of living, that they reduce prices and rents whenever warranted, and that they require comparable sacrifices by business and labor. In addition, the committee bill dropped the provision for ratification of all previous Phase I decisions that had been incorporated in the administration bill. Most of these features remained intact, or were improved upon, during the three days of Senate floor debate on this bill that began November 29. While the committee provision permitting consumer

suits against violators of stabilization rulings was deleted, Proxmire did manage to win Senate support for amendments opening
Pay Board and Price Commission hearings to the public wherever
possible, requiring quarterly presidential reports on the stabilization program, and strengthening the confirmation provision of the
committee bill by stipulating that the *current* chairman of the Pay
Board and Price Commission would be required to submit to
Senate confirmation at the end of sixty days, rather than applying
the confirmation requirement only to future appointees as stipulated in the committee bill.

Administration critics were also somewhat successful in the
House Banking Committee, which completed its own markup sessions on December 7. Although the proposal to require confirmation of Phase II board members failed, the House Committee did
approve retroactive pay increases on prefreeze contracts, a statement of legislative standards for issuance of wage-price guidelines
identical to that in the Senate bill, a requirement that the President must control interest rates whenever he controls wages and
prices, and authority for individual and class action consumer
suits against violators of Phase II regulations. All of these provisions withstood the two days of floor debate that took place on
December 9 and 10, although the retroactive pay increase provision, hotly contested by the administration, was seriously nar-
rowed by an amendment of Democrat Robert Stephens that limited it to cases where funds for the increases had already been
appropriated (as in the case of teachers who had received wage
increases in the spring but had not returned to work until September, after imposition of the freeze), or where productivity increases made them appropriate.

In the House-Senate conference as well, administration critics
managed to hold their gains. The conference committee thus accepted each of the House provisions, and added the Senate confirmation provision as well. Thus amended, the Economic Stabilization Act passed both House and Senate on voice votes on
December 14, 1971.

To read the history of the December 1971 extension of the Economic Stabilization Act as a victory for congressional critics of overreaching executive power, however, is to read it wrongly; for, impressive though the critics' achievements were given the circumstances, they were meager on any absolute scale. The bill that cleared the Senate by 86 to 4 on December 1, and then the House by 326 to 33 on December 10, was essentially and fundamentally the bill the administration had introduced in late October. Except for the proposed ratification of Phase I decisions, each of the key features of the administration bill survived: the extension of the President's control authority to April 30, 1973; the elimination of the prohibition on controls on a single industry; the exemption of the stabilization program from all but the public notice and public hearing provisions of the Administrative Procedures Act; the grant of subpoena powers to the stabilization bodies; and the authorization for the President to delegate the control powers to almost any body he wished, including a group of nongovernmental special interest representatives specifically exempted from the provisions of the conflict-of-interest statutes. Even some of the critics' amendments cited above reflect more the penchant of Congress for deferring to the executive than any vigorous challenge to administration power. Proxmire's "standards" for wage-price guidelines, for example, were stymied until Senator John Tower secured administration assurances that they were sufficiently nebulous to be unobjectionable. By the same token, the House-passed amendment requiring presidential control of interest rates whenever wage and price controls were invoked carried a convenient loophole permitting the President to ignore it whenever he determined that such action was "unnecessary to stabilize the economy." The most the Congress could muster, therefore, was an elaborate shell game of ostensible safeguards that really obscured some very weak reeds. Whenever the critics pushed more boldly, as when Henry Reuss proposed applying the Administrative Procedures Act to the stabilization mechanism, or when Gaylord Nelson (D., Wis.) in the Senate

him not for two months or six months or a year but for about a year and a half. . . . We have turned our back on our economic responsibilities and said let the President do whatever he wishes.[47]

CORALLING THE NINETY-THIRD CONGRESS

These misgivings soon proved well founded. Freed from the constraints of the Administrative Procedures Act, the control apparatus quickly became a legal no man's land, penetrable, if at all, only with the aid of high-powered legal talent able to sift through the increasingly complex and contradictory Pay Board and Price Commission rulings.[48] In addition, labor leaders chafed at the apparent one-sidedness of the controls, their tendency to squeeze labor more than business. The 15 percent rise in corporate profits registered during 1972 gave credence to this view, outdistancing, as it did, the much smaller 5.6 percent increase in nonfarm hourly wages recorded during the same period.[49] In the summer of 1972, moreover, the fatal flaw of the whole control apparatus— its failure to control raw agricultural prices—caught up with it, as meat and other agricultural prices shot up at an alarming rate, carrying the cost of living index with them.

As if this were not sufficient, in January 1973, just as Phase II was beginning to show its worth by limiting the increase in the nonagricultural elements of the Consumer Price Index below 3 percent for the first time since 1967, albeit not without the aid of a healthy boost in economic output, President Nixon summarily ended the Phase II program. On January 11 the President announced he was lifting controls in all areas except processed foods, health, and construction, and was moving back to the original, prefreeze game plan characterized by reliance on traditional fiscal and monetary policy and voluntary wage and price guidelines. With the resulting demise of the Pay Board and Price Commission in mid-January, however, prices headed up again at an accelerating rate, the stock market headed down, and warnings of "impending disaster" issued again from respected professional economists who bewailed the "truly extraordinary folly" of the administration's shift to Phase III at a time when demand pressures in the economy were extraordinarily high.[50]

Although shut out of the decision-making process that led to the premature demise of Phase II, thanks to the extraordinary discretion it had surrendered to the President, Congress did once again have an opportunity to respond to the administration's new change of course. The Stabilization Act was scheduled to expire on April 30, 1973. On the day he announced the shift to Phase III, the President requested a simple one-year extension of the authority, giving Congress another chance to assert its constitutional responsibilities for guiding basic economic policy. But once again Congress dropped the ball.

The Senate proved particularly lacking in backbone. With chairman Sparkman siding with the Republicans, the Banking Committee followed the President's lead and approved a simple extension of the standby authority, giving the President continued broad discretion in economic policy-making despite mounting evidence of poor judgment in the exercise of that discretion. In addition, it granted the President discretionary authority to ration petroleum products. While the committee did depart from administration wishes by requiring public disclosure of reports submitted to Phase III's reconstituted Cost of Living Council, it refused to countenance either a reimposition of rent controls or a proposal by Proxmire that would have restored the crucial Phase II provision requiring major companies and unions to give the government advance notice of significant wage and price increases. During floor debate on March 19 and 20, 1973, the full Senate went along with the committee bill. Though the members agreed to the reimposition of rent controls, they turned aside Proxmire's prenotification provision and roundly defeated proposals to impose an immediate, across-the-board, six-month price freeze; to freeze retail food prices for ninety days; to place raw agricultural products under compulsory price controls; and to freeze interest rates. Instead, despite the hue and cry about premature lifting of the Phase II controls, the Senate chose not to assert any leadership on the economic front, but to line up mutely, as it had in the past, behind the nonpolicy of the President.

The House Banking Committee, in contrast, responded more boldly for the first time. By almost straight party votes, it rejected the President's call for a simple one-year extension of the stabilization authority and, working closely with the House Democratic leadership and the Rules Committee, took matters into its own hands by approving a substitute bill (H.R. 6168) that would: (1) impose an immediate sixty-day freeze on prices and interest rates at levels prevailing on March 16, 1973; (2) establish a "trigger mechanism" tied to the Consumer Price Index for imposing controls automatically in the future whenever prices got out of hand; and (3) create a congressional consumer counsel. The committee's action was the first sign of true congressional initiative in the long history of the anti-inflation effort.

But, as it turned out, it was all for naught. The administration vigorously opposed the committee's bill and mobilized House Republicans to attack it. More important, between April 12, when a revised committee bill was reported out of the Rules Committee, and April 16, when it was considered on the floor, House Democratic leaders suffered massive defections in their own ranks. One reason for this was the active lobbying campaign launched by business groups threatened by the more restrictive committee bill. "The members got all their facts from the lobbyists," observed Banking Committee Democrat Richard Hanna when it was all over. "Beef, lumber, chamber of commerce, and landlords. They got their message through over the weekend and convinced them that this would create chaos."[51] Because of Patman's reputation for wild ideas, many members were afraid to follow him in the face of such united business and administration pressure, especially given the widespread congressional inferiority complex on economic questions. What is more, since the prospects of immediate economic relief seemed remote, many Democrats preferred the opportunistic position of leaving the President with full responsibility for economic decision-making in order to saddle him with the full measure of blame. Whatever the reasons, however, seventy-six Democrats defected on the key vote, defeating the Banking Committee version of the bill, 147 to 258, and clearing the way for ultimate passage, by a vote of 293 to 114, of the Republican measure extending the President's control authority for one year without any conditions. Noted Richard Hanna when the turnabout became final, "Just remember that this day's work will be read . . . as a great indication that the will of Congress has the tensile strength of a wet noodle."[52]

Following a conference with the Senate that led to the elimination of the Senate's rent control provision and acceptance of the Senate's provisions for fuel rationing authority and public disclosure of price increase reports by large corporations, the watered-down extension bill was passed by both houses and signed by the President on April 30, 1973. Once again, Congress reaffirmed its own incapacities and surrendered its authority to the President. Chief White House lobbyist Richard Cook summed up the spectacle well, when, after the administration victory in the House, he nodded his head toward the House Chamber and remarked with a grin, "It's really kind of pathetic, isn't it?"[53]

The rest is denouement. Disregarding critics, the administration held to its Phase III voluntary restraint program. But with controls lifted, prices rose spectacularly in 1973, registering the sharpest annual jump in the Consumer Price Index since 1947. On June 13, with inflation running rampant again, the President reversed course for the fourth time and imposed a temporary freeze, again without any need to consult Congress. On August 14, he launched Phase IV, another price and wage control effort, but on a selective basis and without the benefit of the Pay Board and Price Commission administrative mechanisms. Then, despite price rises throughout 1973, the administration began moving to decontrol segments of the economy one by one in late 1973. When the President proposed in February 1974 that the stabilization authority be extended on a limited scale beyond the scheduled April 30 termination, therefore, Congress finally called a halt to the charade. On March 18, 1974, Patman took the floor in the House to inform his colleagues that support for further extension of the control authority had collapsed. "In my opinion, any consideration of extension of this legislation is on dead center," reported Patman. "Any hope for passage or even committee action appears to be dim, if not dead."[54] Eight days later the Senate Banking Committee concurred, voting, fifteen to zero, to table indefinitely any further consideration of extending the stabilization authority. With that, one of the sorriest chapters in congressional economic policymaking came to an end. But what did not come to an end was the raging inflation and the accompanying economic dislocations that had prompted Congress' fumbling performance in the first place. We can hope, to be sure, that Congress will somehow develop the will and the wisdom to tackle these problems more forcefully in the future, even in the absence of presidential direction. But the story of the effort to stem inflation in the Ninety-first, Ninety-second, and Ninety-third Congresses just recounted hardly inspires confidence that this will occur.

6

The Banking Committees and the Future: Conclusions and Recommendations

In his famous "Senate Establishment speech" of 1963, former Senator Joseph Clark bemoaned the fate to which the Senate leadership had consigned the Banking Committee. "Now I turn to another 'Orphan Annie,' the Committee on Banking and Currency," noted Clark. "What a shame that it is an 'Orphan Annie,' because it is one of the most important committees in the Senate."[1]

From what we have seen, Clark's characterization retains the ring of truth more than a decade later. The Banking committees contain more than their share of hard-working and conscientious

340

legislators with a clear commitment to the public interest. Yet they also suffer particularly severely from some of the fundamental institutional maladies afflicting the Congress as a whole. The purpose of this chapter is to explore four of these maladies and their impact on Banking Committee behavior, and then to speculate on the remedies that might be applied.

THE QUADRUPLE QUANDARY

The Information Gap

Like several other committees, and the Congress as a whole, the Banking committees, as we have seen, confront a gross disproportion between their responsibilities and their resources. No fewer than eleven federal agencies fall under the jurisdiction of these committees in whole or in part, giving the committees responsibility for everything from the Federal Reserve Board's conduct of monetary policy to the future of small businessmen, from wage and price controls to the dynamics of urban development, from the corporate structure of the savings and loan industry to the lending policies of the Export-Import Bank. And the subject matter is not only broad, but also unusually complex. Decisions about the organization of commerical bank fractional reserve requirements, the appropriate lending authorities of savings institutions and commercial banks, the correct rate of money-supply expansion, or the consequences of restrictions on the expansion of one-bank holding companies involve complex economic questions which professional economists, armed with sophisticated mathematical models, have difficulty deciding. In making up their minds about whether to impose wage and price controls, Banking Committee members had to comprehend the limits of the "monetarist" school of economic thought, judge the adequacy of "cost-push" *versus* "demand-pull" explanations of the prevailing economic woes, and assess the potential supply-limiting consequences of restrictions on prices and profits. Even so intrinsically simple a subject as housing involves immensely subtle complexities thanks to its intimate relationship to overall capital flows in the economy and the phenomenon of disintermediation, and because of the elaborate network of indirect program tools Congress has authorized to provide assistance.

Another problem is the secrecy with which the Banking committees must contend. Substantial areas of financial-institution operation are shrouded from official view by the banker dogma of confidentiality. We have already seen, for example, how efforts to assess the concentration of corporate ownership in the hands of bank trust departments was substantially thwarted by the refusal of banks to divulge information about their stock ownership. Perhaps even more frustrating to the committees is the tradition of untouchability that envelops the Federal Reserve Board, which is, after all, a public agency. Backed by the commercial bankers, the Fed takes the position that the details of monetary policy are off limits to the politicians in Congress on the ground that the purity of monetary policy decision-making would otherwise be defiled by unwarranted social and political considerations. In many important respects, therefore, Congress knows more about the operations of the Central Intelligence Agency than it does about those of the Federal Reserve Board.*

To help cope with this jurisdictional smorgasbord and penetrate its complexity and secrecy, the Banking committees have staffs that are hardly adequate. To be sure, staff adequacy is a subjective phenomenon, having to do with the way the staff role is defined, as well as with the numbers and qualifications of the staffers themselves. For the routine function of processing externally initiated legislative proposals, clearing them with the obviously relevant outside interests and with the ideological predispo-

---

* In the early months of the 94th Congress, this situation changed somewhat, with passage of a resolution requiring the chairman of the Federal Reserve Board to testify before the Banking committees several times each year on *anticipated* monetary policy moves. This resolution was itself a moderate substitute, however, for stronger measures that would have given Congress a more substantial role in monetary policy decision-making.

sitions of the members, the twelve professionals on the Senate Banking Committee staff and the twenty-six on the House side are adequate enough. Both of these committees have more than their share of well-qualified and hard-working staff professionals and are burdened with few of the political hacks characteristic of an earlier day. Yet when it comes to initiating policy or developing an independent capacity to evaluate the proposals of others, both committees are at a serious and continuing disadvantage.

This has been especially so in the Senate, where chairman Sparkman chose to disperse staff resources to the members in the interest of committee harmony rather than utilizing them to undertake independent inquiries. Sparkman's staff director, Dudley O'Neal, reflects this lack of leadership and direction. Aside from a generally congenial personality, O'Neal's main claim to fame is his unseemly deference to benefactor Sparkman. ("I wouldn't have been anything on my own. I owe a lot to Sparkman. He is a tremendous man and I appreciate his confidence in me.") A pleasant but generally ineffectual person, O'Neal lacks both the temperament and the ability to mobilize staff resources on behalf of activist policy stances. As he described his role, "I don't take positions on legislation. My job is just to point up the issues. Who am I to suggest to a senator how he should vote?"[2]

Other Banking Committee staffers have fewer inhibitions. The best example is Kenneth McLean, Senator William Proxmire's long-time aide on the Banking Committee and a man who keeps a keen eye out for issues his boss can push. "The senators are really too busy to do much thinking and research," explained McLean. "They hire guys like me to do it for them."[3] By the same token, Carl Coan, Sr., staff director of the Housing Subcommittee, has managed to eke out a substantial area of policy-making autonomy. Yet the overall pattern of staff operations inhibits both of them. Obliged to cover the waterfront for his principal, McLean has quite limited resources with which to develop new areas or explore new ideas. As for Coan, his ties to the generally conservative Sparkman preclude bold innovations. In addition, large chunks of Coan's time are absorbed in handling constituency requests for Sparkman's personal office staff.

The situation in the House, as we have seen, is considerably different. There, under Patman's tutelage, a norm of staff activism has developed, at least within the majority staff. The staff role has been defined to embrace a strong investigative component, and staffers set to work exploring wholly new areas prior to proposals from the standard originators of legislation. Even the Housing Subcommittee, which lies beyond Patman's immediate sphere of influence, has been affected by this activist norm, as the 1970–1971 panel experience suggests. Yet, even in the House committee, the limits of staff resources are clearly in evidence. Staffers like Benet Gellman and Jake Lewis have been highly effective with kamikaze-type raids on particularly ripe and exposed targets, like the Penn Central fiasco and the one-bank holding company phenomenon. But broader inquiries and sustained analysis exceed the committee's capabilities. What is more, the price of husbanding staff resources for centrally directed investigative research has been to deny these resources to other committee members, who frequently need staff help to comprehend the substance of legislation before the committee and participate more effectively in committee affairs.

Compared to the committees' own information sources, those of the administrative agencies and industry groups with which they deal are overwhelmingly more powerful. The Federal Reserve Board, HUD, the American Bankers Association, the National Association of Home Builders, the U.S. Savings and Loan League, and the other movers and shakers with a stake in Banking Committee decisions maintain elaborate research operations geared to the delivery of readily digestible information to genuinely puzzled legislators. In subject areas as complex as those confronting the Banking committees, this information can be particularly decisive, and frequently is. The perennial failure of Patman and Proxmire to secure approval for measures that would channel credit into social priority areas can be attributed in substantial measure to this factor; the bankers have been able to sweep other members off their feet with technical arguments about what such measures would do to general capital flows. So, too, congressional timidity on the anti-inflation front is a product of the same phenomenon. "I don't know any subject where we have less confidence in ourselves than in economics," noted Congressman Richard Hanna at the end of the price control debate in 1973. "When they talk about tinkering with the economy they get scared."[4] The result is to circumscribe the area of committee initiative by making the members institutionally dependent for guidance on the very administrative agencies and private lobbies they are supposed to be overseeing and directing. This is particularly true in view of the fact that on many of the key areas within the committee's jurisdiction, only a few legislators have both the interest and the experience to form an independent judgment: on banking matters, Proxmire and Bennett in the Senate and Patman, Reuss, and Stanton in the House; on housing matters, Sparkman, Tower, Cranston, and Brooke in the Senate, and Barrett, Ashley, Widnall and Brown in the House.

THE FINANCIAL GAP

For many members, this reliance on private lobbies for information and insight is a natural counterpart of reliance on these very same groups for campaign support. Like other congressmen and senators, the members of the Banking committees face the persistent reality of escalating campaign costs and the resulting heavy demands for financial contributions. But membership on these committees places them in a position to be of great service or great harm to some extraordinarily powerful economic groups, most of whom have long since learned how to gain access to Congress. As we have seen, most of the key industry constituents of the Banking committees—the commercial bankers, the savings banks, the home builders, the realtors—maintain active campaign finance operations that channel contributions, speaking fees, and other emoluments into the coffers of interested legislators. In addition, the business interests affected by this committee enjoy unusually broad-based political influence in the members' districts. In most communities, the bankers, builders, and realtors form a strategic political bloc with links to the entire business and legal community. Rare is the politician who can defy this power bloc consistently over an extended period of time and still survive in office. What is more, member dependence on these key special interests is replicated at the staff level as well. Particularly in the Senate committee, as we have seen, a well-worn path leads from committee staff slots to industry lobbying jobs, and back again. Even without accepting the simplistic view that campaign contributions "buy" votes—and most lobbyists complain that they never get their money's worth—it is easy to see that the political-support needs of the members coupled with the information needs of the committees and the career aspirations of staffers guarantee easy access for industry views in the legislative process.

The Publicity Gap

One way legislators can escape the logic of the information gap and the financial gap is to develop a popular following back home. To do so, however, they need a committee assignment that will either provide a source of publicity to lift them out of the obscurity that is the lot of most members of Congress or supply them with some tangible "bacon" to bring home to constituents. On both counts the Banking Committees leave much to be desired.

Even more than most committees, the Banking committees operate in considerable obscurity, unable to attract the front-page coverage the members so desperately desire. Part of the reason for this is the technical complexity of the issues they handle, which relegates most of their stories to the financial press or the real estate pages. And part of the reason is the changing national mood. For a brief period in the middle and late 1960s, with concern about the urban crisis at fever pitch, the Banking committees were in the center of public attention. But, as attention has shifted to environmental issues, they have found themselves increasingly out of the limelight again. HUD Secretary George Romney's explanation of why the Department of Interior, not the Department of Housing and Urban Development (and hence not the Banking committees), assumed prime responsibility for developing a proposed national land-use policy illustrates this point well. Noted Romney:

> We concluded we would be much more likely to get a land use policy under the environmental banner today than we would under the urban banner, because the urban banner had sex appeal politically seven or eight years ago, but it hasn't got sex appeal today politically.[5]

This same phenomenon has also deflated the value of the "bacon" the Banking committees control, and hence the benefits that service on this committee allows a member to provide to his district. During the heyday of urban renewal in the 1950s and early 1960s, Banking Committee members could easily translate committee work into political support back home by stressing how the committee role provided a pipeline into federal urban renewal decision-making. Such urban liberals as Reuss, Ashley, Moorhead, and Sullivan gravitated to the Banking committees for precisely this reason. But as the gleam on urban renewal has tarnished in recent years, the worth of this payoff for committee members has diminished considerably. The willingness of Congress to authorize a block-grant approach to community development programs undoubtedly reflects this fact. There is, indeed, a profound sense, especially on the House side, that previous approaches to urban development and low-income housing have not worked, and that the current alternatives are likewise doomed to failure. The result is an atmosphere of cynicism and despair not conducive to political risk-taking on behalf of social-welfare goals. The harsh treatment of public housing tenants, the rejection of strong community participation provisions in the community development program, and the deletion of Ashley's proposed housing block-grant provisions in the 1972 and 1974 housing acts all reflect this fact.

Since politicians will naturally concentrate their efforts where the political returns are greatest, the consequence of inattention by the press and limited rewards to offer constituents is extensive member disinterest and passivity. As we have seen, particularly on the Senate side, these committees have frequently served as way-stations for ambitious legislators on their way to more powerful assignments. Given the premium on expertise occasioned by the complexity of Banking committee subject matter, the upshot is to reduce the number of members with the self-confidence and support to challenge powerful insiders. The information gap, the financial gap, and the publicity gap, in other words, all work in the same direction. Over time they winnow the field of active participants and reduce the incentive for bold—and risky—policy initiatives by the Congress.

The Jurisdictional Gap

The Banking committees suffer unusually sharply from a fourth institutional malady characteristic of the Congress. In order to retain even what authority it has, Congress has been forced to specialize and decentralize. But the jurisdictional lines dividing committees often bear little relationship to the nature of the problems with which the committees must deal. The result, at best, is uncoordinated action; and, at worst, surrender of authority to the executive branch, which has the institutional capability to put together what Congress seems able to treat only in parts.

The fumbling way in which the Banking committees handled the wage-price stabilization legislation is in large part a reflection of this jurisdictional bedlam. The Banking committees were being asked to consider only one policy tool, but the need for it depended on what happened to several others which lay beyond the committees' reach.

Indeed, only the Joint Economic Committee in Congress has the entire economy in its sights, but the JEC has no legislative responsibilities; it simply gathers information and issues advisory reports. For committees like Banking, the result is a quandary, as Representative Henry Gonzalez pointed out in the House Banking Committee's report on the price control legislation in 1971:

> Unfortunately, for [the Banking] Committee, the economic policy is tied into the tax reduction package. Unless the House, or its committees, examine the whole package of tax write offs plus controls, we will see only its parts. Since we have not considered the package as a whole, we are being asked to approve a program of which we have no more understanding of the true shape than the proverbial blind men feeling an elephant. . . . The sum may be lesser than its parts, or greater—and we have a duty to know. We cannot act responsibly unless and until we at least have a full view of the program. . . . If we are in our present straits because we have failed to act on economic policy as a whole, we may well simply be repeating past mistakes by acting once again in a piecemeal fashion.[6]

A similar problem arises in the housing area. While they can manipulate mortgage terms and authorize various subsidy schemes, the Banking committees have no control over probably the most efficient subsidy mechanism available—the federal income tax—nor do they have any influence over the single federal program with probably the greatest impact on urban development, the interstate highway program. Federal housing policy has, as a consequence, functioned more as a part of counter-cyclical economic policy than it has as a part of some comprehensive and rational national urban policy. Moreover, as the nation's housing problem comes to be defined increasingly as a low-income problem rather than a production problem, the Banking committees stand to lose even more of their responsibilities to committees like

Labor and Public Welfare and Ways and Means–Finance, which handle welfare and income transfer programs.

These jurisdictional gaps naturally produce frustration on the part of committee members, who find themselves perennially obliged to restrict their attention to fragments of problems without any assurance that their decisions will make sense when related to the whole. Under these circumstances, surrendering power to the executive in broad grants of authority frequently comes to seem the most responsible course to follow. "Better impotence than chaos," in other words, becomes the operative norm. The way in which the Banking committees relied on a time limit rather than any more substantive control in their grant of broad authority to the president in the wage and price control area typifies this behavior.

Equally frustrating can be the problem of coordinating action *within* the committees. As we have seen, this problem is less severe in the Senate, where Sparkman has taken pains to accommodate colleagues by decentralizing control of staff slots and encouraging a spirit of compromise. However, the price of this accommodating leadership style has been a certain diffuseness in the resulting policy produced by the committee. The Christmas tree character of omnibus housing bills is a perfect example. As one Senate staffer told us, "Some things get into the housing bill only because one guy stuck it out the longest." In the House committee, by contrast, the integrative norms are badly strained, thanks in large part to the chairman's heavy-handed leadership style and the conspiratorial tone set by his staff. While Patman and his staff justify this caustic and driving style in terms of the chairman's policy goals, it seems clear to us that it is also partially self-defeating, for it discourages some talented potential recruits from seeking Banking Committee membership and produces frustration among members already on the committee. Throughout our interviews, in fact, this sense of frustration was clearly evident, as members complained about Patman's paternalism, his monopolizing of staff resources, his peremptory use of the scheduling power, his failure to consult adequately with other members, and the limited role he consequently left to other committee members.*

ESCAPING THE QUANDARIES: SOME PROPOSALS FOR CHANGE

Viewed in the light of these underlying institutional weaknesses, it cannot be said that the Banking committees have performed all that poorly. There is, in fact, real evidence of vigor and leadership: the push for one-bank holding company regulation, the House committee's urban policy panels and promotion of a national urban-growth policy focus, the increasing attention to consumer finance protections, the House committee's determination to take up wage and price control legislation in the face of administration opposition and then to vote a bill imposing a price freeze in 1973, and the successful tying of community development assistance to the solution of low-income housing problems in the 1974 Housing Act. What former HUD associate general counsel Hilbert Fefferman said of the housing legislation produced by these committees thus applies quite well to their legislative output generally: "I've never seen a A+ or even B+ bill come out of these committees. But at the same time, I've rarely seen an F bill either. Most of what they come up with is C or C+ stuff."[7]

Given the public stake in the work of these committees, however, it seems clear that C or C+ legislation will no longer do. With severe economic distress well under way, with the prospect of persistent inflationary pressures over the next decade at least, with continuing urban unease, with the accelerating growth of consumer finance, and with a total revamping of federal bank regulation law in the offing, the Banking committees must be made to do far better than they have in the past. Achieving this result will not be easy. Indeed, the central theme of this study has been that the behavior of the Banking committees is hardly ran-

---

* Patman's defeat as chairman as the 94th Congress began is attributable in substantial measure to his operating style and the problems cited here.

dom, that it is deeply rooted in a complex set of institutional factors, including the organizational structure of the Congress, the character of the various "policy subsystems" within which the committees operate, the patterns of committee recruitment and the resulting array of ideological predispositions and constituency pressures, the prevailing norms of intracommittee behavior, the obligations among members arising from previous compromises and conflicts, the leadership styles of the chairmen, and the amount of relevant knowledge available. No pat formula or simple tinkering, and no amount of vehement exhortation, is going to alter this situation overnight. Any reform program that ignores these deeply rooted constraints and proceeds as if they did not exist is thus doomed to failure, or may even backfire.

At the same time, however, we have had occasion to note how the systematic constraints on Banking committee behavior can be stretched and bent, how skillful leadership has occasionally been able to alter the traditionally narrow terms of the policy debate and significantly improve the outcome. There is, in short, not only vast *room* and *need* for improvement, but also considerable *opportunity* for it, opportunity that has hardly begun to be tapped. The task of reform, therefore, is to identify these opportunities systematically and build upon them. The proposals outlined below suggest how this might be begun.

Policy Leadership

Perhaps the most fruitful opportunity for altering Banking committee behavior lies in the possibilities for restructuring the constellation of political forces that the committees face. For the most part, as we have seen, the Banking committees operate within relatively closed policy subsystems, effectively cut off from the purifying glare of broad public attention and hence highly susceptible to special-interest pressures. The difficulty these committees have had in attracting progressive, activist legislators and in maintaining the interest and involvement of those it does attract can be attributed in substantial measure to this fact. By failing to provide sufficient opportunities to build a broad public following, the Banking committees fail to provide sufficient incentive to attract the legislators most eager to escape special-interest dominance, and hence most in need of visible, popular issues to champion.*

While this situation is largely a product of external or institutional factors of the sort discussed above, however, it is also partly a consequence of the members' own limited vision. There is, in fact, a kind of vicious cycle at work, as limited public attention discourages member activism, which in turn further limits public attention and solidifies special-interest influence. But this situation is not as fixed as it may appear. The simple fact is that substantial—though certainly not unlimited—opportunities exist to break out of this vicious cycle by appealing over the heads of the traditional special-interest clients and mobilizing a still diffuse but potentially powerful public sentiment newly aroused by the consumer and environmental movements and by the growing economic distress. The House action on the Bank Holding Company Act Amendments of 1970 provided a glimpse of these potentials. But the jurisdiction of the Banking committees offers many more such opportunities, opportunities that, if seized and assiduously nurtured, could begin to rescue the committees from their Orphan Annie status and substantially enrich their policy output by altering the political environment of decision-making. Three examples may help illustrate this point.

1. Housing. Federal housing policy, as we have seen, has traditionally reflected the production needs of the home-building industry and the related demands of counter-cyclical national economic policy. Largely neglected have been the consumers' interests in housing and urban development, both those relating to

---

* This pattern continued in the 94th Congress, which convened in 1975. In the Senate, for example, John Sparkman resigned as chairman to assume the chairmanship of the Foreign Affairs Committee, while six of the other fifteen members left the committee entirely, five of them to take less senior posts on other committees.

the safety, quality, and cost of housing *per se*; and those relating to the broader community context within which housing is located.

On both of these latter points, however, there is considerable public ferment and concern that could be tapped by committee activists to rescue the committees, at least in part, from special-interest dominance. Consumer concerns about product safety and shoddy business practices, for example, are now beginning to focus on housing and home finance, the largest consumer expenditure of all. Ralph Nader has argued, in fact, that:

> the housing issue is going to be in the 70s what the auto issue was in the 60s. There is no question about it, no question at all. . . .
> The problems of safety are involved, the problems of the use of natural resources. In other words it has every characteristic that is necessary for a major consumer effort. It affects people's heavy investments, it affects what they believe should be the one thing that should be right that they buy, their house. It affects something that is not throw-awayable. . . . It is something that stays around. It is something that is involved in many, many hazards and injuries. It is something that is receiving a whole new host of different construction techniques and materials, such as the fiberglass problem. It is something that is going to connect up to the occupational disease areas, construction workers, asbestos—these are going to interlock. . . . And more and more consumers are concerned. They are concerned about housing defects. They are concerned about housing hazards. They are concerned about the rising price of housing. They are concerned about the woeful lack of any government standards or inspection. And more and more consumers are beginning to put these complaints down in writing and send them to their representatives in Washington and at the state level.[8]

The whole process of urban development has also recently come under increasingly critical citizen scrutiny. In the words of a recent task force sponsored by the Rockefeller Brothers Fund, a "new mood" has emerged in the nation questioning traditional assumptions about the desirability and character of urban development:

> This new mood represents a force of great energy. On the one hand it presents an opportunity; finally a broad popular concern for planning and regulating land use has emerged that can be offset against the one-sided, purely economic values that have characterized much development pressure. On the other hand it presents a challenge, for it encompasses a range of negative attitudes that are sometimes confused and even hostile to the needs of our society for new development.
>
> Nevertheless, this new mood is the most hopeful portent we see. Although it expresses a range of anxieties and discontents, it can be used as a lever to achieve the changes in land-use planning and control that will make possible a qualitatively different future for us and for American generations to follow.[9]

Nor are these concerns likely to subside over the next decade or two. During the 1970s and 1980s, in fact, the demands on the housing and urban land market are likely to accelerate. Although the overall American population growth rate has slowed, a dramatic increase is expected in the number of households, as the offspring of the postwar baby boom leave school, marry, and settle down. What was a public education crunch in the 1950s and 1960s will thus become a housing crunch in the 1970s and 1980s. During the 1970s alone, the number of households is expected to increase 22 percent, almost double the projected 11 to 15 percent increase in the total population expected during the decade.[10] These pressures are already finding reflection in rapidly rising home-ownership and land costs. Between 1967 and 1972, for example, home-ownership costs rose 40.1 percent, more than one and one-half times the 25.3 percent increase registered by the overall consumer price index. During this same period, moreover, the land cost per square foot for new housing sites jumped 58 percent.[11] Although lot sizes will likely decline somewhat as a consequence, the amount of new, undeveloped land likely to be converted to urban uses during the remainder of this century promises to be immense. According to one estimate, in fact, urban development will consume during the next thirty years a land area equal to that now encompassed in the nation's present 228 standard metropolitan statistical areas.[12] In addition, the composition of the housing stock is changing dramatically, with a vast increase in the reliance on multifamily dwellings and mobile homes, both of which raise even more severe consumer issues than the single family home.

These developments imply important opportunities for policy leadership on the part of Banking Committee members, opportunities that, if properly developed, could substantially change the situation so far as housing and urban development policy formation is concerned. Congressman Lud Ashley's initiatives on behalf of a national urban growth policy suggest the potentials that exist, yet these initiatives have only begun to scratch the surface and have not succeeded in mobilizing support on the Senate side. Indeed, the Banking committees have generally looked on passively while other committees, especially Interior under Senator Henry M. Jackson (D., Wash.), have developed many of these issues instead, thus further splintering an already fragmented policy sphere. Nevertheless, there are still vast opportunities here for policy leadership, leadership that could tap important new reservoirs of public concern and hence alter the constellation of political forces impinging on committee members in the housing sphere.

2. *Consumer Finance*. A second area in which policy leadership could help rescue the Banking committees from special-interest dominance is consumer finance. Consumer finance is the fastest growing of all types of credit and represents, in dollar terms, probably the single largest consumer issue except for housing. To be sure, the Banking committees have been active in this field since the early 1960s, when Senator Paul Douglas began his truth-

in-lending legislation. Following Douglas' defeat and the subsequent passage of the truth-in-lending law in 1968, moreover, Senator William Proxmire and Congresswoman Leonor Sullivan have continued to work in this area. Consumer finance is an excellent example of the feasibility of appealing over the heads of traditional committee clients to mobilize broader publics on behalf of committee initiatives.

Yet all of this is only just a beginning. Properly conceived, the consumer finance issue embraces much more than credit card transactions and the troubling growth of credit bureau personal data banks. It also covers the whole gamut of consumer interactions with financial institutions, including the problems of excessive closing costs, the use of "discount points" in mortgage loans, the lack of rate competition for savings, the use of carrying charges, the patterns of credit allocation, the extent of bank concentration, and the costs of credit for various uses. All of these are increasingly important issues that Banking committee activists could use to generate public attention to committee activities. The creation of a consumer finance subcommittee headed by William Proxmire in the Senate Banking Committee during the Ninety-third Congress, and Proxmire's subsequent elevation to the full-committee chairmanship in the Ninety-fourth Congress, augur well for this. But the subject must be developed more broadly and pushed more vigorously.

3. *Economic Policy.* The Banking committees could also assume a greater leadership role in the conduct of economic policy. Historically, as we have seen, despite the objections of Wright Patman, the committees have willingly accepted a back-seat role in the conduct of monetary policy, surrendering to the Federal Reserve Board, the Treasury Department, and the private banking system wide latitude in the direction of the nation's monetary affairs. The accelerating inflation, widespread economic dislocations, and escalating interest rates that took place in the latter 1960s and early 1970s, however, have challenged the wisdom of this approach, particularly since the decisions made by the mone-

tary authorities have been blamed by some as a large part of the problem. Moreover, there is every prospect that these inflationary pressures will continue into the foreseeable future, necessitating additional difficult decisions about the social priorities to be served by the nation's capital resources, and about possible wage and price controls. In recent years, Congress has taken substantial steps to enlarge its role in economic policy formation, most notably with the creation of House and Senate Budget committees. But these steps affect fiscal policy only. In the field of monetary policy, Congress remains as impotent as ever. While the arguments for monetary authority independence have merit, we think they have been substantially overdrawn and that the Congress, through the Banking committees, could usefully reassert a greater measure of public control. Were this to be done, the Banking committees could take their place alongside the Finance–Ways and Means and newly created Budget committees as premier economic policy formulators in Congress, overseeing monetary policy much as these other committees oversee fiscal policy. The result could be to galvanize political support for a broader range of financial-institution reforms as well.

There are, in short, some real opportunities for altering the constellation of political forces impinging on Banking committee members by mobilizing the latent power of public sentiment. We do not suggest that this is a simple strategy, or a panacea for the Banking committees' ills. Yet the civil rights and consumers' movements of the 1960s and 1970s suggest the real possibilities for substantial innovation when policy entrepreneurs seek out public concerns and frame programs to respond to them. Our argument here is only that Banking committee members, with some notable exceptions, have been far too timid in exploring such possibilities within their own bailiwicks. Were they to do so more effectively, they could escape some of the bondage they now experience in most policy spheres and alter the incentive structure for member participation in committee affairs.

Staffing

Policy leadership of the sort just proposed is not likely to result from mere exhortation, however. Additional changes will also be required. Foremost among these are changes in staffing patterns. As we have noted, congressional subservience to special-interest pleadings and executive pressures is in large part a function of Congress' dependence on these agencies for information. At the very least, in a field as complex as banking and housing, there is little prospect for bold initiatives in the absence of independent sources of information and analysis. Yet the traditional information-gathering mechanism in Congress, the public hearing process, is singularly inappropriate for this purpose. Hearings are useful for building a case or determining official administration and special-interest positions on proposals. But they are far less satisfactory for gathering information and exploring complex policy options. As one lobbyist told us, "There is simply no incentive for candor in the hearings. The other guys are tooting their organizational horns in their testimony, so I have to, too."

The provision of committee staffs was designed to remedy this situation, but it has done so only in part. The problem is less one of staff competence or numbers, moreover, than one of proper utilization. For the most part, as we have seen, the staff function is largely a passive one, collecting input on legislative proposals from the relevant lobbies and working out the appropriate compromises. This has been particularly true on the Senate committee, where policy leadership has been rather limited and staff functions restricted. The result is to leave the committees at the mercy of external sources of information and give them little foundation for independent initiatives.

If Congress is to hold its own in the interinstitutional donnybrook that is the American political system, it must gain access to the more high-powered policy analysis and evaluation increasingly prevalent in the executive agencies. In practice, this means a far more active committee research and analysis role, either on the part of the staff itself or on a subcontracting basis under the staff's supervision. The executive agencies are already spending millions of dollars on this type of analysis, giving them the capacity to generate presumably "scientific" rationales for their policy prescriptions, to which the members of Congress have little choice but to respond with uncomprehending assent. Would it not make more sense to give Congress—and particularly the substantive committees—a major share of the responsibility for this policy and evaluative research? Certainly Congress should be equipped to conduct most of the evaluative research on ongoing programs. In addition, the committees should be equipped to authorize specialized studies on particular policy areas or to organize semiformal briefings by its own experts. Congressional committees could, for example, contract with consumer groups or public-interest law firms, as well as with traditional contract research organizations, to monitor administrative agencies, evaluate program outputs, or devise alternative policy options. In this way, they could secure control over data as persuasive as those fed to them by the agencies and special interests, and could stimulate policy research in areas ignored by the executive branch.

The House Banking Committee has already taken some important steps in this direction. We have noted the policy role played by the staff studies Patman instigated on trends in commercial bank structure, and by the panel experience organized by staffers in the House Banking Committee's Housing Subcommittee. These examples illustrate the importance such staff research efforts can have. But there is a need to go well beyond this, to systematize the committees' policy research function and thus generate the capacity for more than crash investigations and hastily assembled collections of existing knowledge. To be sure, this will naturally require somewhat different staff skills—fewer legal generalists and more persons skilled at interpreting complex pieces of policy research. It will also require expanded committee budgets to finance the necessary inquiries. But the contribution this could make to congressional independence in the policy process would be well worth the cost. At a minimum, to talk of congressional independence in the absence of such a capacity is to talk nonsense.

Campaign Financing and Conflict of Interest

Even with a vast improvement in the information available, however, the accommodationist character of Banking committee decision-making will not be eliminated without some attention to the financial gap confronting members. To be sure, we have rejected the simplistic notion that campaign contributions automatically buy votes. Committee members, and members of Congress generally, have substantially more leeway in defining their roles and balancing competing pressures than any such notion would suggest. Yet there is also no denying that such contributions do have an effect. At a minimum, they establish the basic parameters of the "acceptable" options. They typically guarantee access for special-interest views. And in numerous cases they decisively tip the voting balance.

Although hardly seeing it as a cure-all, therefore, we are persuaded of the need for far greater controls on campaign contributions. The optimum solution is some system of public financing of campaigns, either in whole or in part. Failing that, the campaign finance reporting requirements must be substantially strengthened to increase the amount of information reported, ensure public access, require permanent retention of the records, set harsher penalties for infractions, and streamline enforcement. Otherwise, public trust in Congress will remain at its current low ebb and public support for congressional initiatives will continue to decline. There is simply no way for Congress to regain power unless it somehow regains public esteem, and it is doubtful it can regain public esteem without revolutionizing the pattern of campaign finance.

Democratization

Banking committee operations could also be significantly improved by further democratization in internal committee life. To be sure, as we have seen, neither House nor Senate committee resembles the archtypical congressional committee in this respect: neither has an obdurate, conservative chairman steadfastly resisting all progressive or liberal initiatives. But, from the point of view of member incentives and opportunities to participate, what they have had has been only partially better. In the Senate, John Sparkman has willingly accommodated other colleagues, but at the price of denying the committee any overall policy leadership. In the House, Wright Patman has done just the reverse: actively promoting a policy program but denying other members meaningful leadership roles and opportunities for active participation in the process.

We reject both of these styles for the future. What is needed instead is a pattern of committee leadership that is conscious of the need for *both* policy activism and meaningful opportunities for member participation in committee affairs. One way to accommodate these twin goals might be through more active use of subcommittees. Needless to say, there are risks involved in this tactic, since subcommittees can further splinter a committee's policy focus. Yet subcommittees afford a chairman a way to encourage member interest in committee affairs. If the full-committee chairman made a practice of reserving subcommittee chairmanships for those colleagues eager to take the initiative in policy, irrespective of seniority, moreover, the subcommittees could also become vehicles for promoting committee independence and mobilizing broader public support. To do so, however, they would have to be equipped with their own staff and research capabilities, but tied in to full-committee operations through frequent consultations and ultimate full-committee budget, assignment, and review controls.

The elevation of William Proxmire to the Senate Banking

Committee chairmanship in the Ninety-fourth Congress suggests that some such pattern of committee leadership may be emerging on the Senate side already. But much will depend on the interest that Proxmire actually takes in Banking Committee business, and the success he has in inspiring other members to do the same. In the House, the defeat of Patman and the accession of Henry Reuss to the chairmanship as the Ninety-fourth Congress convened raises the possibility for real democratization there at long last. What should be avoided, however, is the manipulation of the slogan of democratization to sap the committee of the capacity for policy initiatives altogether and thus deliver it more fully to special-interest control. The goal, rather, is to strike a better balance, to promote policy leadership, but to do so in ways that allow broader, more meaningful member participation and hence greater incentives for members to work at mobilizing the needed public support.

Committee Jurisdiction

One of the thorniest reform issues to evaluate in the context of the Banking committees is that of committee jurisdictional reform. We have had occasion to note how jurisdictional gaps frustrate Banking committee policy-making in numerous areas, most notably housing and economic policy. Several commentators have proposed, in fact, that the Banking committees be discharged from their urban responsibilities and a new congressional committee focused exclusively on the urban scene be created to provide an urban counterpart to the Agriculture committees and an arena where the full range of federal urban programs—from welfare assistance to housing—could be considered.

We are frankly skeptical of such proposals. Too often in the past reform efforts have been sidetracked by pursuit of organizational changes that turned out to produce wholly unintended results because the reformers failed to alter the political forces lying behind the institutional structures they were changing. In the case of the Banking committees, the real problem has not been lack of jurisdiction but failure to exploit the jurisdiction that is available. And this is less a product of congressional committee organization than of more basic political factors of the sort already discussed. What is more, there is strong reason to resist separating authority over housing and urban development programs from authority over banking and monetary policy, since the current setup at least makes it possible to move away from the present reliance on cumbersome, indirect devices and treat basic housing and urban development problems at their source, in the operations of the private capital markets. Furthermore, such a split would thoroughly upset the logic of the reform strategy we have propounded here, since it would further reduce, instead of expanding, the incentives for greater involvement by congressional progressives in Banking committee affairs and thus further diminish the prospects for substantially opening the closed policy subsystems within which these committees operate. A more productive approach would be the one outlined above, beefing up the Banking committees by equipping them with whatever authority they lack to handle the important issues of urban development and monetary affairs. But even so, euphoric hopes pinned to organizational reforms seem doomed to continued failure unless amply supplemented by changes aimed at the underlying political dynamics as well.

Recruitment

The whole thrust of the proposals outlined here has been to increase the attractiveness of the Banking committees to progressive, activist legislators by encouraging the development of currently untapped issues that can generate broader public support, and by enlarging the opportunities for meaningful member participation. This scheme will not work, however, if the committee assignment process continues to be dominated by parochial concerns inordinately responsive to special-interest pressures. The tendency to assign former bankers to the Banking committees, for example, should be stopped. More important, as the political appeal of the Banking committees increases, so too must the willingness to assign competent, independent, activist legislators to them. Otherwise, stagnation and dependence will persist. It is hoped that the decision of the Democratic Caucus at the beginning of the Ninety-fourth Congress to strip the Ways and Means Committee of control over Democratic committee assignments in the House will help achieve this goal. But this must now be followed by a similar democratization of the assignment process in the Senate and by a similar set of reforms at the committee level, to ensure that slavish adherence to seniority does not bar interested legislators from subcommittees most germane to their constituents.

These proposals do not, of course, exhaust the list of reforms we could propose to improve Banking committee performance. Greater utilization of the seminar format in place of hearings, creation of a permanent evaluation staff and subcommittee, continued use of the open executive session format adopted in the Ninety-third Congress, more coherent and evenly paced scheduling of action on legislation that comes up for renewal every year or two—all of these, and several others, fall within the general approach we are endorsing here. We have argued that the shortcomings the Banking committees suffer are not the product of ephemeral phenomena easily dissipated by the mumbling of some rhetorical formula or the manipulation of a few institutional forms. We have traced these shortcomings instead to more fundamental problems related to the context of political pressures within which these committees have traditionally functioned and certain deep-seated structural faults in internal committee operations. At the same time, however, we have argued that there is far more slack in the system than is now being exploited, that important opportunities exist for members to alter the political context of committee decision-making and thus free themselves more fully from agency and special interest dominance. Our suggestions for change have been designed to promote such alterations, to en-

Notes

CHAPTER 1.   WHY THE BANKING BUSINESS IS
EVERYONE'S BUSINESS

---

1. U.S. Savings and Loan League, *1975 Savings and Loan Fact Book*, p. 95.
2. U.S., Congress, Senate, Committee on Banking, Housing and Urban Affairs, *Financial Structure and Regulation: Hearings*, 93rd Cong., 1st sess. (Nov. 1973), p. 21.
3. Paul M. Horvitz, *Monetary Policy and the Financial System* (Englewood Cliffs, N.J.: Prentice-Hall, 1969), p. 12.
4. Eli Shapiro, Ezra Solomon, and William L. White, *Money and Banking*, 5th ed. (New York: Holt, Rinehart, and Winston, 1968), p. 69.
5. Board of Governors of the Federal Reserve System, *Annual Report, 1973*, p. 298.
6. Edward C. Ettin, "The Development of American Financial Intermediaries," in J. V. Fenstermaker, ed., *Readings in Financial Markets and Institutions* (New York: Appleton-Century-Crofts, 1969), p. 245.
7. *U.S. Statistical Abstract*, 1973, p. 451.
8. Shapiro, Solomon, and White, *Money and Banking*, pp. 286, 288.
9. *U.S. Statistical Abstract*, 1973, p. 449.
10. U.S., Congress, House, Committee on Banking and Currency, *Control of Commercial Banks and Interlocks Among Financial Institutions*, Staff Report, 90th Cong., 1st sess. (July 31, 1967), pp. iii, 62–63.
11. U.S., Congress, Senate, Committee on Government Operations, *Disclosure of Corporation Ownership*, Staff Report, 93rd Cong., 1st sess. (Dec. 27, 1973), pp. 6, 115–116. Emphasis added.

12. *Fortune*, May 1972, pp. 190, 270.
13. *Report of the President's Commission on Financial Structure and Regulation* (Washington: U.S. Government Printing Office, 1972), pp. 102–103. (Hereafter cited as Hunt Commission Report.)
14. Martin Lybecker, "Regulation of Bank Trust Department Investment Activities," *Yale Law Journal*, Vol. 82 (Apr. 1973), p. 997.
15. Kenneth Crowe, "Corporate Closeness: LILCO Is a Case in Point," *Newsday*, Mar. 22, 1973, reprinted in Senate Government Operations Committee, *Disclosure of Corporate Ownership*, pp. 10, 387–391.
16. Hunt Commission Report, p. 105.
17. U.S., Congress, House, Committee on Banking and Currency, *The Penn Central Failure and the Role of Financial Institutions*, 92nd Cong., 1st sess. (Jan. 1971), p. 4.
18. U.S., Congress, House, Committee on Banking and Currency, *The Growth of Unregistered Bank Holding Companies*, Staff Report, 91st Cong., 1st sess. (Feb. 11, 1969), p. 2.
19. Cited in U.S., Congress, House, Committee on Banking and Currency, *The Federal Reserve System After Fifty Years*, Staff Report, 88th Cong., 2nd sess. (Aug. 1964), pp. 10–11.
20. For an excellent analysis of how these mechanisms work, see Shapiro, Solomon, and White, *Money and Banking*, pp. 171–235.
21. *Congressional Record*, Aug. 15, 1972.
22. See, for example, *Congressional Record*, May 30, 1974, p. H4555.
23. Professor John Gurley, cited in House Banking Committee, *The Federal Reserve System After Fifty Years*, p. 28.
24. Thomas Havrilevsky, William P. Yohe, and David Schirm, "The Economic Affiliations of Directors of Federal Reserve District Banks," *Social Science Quarterly*, Vol. 54, No. 3 (Dec. 1973), pp. 608–622.
25. Quoted in House Banking Committee, *The Federal Reserve System After Fifty Years*, p. 67.
26. Jack M. Guttenbag, "The Short Cycle in Residential Construction, 1946–1959," *American Economic Review*, Vol. 51, No. 3 (June 1961), quoted in U.S., Congress, House, Committee on Banking and Currency, *The Residential Mortgage Financing Problem*, by Henry B. Schechter, Staff Report, 92nd Cong., 1st sess. (Sept. 1971), p. 8.
27. U.S. Savings and Loan League, *1972 Savings and Loan Fact Book*, p. 32.
28. S. Lee Booth, *1972 Finance Fact Book* (Washington: National Consumer Finance Association, 1972).
29. Personal interview, July 17, 1972.
30. *Congressional Record*, Feb. 19, 1963.
31. *Law and Contemporary Problems*, Vol. 32, No. 4 (Autumn 1966), p. 637.
32. *New York Times*, Oct. 9, 1972.
33. Personal interview, June 27, 1972.
34. Personal interview, July 17, 1972.

CHAPTER 2. THE ARENA: THE BANKING COMMITTEES AND THEIR LEGISLATIVE CONTEXT

1. Harold Seidman makes this point convincingly in *Politics, Position and Power* (New York: Oxford University Press, 1971).
2. *Congressional Record*, Jan. 6, 1932, p. 1400; Feb. 29, 1933, p. 4966.
3. Personal interview, June 27, 1973.
4. See, for example, U.S., Congress, House, Select Committee on Small Business, *Banking, Chain, Stockholder and Loan Links of 200 Largest Member Banks* (1963); *Foundations, Tax-Exempt and Charitable Trusts: Their Impact on Our Economy* (1962), Second Installment (1963), Third Installment (1964); *Banking Concentration and Small Business: Interlocking Directors and Officials of 135 Large Financial Companies of the United States* (1957); *The Monopoly Problem, Congress and the Fifty-Six Years of Antitrust Development, 1900–1956* (1957).
5. *Congressional Record*, Aug. 3, 1964.
6. "Letter from ABA President Reno Oldin to Chief Executive Officers of Member Banks," Dec. 1, 1964. (A copy of this letter is in Congress Project files.)
7. U.S., Congress, House, Committee on Banking and Currency, *The Federal Reserve System After Fifty Years*, Staff Report, 88th Cong., 2nd sess. (Aug. 1964).
8. U.S., Congress, House, Committee on Banking and Currency, *Acquisitions, Changes in Control, and Bank Stock Loans of Insured Banks*, Staff Report, 90th Cong., 1st sess. (June 1967).
9. U.S., Congress, House, Committee on Banking and Currency, *Bank Holding Companies: Scope of Operations and Stock Ownership*, Staff Report, 88th Cong., 1st sess. (May 1963); *Growth of Unregistered Bank Holding Companies—Problems and Prospects*, Staff Report, 91st Cong., 1st sess. (Feb. 1969).
10. U.S., Congress, House, Committee on Banking and Currency, *Control of Commercial Banks and Interlocks Among Financial Institutions*, Staff Report, 90th Cong., 1st sess. (July 1967).
11. *Congressional Record*, May 30, 1974, p. H4560.
12. U.S., Congress, House, Committee on Banking and Currency, *The Banking Reform Act of 1971: Hearings*, 92nd Cong., 1st sess. (1971), p. 25.
13. *Congressional Record*, Aug. 3, 1964, pp. 17838–17840.
14. *Congressional Record*, May 30, 1974, p. H4563.
15. See, for example, "Letter of Transmittal" in House Banking Committee, *Control of Commercial Banks*, pp. iii–iv.
16. Personal interview, Aug. 17, 1972.
17. U.S., Congress, House, Committee on Banking and Currency, *Bank*

Holding Company Act Amendments: Hearings, 91st Cong., 1st sess. (Apr. 1969), p. 1.

18. *Congressional Record*, May I, 1935, p. 6972.
19. See, for example, "Letter of Transmittal," House Banking Committee, *Federal Reserve Structure* (1971), p. iii.
20. *Congressional Record*, May. 30, 1974, p. H4557.
21. *New York Times*, July 21, 1974.
22. *Congressional Record*, Aug. 3, 1964.
2³. *Congressional Record*, May 30, 1974, p. H4557.
24. Personal interview, Aug. 17, 1972.
25. Ibid.
26. Charles McNeil, director, Governmental Relations Division, American Bankers Association, personal interview, July 24, 1972.
27. For a description of the "consensus chairman," "service chairman," and "minority and restraining chairman" roles delineated by John Bibby in a study of the Senate Banking Committee, see John Bibby and Roger H. Davidson, *On Capitol Hill* (New York: Holt, Rinehart and Winston, 1967).
28. *Congressional Record*, Mar. 1, 1972, p. H1621.
29. Thomas L. Ashley, personal interview, July 19, 1972.
30. U.S., Congress, House, *The Penn Central Failure and the Role of Financial Institutions*, 5 parts (Nov. 1971–Mar. 1972).
31. Benet Gellman, personal interview, July 20, 1972.
32. S. 2591, introduced on October 18, 1973.
33. U.S., Congress, House, Committee on Banking and Currency, *Financial Institutions: Reform and the Public Interest*, Staff Report, 93rd Cong., 1st sess. (Aug. 1973).
34. The foregoing observations are based on interviews with approximately two-thirds of the members of the House Banking Committee during the summer of 1972.
35. U.S., Congress, House, Committee on Banking and Currency, *Housing and the Urban Environment; Report and Recommendations of Three Study Panels of the Subcommittee on Housing*, 92nd Cong., 1st sess. (June 1971); *Papers Submitted to Subcommittee on Housing Panels on Housing Production, Housing Demand, and Creating A Suitable Living Environment*, 92nd Cong., 1st sess. (June 1971) (2 volumes).
36. Computed from U.S., Congress, House, Committee on Banking and Currency, *Legislative Calendar*, 92nd Cong., 1st sess. (Dec. 17, 1971).
37. Personal interview, Aug. 17, 1972.
38. House Banking Committee, *Banking Reform Act Hearings*, pp. 308–320.
39. Ibid., pp. 743–745.
40. The author personally witnessed this exchange.
41. Gellman interview.
42. Washington *Post*, July 16, 1974.
43. Gellman interview.
44. House Banking Committee staffer, personal interview, Mar. 12, 1974;

Dr. James Tobin (member of Council of Economic Advisers, 1963–1964), personal interview, Apr. 1974.

45. Personal interview, Aug. 17, 1972.
46. Personal interview, July 1972.
47. Personal interview, Aug. 17, 1972.
48. McNeil interview.
49. *American Banker*, June 2, 1972.
50. Based on reports filed with the Clerk of the House.
51. See, for example, H.R. 7440 (92nd Cong., 1st sess.), "A Bill to clarify and expand the authority of the Federal Home Loan Bank Board to regulate conflicts of interest in the operation of insured savings and loan associations," introduced by Sullivan in April 1971.
52. Personal interview (name withheld on request).
53. Personal interview, July 19, 1972.
54. Ibid.
55. The foregoing discussion was based on interviews with committee members Patman, Ashley, and Moorhead, and with staffers Paul Nelson, Benet Gellman, and Orman Fink.
56. William Frenzel, personal interview, July 1972.
57. U.S., Congress, House, Committee on Banking and Currency, *Emergency Home Financing Act of 1970: Hearings*, 91st Cong., 2nd sess.
58. Quoted in William Bradford Huie, "Draughts of Old Bourbon: The Sparkman Legend," *American Mercury*, Vol. 75, No. 3 (Oct. 1952), p. 126.
59. Quoted in *National Journal*, Feb. 27, 1971.
60. Compiled by Congress Project staff from quarterly reports of the secretary of the Senate.
61. Paul Douglas, *In the Fullness of Time* (New York: Harcourt, Brace, Jovanovich, 1972), pp. 523–535.
62. *Congressional Record*, Feb. 3, 1972, p. S1147.
63. John Evans, personal interview, Aug. 1, 1972.
64. Dudley O'Neal, personal interview, June 27, 1972.
65. John Sparkman, personal interview, Aug. 5, 1972.
66. Jack Woolley, personal interview, July 20, 1972.
67. U.S., Congress, Senate, Committee on Banking, Housing and Urban Affairs, *State and Local Taxation of Banks* (Report prepared by the Board of Governors of the Federal Reserve System), 92nd Cong., 2nd sess. (June 1972), p. 3.
68. O'Neal interview.
69. Ibid.
70. Personal interview, Aug. 15, 1972 (name withheld on request).
71. John Bibby, "Legislative Oversight of Administration: A Case Study of a Congressional Committee," (Ph.D. diss., University of Wisconsin, 1963), p. 125.
72. U.S., Congress, Senate, Committee on Banking, Housing and Urban Affairs, *Legislative Calendar*, 92nd Cong., 1st sess.
73. *Congressional Record*, Feb. 3, 1972, pp. S1146–1147.

74. U.S., Congress, Senate, Committee on Banking, Housing and Urban Affairs, *Summary of Activities*, Committee Print (Dec. 1973), p. v.
75. Personal interview, Mar. 11, 1974.
76. Senate Banking Committee, *Summary of Activities* (Dec. 1973), pp. 14–27.
77. Douglas, *In the Fullness of Time*, p. 20.
78. George Goodwin, *Little Legislatures* (Amherst: University of Massachusetts Press, 1970), pp. 112–113.
79. John Bibby, "The Congressional Committee: The Politics of the Senate Committee on Banking, Housing, and Urban Affairs," in Bibby and Davidson, *On Capitol Hill*, p. 195.
80. U.S., Congress, Joint Economic Committee, *The Economics of Federal Subsidy Programs*, Staff Study (Washington: Government Printing Office, Jan. 11, 1972), p. 152.
81. Morton Grodzins, *The American System* (Chicago: Rand McNally, 1966), p. 255.
82. William J. Keefe and Morris Ogul, *The American Legislative Process* (Englewood Cliffs, N.J.: Prentice-Hall, 1973), pp. 46–47.
83. Personal interview, July 13, 1972.

CHAPTER 3. BANKING ON CONGRESS: THE BANK HOLDING COMPANY ACT OF 1970

1. U.S., Congress, House, Committee on Banking and Currency, *The Growth of Unregistered Bank Holding Companies—Problems and Prospects*, Staff Report, 91st Cong., 1st sess. (Feb. 11, 1969), p. 7.
2. Ibid., pp. 8–9.
3. Ibid., p. 1.
4. See chapters by Arlt, Golembe, Keefe, Randall, and Camp in Herbert V. Prochnow, ed., *The One Bank Holding Company* (Chicago: Rand McNally, 1969).
5. Probably the clearest summary of arguments against bank holding companies can be found in House Banking Committee, *Growth of Unregistered Bank Holding Companies*, pp. 1–5.
6. 12 U.S.C. Sec. 371 (a) (1964); 12 U.S.C.R. Sec. 128(g) (Supp. 1966).
7. Clifton Kreps, "Modernizing Bank Regulation," *Law and Contemporary Problems*, Vol. 31, No. 4 (Autumn 1966), pp. 660–661.
8. U.S. Savings and Loan League, *1973 Savings and Loan Fact Book*, pp. 32, 35, 53.
9. U.S., Congress, House, Committee on Banking and Currency, *Financial Institutions: Reform and the Public Interest*, Staff Report, 93rd Cong., 1st sess. (Aug. 1973), p. 1.

10. Gerald C. Fischer, *American Banking Structure* (New York: Columbia University Press, 1968), p. 31.

11. Ibid., p. 174.

12. 49 Stat. 684 (1935), Title I (g).

13. Quoted in Fischer, *American Banking Structure*, p. 232. See also Kreps, "Modernizing Bank Regulation," pp. 655–656.

14. See Fischer, *American Banking Structure*, Table 41, p. 130.

15. Ibid., p. 130; Board of Governors of the Federal Reserve System, *60th Annual Report*, 1973, p. 298.

16. *U.S. Statistical Abstract*, 1973, p. 446.

17. Fischer, *American Banking Structure*, p. 128.

18. Jerry S. Cohen, "The Antitrust Laws Applied to Bank Mergers: Reciprocity and Tie-In Arrangements," *Business Lawyer*, Sept. 1970, p. 2.

19. Federal Deposit Insurance Corporation, *Annual Report*, 1970, p. 176.

20. U.S., Senate, Select Committee on Small Business, *Recent Changes in Banking Structure in the United States*, Staff Report, 92nd Cong., 1st sess. (Mar. 1970), p. 21.

21. *U.S. Statistical Abstract*, 1973, p. 449.

22. On these points, see U.S., Congress, House, Committee on Banking and Currency, *Chain Banking, Stockholder and Loan Links of 200 Largest Member Banks* (May 1963), *Bank Stock Ownership and Control* (Dec. 1966), *Control of Commercial Banks and Interlocks Among Financial Institutions*; and Fischer, *American Banking Structure*, pp. 247–255, 273.

23. Fischer, *American Banking Structure*, p. 161.

24. William T. Lifland, "The Supreme Court, Congress, and Bank Mergers," *Law and Contemporary Problems*, Vol. 32, No. 1 (Winter 1967), p. 16.

25. Ibid., p. 17.

26. Fischer, *American Banking Structure*, pp. 161–162.

27. George R. Hall and Charles F. Phillips, Jr., *Bank Mergers and Regulatory Agencies: Application of the Bank Merger Act of 1960* (Washington: Federal Reserve Board, 1964), pp. 27, 47, 60.

28. *U.S. v. Philadelphia National Bank*, 374 U.S. 321, 372 (1963), quoted in Fischer, *American Banking Structure*, pp. 292–293.

29. 12 U.S.C. 1828 (c), paragraphs 5 and 7(B), as amended February 1966.

30. Emmett S. Redford, "Dual Banking: A Study in Federalism," *Law and Contemporary Problems*, Vol. 31, No. 4 (Autumn 1966), pp. 749–773.

31. Ibid., p. 757.

32. *New York Times*, July 24, 1974.

33. Cited in Redford, "Dual Banking," p. 771.

34. Guy Fox, "Supervision of Banking by the Comptroller of the Currency," in Emmett S. Redford, ed., *Public Administration and Policy Formation* (Austin: University of Texas Press, 1956), p. 143, n. 58.

35. House Banking Committee, *Growth of Unregistered Bank Holding Companies*, pp. 1–2.
36. Eli Shapiro, Ezra Solomon, and William L. White, *Money and Banking*, 5th ed. (New York: Holt, Rinehart, and Winston, 1968), pp. 110–113.
37. U.S., Congress, Senate, Committee on Banking and Currency, *One Bank Holding Company Legislation of 1970: Hearings*, 91st Cong., 2nd sess. (1970), p. 238.
38. Fischer, *American Banking Structure*, p. 7.
39. The landmark work advancing these conclusions was David Alhadeff's study, which drew most of its data from California. See David Alhadeff, *Monopoly and Competition in Banking* (Berkeley: University of California Press, 1954), pp. 55–128, pp. 213–214.
40. George Kaufman, "Bank Market Structure and Performance: The Evidence from Iowa," *Southern Economic Journal*, Vol. 32, No. 4 (Apr. 1966), pp. 429–439; F. R. Edwards, "Bank Mergers and the Public Interest," *Banking Law Journal*, Vol. 85, No. 9 (Sept. 1968), pp. 753–796.
41. Alhadeff, *Monopoly and Competition in Banking*, p. 232.
42. William B. Camp, "Need to Encourage the Pioneering Spirit," in Prochnow, *The One Bank Holding Company*, pp. 32–33.
43. U.S., Congress, House, Committee on Banking and Currency, *Bank Holding Company Act of 1955*, Report No. 609, 84th Cong., 1st sess. (May 20, 1955), p. 5.
44. Ibid., p. 8.
45. Fischer, *American Banking Structure*, p. 98.
46. Camp, "Pioneering Spirit," p. 34.
47. *House Report on the Bank Holding Company Act of 1955*, pp. 4, 8. (The House report credits Transamerica with only six banks, but this is undoubtedly a misprint).
48. Carl T. Arlt, "Background and History," in Prochnow, *The One Bank Holding Company*, p. 18.
49. Cited in U.S., Congress, Senate, Committee on Banking and Currency, *Control of Bank Holding Companies*, Report No. 1095, 84th Cong., 1st sess. (July 25, 1955), p. 2.
50. Fischer, *American Banking Structure*, p. 98.
51. *Transamerica Corporation v. Board of Governors of the Federal Reserve System*, 206 f. 2d 163 (1953).
52. 70 Stat. 133 (1956). Emphasis added.
53. U.S., House, Committee on Banking and Currency, *Control and Regulation of Bank Holding Companies: Hearings*, 84th Cong., 1st sess. (1955), p. 15.
54. These exemptions are detailed in House Banking Committee, *Growth of Unregistered Bank Holding Companies*, p. 3.
55. George Eccles, "Registered Bank Holding Companies," in Prochnow, *The One Bank Holding Company*, p. 96.
56. Cited in ibid.

57. Ibid., p. 96–97.
58. Fischer, *American Banking Structure*, p. 148.
59. House Banking Committee, *Growth of Unregistered Bank Holding Companies*, pp. 5–6.
60. Ibid., pp. 5–6.
61. Arlt, "Background and History," p. 22.
62. Carter Golembe, "One Bank Holding Companies," in Prochnow, *The One Bank Holding Company*, p. 72.
63. Ibid.; Harry V. Keefe, Jr., "The One Bank Holding Company—A Result, Not a Revolution," in Prochnow, *The One Bank Holding Company*, pp. 121–122.
64. Keefe, "The One Bank Holding Company," p. 125. Emphasis added.
65. House Banking Committee, *Growth of Unregistered Bank Holding Companies*, pp. 50–51.
66. *New York Times*, Sept. 20, 1972.
67. See Camp, "Pioneering Spirit," esp. pp. 46–48.
68. K. A. Randall, "An Evolutionary Process in Banking," in Prochnow, *The One Bank Holding Company*, p. 49.
69. "Letter of Transmittal," House Banking Committee, *Growth of Unregistered Bank Holding Companies*, p. iii.
70. A copy of H.R. 6778 can be found in U.S., Congress, House, Committee on Banking and Currency, *Bank Holding Company Act Amendments: Hearings*, 91st Cong., 1st sess. (Apr.–May 1969), pp. 3–6. (Cited hereafter as *House Holding Company Hearings*.) An analysis of the bill is provided on pp. 165–166.
71. Cited in U.S., Congress, House, Committee on Banking and Currency, *Bank Holding Company Amendments*, Report No. 91–174 (Dec. 15, 1970), p. 11.
72. *House Holding Company Hearings*, pp. 78–81.
73. Ibid., p. 199.
74. Ibid., pp. 195–196.
75. Ibid., p. 88.
76. Ibid.
77. Ibid., p. 8. Emphasis added.
78. Ibid., pp. 88–89.
79. See Camp, "Pioneering Spirit," pp. 46–48; and Randall, "Evolutionary Process," p. 49.
80. *House Holding Company Hearings*, p. 90.
81. Ibid., pp. 164–165.
82. Ibid., pp. 71–72.
83. Ibid., p. 490.
84. Washington *Evening Star*, Mar. 5, 1969; *The American Banker*, Mar. 6, 1969; *The American Banker*, Mar. 7, 1969, reprinted in *House Holding Company Hearings*, pp. 118–120.
85. Washington *Evening Star*, Mar. 4, 1969, reprinted in *House Holding Company Hearings*, p. 118; testimony of Comptroller Camp, in ibid., pp. 1236–1238.

86. *House Holding Company Hearings*, pp. 199–202.
87. Ibid., p. 220.
88. Peter N. Toulmin, *An Analysis and Evaluation of One Bank Holding Companies* (New Brunswick, N.J.: Stonier School of Banking, Rutgers University, 1971), p. 196.
89. *The American Banker*, Apr. 10, 1969.
90. Testimony of ABA President Nat Rogers, in *House Holding Company Hearings*, p. 543.
91. *House Holding Company Hearings*, pp. 541–544.
92. "Memorandum from Charles R. McNeil, Director of the Washington Office, ABA, to Contact Bankers for House Banking and Currency Committee Members," May 6, 1969. (A copy of this memo is in Congress Project files.)
93. Based on records filed with the Clerk of the House.
94. "Memorandum from Charles McNeil, Director of the Washington Office, American Bankers Association, to All Contact Bankers for the House of Representatives," Oct. 24, 1969. (This memo is in Congress Project files.) Original emphasis.
95. Personal interview, House Banking Committee staff member, Aug. 18, 1972.
96. *Congressional Record*, Nov. 5, 1969, p. 32900.
97. Ibid., p. 33133.
98. Ibid., p. 33139.
99. Ibid., p. 33153–33154.
100. Benet Gellman, personal interview, July 13, 1972.
101. Frank Fowlkes, "Big Bank Lobby," *National Journal*, July 18, 1970, pp. 1541–1542; personal interview, Senate Banking Committee staff member, July 13, 1972.
102. Personal interviews, Donald L. Rogers, executive director and secretary; Forrest J. Prettyman, counsel; Don L. Waage, public affairs assistant, Association of Registered Bank Holding Companies, July 24, 1972.
103. Personal interview, Steve Paradise, Senate Banking Committee staff member, July 26, 1972.
104. U.S., Congress, Senate, Committee on Banking, Housing and Urban Affairs, *Bank Holding Company Act Amendments of 1970: Hearings*, 91st Cong., 2nd sess. (May 1970), p. 681. (Cited hereafter as *Senate Holding Company Hearings*.)
105. Ibid., pp. 17–18.
106. Personal interview, July 24, 1972.
107. Senate Banking Committee, *Bank Holding Company Act Amendments*, Print No. 1, June 23, 1970.
108. Personal interview, Senate Banking Committee staffer, July 19, 1972.
109. U.S., Congress, Senate, Committee on Banking, Housing and Urban Affairs, *Bank Holding Company Act Amendments of 1970*, Report No. 91–1084 (Aug. 10, 1970), p. 6.
110. *Congressional Record*, Sept. 16, 1970, p. 32104.

111. "Action Letter to Contact Bankers for the Senate from Willis W. Alexander, Executive Vice President, American Bankers Association," Sept. 2, 1970. (A copy of this letter is in the Congress Project files.)
112. *American Banker*, July 21, 1970.
113. *Congressional Record*, Sept. 16, 1970, p. 21233.
114. Ibid., p. 32135.
115. See ABA Action Letter, Sept. 2, 1970, note 111.
116. *Congressional Record*, Sept. 16, 1970, p. 32133.
117. Personal interview, House Banking Committee staffer, July 1972.
118. *Moody's Bank and Finance Manual*, 1970, p. 453.
119. "Action Letter to Contact Bankers, from Willis W. Alexander, Executive Vice President, American Bankers Association," Nov. 6, 1970. (This letter is available in Congress Project files.)
120. Based on interviews with three House and two Senate staffers, July–Aug., 1972 (names withheld on request).
121. Quoted in Hamilton Potter, *The New Bank Holding Co. Act of 1970*, (New York: Practicing Law Institute, 1971), p. 119.
122. Personal interview, July 13, 1972.
123. U.S., Congress, House, Committee on Banking and Currency, *Conference Report on H.R. 6778*, Report No. 91-1747 (Dec. 15, 1970), p. 5. Emphasis added.
124. Ibid., p. 22.
125. *Congressional Record*, Dec. 18, 1970, pp. 42422–42423.
126. *Regulation Y*, 12 C.F.R., Feb. 1972.
127. *Conference Report* No. 91-1747, pp. 27–28.
128. Association of Registered Bank Holding Companies, *Bank Holding Company Facts* (Mar. 1972), pp. 2–3.
129. Herbert Marks, personal interview, July 10, 1972.
130. John Evans, personal interview, Aug. 1, 1972.

CHAPTER 4.   BRICK BY BRICK: HOUSING AND URBAN POLICY

1. Lawrence Friedman, "Government and Slum Housing: Some General Considerations," *Law and Contemporary Problems*, Vol. 32, No. 2 (Spring 1967), p. 362.
2. U.S., National Commission on Urban Problems (Douglas Commission), *Building the American City*, Report to the Congress and to the President of the United States, House Doc. No. 91–34, 91st Cong., 1st sess. (Washington: Government Printing Office, 1968), p. 9.
3. *Report of the National Advisory Commission on Civil Disorders* (Washington: Government Printing Office, Mar. 1, 1968), p. 257.

4. Douglas Commission, *Building the American City*, p. 11.
5. Washington *Post*, June 19, 1974; U.S. Savings and Loan League, *1973 Savings and Loan Fact Book*, p. 24.
6. For data on these fluctuations, see U.S., Congress, House, Committee on Banking and Currency, *The Residential Mortgage Financing Problem*, by Henry Schechter, 92nd Cong., 1st sess. (Sept. 1971), p. 3.
7. *1973 Savings and Loan Fact Book*, p. 31.
8. Ibid., p. 32.
9. George Sternlieb, "Abandonment and Rehabilitation," in U.S., Congress, House, Committee on Banking and Currency, *Papers Submitted to the Subcommittee on Housing Panels*, 92nd Cong., 1st sess. (June 1971), p. 334.
10. Jack M. Guttentag, "The Short Cycle in Residential Construction, 1946–59," *The American Economic Review*, Vol. 51, No. 3 (June 1961), p. 292, quoted in House Banking Committee, *Residential Mortgage Financing Problem*, p. 8.
11. U.S., Commission on Mortgage Interest Rates, *Report* (Washington: Government Printing Office, 1969), p. 23.
12. House Banking Committee, *Residential Mortgage Financing Problem*, p. 24.
13. *Congressional Record*, Feb. 25, 1970.
14. *Report of the Commission on Mortgage Interest Rates*, p. 32; U.S., Commission on Civil Rights, *Mortgage Money: Who Gets It? A Case Study in Mortgage Lending Discrimination in Hartford, Connecticut* (Washington: Government Printing Office, June 1974).
15. Morton Isler, *Thinking About Housing* (Washington: Urban Institute, 1970), p. 15. For evidence on the extent of abandonment, see Sternlieb, "Abandonment and Rehabilitation," pp. 332–333.
16. U.S., Congress, House, Committee on Banking and Currency, *Emergency Home Financing: Hearings*, 91st Cong., 2nd sess. (1970), p. 256.
17. Ibid., p. 407.
18. For an account of the early history of government involvement in housing in the United States, see Lawrence Friedman, *Government and Slum Housing* (Chicago: Rand McNally, 1968).
19. *1973 Savings and Loan Fact Book*, p. 53.
20. For a discussion of the legislative history of the Home Loan Bank System focusing particularly on the role of the savings banks in promoting the concept, see Josephine Hedges Ewalt, *A Business Reborn: The Savings and Loan Story, 1930–1960* (Chicago: American Savings and Loan Institute Press, 1962), pp. 49–72.
21. Ibid., p. 90. Emphasis added.
22. *1973 Savings and Loan Fact Book*, p. 53.
23. Ibid., p. 37.
24. See Douglas Commission, *Building the American City*, p. 96.
25. Michael Stone, "The Politics of Housing: Mortgage Bankers," *Society*, Vol. 9, (July/Aug. 1972), p. 27.

26. On the origins of the urban renewal program, see Ashley Foard and Hilbert Fefferman, "Federal Urban Renewal Legislation," in James Q. Wilson, ed., *Urban Renewal: The Record and the Controversy* (Cambridge: MIT Press, 1966), pp. 71–125.

27. Douglas Commission, *Building the American City*, pp. 152–169. See also Friedman, "Government and Slum Housing"; Martin Anderson, *The Federal Bulldozer* (Cambridge: MIT Press, 1969); and Wilson, *Urban Renewal.*

28. U.S., Congress, Joint Economic Committee, *Economics of Federal Subsidy Programs*, Staff Study, 92nd Cong., 1st sess. (1972), p. 152. For a discussion of income tax impacts on urban development activity, see Richard Slitor, "Taxation and Land Use," in C. Lowell Harris, *The Good Earth of America* (Englewood Cliffs, N.J.: Prentice Hall, 1974), pp. 67–88.

29. For an official view of the accomplishments of FHA, see "Report on Programs and Goals of HUD," in U.S., Congress, Senate, Committee on Government Operations, *Federal Role in Urban Affairs*, Appendix I (Dec. 1966).

30. Douglas Commission, *Building the American City*, p. 107.

31. *Savings and Loan Fact Book*, pp. 34, 43; Washington *Post*, Aug. 12, 1972.

32. See, for example, Jeanne R. Lowe, *Cities in a Race with Time* (New York: Vintage Books, 1967).

33. William Slayton, "The Operation and Achievements of the Urban Renewal Program," in Wilson, *Urban Renewal*, pp. 189–230.

34. Bernard Frieden, "Housing and Urban Goals: Old Policies and New Realities," in James Q. Wilson, ed., *The Metropolitan Enigma* (Garden City, New York: Anchor Books, 1970), p. 199.

35. U.S., Department of Housing and Urban Development, *1970 HUD Statistical Yearbook* (Washington: Government Printing Office, 1971), Tables 162 and 163.

36. HUD Audit Report, Dec. 19, 1971, reprinted in U.S., Congress, House, Committee on Banking and Currency, Subcommittee on Housing, *Hearings on Housing and Urban Development Legislation of 1972*, 92nd Cong., 2nd sess. (1972), p. 84.

37. "Programs and Goals of HUD," in Senate Government Operations Committee, *Federal Role in Urban Affairs*, pp. 42–43.

38. Douglas Commission, *Building the American City*, p. 100.

39. *1970 HUD Statistical Yearbook*, Table 194, p. 194.

40. Ibid., pp. 257, 259.

41. Douglas Commission, *Building the American City*, p. 163.

42. Senate Government Operations Committee, *Federal Role in Urban Affairs*, Appendix I, p. 37.

43. *Report of the President's Commission on Financial Structure and Regulation* (Hunt Commission Report) (Washington: Government Printing Office, 1971), p. 37.

44. These figures were adopted from those offered in testimony before the

Senate Banking, Housing and Urban Affairs Committee and reported in U.S., Congress, Senate, Committee on Banking, Housing and Urban Affairs, *Hearings: Housing and Urban Development Legislation of 1970*, 91st Cong., 2nd sess. (1970).

45. U.S., Congress, Senate, Special Committee on Aging, *Adequacy of Federal Response to Housing Needs of Older Americans: Hearings*, 92nd Cong., 1st sess. (1971), pp. 18–20, 71.

46. *NAHB Journal of Homebuilding*, July 1972, p. 6.

47. U.S., Congress, House, Committee on Banking and Currency, *Housing and Urban Development Legislation—1970: Hearings*, 91st Cong., 2nd sess. (1970), p. 8947.

48. George Romney, speech before the National Association of Home Builders, January, 1973.

49. Friedman, "Government and Slum Housing," p. 368.

50. Henry Aaron, *Shelter and Subsidies: Who Benefits from Federal Housing Policies?* (Washington: Brookings Institution, 1972).

51. *Congressional Record*, Apr. 16, 1970, p. 12206.

52. Richard Fenno, *The Power of the Purse* (Boston: Little, Brown, 1966).

53. For an analysis of the growing significance of uniquely "suburban" issues and of the growing power of the "suburban bloc" in Congress, see *Congressional Quarterly Weekly Report* (Apr. 6, 1974), pp. 878–880.

54. Personal interview, Aug. 5, 1972.

55. Ibid.

56. Personal interview, Aug. 1, 1972 (name withheld on request).

57. Personal interview, Aug. 10, 1972 (name withheld on request).

58. House Banking Committee, *Emergency Home Financing Hearings*, p. 3.

59. Personal interview, July 19, 1972.

60. Title VII of the Housing and Urban Development Act of 1970. The hearings resulted in three published volumes: U.S., Congress, House, Committee on Banking and Currency, *Hearings Before the Ad Hoc Subcommittee on Urban Growth*, 91st Cong., 1st and 2nd sess. (1969–1970).

61. U.S., Congress, House, Committee on Banking and Currency, *Housing and the Urban Environment: Report and Recommendations of Three Study Panels of the Subcommittee on Housing*, 92nd Cong., 1st sess. (June 1971).

62. Gerald McMurray (Staff Director, Housing Subcommittee), personal interview, June 20, 1972.

63. Personal interview, June 27, 1972.

64. Dudley O'Neal, personal interview, June 28, 1972.

65. U.S., Congress, House, Committee on Banking and Currency, *Housing and Urban Development Act of 1972*, Report No. 92-1429, 92nd Cong., 2nd sess. (1972), p. 319.

66. Personal interview, July, 1972.

67. House Banking Committee, *Housing and the Urban Environment* (Study Panels Report), p. 1.
68. Coan interview, June 27, 1972.
69. Personal interview, Senate staffer, Aug. 10, 1972 (name withheld on request).
70. Personal interview, Aug. 1, 1972 (name withheld on request).
71. Personal interview, Aug. 10, 1972.
72. Personal interview, June 13, 1972 (name withheld on request).
73. Personal interview, Aug. 10, 1972 (name withheld on request).
74. Personal interview, Aug. 18, 1972.
75. William Moorhead, personal interview, Aug. 17, 1972.
76. Friedman, "Government and Slum Housing," p. 14.
77. See Suzanne G. Farkas, *Urban Lobbying* (New York: New York University Press, 1971).
78. Robert Wood, *The Necessary Majority* (New York: Columbia University Press, 1972).
79. For a brief discussion of the Home Owners Loan Corporation and bank opposition to it, see Ewalt, *A Business Reborn*, pp. 36–43, 62–63.
80. U.S., Congress, Senate, Committee on Banking and Currency, *Hearings: Housing and Urban Development Legislation of 1968*, 90th Cong., 2nd sess. (1968), pp. 1248–1249. For a similar argument from the Mortgage Bankers Association, see pp. 400–404.
81. On banker support for low income limits on subsidy programs, see testimony by the Mortgage Bankers Association and the U.S. Savings and Loan League in the Senate Hearings on the 1968 Housing Act, ibid., pp. 402 and 1427.
82. Mortgage Bankers Association of America, *Statement of Public Policy, 1971*, p. 5. Emphasis added.
83. For a detailed description of these various financial institutions, see Eli Shapiro, Ezra Solomon, and William L. White, *Money and Banking* (New York: Holt, Rinehart, and Winston, 1968), Chap. 12.
84. *Statistical Abstract of the United States*, 1973, pp. 447–451. Data are for 1972.
85. *1973 Savings and Loan Fact Book*, pp. 35–36. Data cover 1972.
86. Statement of USS&LL vice-president Norman Straub in House Banking Committee, *Emergency Home Financing Hearings*, p. 46.
87. Personal interview, Aug. 1, 1972.
88. Personal interview, Aug. 17, 1972.
89. Personal interview, Aug. 10, 1972.
90. Personal interview, Aug. 15, 1972.
91. "Report of Savings Association Political Elections Committee to the United States House of Representatives, Schedule of Expenditures for the Period March 1, 1972 through May 31, 1972," Section B, Part 9.
92. Personal interview, Aug. 15, 1972.
93. *Congressional Quarterly Weekly Report*, Vol. 31, No. 26, June 30, 1973.

94. Personal interview, Aug. 15, 1972.
95. Personal interviews, Nathaniel Keith and Oliver Jones, Aug. 10 and July 28, 1972.
96. Personal interview, Aug. 15, 1972.
97. Ibid.
98. Personal interview, July 28, 1972.
99. Oliver Jones, personal interview, July 28, 1972.
100. Congress Project files.
101. *Congressional Quarterly Weekly Report*, Vol. 31, No. 26, June 30, 1973, p. 2.
102. Personal interview, July 28, 1972.
103. Personal interview, Aug. 1, 1972.
104. House Banking Committee, *Emergency Home Financing Hearings*, p. 20.
105. See, for example, ibid., pp. 244, 405.
106. U.S., Congress, Senate, Committee on Banking and Currency, *Secondary Mortgage Market and Mortgage Credit: Hearings*, 91st Cong., 2nd sess. (1970), p. 205.
107. *Congressional Record*, June 25, 1970, p. 21605.
108. *1970 HUD Statistical Yearbook*, Table 160, p. 147; Douglas Commission, *Building the American City*, p. 100.
109. U.S., Congress, House, Committee on Banking and Currency, *Housing and Urban Development Act of 1968*, Report No. 1585, 90th Cong., 2nd sess. (1968), p. 8.
110. Testimony of National Association of Home Builders President Lloyd Clarke, in Senate Banking Committee, *Hearings: Housing and Urban Development Legislation of 1968*, pp. 291–292.
111. *1970 HUD Statistical Yearbook*, Table 160, p. 147.
112. *National Journal*, Vol. III, No. 9, Feb. 27, 1971, p. 437.
113. Ibid.
114. Executive Session Transcripts, Mar. 15, 1972.
115. Personal interview, Aug. 1, 1972.
116. Personal interview, Sept. 7, 1972.
117. Jake Lewis, personal interview, June 13, 1972.
118. Personal interview, Aug. 10, 1972.
119. Personal interview, Sept. 8, 1972.
120. Senate Banking Committee, *Hearings: Housing and Urban Development Legislation of 1970*, pp. 752–753.
121. See, for example, *NAREB Statement of Policy*, 1972, p. 6.
122. Personal interview, Sept. 8, 1972.
123. Ibid.
124. Ibid.
125. Ibid.
126. Ibid.
127. Personal interview, Aug. 1, 1972.
128. Win Skiles, personal interview, Sept. 8, 1972.
129. Personal interview, Sept. 6, 1972.

130. Ibid.
131. "Legislative Process: Federal Substantive Laws" (internal HUD document), Aug. 20, 1971. Emphasis added.
132. Personal interview, Aug. 17, 1972.
133. Personal interview, Aug. 15, 1972.
134. Ibid.
135. James interview, Aug. 18, 1972.
136. Personal interview, Aug. 17, 1972.
137. Personal interview, Aug. 17, 1972.
138. Personal interview, Aug. 10, 1972.
139. Personal interview, Aug. 17, 1972 (name withheld on request).
140. NAHRO membership brochure, p. 1.
141. Ibid.
142. Personal interview, July 25, 1972.
143. Ibid.
144. For a discussion of the differences between the presidential and congressional wings of the Democratic Party, see James McGregor Burns, *The Deadlock of Democracy: Four Party Politics in America* (Englewood Cliffs, N.J.: Prentice-Hall, A Spectrum Book, 1963).
145. "Accomplishments of HUD, 1969–1972," *Challenge*, Feb. 1972.
146. U.S., Congress, House, Committee on Appropriations, *Hearings Before a Subcommittee of the Committee on Appropriations on Independent Offices and Department of Housing and Urban Development Appropriations for 1971*, 91st Cong., 2nd sess. (1970), p. 6.
147. House Appropriations Committee, *Hearings on 1970 HUD Budget*, p. 9.
148. House Appropriations Committee, *Hearings on 1971 HUD Budget*, p. 2. For a recent discussion of the heavy emphasis on production under Romney, see Anthony Downs, "The Successes and Failures of Federal Housing Policy," in Eli Ginzberg and Robert M. Solow, eds., *The Great Society: Lessons for the Future* (New York: Basic Books, Inc., 1974), pp. 124–144.
149. *NAHB Policy Statement* 1972, p. 3.
150. House Banking Committee, *Emergency Home Financing Hearings*, p. 486. Emphasis added.
151. Personal interview, June 13, 1972.
152. O'Neal interview, June 28, 1972.
153. Senate Report 91-698 (Feb. 9, 1970). See also U.S., Congress, Senate, Committee on Rules and Administration, *Study of Federal Housing Programs*, Report No. 15, 89th Cong., 1st sess. (Feb. 1, 1965), p. 1; U.S., Congress, Senate, Committee on Banking and Currency, *Study of Federal Housing and Urban Development Programs*, Report No. 91-2, 91st Cong.; Senate Committee on Rules and Administration, *Authorizing Additional Expenditures by the Committee on Banking, Housing and Urban Affairs for Inquiries and Investigations*, Report No. 92-650, 92nd Cong., 2nd sess. (Feb. 28, 1972).

154. House Banking Committee, *Housing and the Urban Environment*, p. 2.
155. Quoted in U.S., Congress, House, Committee on Government Operations, *Defaults on FHA Insured Home Mortgages—Detroit, Michigan*, House Report No. 92-1152, 92nd Cong., 2nd sess. (1972), p. 55.
156. *National Journal*, Jan. 1, 1972.
157. House Government Operations Committee, *Defaults on FHA-Insured Home Mortgages—Detroit*, p. 3.
158. Cited in Brian D. Boyer, *Cities Destroyed for Cash* (Chicago: Follett, 1973), pp. 6–7.
159. Hewes interview, Aug. 1, 1972.
160. Personal interview, July, 1972.
161. Reported in U.S., Congress, House, Committee on Appropriations, "Surveys and Investigations Staff Report on Housing Programs in the Department of Housing and Urban Development," in *Hearings: HUD-Space-Science-Veterans Appropriations for 1973*, 92nd Cong., 2nd sess. (Apr. 10, 1972), Part 3, p. 1314.
162. U.S., Congress, House, Committee on Banking and Currency, *Investigation and Hearing of Abuses in Federal Low- and Moderate-Income Housing Programs*, Staff Report, 91st Cong., 2nd sess. (Dec. 1970). For background on the investigations, see U.S., Congress, House, Committee on Banking and Currency, *Interim Report on HUD Investigation of Low- and Moderate-Income Housing Programs: Hearings*, 92nd Cong., 1st sess. (Mar. 31, 1971), pp. 1–3.
163. House Banking Committee, *Hearings on Interim Report on HUD Investigation of Housing Programs*, p. 2.
164. See Romney testimony before the House Appropriations Subcommittee on HUD in April 1972 in House Appropriations Committee, *Hearings: HUD-Space-Science-Veterans Appropriations for 1973*, p. 69.
165. Barrett interview, July 19, 1972; Hewes interview, Aug. 1, 1972.
166. Personal interview, July 6, 1972.
167. Personal interview, June 26, 1972.
168. U.S., Congress, Senate, Committee on Banking, Housing and Urban Affairs, *Summary of Activities*, 1971, Report, 92nd Cong., 2nd sess. (1972), pp. 23–24.
169. Personal interview, Aug. 19, 1972.
170. Carl Coan, Jr., personal interview, Aug. 1972.
171. U.S., Congress, Senate, Committee on Banking, Housing, and Urban Affairs, *Oversight on Housing and Urban Development Programs*, 93rd Cong., 1st sess. (Apr. 1973), p. 1.
172. James interview, Aug. 18, 1972.
173. U.S., Congress, House, Committee on Banking and Currency, Subcommittee on Housing, *Housing and Urban Development Legislation—1970, Hearings*, 91st Cong., 2nd sess. (June 1970), p. 5.
174. For a complete listing of these changes, see ibid., pp. 103–104.
175. H.R. 16643, 91st Cong.

176. House Banking Committee, *Hearings on 1970 Housing Legislation*, pp. 24–25.
177. Ibid., p. 7.
178. James interview, Aug. 18, 1972.
179. House Banking Committee, *Hearings on 1970 Housing Legislation*, pp. 29–31.
180. James interview, Aug. 18, 1972.
181. Coan interview, June 28, 1972.
182. James interview, Aug. 18, 1972.
183. Senate Banking Committee, *Hearings: Housing and Urban Development Legislation of 1970*, p. 399.
184. Ibid., pp. 328–329.
185. Ibid., pp. 590–592.
186. See the testimony of Nathaniel Goldfinger of the AFL–CIO, in ibid., pp. 618–621.
187. Ibid., pp. 878–880.
188. Ibid., p. 326.
189. Ibid., p. 620–621.
190. James interview, Aug. 18, 1974.
191. Personal interview, Aug. 1, 1972.
192. Personal interview, July 25, 1970.
193. "NAHRO Proposes Community Development Program and Comprehensive Housing Assistance Program," reprinted in U.S., Congress, Senate, Committee on Banking, Housing and Urban Affairs, Subcommittee on Housing, *Hearings: 1971 Housing and Urban Development Legislation*, 92nd Cong., 1st sess. (Aug. 1971), pp. 126–131.
194. Ibid.
195. Stenson interview, June 29, 1972.
196. James interview, Aug. 18, 1974.
197. Ibid.
198. U.S., Congress, Senate, Committee on Banking, Housing and Urban Affairs, *Agenda for Subcommittee Consideration of Pending Housing and Urban Development Bills and Proposals*, Part II, 91st Cong., 2nd sess. (Feb. 4, 1972), p. 3.
199. Hewes interview, August 1, 1972.
200. U.S., Senate, Committee on Banking, Housing, and Urban Affairs, *Housing and Urban Development Act of 1970*, Report No. 92-647, 92nd Cong., 2nd sess. (1972), p. 24.
201. *Congressional Record*, Mar. 1, 1972, p.S.3049; Mar. 2, 1972, pp. S. 3102–3152.
202. Coan interview, June 28, 1972.
203. Testimony of Robert W. Mafflin, Executive Director of NAHRO, in Senate Banking Committee, *Hearings on 1971 Housing Legislation*, p. 105.
204. Ibid., p. 882.
205. Ibid., pp. 74, 103.

206. Ibid., p. 753.
207. Testimony of Kenneth F. Phillips, Director, National Housing and Economic Development Law Project, University of California, Berkeley, in ibid., pp. 881–883.
208. *Senate Banking Committee Report on Housing and Urban Development Act of 1972*, Report No. 92-642, 92nd Cong., 2nd sess. (1972), p. 47.
209. Ibid., p. 128.
210. U.S., Congress, House, Committee on Banking and Currency, *Financing of Inner City Housing*, Hearings Before an Ad Hoc Subcommittee, 91st Cong., 1st sess. (1969).
211. Hugh Mields, personal interview, Aug. 1972.
212. Personal interview, July 25, 1972.
213. Representative Garry Brown, personal interview, June 26, 1972.
214. McMurray interview, June 20, 1972.
215. House Banking Committee, *Housing and the Urban Environment*, p. 23.
216. Ibid., pp. 34–35.
217. Ibid., p. 23.
218. Ibid., p. 14.
219. Ibid., p. 14.
220. Ibid., p. 13. (Original emphasis.)
221. Ibid., p. 2.
222. U.S., Congress, House, Committee on Banking and Currency, Subcommittee on Housing, *Housing and Urban Development Legislation—1971: Hearings*, 92nd Cong., 1st sess. (1971), p. 1063.
223. Ibid., p. 74.
224. 36 *F.R.* 1931620, Oct. 2, 1971.
225. House Banking Committee, *Hearings on 1971 Housing Legislation*, pp. 298, 278.
226. Ibid., p. 1244.
227. Ibid., p. 1259. (Emphasis added.)
228. Ibid., p. 1244.
229. Ibid., p. 1242.
230. See, for example, ibid., p. 304.
231. Ibid., p. 1245.
232. Ibid., pp. 495–496.
233. Ibid., p. 674.
234. Ibid., p. 505.
235. Ibid., pp. 970–985.
236. Ibid., p. 1014.
237. Ibid., pp. 502, 991.
238. The coolness of the mayors toward both of these ideas is reflected in ibid., p. 512. For the opposition of the Investment Bankers Association and the American Bankers Association to the urban development bank idea, see ibid., pp. 782–791, 1335–1336.
239. Personal interview, July 25, 1972.

240. House Banking Committee, *Hearings on 1971 Housing Legislation*, p. 535.
241. For an interesting description of the resulting liberal dilemma, see the speech of Congresswoman Sullivan in *Congressional Record*, Apr. 6, 1972.
242. Stenographic Minutes, *Executive Sessions of the Subcommittee on Housing of the Committee on Banking and Currency on Housing and Urban Development Legislation of 1972.*
243. Ibid.
244. Ashley interview, July 19, 1972.
245. Stenographic Transcripts, *House Housing Subcommittee Executive Sessions.*
246. Personal interview, July 19, 1972.
247. Stenographic Transcripts, *House Housing Subcommittee Executive Sessions.*
248. Ibid.
249. Ibid.
250. House Banking Committee, *Hearings on 1971 Housing Legislation*, p. 338.
251. Stenographic Minutes, *House Housing Subcommittee Executive Sessions.*
252. Ibid.
253. Ibid.
254. U.S., Congress, House, Committee on Banking and Currency, *Housing and Urban Development Act of 1972: Hearings*, 92nd Cong., 2nd sess. (1972), p. 1.
255. Ibid., pp. 613–617; Hilbert Fefferman, personal interview, Sept. 6, 1972.
256. House Banking Committee, *Hearings on 1972 Housing Act*, p. 534.
257. Ibid., pp. 276–277.
258. Ibid., 539–540.
259. Personal interview, Aug. 17, 1972.
260. Personal interview, Aug. 10, 1972.
261. Washington *Post*, Aug. 10, 1972.
262. Personal interview, June 13, 1972.
263. U.S., Congress, House, Committee on Banking and Currency, *The Housing and Urban Development Act of 1972*, Report No. 92-1429, 92nd Cong., 2nd sess. (Sept. 21, 1972), pp. 6–9.
264. Personal interview, Aug. 19, 1972.
265. Richard Nixon, Message to the Congress, Sept. 19, 1973.
266. Ibid.
267. U.S., Congress, Senate, Committee on Banking, Housing and Urban Affairs, *Oversight on Housing and Urban Development Programs*, Hearings Before the Subcommittee on Housing and Urban Affairs, 93rd Cong., 1st sess. (Apr. 1973), p. 317.
268. *Congressional Quarterly Weekly Report*, Mar. 9, 1974.
269. Senate Report, No. 93-693, reprinted in U.S., Congress, House, Com-

mittee on Banking and Currency, *Compilation of the Housing and Community Development Act of 1974*, 93rd Cong., 1st sess. (Oct. 1974), p. 612.

270. Ibid., p. 744.
271. Ibid., p. 740.
272. U.S., Congress, House, Committee on Banking and Currency, *Housing and Community Development Legislation—1973: Hearings*, 93rd Cong., 1st sess. (Oct. 1973).
273. Ibid., p. 1267.
274. House Report No. 93-114, in *Compilation of the Housing and Community Development Act*, p. 551.
275. *Congressional Record*, June 20, 1974, p. H. 5394.

CHAPTER 5.   COWBOYS WHO LASSO THEMSELVES: THE BATTLE AGAINST INFLATION

1. The report was issued March 25, 1970. *National Journal*, Apr. 4, 1970, p. 745.
2. U.S., White House, "President Nixon's Speech on the Economy," June 17, 1970.
3. Rule XXV of the *Standing Rules of the Senate*; Part 4 of Rule XI of the *Rules of the House of Representatives*.
4. U.S., Congress, House, Committee on Banking and Currency, Letter from Wright Patman to Richard Nixon, May 20, 1970.
5. U.S., Congress, House, Committee on Banking and Currency, *To Extend the Defense Production Act of 1950, as Amended: Hearings on H.R. 17880*, 91st Cong., 2nd sess. (1970), pp. 5–6.
6. Ibid., pp. 4, 67.
7. Ibid., p. 111.
8. Ibid., p. 159.
9. Ibid., p. 23.
10. U.S., Congress, House, Committee on Banking and Currency, *Defense Production Act Extension and Economic Stabilization Act*, House Report 91-1330, 91st Cong., 2nd sess. (1970), Minority Views.
11. *Congressional Record*, July 31, 1970, p. 26839.
12. Ibid., pp. 26824–26825.
13. Ibid., p. 26813.
14. Quoted in *National Journal*, Aug. 22, 1970, p. 1834; *Congressional Quarterly Weekly Report*, Aug. 21, 1970, p. 2091.
15. Cited in U.S., Congress, Senate, Committee on Banking, Housing and Urban Affairs, Subcommittee on Financial Institutions, *Hearings: Selective Credit Policies and Wage-Price Stabilization*, 92nd Cong., 1st sess. (1971), p. 74.

16. *National Journal,* Dec. 12, 1970, p. 2724.
17. *National Journal,* Nov. 28, 1970, p. 2615; Dec. 19, 1970, p. 2782.
18. See, for example, *National Journal,* Apr. 4, 1970, p. 746.
19. Cited in *National Journal,* May 30, 1970; *Congressional Quarterly Almanac,* 1971, p. 427.
20. Quoted from *Congressional Quarterly Almanac,* 1971, p. 20-H.
21. U.S., Congress, House, Committee on Banking and Currency, *To Extend Standby Powers of the President to Stabilize Wages and Prices and the Authority of the Federal Reserve Board and the Federal Home Loan Bank Board to Establish Flexible Interest Rates on Time Deposits: Hearings on H.R. 4246,* 92nd Cong., 1st sess. (1971), p. 5. (Emphasis added.)
22. Senate Banking Committee, *Hearings on Selective Credit Policy and Wage-Price Stabilization,* p. 3.
23. Ibid., p. 79.
24. Quoted in *Congressional Quarterly Almanac,* 1971, p. 428.
25. *Congressional Record,* Mar. 10, 1971, p. H 1385.
26. Cited in *National Journal,* Oct. 2, 1971.
27. Senate Banking Committee, *Hearings on Selective Credit Policies and Wage-Price Stabilization,* pp. 2–3.
28. Testimony of Charles Walker in ibid., p. 43.
29. See ibid., pp. 80–82.
30. *Congressional Record,* May 3, 1971, pp. S 6135–6136.
31. *Executive Order 11615,* Aug. 15, 1971, Section 2.
32. *Executive Order 11617,* Oct. 15, 1971.
33. See, for example, "Prices: The Freeze Has Been Dripping All Over the Place," *New York Times,* Oct. 31, 1971.
34. *Congressional Record,* Sept. 8, 1971, p. H 8199.
35. *Congressional Record,* Sept. 16, 1971, p. S 14404–14405.
36. *National Journal,* Oct. 2, 1971, p. 2019.
37. U.S., Congress, House, Committee on Banking and Currency, *Oversight Hearings on the Operation of the Economic Stabilization Act of 1970,* 92nd Cong., 1st sess. (Oct. 4–7, 1971).
38. U.S., Congress, House, Committee on Banking and Currency, *Economic Stabilization, Part II: Hearings on H.R. 11309, To Extend and Amend the Economic Stabilization Act of 1970,* 92nd Cong., 1st sess. (1970), p. 312.
39. Testimony of Andrew Biemiller, AFL–CIO, in ibid., p. 371.
40. Ibid., p. 375.
41. Ibid., pp. 503–505.
42. Ibid., pp. 328–329.
43. Ibid., pp. 309–310.
44. U.S., Congress, Senate, Committee on Banking, Housing and Urban Affairs, *Economic Stabilization Legislation: Hearings on S. 2712,* 92nd Cong., 1st sess. (Nov. 1971), p. 26.
45. *Congressional Record,* Dec. 9, 1971, pp. H 12163–12165.
46. House Report 92-714, p. 25.

47. *Congressional Record*, Dec. 1, 1971, pp. S 19985-19986.
48. *National Journal*, Jan. 6, 1973, pp. 11–15.
49. U.S., Congress, House, Committee on Banking and Currency, *Economic Stabilization—1973: Hearings*, 93rd Cong., 1st sess. (Mar. 1973), p. 221. For a similar conclusion from an academic economist, see ibid., p. 174.
50. Details on price rises and stock market activity from *Congressional Quarterly Almanac*, 1973, p. 202. See also testimony of Professor Robert Lekachman, House Banking Committee, *1973 Economic Stabilization Hearings*, pp. 152–154.
51. Quoted in *Congressional Quarterly Almanac* (1973), p. 216.
52. Quoted in ibid., p. 215.
53. Quoted in "House Rules Out Price Rollback by 258–147 Vote," *New York Times*, Apr. 17, 1973.
54. *Congressional Record*, Mar. 18, 1974, p. H 1837.

CHAPTER 6. THE BANKING COMMITTEES
AND THE FUTURE: CONCLUSIONS
AND RECOMMENDATIONS

1. *Congressional Record*, Feb. 19, 1963.
2. Personal interview, June 27, 1972.
3. Personal interview, July 1972.
4. *Congressional Quarterly Almanac*, 1973, p. 216.
5. U.S., Congress, House, Committee on Banking and Currency, *Housing and Urban Development Legislation—1971: Hearings*, 92nd Cong., 1st sess. (1971), p. 322.
6. House Report No. 92-714 (1971), pp. 34–35.
7. Personal interview, Aug. 1972.
8. Ralph Nader, "Speech to the National Conference of the Plumbing-Heating-Cooling Industry," Apr. 6, 1972, Arlington, Va.
9. William K. Reilly, ed., *The Use of Land: A Citizens' Policy Guide to Urban Growth*, A Task Force Report Sponsored by the Rockefeller Brothers Fund (New York: Thomas Y. Crowell, 1973), p. 19.
10. U.S., Department of Housing and Urban Development, *Housing in the Seventies*, Report of the National Housing Policy Review, reprinted in U.S., Congress, House, Committee on Banking and Currency, Subcommittee on Housing, *Hearings: Housing and Community Development Legislation—1973*, 93rd Cong., 1st sess. (1973), Part 3, p. 2260.
11. HUD, *Housing in the Seventies*, pp. 2320, 2325.
12. U.S., Congress, Senate, Committee on Interior and Insular Affairs, *Land Use Policy and Planning Assistance Act*, Report No. 93-197, 93rd Cong., 1st sess. (1973), p. 36.

Index

Aaron, Henry, 174n
Administrative Procedures Act, 328, 333, 335
AFL-CIO, 281
Alioto, Joseph, 268n
Allen, James V., 232
American Banker, 128–29, 135–36
American Bankers Association (ABA), xxvi, 101, 201, 205, 207, 344
  bank holding companies and, 121–29, 131, 134, 135, 136, 138
  congressional influence of, 52, 65, 66, 67
  functions of, 23
Americans for Constitutional Action, 48, 72
Americans for Democratic Action, 48, 53, 72
American Institute of Planners, 281
Anderson, Jack, 126
Annunzio, Frank, 216
Appropriations Committee (House of Representatives), 181–84
  ideology and constituency of members of, 184 (table)
Appropriations Committee (Senate), 79

Appropriations Subcommittee on Foreign Operations (Senate), 185
Archer, Bill, 51, 286
Ashley, Thomas L., 52, 53–54, 345, 347, 356
  federal housing policy and, 186, 189, 205, 224
  Housing Act (1972) and, 272–74, 279, 283–87
  Housing Act (1974) and, 303–5
Association of Corporate Owners of One Bank, 122, 123
Association of Registered Bank Holding Companies, 66, 110, 129

Badillo, Herman, 334
"Balance of Payments Problem" hearing (1965), 67
Baldwin-Central bank holding company, 137
Bank Holding Company Act (1956)
  Amendments (1966), 110
  Amendments (1970), 85, 86, 137–43, 353
  bank regulation proposals and, 115–29
  purpose of, 107–10

391

Bank Holding Company Act (1970), xxiv, 15, 36, 55, 70, 104
Bank Merger Act (1960), 96, 97, 98 (table)
  Amendments (1966), 44, 54, 98–99, 110
Bank of America, xxii, 9, 52
  assets of, 10 (table)
Bank of New York, 11
Bank Reform Act (1971), 37, 41, 43
Bank Supervision and Insurance subcommittee (House of Representatives), 40
Bankers Political Action Committee, 23–24, 52
Bankers Trust Company, xxii, 11, 13
Banking, Housing, and Urban Affairs Committee (Senate), 2, 20, 81
  Bank Holding Company Act and, 129–43
  budget of, 61 (table)
  defense contracts (1970) and, 314–15
  democratization of, 363–64
  hearings by, 67–68
  Housing Act (1974) and, 299–300
  jurisdiction of, 72–79, 363–64
  leadership of, 57–61
  lobbies and, 22–23, 346
  mandated agency reports issued by (1965–72), 64 (table)
  membership of, 71–76
  policy-change proposals for, 351–58
  policy initiation by, 342–44
  recruitment proposals for, 364–65
  staff function of, 61–67
  subcommittees of, 68–71
  voting blocks of, 74 (table)
  wage-price controls and, 318–19, 331–32, 336–37
  workload of, 82–83
  See also Housing and Urban Affairs subcommittee (Senate)

Banking Act (1863), 99
Banking Act (1933), 88, 105, 143
Banking Act (1935), 31, 88, 91
Banking and Currency Committee (House of Representatives), 2, 22–23, 85
  bank holding companies and, 115–29, 137–43
  budget of, 61 (table)
  democratization of, 362–63
  hearings by, 43–46
  jurisdictional change proposals for, 363–64
  membership of, 47–57
  name change of, 307
  Patman's leadership of, 27–33
  policy-change proposals for, 351–58
  policy initiation by, 342, 344–45
  policy limitations of, 349
  recruitment proposals for, 364–65
  research reports issued by (1963–72), 34–35 (table)
  staff-change proposals for, 359–61
  staff functions of, 33–40
  subcommittees of, 40–43
  wage-price controls and, 315, 317–18, 320, 332, 337–39
  See also Housing and Urban Affairs subcommittee (House of Representatives)
Banking industry
  branching and, 92–93
  chartering and, 91–92
  consumer credit and, 20–21
  corporate stockholders in NYC banks, 13–14 (tables)
  credit distribution and, 18–20
  dual banking system and, 99–102
  economic concentration and, 3–15
  financial intermediaries of, 8 (table)
  FRS influenced by, 18
  holding company formation by, 15, 84–89, 103–15
  housing development and, 152–

57, 161, 165–72, 199–210
mergers and, 93–99
nonbanking business and, 102–3, 112–14
protected markets of, 89–91
types of commercial banks and, 6 (table)
U.S. economy and, 1–2
See also American Bankers Association
Banking Profession Political Action Committee (BankPAC), 23–24, 52
Barrett, William, 39, 42, 52, 138, 345
  federal housing policy and, 186–89, 195, 205, 215, 238
  Housing Act (1972) and, 273, 284, 285, 287, 289, 291, 293, 295
  Housing Act (1974) and, 305
Basic Compilation of Authorities on Housing and Urban Development (Banking Committee, House of Representatives), 172
Beall, J. Glenn, 125, 127
Beckman, Norman, 263
Bennett, Wallace F., 60, 73–74, 75, 177, 345
  bank holding companies and, 133, 136, 138, 139, 145
Bevill, Tom, 125
Bingham, Jonathan, 318
Blackburn, Benjamin B., 49, 55, 125, 127
  federal housing programs and, 173, 205, 285, 287
  wage-price controls and, 317–18
Blount, Winston, 59*n*
Bolling, Richard, 78*n*
Brandeis, Louis D., xxvi
Brann, Charles F., 137
Brennan, William J., 97–98
Brock, William E., III, 60, 73, 74, 127, 261, 270, 302
Brooke, Edward, 72, 75, 76, 133, 345

federal housing and, 186, 205, 216, 254–55, 258, 260, 270, 289, 300
Brooke Amendment (1969), 255, 256, 289
Brown, Garry E., 53, 56, 125, 127, 345
  federal housing and, 205, 285, 295, 304
  wage-price control and, 317–18, 322
Brownstein, Philip, 217, 225, 235
Buckley, William, 327
Builders Political Action Committee (BIPAC), 215–16
Building industry
  economic recession and, 299
  housing and, 211–18, 353
Burdick, Quentin, 137
Burlington Northern Railroad, 11
Burns, Arthur F., 43, 151, 313, 320
  on Economic Stabilization Act, 372

Carson and Company, 11
Cash, James B., 67, 129
Celler-Kefauver Act (1950), 96
Central Bank and Trust Company (Denver), 137
Chappell, Bill, Jr., 49
Chase Manhattan Bank, xxii, 9, 11, 13, 43
  assets, 10 (table)
Chemical Bank, xxii
Chrysler Corporation, 9, 10
CIT Financial Corporation, 66, 129
Clark, Joseph, 22, 69, 72, 340
Clayton Anti-Trust Act, 54
  bank mergers and, 95–96, 107
Cleveland Trust Company, 52
Coan, Carl A. S., Sr., 63, 65, 343–44
  federal housing policy and, 191–94, 224, 225, 238, 249–50, 254, 262, 269, 300
Coan, Carl A. S., Jr., 65, 194, 214, 216, 254

Commerce, Department of, 82
Commerce Committee (House of Representatives), 35
Commerce Committee (Senate), 78
Commission on Financial Structure and Regulation, President's (Hunt Commission), 12, 38, 130, 145, 166
Committee on Political Education, 48, 72
Committee to Re-elect the President, 37
Community development programs, 261–72
Comptroller of the Currency, xxii, 100, 119
    bank holding companies and, 123
    bank mergers and, 97
Conference committees, 137–38
Conference of Mayors, U.S./National League of Cities, 197, 229, 265, 270, 281, 292
Conglomerate bank holding companies, 134–35
Connally, John, 320
Consumer Affairs subcommittee (House of Representatives), 40
Consumer credit, 20–21
    new federal policy proposals for, 256–57
Consumer Credit subcommittee (Senate), 70
Cook, Richard, 338
"Cost and Adequacy of Fuel Oil" hearing (1971), 68
Cost of Living Council, 326–27, 329–30, 336
Council of Economic Advisers, 17
Council of Housing Producers, 217, 225
Cowger, William, 125
Cranston, Alan, 74, 133, 177, 300, 331, 345
Cudd and Company, 11

Davis-Bacon Act, 197, 320, 321
Dean, John, 37

Defense Producers Act (1950), 314
    extension (1970), 314–15
Democratic Caucus, 365
Demonstration Cities and Metropolitan Development Act (1966), 235
Detroit, FHA foreclosures in, 236
Domestic Finance subcommittee (House of Representatives), 40
Douglas, Paul, 60, 71, 72, 356, 357
Douglas Commission (National Commission on Urban Problems), 147, 164
Dwyer, Florence P., 125, 127, 181

Economic Stabilization Act (1971), 38, 41, 315
    passage of, 320–23
    Phase II extensions of, 324–35
    Phase III extensions of, 335–39
"Effect of Railroad Mergers on Commuter Transportation" hearings (1971), 68
Emergency Home Finance Act (1970), 168, 209–10, 234
Emergency Loan Guarantee Act (1971), 41
Emergency Middle Income Housing Act (1975), 308–10
Englehart, William, 139
Englehart Industries, 139
Equity and Morris Plan Corporation, 106
Evans, Rowland, 70, 293, 295
Evans, John, 203, 263

Fair Credit Billing Act (1972), 66
Fair Credit Reporting Act (1970), 42, 81
Federal Deposit Insurance Corporation, 5, 82, 91, 100, 119
Federal Home Loan Bank Board (FHLBB), 82
    federal housing policy and, 153, 154, 160–61, 194, 200, 204, 206–7, 210, 230

Federal Home Loan Bank System, 153

Federal Housing Administration (FHA), 20, 65
  established, 199
  federal housing policy and, 211–14
  HUD and, 227
  low-income housing scandal and, 235–27, 239
  mortgage guarantees and, 155–57, 160–62, 165, 167–68, 195, 201, 207–8, 210
  subsidy program reorganization of, 241–44
  Santa Maria Del Mar project (Biloxi, Miss.) of, 171 (table)

Federal National Mortgage Association (FNMA), 155–56

Federal Power Commission, 11

Federal Reserve Banks, 16–18

Federal Reserve Board, 64, 91, 313
  bank reorganization as holding companies and, 95, 97, 101–2, 106–10, 112, 117–19, 123
  GAO audit of, 29, 31, 80–81
  housing development and, 149, 150–51, 200, 210
  regulatory function of (1913), 100
  untouchability of, 342

Federal Reserve System, xxii–xxiii, xxv, 36, 46, 53, 82, 91, 202
  bank holding companies and, 142
  creation of, 5
  credit distribution and, 18–20
  function and membership of, 16
  GAO audit of, 29, 31, 80–81, 295
  monetary policy and, 16–18
  Open Market Committee of, 17, 18, 31, 43
  regulatory function of (1913), 100
  restrictive monetary policy and, 312n–13n
  structure of, 16–17

Federal Trade Commission, 37, 96

Fefferman, Hilbert, 222, 351

FHA, *see* Federal Housing Administration

Financial Institutions Act (1973), 38, 66, 70–71

Financial Institutions subcommittee (Senate), 323

Firing Line, 327

First National City Bank, xxii, 13, 45, 52, 66, 113, 129
  assets, 10 (table)
  reorganization of, 84

First National City Corporation, 129, 144

Fisher, Gerald, 103n

Foard, Ashley, 222

Ford, Gerald, 307

Ford Motor Company, 9, 10

"Foreign Trade Zone Application of the State of Maine" hearings (1968), 68

Frenzel, William, 55

Frieden, Bernard, 161

Friedman, Lawrence, 146, 173–74, 196

FRB, *see* Federal Reserve Board

FRS, *see* Federal Reserve System

Fulbright, J. William, 57, 77–78

Galifianakis, Nick, 125

Garrison, David, 262

Gellman, Benet, 140, 344

General Accounting Office (GAO), xxiii
  FRS audit by, 29, 31, 80–81

General Mills, 144

General Motors, 9, 10

Genoy and Company, 11

Gettys, Tom S., 51, 125, 205

Glass-Steagall Act (1933), 102

Giaimo, Robert N., 183

Goldfinger, Nathaniel, 253

Gonzalez, Henry B., 285, 288–89
  on limitations of Banking Committee, 349
  on wage-price controls, 334

Goodell, Charles, 72, 133
Government Operations Committee (Senate)
  economic concentration and, 11
  report by (1973), 8
  "Green Stamp Amendment," 134–35, 137–40
  See also Bank Holding Company Act (1956)
Griffin, Charles H., 125
Gross, George, 215, 238, 272
Growth of Unregistered One Bank Holding Companies, The (1969), 115
Grueninger, O. G., 121
Gulf of Tonkin Resolution (1964), 311
Gulledge, Eugene A., 215, 231
Gunther, John, 203, 293

Haldeman, H. R., 37
Hale, Matthew, 129
Hanley, James M., 208
Hanna, Richard, 51, 53, 127, 345
  federal housing policy and, 181, 205, 214, 216
  wage-price controls and, 337, 338
Hart, Philip, 238
Heckler, Margaret M., 125, 127, 181, 285
Heller, Walter, 313
Herbers, John, 22, 24, 191–92, 237
Hewes, Alexander, 243, 255, 257
"High Cost of No. 2 Heating Oil, The" hearings (1970), 68
Highway programs, 159–60
Hollings, Ernest, 133
Home Manufacturers Association, 217
Home Owners' Loan Corporation, 199, 209
Housing
  banking industry and, 152–57, 161, 165–72, 199–210
  building industry and, 211–18
  conditions of, 146–52
  congressional oversight and, 233–40
  credit distribution and, 19–20
  federal housing development policy and, 152–64, 172–76, 190
  federal policy proposals for, 353–56
  HUD and, 221–31
  in the 1960s, 165–72, 196–99, 355–56
  real estate brokers and, 218–21
  See also Housing and Urban Affairs subcommittee (House of Representatives); Housing and Urban Affairs subcommittee (Senate); and specific listings
Housing Act (1934), 309
Housing Act (1949), 158, 163, 226
Housing Act (1961), 166
Housing Act (1968), see Housing and Urban Development Act (1968)
Housing Act (1972), 191, 215
  House of Representatives action on, 251, 272–89
  James, Ray, and, 222
  Senate activity on, 249–72
Housing Act (1974), see Housing and Urban Development Act (1974)
Housing and Home Finance Agency (HHFA), 166, 194
  HUD and, 225–27, 230
Housing and Urban Affairs subcommittee (House of Representatives), 176–77
  builders' influence in, 214–17
  Housing Act (1972) and, 251, 272–89
  Housing Act (1974) and, 248, 302–7
  ideology and constituency base of members of, 182 (table)

leadership and operating style of, 186–89

membership of, 180–83

omnibus approach of, 190–95

oversight and, 234, 237–40

power of, 40–42

real estate brokers and, 221

Housing and Urban Affairs subcommittee (Senate), 59, 68, 69, 176–77

    Housing Act (1972) and, 249–72

    Housing Act (1974) and, 248, 299–302, 306–7

    leadership and operating style of, 185–86

    ideology and constituency base of members of, 179–80 (table)

    membership of, 177–80

    oversight and, 233–34, 237–40

Housing and Urban Development Act (1968), 148, 167, 168, 197, 212–13, 228, 252, 274

    section 202 program, 169–71, 171 (table)

    sections 235 and 236 programs, 168–71, 171 (table), 197, 212, 213, 230, 235, 239, 243–44

Housing and Urban Development Act (1974), 229, 241

    House of Representatives action on, 248, 302–7

    Romney's initiative for, 242–49

    Senate action on, 248, 299–302, 306–7

Housing and Urban Development, Department of (HUD), 20, 82, 162, 193, 198

    appropriations for, 181–84

    community development and, 266–67

    congressional oversight over, 233, 237, 239

    creation of, 166, 207, 211, 227, 230

    federal housing policy and, 215, 216, 221–25

Housing Act (1972) and, 258–59, 277–80, 290, 295

Housing Act (1974) and, 241–48, 254, 299, 300–2

Housing for the Aged subcommittee (Senate), 169

Hughes, Harold E., 76, 133

Hunt Commission (President's Commission on Financial Structure and Regulation), 12, 38, 130, 145, 166

Independent Bankers Association, 121

Interior Department, 347

Internal Revenue Code, 154

International Finance subcommittee (House of Representatives), 40

International Trade subcommittee (House of Representatives), 40

Interstate Commerce Commission, 11

Jackson, Henry M., 356

James, Ray, 194, 222, 224, 251, 260, 268

Javits, Jacob, 72, 76, 271

Johnson, Albert W., 125, 138, 205, 216

Johnson, Lyndon B., 168, 198, 211, 294, 311, 312

Joint Economic Committee, 349

    wage-price action report by (1970), 313

Jones, Oliver, 208

Judiciary Committee (House of Representatives), 306

Justice Department, bank mergers and, 95–97

Kane and Company, 11

Keith, Nathaniel, 225

Kennedy, David M., 116, 117, 320

Kerner Commission (National Advisory Commission on Civil Disorders), 147

Koch, Edward I., 42, 42n, 188, 305

Labor and Public Welfare Committee (Senate), 76, 186, 350
Lake County National Bank (Painesville, Ohio), 126
Legislative Reorganization Act (1946), 36
Lewis, Jake, 294, 344
Lindsay, John V., 55, 230
Lobbies
  bank holding companies and, 121–29
  congressional reliance on, 345–46
  housing and, 211–21
  Housing Act (1972) and, 227–29, 255–58, 280–81, 296
  Housing Act (1974) and, 300
  influence of, 22–23
  See also Banking industry; Building industry; and specific listings
Long Island Lighting Company (LILCO), 11, 12
Low-income housing during 1960s, 167, 168–70, 173
  eligibility criteria for, 243–44
  federal policy for, 187, 347
  Housing Act (1972) and, 286
  scandal in (1972), 235–40

McCormack, John, 54
McGovern, George, 137
McGuire, John, 257
McIntyre, Thomas J., 68, 133, 186
McLean, Kenneth, xxvi, 65, 66, 343
McMurray, Gerald, 272
McMurray, Joseph, 194, 272
McNeil, Charles, 122n, 132
Maffin, Robert, 262, 268n
Malakoff, Robert, 192
Martin, William McChesney, Jr., 107, 109, 117, 214
Mellon, Andrew, 28
Metcalf, Lee, 8, 11–12, 137
Mields, Hugh, 263
Miller, Arthur, 327

Mills, Wilbur, xxv
Minish, Joseph G., 181, 208, 216, 285
Minnesota Mining and Manufacturing (3M) Company, 134
Minting and Mining subcommittee (Senate), 70
Mitchell, Parren J., 42, 188, 305
Mize, Chester, 125, 127
Mobile Home Manufacturers Association, 217
Model Cities program, 20, 166, 197, 246, 270
Monagan, John S., 238
Mondale, Walter F., 133–34, 331
  Banking Committee and, 72, 75, 76
  federal housing policy and, 186, 205, 208, 216, 257, 260, 289
Moorhead, William S., 127, 347
  Banking Committee and, 47, 51, 53, 54
  federal housing policy and, 195, 205, 208, 216, 225, 239, 270, 273, 276, 284, 289, 296
  wage-price controls and, 323
Morgan Guaranty Trust Company, xxii, 9, 11, 13
Mortgage Bankers Association (MBA), 194, 200, 207
Moskoff, Howard, 263
Muskie, Edmund S., 76, 133, 205

Nader, Ralph, xxii–xxvi, 329
  on housing needs, 354
National Advisory Commission on Civil Disorders (Kerner Commission), 147
National Aeronautics and Space Administration, 181
National Association of Home Builders (NAHB), 65, 344
  Housing Act (1972) and, 280–81, 286
  lobbying influence of, 173, 194, 213–18, 230, 232

National Association of Housing and Redevelopment Officials (NAHRO), 197, 227, 252
  community development and, 263–65, 270
  Housing Act (1972) and, 255–58, 279, 282, 296
  Housing Act (1974) and, 299, 303
  purpose of, 227–29
National Association of Insurance Agents (NAIA), 126–27
National Association of Real Estate Boards (NAREB), 218–21
National Commission on Urban Problems (Douglas Commission), 147, 164
National Development Bank, 29, 294
National Farmers Union, 137
National Housing Conference, 197
National Institute of Building Sciences, 248, 275
National Journal, 214
National League of Cities/U.S. Conference of Mayors, 197, 229, 265, 270, 281, 292
Neighborhood Preservation Assistance Program, 275
Nelson, Gaylord, 333
Nelson, Paul, 294
Nenno, Mary, 228, 255, 273, 283
New Economic Policy, 325–26
Nixon, Richard M., 12, 38, 116, 130, 311
  Economic Stabilization Act and, 315–23
  federal housing policy and, 215, 246, 262, 298–99, 307
  Phase II extensions and, 324–28, 330
  Phase III extensions and, 335–36, 338
  restrictive monetary policy and, 312
Northwest Bancorporation, 106
Novak, Robert, 70, 293, 295

O'Brien, Lawrence, 313
Odum, Lewis G., 129
Office of Emergency Preparedness, 82
Office of Management and Budget (OMB), 17, 239
  Housing Act (1972) and, 245–46, 248, 258, 270, 290, 292
Omnibus Financial Institutions Act (1973), 71
O'Neal, Dudley, 62, 65, 67, 343
Open Market Committee (Federal Reserve Board), 17, 18, 31, 43

Packwood, Bob, 133, 302
  wage-price controls and, 325
Patman, Wright, xxi, xxiv, 58, 181, 308, 357
  bank holding companies and, 98, 114–17, 120, 121, 125, 126, 128, 131, 138
  Bank Merger Act and, 54–55
  federal housing policy and, 187–89, 191, 203–4, 205, 209, 214, 216, 237–39
  Housing Act (1972) and, 288, 291, 293–96
  GAO audit of FRS and, 80–81, 295
  hearings and, 43–46
  leadership of, 27–39, 344, 345, 350–51, 362, 363
  subcommittees and, 40–43
  wage-price controls and, 315–16, 327, 330, 332, 337, 339
Penn Central Railway, 12, 36–37, 43, 344
Percy, Charles H., 76, 133, 205, 216, 257
Philadelphia, FHA foreclosures in, 236
Philadelphia Bank case (1963), 97, 99
"Primer on Money" (Patman), xxv

"Problems of Small Domestic Shoe Manufacturers, The" hearings (1969), 68

Progress Report on Federal Housing Programs (Senate Housing subcommittee), 233

Proxmire, William, xxv, xxvi, 145, 344, 345, 357
  bank holding companies and, 130, 133, 135–37, 143
  Banking Committee and, 57, 66, 67, 69–70, 72, 74–75, 362–63
  defense contractors and, 314–15
  federal housing and, 185–86, 205, 210, 300
  wage-price controls and, 321, 323–25, 327, 330, 331–32, 334–36

Public housing, 157–58

Public Housing Administration, 227

Public Works Committee (House of Representatives), 35

Public Works Committee (Senate), 78

Rains, Albert, 39–41, 59
  federal housing policy and, 186, 195, 214

Real estate brokers, 218–21

Real Estate Political Education Committee, 220

Realtors' Washington Committee, 218, 219

Rees, Thomas M., 53, 127, 205

Reing and Company, 11

Reuss, Henry S., xxv, 138, 345, 347
  Banking Committee and, 42, 51, 52, 308, 363
  federal housing policy and, 284, 285, 289
  wage-price controls and, 315–16, 321, 324n, 327, 333

Robertson, A. Willis, 60, 69

Rockefeller, David, 43

Rockefeller Brothers Fund, 354

Rodgers, Donald, 129

Rogg, Nathaniel, 214

Romney, George W., 43–44, 173, 299
  FHA subsidy program reorganization and, 241–42, 244, 246
  Housing Act (1972) and, 251, 259, 260, 278–79, 285, 291–92, 293
  HUD and, 230–31, 235, 237–38
  on national land use policy, 347

Roth, William V., Jr., 75, 177

Rousselot, John H., 49, 181

Rules Committee (House of Representatives), 81

St. Germain, Fernand J., 189, 205, 285, 287

Salamon, Lester, xxii

Savings Political Education Committee (SPEC), 204–5

Saxon, John, 101n

Schechter, Henry, 263

Schultz, George, 312

Securities and Exchange Commission, 181

Security subcommittee (Senate), 68

Select Committee to Investigate the Problems of Small Business (House of Representatives), 28, 33

Selective Service System, 181

Semer, Milton, 217–18

Sherman antitrust laws, 54

Simon, William E., 3

Skiles, Win, 193, 269

Slipher, Stephen, 204–6

Small Business Administration, 82, 312

Small Business subcommittee (House of Representatives), 40

Small Business subcommittee (Senate), 68

Smith, Hugh, 66, 129, 132, 134, 135, 139

Society Corporation, 126
Southeastern Underwriters case (1944), 96
Sparkman, John, xxv, xxvi, 27, 145, 350
  bank holding companies and, 129–32, 135, 138, 142
  committee staff and, 61–67
  federal housing policy and, 174, 178, 185, 189, 193, 195, 205, 208, 213, 215, 224, 225, 233, 239, 340
  hearings and, 67–68
  Housing Act (1972) and, 249, 253–54, 258, 261, 265, 271
  Housing Act (1974) and, 300
  leadership of, 57–60, 79, 343, 345
  subcommittees and, 68–71
  wage-price controls and, 336
Spense, Brent, 32–33, 35, 40
Staats, Elmer B., 268
Stahl, David, 263
Stanton, William, 51, 52, 285, 287*n*, 345
  bank holding companies and, 124–26, 127, 138
Stark, Pete, 307
"State of the National Economy" hearings (1971), 67
State Street Bank (Boston), 11
Steagall, Henry, 33
Stein, Herbert, 313
Stenson, Gary, 257
Stephens, Robert G., 49, 51, 79, 125, 214, 284, 285, 332
Sternlieb, George, 149
Stevenson, Adlai E., 58
Stevenson, Adlai E., III, 76, 331
  federal housing policy and, 186, 240*n*, 300
Sullivan, Leonor K., 138, 140, 347, 357
  Banking Committee and, 42, 49–52
  federal housing policy and, 186, 189, 209, 210, 215

Housing Act (1972) and, 273, 286–89, 294
Supreme Court, 44, 54
  bank mergers and, 95–97, 107

Taft, Robert, Jr., 75, 205, 216, 271, 300, 301
Taylor, Ralph, 263
Tower, John G., 345
  bank holding companies and, 133, 138
  Banking Committee and, 60, 63, 65, 73–75, 80
  federal housing program and, 177, 193, 205, 208, 213, 215, 239, 253–54, 270, 271, 300, 302
  wage-price controls and, 324, 333
Transamerica case (1953), 96, 107
Transamerica Corporation, 107
Treasury, Department of, 82
Truth-in-Lending Act (1968), 60

Unions, low-income housing and, 197–98
United States Savings and Loan League (USS&LL), 203–4, 207, 248, 344
U.S. v. *Morgan* case (1953), 96
Urban Development Bank, 276
Urban Homestead Loan Program, 274
Urban League, 197
Urban Mass Transit Assistance Act, 131
Urban renewal, 20, 158–59
  during the 1960s, 167
Urban Renewal Administration, 227

Veterans Administration, 181
  housing and, 157, 160–61, 165, 201, 210

Wage-price controls
  Defense Production Act extensions and, 312–19

Wage-price controls *(Continued)*
  Economic Stabilization Act and, 320–23
  Phase II extensions and, 325–34
  Phase III extensions and, 335–39
Walker, Charls E., 38, 65
  federal housing and, 117, 123, 124, 128, 131
Walsh, Albert, 262, 282, 292
Waranch, Stanley, 292
Watergate Committee (Senate), 37
Ways and Means Committee (Senate), 350
  assignment powers stripped from, 365
Weaver, Robert C., 288
Wells Fargo Bank, 9
Western Reserve Bank of Lake County (North Madison, Ohio), 126
Widnall, William B.
  bank holding companies and, 118, 124, 125, 127, 138

Banking Committee and, 49, 56, 79
  federal housing policy and, 205, 215, 283, 284, 295
  wage-price controls and, 322, 334
Williams, Harrison J., 178, 186, 300, 331
  bank holding companies and, 131, 134, 138, 139
  Banking Committee and, 62, 67, 69, 74, 78
Williams, John Skelton, 101n
Williams, Lawrence G., 125
Williamson, John, 218–20
Wood, Burton, 214, 225
Wood, Robert, 198
Woodcock, Leonard, 317
Woolley, Jack, 224
Wylie, Chalmers P., 125, 127, 128, 318

Yale Law Journal, 10
Yingling, John, 129